ON MUSIC THEORY
AND MAKING MUSIC MORE WELCOMING FOR EVERYONE

MUSIC AND SOCIAL JUSTICE

Series Editors: William Cheng and Andrew Dell'Antonio

From Plato to Public Enemy, people have debated the relationship between music and justice—rarely arriving at much consensus over the art form's ethics and aesthetics, uses and abuses, virtues and vices. So what roles can music and musicians play in agendas of justice? And what should musicians and music scholars do if—during moments of upheaval, complacency, ennui—music ends up seemingly drained of its beauty, power, and even relevance?

Created by editors William Cheng and Andrew Dell'Antonio, this endeavor welcomes projects that shine new light on familiar subjects such as protest songs, humanitarian artists, war and peace, community formation, cultural diplomacy, globalization, and political resistance. Simultaneously, the series invites authors to critique and expand on what qualifies as justice—or, for that matter, music—in the first place.

ON MUSIC THEORY

AND MAKING MUSIC

MORE WELCOMING

FOR EVERYONE

Philip Ewell

University of Michigan Press
Ann Arbor

Copyright © 2023 by Philip Ewell

For questions or permissions, please contact um.press.perms@umich.edu

Published in the United States of America by the
University of Michigan Press
Manufactured in the United States of America
Printed on acid-free paper
First published April 2023

A CIP catalog record for this book is available from the British Library.

Library of Congress Control Number: 2023931729
LC record available at https://lccn.loc.gov/2023931729

ISBN 978-0-472-07502-7 (hardcover : alk. paper)
ISBN 978-0-472-05502-9 (paper : alk. paper)
ISBN 978-0-472-12943-0 (e-book)

Марине и Казимиру, с любовью

Contents

Digital materials related to this title can be found on
the Fulcrum platform via the following citable URL:
https://doi.org/10.3998/mpub.12050329

Acknowledgments

I imagine the hardest thing I will write in *On Music Theory*, among many hard things, will be these acknowledgments. Over the past few years I have been contacted, quite literally, by thousands of people from all over the planet—from countries like Australia, Benin, Bolivia, Brazil, Canada, China, Ecuador, Israel, Japan, Mexico, New Zealand, Nigeria, Oman, Russia, South Africa, South Korea, Turkey, United Arab Emirates, *many* countries in Europe, and elsewhere—concerning my race scholarship in music theory, and I could, and should, rightly acknowledge these folks here. The problem is that I'll most certainly forget to mention some who were helpful, supportive, and inspirational, and for that I must apologize in advance. So, to all those unmentioned folks, thank you! I have been truly humbled by the outpouring of support that this work has brought about.

One rather strange acknowledgment I have to make straight away is of Russia's invasion of Ukraine in late February 2022. As a Russianist who has spent some seven years there, and who married a Russian in Moscow in 2002, the war in Ukraine has had an enormous effect on me personally, though my suffering pales in comparison to the unspeakable horrors that Ukrainians are enduring every day. I acknowledge this war since there are several vignettes from Russia peppered throughout the pages of *On Music Theory* and, though they were written before the war, they may not sound so innocent now. Yet it's worth pointing out that there are literally millions upon millions of Russian citizens who wholeheartedly reject Russia's invasion of Ukraine, many of whom have left Russia on a one-way ticket elsewhere, which is important to bear in mind. It's also worth noting that Russia, inadvertently, has breathed new life into the concept of "the west," which had become quite fractured before the war. This is important insofar as I am quite critical of the west in chapter 2, yet now it has clearer contours.

This does not change the gist of my arguments, however, and chapter 2 remains virtually unchanged from how I wrote it in 2021. Finally, I acknowledge the simple fact that my time in Russia has given me, a mixed-race black American, a unique perspective on the United States, one in which I openly acknowledge the beauty of our country and through which I believe I can help to unlock some of the keys to understanding the racialized ways of how we teach music in hopes of making music more welcoming for all. The same racialized structures exist in Russia, of course, with certain local nuances, and it has been crucial for me to see how another significant musical culture deals with the racialized aspects of making music. Of the folks in Russia who've helped me think through some of the ideas contained herein I thank Levon Akopyan, Tatiana Bershadskaya (RIP), Valentina Kholopova, Marina Karaseva, Tatiana Kiuregian, Andrei Konovalov, Grigory Lyzhov, Charles Maynes, Anna Morozova, Alan Moseley, Dana Nagina, Mohamed Saleh, Daniil Shutko, Tatiana Tsaregradskaya, Marina Voinova, and Konstantin Zenkin.

Before I began work on this monograph I had to endure a two-year tenure battle at Hunter College in 2014–2016, which I discuss briefly in the Intro, and many people helped me through this trying time. First is Joe Straus, who was by my side every step of the way. Joe never wavered in his support for me throughout that time, and I will be forever grateful to him for all he's done for me in my career. Next would be Poundie Burstein, who was also unwavering in his support, and I'm deeply grateful to him. Suzanne Farrin, who came on board as chair to right the ship of the Hunter Department of Music in 2015, has become a close friend, and I always learn from our conversations about making music more welcoming for everyone. Others at Hunter and CUNY who were crucial to my success during those trying times were Anthony Brown, Richard Burke (RIP), Laura Hertzog, Renee Lasher, Shafer Mahoney, Andy Polsky, Jennifer Raab, Vita Rabinowitz, Jewel Thompson, and Mariann Weierich, and I owe my very career to these friends and colleagues. Finally, my best friend in music theory, Andrew Pau—he and I played a cello-piano recital at Stanford University as undergrads in the late 1980s, when neither of us knew of the existence of music theory as a field—helped me enormously during my tumultuous tenure battle, and I can't thank him enough for his steadfast support and lawyerly advice at that time, and beyond.

The first chance I had to get some of *On Music Theory*'s ideas out of my head and onto paper came with the invitation, from my friend Noriko Manabe early in 2018—which is when I first envisioned the outlines of the current monograph—to write an introduction to a symposium on Kendrick Lamar's *To Pimp a Butterfly* for *Music Theory Online*. I ended up submitting a different response then, but the feedback I got on my original submission from the symposium authors—Noriko along with Robin Attas, James Bungert, John Mattessich, and Mitch Ohriner—was invaluable, and put me on a path that led to the current publication, so thanks to these five. I was able to further workshop these ideas at a conference in Ireland in September 2018, and I thank all those who gave valuable feedback then, especially Will Fourie, Wolfgang Marx, Fred Maus, and Linda Shaver-Gleason, whom I was honored to have met before her untimely death in January 2020.

I took part in two writing workshops, one in fall 2018, the other in spring 2019, and I'm thankful to all who helped me work on the ideas contained in *On Music Theory*, especially Juan Battle, Lawrence Kowerski, Annemarie Nicols-Grinenko, and Shanti Thakur. My dear friend Rob Cowan helped in one of those writing workshops, and has been at my side through some of the most trying times in my career—his friendship and insight have gotten me out of more than one bind over the years. In the spring 2019 workshop I was honored to have as my mentor Jessie Daniels, from whom I learned so much about basic aspects of working on antiracist and antisexist topics. Her counsel has greatly improved my work here, and I am deeply indebted to Jessie for her support and mentoring. It was Jessie, who had been a mentee of Joe Feagin years ago at the University of Texas, who first told me of Joe's groundbreaking work in sociology, and I have since become good online friends with Joe as a result, and I am so very thankful for his support, friendship, and advice over these past few years.

One point I often make as I've delved deep into matters of social justice in American music theory is that I've learned so much from colleagues who are junior to me, often students themselves, and sometimes junior faculty. Such colleagues, to whom I'm greatly indebted, include but are not limited to Knar Abrahamyan, Catherine Adoyo, Charlotte Alkoppa, Brock Bahler, Chandler Blount, Clifton Boyd, Sergio Bragatte, Daniel Cho, Jacob Cohen, Jade Conlee, Gabby Cornish, Jacey Denny, Patrick Doane, Michèle Duguay, Collin Edouard, Sarah Ellis, Sara Everson, Sam Falotico, Daniel Fox, Pala Garcia, Gillian Gower, Pheaross Graham, Brittany Green, Vincent Guarna, Marc Hannaford, Kristi Hardman, Dani Hawkins, Charles Hsueh, Nikhil James, Tom Johnson, Alessandra Jones, Tara Jordan, Noah Kahrs, Patrick Kennedy, Kylie Ketchner, Thomas Kirkegaard, Tatiana Koike, Hannah Krall, Dennis Krolevich, Zane Larson, Stephen Lett, Megan Lyons, Anabel Maler, Ryan McCulloch, Thornton Miller, Toru Momii, Marcus Moone,

Aaron Mulder, Jason Mulligan, Ameera Nimjee, Nathan Pell, Erin Pratt, Marcelo Rebuffi, Alissandra Reed, Joshua Rosner, Garrett Schumann, Gavin Shaw, Zac Stewart, Bryan Terry, Sarah Thomas, Noel Torres-Rivera, Rasheed Townes, John Vandevert, Anna Yu Wang, Jacob Wendt, Mauro Windholz, and Diana Wu. Also, Miriam Piilonen had the great idea of introducing me to her friend Adam Neely, and the Neely YouTube video in which I appeared, which has been viewed over two million times, has made me, arguably, the most recognizable music theorist in the country.[1] (I can count at least five times that I've been recognized by strangers on the street, probably because of this video.) I thank Adam not only for that video, but for all he does to hold music theory to account. And speaking of helpful folks who are junior to me, my Spring 2022 Advanced Music Theory graduate class at Hunter College, in which we read a draft of the current book, was enormously helpful in putting the final touches on *On Music Theory*, so I thank all students in this class for their many great comments.

One event that made the work that I'm doing in this book possible was my short plenary talk at the November 2019 Annual Meeting of the Society for Music Theory. I'd like to thank my co-panelists there, Ellie Hisama, Joe Straus, and Yayoi Uno Everett, and also our moderator, Betsy Marvin, and the chair of the program committee that year, Danny Jenkins. I remember my Zoom discussion with Betsy and Danny well, when I introduced some of the ideas I was putting forth, and I'm humbled that they thought them significant enough to include on that program. One direct result of my plenary talk was an invitation to be a Virtual Scholar in Residence at the University of the Pacific during the 2020–2021 academic year. This was an utterly invaluable experience during which I was able to workshop many new ideas with the entire UOP community, and they were so gracious in their reception of my work. I thank Dean Peter Witte and everyone else at the UOP Conservatory of Music for their eagerness to engage with me on difficult topics in the music academy.

Summer 2020 saw great upheaval in music theory because of the publication of volume 12 of the *Journal of Schenkerian Studies*, which I discuss in detail below. With the ensuing controversy, countless people spoke out in support of me and my scholarship. For their statement of support I wish to thank the Executive Board of the Society for Music Theory at the time, namely, Inessa Bazayev, Anna Gawboy, Patricia Hall, Robert Hatten, Julian Hook, Gretchen

---

1. You can watch the video, "Music Theory and White Supremacy" (September 7, 2020), on Adam Neely's YouTube channel here: https://youtu.be/Kr3quGh7pJA

Horlacher, Jennifer Iverson, Jocelyn Neal, Philip Stoecker, Leigh VanHandel, and Nancy Yunhwa Rao. For the statement of support from the Department of Music at Yale University, I wish to thank Ian Quinn and all my friends and supporters at Yale, my doctoral alma mater. For their brave 2020 open letter to the Society for Music Theory on how we might begin antiracist actions in the field I thank Edward Klorman, Stephen Lett, Rachel Lumsden, Mitch Ohriner, Cora Palfy, Nathan Pell, Chris Segall, and Daniel Shanahan. And to all those who wrote in support of me that summer and fall, including but not limited to friends and colleagues at the University of North Texas, the University of Toronto, and the Music Theory Society of New York State, a heartfelt thanks. I thank authors/journalists Jeffrey Arlo Brown, Colleen Flaherty, Olivia Giovetti, Beth Harpaz, Lauren Ishida, Alex Ross, Hannah Schmidt, Jacqueline Warwick, and Jeffrey Yelverton for their honest accounting of the events from summer 2020 and of my music theoretical work. I'd also like to thank the five good-faith authors who responded to my scholarship in volume 12 of the *Journal of Schenkerian Studies*, namely, Richard Beaudoin, Suzannah Clark, Stephen Lett, Rich Pellegrin, and Chris Segall.

Having just mentioned the *Journal of Schenkerian Studies*, I must acknowledge the Schenkerian scholars who have reached out to me to have meaningful conversations about a path forward. I thank Joel Lester, Frank Samarotto, and Janet Schmalfeldt for congratulating me after my 2019 talk, and I thank Frank for some follow-up email exchanges as well. Jason Hooper has been extremely helpful in our several exchanges, and I thank him for his help with this project. I thank Matthew Brown and Eric Wen for reaching out to me and for our subsequent email exchanges and Zoom calls, during which we were able to think deeply about issues affecting our field. I also thank Bill Rothstein for our meaningful email exchanges, as well as Wayne Alpern for similar exchanges that led to a nice in-person night out in Manhattan (dinner and drinks are on you next time, Wayne). Outside of Schenkerism, I'd like to thank Richard Taruskin, who gave me great advice on this project at three moments: at a Slavic-languages conference in San Francisco in late November 2019, during the Q&A of a Zoom presentation I gave at the University California, Berkeley, in October 2020, and in various email exchanges. I'm saddened that Richard was not able to see the final version of this work before his untimely passing on July 1, 2022.

Other scholars, friends, and colleagues with whom I've had meaningful exchanges or who have shown support for my work, and from whom I have drawn inspiration, include but are not limited to Cheryl Abram, Kofi Agawu, Shazia Ali, Khyam Allami, Shawn Allison, Adrienne Alton-Gust, Stephen

Amico, Farzad Amoozegar, Cory Arnold, Paul Austerlitz, Jacqueline Avila, Tom Baker, Ellen Bakulina, Wesley Baldwin, Kelly Ballard, Alyssa Barna, Taylor Barnett, Anthony Barone, David Bashwiner, Sophia Bass, Eliot Bates, Leah Batstone, Jennifer Beavers, Jonathan Bellman, Paul Benzaquin, Mark Bergman, Rachel Bergman, Daniel Bertram, David Bevilacqua, Nicole Biamonte, Sally Bick, Ben Bierman, John Biewen, Sanne Bijker, Michael Binder, Ed Bingham, Adem Merter Birson, Susan Bisson, Reuben Blundell, Judith Bose, Linsey Bostwick, Patrick Boyle, Tara Boyle, Jill Brasky, Danielle Brown, Joshua Clement Broyles, Michael Buchler, Geoff Burleson, Chelsea Burns, Lori Burns, Michele Cabrini, Zac Cairns, Michael Callahan, Vincenzo Cambria, Clement Cano, Bill Caplin, Guy Capuzzo, Norman Carey, Omar Carmenates, Devin Chaloux, Thomas Christensen, Stacy Christofakis, Andrew Chung, Tim Clarkson, Jane Clendinning, Kevin Clifton, Ed Cohn, Andrew Conklin, Bryan Cooperrider, Arnie Cox, Cody Coyne, Jonathan Cross, Suzanne Cusick, Michael Cuthbert, Andrew Davis, Rob Deemer, Valeda Dent, Johanna Devaney, Benjamin Dobbs, Stephanie Doktor, Alexander Douglas, Wayne du Maine, Patrick Effiboley, Laura Emmery, James Falzone, Dave Flynn, Frank Fontaine, Kenneth Forkert-Smith, Murray Forman, Karen Fournier, Aaron Fox, Chris Freitag, David Fulmer, Rachel Gain, Christine Gangelhoff, David Garcia, Mariana Gariazzo, Kyra Gaunt, Chuck Gerardo, Sarah Gerk, Benjamin Givan, Andrew Glendening, Cynthia Gonzales, Sumanth Gopinath, Carma Gorman, Joshua Grayson, Jeannie Guerrero, Erin Guinup, Sarah Haefeli, Aaron Harcus, Phil Harper, Robert Hasegawa, Robert Hatten, Ryan Hepburn, Steve Hinds, Norman Hirschy, Hubert Ho, Steve Holley, Steve Holtsford, Erika Supria Honisch, Martha Horst, Christoph Hust, Ashley Jackson, Susan Jackson, Kristina Jacobsen, Robin James, Stephanie Jensen-Moulton, Emily John, James John, Steven Jouanny, Emil Kang, Ema Katrovas, Mark Katz, Inderjit Kaur, Tammy Kernodle, Joe Kerr, Daniel Ketter, Hae Joo Kim, Paul Kirby, Michael Klein, J. Marchand Knight, Ellen Koskoff, Steven Laitz, Sterling Lambert, Tom Langehaug, Matthew Lasner, Megan Lavengood, Imogen Lawlor, Merrin Lazyan, Gavin Lee, Ji Yeon Lee, Maryse Legault, Javier Leon, Siv B. Lie, Eva Lipton-Ormand, Charity Lofthouse, Paul Lombardi, Justin London, João Luiz, Dana Lyn, Rebecca Magill, Victoria Malawey, Alicia Pashby Maul, Paula Maust, Desirée Mayr, Paul Miller, Ana Alonso Minutti, Jan Miyake, Mark Mobley, Hafez Modirzadeh, Otto Muller, Nancy Murphy, Luisa Nardini, Janet Neary, Jeff Nichols, Lonán Ó Braian, Kate O'Brien, Carl Oser, Karen Painter, Olga Panteleeva, John Peterson, Dan Posen, Bruce Quaglia, Maarten Quanten, Steven Rajam, Shana Redmond, Alex Reed, Sam Reenan,

Alex Rehding, Maria Reich, Michael Reingold, Steven Rings, Miguel Roig-Francoli, Griff Rollefson, Daniel Bernard Roumain, Brandon Scott Rumsey, Jon Russell, Bruno Ruviaro, Rebecca Ryan, Lauryn Salazar, Reggie Sanders, Felicia Sandler, Matt Schullman, Marcia Sells, August Sheehy, Michael Sheetz, Braxton Shelley, Dong Jin Shin, Lawrence Shuster, Maya Shwayder, Jon Silpayamanant, Adam Silverman, Michael Silvers, Ayana Smith, Jenny Snodgrass, Danielle Shlomit Sofer, Mark Spicer, Jamie Spillane, Amy Stewart, Anne Stone, Jane Sugarman, Nina Sun Eidsheim, Gary Swift, Hans Tammen, Benjamin Tausig, Matthew Taylor, Kira Thurman, Louise Toppin, Fatiah Touray, John Turci Escobar, Dmitri Tymoczko, Cameron Vohr, Ben Wadsworth, Danny Walden, Levi Walls, Sarah Waltz, Patrick Warfield, Robert Wason, Susan Weiss, Marianne Wheeldon, Cord Whitaker, Chris White, Jon Wild, Brian Wright, James Wright, Seiji Yamashita, Eli Yamin, George Yancy, Mina Yang, David Yearsley, Jeff Yunek, Christina Zanfagna, Emily Zazulia, and Karen Zorn. There are surely names I'm forgetting here, and I feel horrible about it, but please know that if I've forgotten your name it does not mean that your support or influence has not been consequential—it has. It only means that, once things went sideways in summer 2020, it has been difficult to keep track of everything that's gone on in my career, so I ask for your indulgence here.

I'm currently coauthoring a new undergraduate music theory textbook, and my three coauthors, Rosa Abrahams, Aaron Grant, and Cora Palfy, have taught me so much about rethinking American music theory. Our weekly Zoom sessions have proven to be some of the most invigorating moments in my career, so huge thanks are due to them. Further, Rosa, along with another dear friend, Ed Klorman, read a draft of *On Music Theory* cover to cover, and they both gave outstanding feedback, for which I am deeply grateful. Another friend and colleague, Daniel Goldmark, gave great feedback on about half of the monograph, and for his compelling commentary I give thanks.

In June 2022 I co-convened a conference, "Theorizing African American Music," in Cleveland, and my interactions with many people have influenced my work in *On Music Theory*. I especially thank my co-convenor, Chris Jenkins, and all the scholars on the steering and program committees that made this conference, and this work, possible: Naomi André, Fredara Hadley, Marc Hannaford, Eileen Hayes, Travis Jackson, Mark Pottinger, Teresa Reed, and Rosita Sands. A final member of the steering committee, Horace Maxile, deserves special mention. I remember the cognitive dissonance I felt meeting him, another black music theorist, at a conference in about 2004. I didn't know whether I should run up to Horace and hug him, or run up to Horace and kill him. Fortunately, for everyone, I chose the former, and he's been a close friend ever since. When I visited Horace at the Center for Black Music Research in about 2008 in Chicago, where he was working at the time, he introduced me to all the black music scholars who came before us—the Horace Boyers, Samuel Floyds, and Eileen Southerns of our field—scholars who have been erased from the academic mainstream for all the wrong reasons. For that introduction, I especially thank Horace.

I'd like to thank everyone at the University of Michigan Press, and especially my two editors, Will Cheng and Andrew Dell'Antonio, and my managing editor, Sara Cohen, all of whom read my work and provided valuable feedback. It's truly been an honor to work with you all. I should also acknowledge Will's *Loving Music Till It Hurts* as a great model for socially responsible and meaningful musicological research. I thank Editorial Associate Anna Pohlod, who so expertly shepherded *On Music Theory* through the publication process, and thanks also are due to production editor Kevin Rennells and copyeditor Richard Isomaki for their eagle-eyed edits. I thank Lisa DeBoer for her brilliant indexing, and I am grateful to Michigan's Associate General Counsel Jack Bernard for his keen lawyerly advice and helping me dial back my language when necessary. Lawyers have such a wonderfully dispassionate take on passionate affairs, something I learned firsthand when I worked as a translator and editor at the Moscow office of the American law firm White & Case in the early 2000s, a firm that has, sadly, shuttered operations due to Russia's invasion of Ukraine in February 2022. Speaking of lawyers, I also thank Richard Painter for his sagacious advice and general support. I thank the two anonymous reviewers for *On Music Theory*, one of whom later self-identified as Loren Kajikawa, for their excellent suggestions. Loren's interventionist work itself has provided another great model for how to envision musical academic work in the twenty-first century, and I'm honored to have had contact with, and advisement from, Loren on occasion over the past few years.

Institutional support has proven to be key to the success of this project. At Hunter College I've received funding from the Presidential Fund for Faculty Advancement and the Presidential Travel Grant Fund. In 2016–2017 I was a fellow with Hunter's Academic Center for Excellence in Research and Teaching, which allowed me to meet many forward-thinking pedagogues who made me think deeply about what I do in the classroom and how I might relate that work to musical race scholarship. In spring 2019 I took part in the CUNY Mid-Career Faculty Fellowship Program, which was crucial on my path to becoming a full professor in August 2021. In 2020–2021, I was the Susan McClary and Robert Walser Fellow of the American Council of Learned Societies, which allowed me to become online friends with both Susan and Robert. Especially Susan has become a dear friend and mentor, and she has been a constant presence in the background of my writings. In short, there would be no *On Music Theory* were there no Susan McClary, and I am honored to count an icon like her as a friend. Joy Connolly and James Shulman have been extremely helpful behind the scenes at ACLS, and I thank them both for everything they do. I thank the Atlantic Center for the Arts, where I was a Mentoring Artist in May–June 2022 and, especially, Ivan Riascos and my six Associate Artists, Lydia Bangura, Gia Dreyer, Itza Garcia Ordoñez, Monica Hershberger, Kim Loeffert, and Skye Steele, all of whom have helped to strengthen the arguments contained herein. I'd also like to acknowledge two music theory societies that have provided support over the years, namely, the Music Theory Society of New York State and the Society for Music Theory, the latter of which provided funding for the indexing of this work. The reader will notice that I'm quite critical of SMT at times in *On Music Theory*, but my criticism is only in hopes of making that society a better version of itself by holding it to account, and it is in this light that I hope the reader bears my criticisms in mind.

Lastly, my family. I thank the memory of my parents, John and Viola Ewell, who had to endure such horrors in the United States as an interracial couple married in 1960 in California. By some miracle they stayed together until John passed in 2007, and I am deeply grateful that I had such loving parents who afforded me freedoms to truly find myself in this life. I thank my brother and sister, Lars and Ginger Ewell, who made me the man am I today in ways large and small, as I thank my brother-in-law and nephew, Gunnar and Henning Schade. My extended family in Russia, especially Tatiana Vytovtova and Sergei Mrezhin, has provided great support over these past years, for which I am grateful. Most important, I thank my wife, Marina Vytovtova, and our son, Kazimir Ewell—without them I would not have made it through the tough times, and it is to them that I dedicate *On Music Theory*. Казик и Зайчик, я вас люблю больше жизни. Без вас я бы просто погиб. Но когда вы рядом, нет ничего, чего я не мог бы достичь.

On *On Music Theory*

And, well, how do I put this delicately? I've never met him before, so perhaps I'm being presumptuous. But I doubt the Road Runner, after a day of outrunning, outscheming and outlasting Wile E. Coyote, wishes to come home and explain coyote supremacy to the liberal coyotes who live in his neighborhood.[1]

Being a black person in a white space is *exhausting*. We must constantly walk a fine line between our blackness, on the one hand, and white expectations on the other. And as far as the academic study of music goes in the United States, music theory is arguably the whitest space of all. I was reminded of this in December 2020 as I spoke with a fellow black music scholar on Zoom. The ease with which I could speak my mind was exhilarating, emancipating. I felt I could exhale, and I didn't have to walk on eggshells or coddle whiteness, because they had none. We finished each other's sentences and commiserated over how difficult it was to explain what was actually happening with respect to race to our white colleagues. Ultimately, we left the call knowing that we'd once again need to don our battle armor in order to shield ourselves, from the smallest antiblack microaggression to the most overt and ugly forms of antiblackness.

To a large extent, *On Music Theory* reframes the field as practiced in the United States from my perspective, which is a black African American

---

1. Damon Young, "Yeah, Let's Not Talk about Race: Unless You Pay Me," *New York Times*, July 10, 2020.

perspective.[2] That is, my race is black, and my ethnicity is African American. I will tell my version of events, some aspects of which have been well researched and discussed previously—others appear here for the first time. Of course, any inaccuracies are mine and mine alone. This reframing is paramount for one primary reason: since its inception in the mid-twentieth century, American music theory has been framed almost exclusively by white men. Consequently, whiteness and maleness have been not simply overrepresented in the field, but nearly completely monopolistic. In both subconscious and conscious fashion, white men have shunted to the side nonwhite and nonmale voices, as well as the music-theoretical work of those voices. Thus one of my main goals with this book is to create a space in which those who have been marginalized by white men in music theory can thrive.

However, bringing to light marginalized voices, which generally falls under the rubric of "diversity, equity, and inclusion," or "DEI," is not my main goal. Journalist Kalefa Sanneh places the beginning of "diversity" in June 1978, with the US Supreme Court decision in *Regents of the University of California v. Bakke,* the landmark court case brought by Allan Bakke, a white military veteran, against the University of California, Davis.[3] Since then, diversity has morphed into DEI, and there has been a great surge in DEI positions not only in academia, such as the fall 2021 announcements for chief diversity officers at the University of Michigan's School of Music, Theatre, and Dance and at the Eastman School of Music, but also in nonacademic music institutions, like the recent hire of Chief Diversity Officer Marcia Sells at New York's Metropolitan Opera in January 2021, or the announcement, in May 2021, of such a search at the New York Philharmonic.

Generally, DEI can be useful, but it can also be a smokescreen. The great surge in adding, for instance, black composers and artists to rosters of music institutions or music academies generally falls under the rubric of DEI. However, this "additive activity," as I call it, does not really threaten the white-male structure of the academic study of music; that structure remains

---

2. Much has been made of the capitalization of "black," "white," and other races (see John Eligon, "A Debate over Identity and Race Asks, Are African-Americans 'Black' or 'black'?," *New York Times,* June 26, 2020). Generally, I'll lowercase both "black" and "white" in this work.

3. Kalefa Sanneh, "The Limits of 'Diversity,'" *New Yorker,* October 9, 2017. For more on the *Bakke* decision, see Anthony Lewis, "'Bakke' May Change a Lot While Changing No Law," *New York Times,* July 2, 1978.

intact and in control.[4] If I focused on, say, forgotten operas written by African American composers—like John Thomas Douglass's *Virginia's Ball* (1868), Harry Lawrence Freeman's *Epthelia* (1891), Scott Joplin's *Treemonisha* (1911), or Zenobia Powell Perry's *Tawawa House* (1985), which were all staged but none of which made it to America's premiere opera house, New York's Metropolitan Opera—white men would heave a sigh of relief and, potentially, throw money at projects that focus on these unrecognized gems.[5] However, examining and exposing how and why white men excluded these operas by African American composers in the first place is quite a bit more threatening, which is why white men (and many others, not insignificantly) can lash out at this type of exposé, which falls under the rubric of "antiracism." In short, DEI leaves white structures intact and in control, while antiracism dismantles those structures. For the most part, *On Music Theory*'s focus is antiracism and not DEI.[6] To put this another way, DEI focuses on BIPOC figures who have been erased by white structures, while antiracism focuses on the anti-BIPOC activities undertaken by white structures that kept whiteness in power.[7] And, as I like to say, *if there's anything worse than the erasure of blackness in American history, it's the erasure of antiblackness*, a point I highlight often in this work. Thus, perhaps my main goal in *On Music Theory* is antiracism, which I come by through exposing what music theory looks like from the vantage point of a person it was designed to ignore. And if you disagree that music theory was designed to ignore blackness, just ask yourself why jazz (music) theory has evolved entirely outside of the music theory mainstream?

More generally, however, my own identities are, of course, relevant to my version of events. In addition to being black—my father was an African American—I am a cisgender straight man, which gives me quite a bit of privilege in American society, and I'm mindful of this privilege. I've always felt that those who gain the most privilege from a given structure or institu-

---

4. Ethnomusicologist Dylan Robinson calls this additive activity "additive inclusion." See Robinson, "To All Who Should Be Concerned," *Intersections* 39, no. 1 (2019): 137–44.

5. The Metropolitan Opera had never staged an opera written by an African American in its 138-year history until it staged Terrance Blanchard's *Fire Shut Up in My Bones* in September 2021.

6. For more on the distinction between DEI and antiracism, see my "Erasing Colorasure in American Music Theory, and Confronting Demons from Our Past" (RILM's *Bibliolore* blog series, March 25, 2021).

7. BIPOC stands for "black, indigenous, and people of color." I use "BIPOC" and "nonwhite" synonymously in *On Music Theory*.

tion are those most responsible for any possible infractions or misconduct that may occur based on this privilege. Thus, as a cisgender straight man, I feel a responsibility to confront male entitlement and privilege, insofar as I know that I am the beneficiary of male structures that enshrine this privilege.[8] I have one other identity that may surprise the reader: white. My mother, Viola Lavik, was an immigrant from Norway who lived through the Nazi occupation of her country during World War II as a teen in her hometown of Bergen and who arrived in the United States in 1959 on a boat, in New York City, just a few miles from my Brooklyn apartment where I now write. My mom—who became a green-card holder through marriage to my African American dad in California in late 1960, seven years before *Loving v. Virginia* struck down all anti-miscegenation laws across the country—never became a US citizen, but remained only a Norwegian passport holder until her death in 2010 at age eighty-six. I have friends and relatives in Norway, speak some of the language, and have spent good amounts of time there. But in a country such as the United States, as well as in Norway, to be clear, I will never be thought of as white—I have too much melanin in my skin and naps in my now-thinning, graying hair—so I am happy, and proud, to call myself African American. And though I don't consider myself white, nor would the United States of America consider me white, I am equally proud of my Norwegian heritage.

Having stated my own identities, I must also state some obvious caveats with respect to my table of contents. As a black person it is not difficult to understand why I wish to confront racism in music theory. But no less important is what I wish to confront in the field with respect to those identities I cannot claim. Aside from racism, *On Music Theory* most directly confronts sexism and antisemitism, yet I hope that, by clearly showing structural forms of hate, I will enable others to use the arguments I set forth to aid in other struggles, like confronting discrimination against LGBTQ+ folks or those living with disabilities in music theory. I sometimes draw on feminist authors who have confronted sexism in music studies in order to draw parallels to my music-theoretical race scholarship. For instance, in confronting sexism in American jazz, Sherrie Tucker writes:

> Usually, when I tell people that I'm interested in gender and jazz, they think that means that I am interested in reclaiming the "lost" histories

---

8. See here Kate Manne's *Entitled: How Male Privilege Hurts Women* (Crown Publishers, 2020).

of women who played jazz. And I am. Or in exposing the ways that sexism affects women who play jazz today. And I am. But in addition to these interests, and in part because of them, I am also interested in gender as an analytic category for understanding how power is organized, maintained, and challenged, and how change occurs. Historical and professional invisibility is one way that hierarchical power is attained. But how? Gender analysis would seek such explanations. This requires meticulous historical study, since successful invisibility is attained not just once, but over and over and over again.[9]

In speaking of my own work here, and taking this quotation as a model, I could simply substitute "gender" with "race," "jazz" with "music theory," and "women" with "BIPOC." And, as with Tucker, when I tell people that I'm interested in examining race in music theory, one common response is that I must be interested in "lost" or erased BIPOC figures in music theory, and I am.[10] Or that I wish to expose how racism affects BIPOC in music theory, and, again, this interests me. But perhaps more than anything, I'm interested in one concept, power, and how it is "organized, maintained, and challenged" in music theory. That is, I treat race as an analytical category within music theory, and I underscore historical aspects of the field to reveal how music-theoretical power is achieved. Such parallels can be extremely useful to make, since they help minoritized others who struggle against injustice in the academic study of music, and underscore common struggles to recognize our shared humanity. That is, illumination helps other minoritized peoples to be seen.

An obvious problem arises when I, for example, as a non-Jew, speak of confronting antisemitism in American music theory. What right do I have to address such issues, coming from outside? This is a legitimate concern, and I am mindful of the problems. However, being a member of a marginalized group myself, I believe I can shed an important light on how music theory has marginalized many groups, all in the service of glorifying the many white-male ideas in the field that we have been taught, usually by white cisgender men themselves, are the only ideas that mattered in music's history. I believe that an examination of music theory's antisemitism pro-

---

9. Sherrie Tucker, "Big Ears: Listening for Gender in Jazz Studies," *Current Musicology* 71–73 (2001–2): 386. Notably, I could offer the same mantra about America's historical erasure of women that I did with the erasure of blackness: *if there's anything worse than the erasure of feminism in American history, it's the erasure of antifeminism.*

10. See again my RILM blog post, "Erasing Colorasure in American Music Theory."

vides instructive precedents to music theory's antiblackness and other forms of discrimination in the field—there are more points of *convergence* here than *divergence*. I also happen to believe that anyone, of any identity, has the right to comment on anyone's relationship to a given field, so long as those comments are made in a collegial and respectful manner and are not incendiary or based on the false logic of white supremacy and patriarchy. Sadly, many proponents of America's white supremacist patriarchy and patriarchal white supremacy use the idea of "free speech" to peddle false ideas of racial and gender superiority and inferiority, usually masked in a colorblind, gender-neutral meritocracy, and the common twenty-first-century notion that "both sides" of the issue merit consideration.[11] For the record, white supremacy and patriarchy do not merit consideration as legitimate structures in a just, civil, and democratic society.

I occasionally use "cisgender" to evoke cisnormativity, which arises from the false belief that all people are cisgender (i.e., not queer, trans, or gender nonconforming) and that their gender is determined at birth and of only two types, male and female, known as the gender binary, something that cultures, societies, and religions worldwide have, with remarkable consistency, perpetuated. But this gender binary is a mythology, one that shares many similarities with the mythologies surrounding race and racial hierarchies in the roughly five-hundred-year history of white supremacy.[12] The main problem of the binary-gender myth is that is erases other gender identities from consideration, an erasure that can create hostile environments for those who do not fit neatly into what are commonly known as "male" and "female" identities and, subsequently, what are commonly known as cisnormative structures. And these hostile environments create harassment and other forms of physical and nonphysical discrimination.

American music theory is cisnormative, yet this is something that has been discussed very little indeed.[13] (American music theory is also hetero-

---

11. "Bothsidesing," like "whataboutism" or "whataboutery," has become quite common ever since Donald Trump's famous statement that there were "very fine people on both sides" of the protests in Charlottesville, Virginia, at the "Unite the Right" rally on August 11–12, 2017. In general, when our white racial frame tries to bothsides an argument, it is often trying to excuse or legitimize the white supremacy that is baked into the system. But this binary system is ultimately meant to stall or stop conversations about race.

12. See Naseem Jamnia, "The Dangers of the Gender Binary," Medium.com, January 9, 2016 (https://medium.com/the-coffeelicious/the-myth-of-the-gender-binary-72ed2428 c955).

13. One notable exception is Gavin Lee, "Queer Music Theory," *Music Theory Spectrum* 42, no. 1 (Spring 2020): 143–53. Many issues of sexuality were discussed in the "New Musi-

normative, and though this is something I do not discuss directly in *On Music Theory*, I hope that my intersectional arguments can help those who wish to confront music theory's heteronormativity.) What this means for LGBTQ+ friends and colleagues is that the field can create hostile environments for those who wish to consider issues that affect them directly in hopes of dismantling music theory's cisnormative structures. As a cisgender man, I am an imperfect vessel to carry this particular message of dismantling, yet I do. And I vow to work at becoming the best ally I can possibly be to everyone in the LGBTQ+ community.

While I use singular "they" freely when referring to hypothetical persons—in so doing I seek to be inclusive of gender-nonconforming persons—I do use the gendered pronouns "he/him" and "she/her" for named authors, even when I don't know for sure the nature of their gender or sex. Sometimes this is easy, with historical figures like Ida B. Wells or Richard Wagner. It's also easy when I'm quoting someone who's still alive, whom I know personally or who has stated their preferred pronouns. But at times I will make assumptions, imperfect though they might be, usually based on names or other information one can find online. This is a fine line to walk—my intention is to be as gender appropriate and inclusive as possible in my writing—in determining where, and with what person, one moves from "he/she" to "they" or vice versa.[14]

Some will criticize this book for its paucity of musical examples, saying, "How can this be about music theory?" "Where are the graphs?" "Where are the notes on the page?" But this dismissal of my work as "not music theory" is precisely why I've chosen the title I have. This is a book about American music theory, plain and simple, and no one will convince me otherwise. Though at times I'll discuss the academic study of music generally, music

---

cology" that swept that field in the 1990s, and many of the issues raised by scholars such as Susan McClary, Philip Brett, Elizabeth Wood, and Gary Thomas directly applied to music theory, though music theory successfully stifled any incursions of New Musicology into music theory in the 1990s. See, for instance, McClary, *Feminine Endings: Music, Gender, and Sexuality* (University of Minnesota Press, 1991), and Brett, Wood, and Thomas, eds., *Queering the Pitch: The New Gay and Lesbian Musicology* (Routledge, 1994).

14. For an interesting dialogue about the use of singular "they," see Abigail C. Saguy and Juliet Williams, "Why We Should All Use They/Them Pronouns," *Scientific American, Voices* blog, April 11, 2019 (https://blogs.scientificamerican.com/voices/why-we-should-all-use-they-them-pronouns), and the response by Alex Hanna, Nikki L. Stevens, Os Keyes, and Maliha Ahmed, "Actually, We Should *Not* All Use They/Them Pronouns," *Scientific American, Voices* blog, May 3, 2019 (https://blogs.scientificamerican.com/voices/actually-we-should-not-all-use-they-them-pronouns).

theory remains at the core of my study. The reason that some will question whether this is music theory lies in the simple fact that, since its inception in the mid-twentieth century, the field has been defined almost exclusively by white cisgender men, and it is their definition of the field that I violate with my book. But that doesn't mean that this is not a book about music theory. What it means is that those who think it is not have been taught only a small slice of music theory's full potential, only a narrow view of what the field could actually do or be. In other words, those who say my work is not music theory have, to a significant extent, lived an impoverished music-theoretical life—I count myself, regrettably, among such impoverished music theorists—and I hope that my work here can help to expand the field in ways beyond the exclusivist white-male world we have, of necessity, mostly inhabited.

On Music Theory originated in my tenure battle at Hunter College in 2014–2016. The chair of the music department at that time, for what I believe was antiblack racism, decided that I should be let go and worked tirelessly behind the scenes to make that happen. Fortunately, because of my strong circle of advisers, the City University of New York's strong union, family support, and Hunter College's outstanding administration, I was able to fend off my chair's intense efforts and, ultimately, emerged victorious. But what happened to me is all too common among BIPOC scholars in our American colleges and universities. How often have you heard some variation of the following: "We will judge the qualifications of this candidate (or dissertation, article, proposal, etc.) based solely on the merits of the case—race has nothing to do with it." This brings up what Patricia Matthew calls the "false meritocracy" of academia or what Eduardo Bonilla-Silva calls "a meritocratic way of defending white privilege."[15] This statement also makes white-male power structures feel righteous—after all, they will only look at the candidates' merits and nothing else. But, as Matthew writes, "There has yet to be a denial of tenure that begins, 'We are denying Candidate X tenure because she is Hispanic' or 'Because Professor X is Black, we'd rather not grant him a lifetime appointment,'"[16] which is a beautiful way of saying that the "merits" of any candidate are more about how they are defined and interpreted, and not objective. Ask yourself why these "merits" have, with

---

15. See Matthew, *Written/Unwritten: Diversity and the Hidden Truths of Tenure* (University of North Carolina Press, 2016), 8; and Bonilla-Silva, *Racism without Racists: Color-Blind Racism and the Persistence of Racial Inequality in America*, 5th ed. (Rowman & Littlefield, [2003] 2018), 60ff.

16. Matthew, *Written/Unwritten*, 14.

remarkable consistency, benefited and yielded white men above all others. For example, one study from Matthew's book, on tenure cases at the University of Southern California from 1998 to 2012, showed that, of 106 assistant professors going up for tenure at USC in the social sciences and humanities, 91% of white-male professors received tenure while only 55% of all others did.[17] I think it's reasonable to state that the white men were not 91/55 times more meritorious than their nonwhite-nonmale counterparts.

I've never been so naive as to believe that racism doesn't exist in the United States, but of all the racism, and antiblackness, I've endured over my lifetime, nothing had come close to the significance of my tenure battle at Hunter College. Consequently, I began reading race scholarship. The treatment I received from my chair back then is summed up by sociologist Elijah Anderson as the "nigger moment," in which whiteness asserts its power over blackness in an effort to "put the black person 'back in his place.'"[18] I attended a talk on the subject given by Anderson at Columbia University on September 26, 2019, and he asked the audience of about fifty, a majority of whom were black, whether they had ever experienced a nigger moment. Of all the black people in the room, I think 100% raised their hands. The injury caused by this moment is often devastating and demoralizing, which is usually the point in a white space such as academia. For instance, during my tenure battle my Russian wife and I were making plans for a one-way move to Moscow, where we have family and I have worked successfully as an editor and (simultaneous) translator in business. To be clear, the nigger moment is not when a white person calls a black person a nigger to their face, something that has happened to me only twice in my life. Rather, it is about power, and whiteness's exertion of that power over black persons. It is an all-too-common occurrence for blacks in white spaces. It is the high-profile denial of tenure for icons like Cornel West at Harvard University, or Nikole Hannah-Jones at the University of North Carolina, Chapel Hill, both of which happened in spring 2021.[19] And it is the pedestrian notion

---

17. Matthew, *Written/Unwritten*, 269–75.

18. Elijah Anderson, "The White Space," *Sociology of Race and Ethnicity* 1, no. 1 (2015): 14. See also his *Black in White Space: The Enduring Impact of Color in Everyday Life* (University of Chicago Press, 2022).

19. On June 30, 2021, the UNC Board of Trustees voted nine to four to grant Hannah-Jones tenure with her appointment as the Knight Chair in Race and Investigative Journalism at the Hussman School of Journalism and Media at UNC. Hannah-Jones ultimately declined UNC and decided to join the faculty at Howard University, a historically black college in Washington, DC.

that unemployed working-class whites are somehow owed something by American society, while unemployed working-class blacks are not. Anderson writes:

> The injury [caused by the nigger moment] most often has the same [disrespectful] effect: deflation and a sense of marginalization, regardless of the black person's previous negotiations, putative achievements, or claims to status; the person is reminded of her provisional status, that she has much to prove in order to really belong in the white space.

One of the first books I read after my tenure and promotion victory was James Whitman's *Hitler's American Model: The United States and the Making of Nazi Race Law*, a fascinating account of how influential American race law was to Nazi jurists and legislators as they crafted their notorious Nuremberg Laws, whose main intent was to deny full citizenship to Jews and determine what bloodlines constitute Jewishness.[20] Whitman begins with a chilling quotation in which Nazi judge and jurist Roland Freisler, in a June 1934 meeting meant to begin drafting those laws, cites American race law: "This [American] jurisprudence would suit us perfectly, with a single exception. Over there they have in mind, practically speaking, only coloreds and half-coloreds, which includes mestizos and mulattoes; but the Jews, who are also of interest to us, are not reckoned among the coloreds."[21] I thought to myself that if Nazi lunacy, to any extent at all, were based on American race law, then I really have to do a deep scholarly dive into the literature and see what I find. Once I realized how whiteness works hand in glove with maleness in order to suppress both nonwhiteness and nonmaleness, I began to read feminist scholarship, since, as I like to say, white supremacy is the child of patriarchy, not its parent.[22] I read race scholarship, feminist scholarship, queer scholarship, and anything else that might help me understand how and why music theory, a field I love, remained so stubbornly white, male, and cisnormative despite its stated goals of diversity and inclusivity.

In spring 2019 I took part in the City University of New York's Mid-Career Faculty Fellowship Program, which provided a structured writing

---

20. James Q. Whitman, *Hitler's American Model: The United States and the Making of Nazi Race Law* (Princeton University Press, 2017).

21. Whitman, *Hitler's American Model*, 1.

22. This I base on Ta-Nehisi Coates's aphorism, "Race is the child of racism, not the father." See Coates, *Between the World and Me* (Spiegel & Grau, 2015), 7.

environment for mid-career scholars. I was fortunate to have Hunter College sociologist Jessie Daniels as my mentor for this program. Since she herself was a former mentee of Texas A&M sociologist Joe Feagin, Daniels recommended applying his work on white racial framing, and his language, to my critical race analysis of music theory, and it was at this point that I settled on "Music Theory's White Racial Frame" as the title for this work.[23] Because Joseph Straus, my colleague at CUNY's Graduate Center, considered my race scholarship important, he suggested to the Program Committee for the Society for Music Theory that I be included in the SMT plenary for the fall 2019 annual meeting, a session entitled "Reframing Music Theory." The talk, "Music Theory's White Racial Frame," which I gave on November 9, 2019, was thus based on work that I had been doing dating back to my tenure battle at Hunter College, which started in February 2014. More important, my talk was based on the roughly eighteen-thousand-word article on the topic that I submitted to *Music Theory Online* on June 10, 2019, an article that appeared in that journal in June 2020. In an attempt to "reframe" music theory, I began my SMT talk with four simple words: "Music theory is white," thus giving voice to a nonwhite perspective on the field. This was significant because one of the core beliefs of white racial framing has been to never name whiteness as such, but to use coded language instead.[24] If I had used such coded language, I would have begun, "Music theory lacks diversity," the white-framed agreed-upon wording to say the same thing and an obfuscating tactic that has allowed whiteness to avoid direct confrontations with respect to race. So right from the start the SMT audience could tell that this talk was going to be different. Finally, as a follow-up to my plenary talk I wrote and self-published a six-part blog, "Confronting Racism and Sexism in American Music Theory."[25]

What happened after my SMT plenary talk—when certain faculty at the University of North Texas and, specifically, their *Journal of Schenkerian Stud-*

---

23. I note that, while "Music Theory's White Racial Frame" is the title of the plenary talk I gave at the Annual Meeting of the Society for Music Theory in November 2019, I altered the title of the long article to "Music Theory and the White Racial Frame" in order to avoid confusion with the plenary talk. See also Joe Feagin, *The White Racial Frame: Centuries of Racial Framing and Counter-framing*, 2nd ed. (Routledge, [2009] 2013).

24. In *Mythologies*, philosopher Roland Barthes calls this process "exnomination," that "outside of naming" aspect of a domination system. See Barthes, *Mythologies* (Les Lettres nouvelles, 1957).

25. See "Confronting Racism and Sexism in American Music Theory" (musictheoryswhiteracialframe.com).

ies, decided to launch a response symposium in that journal—ultimately became national and international news and changed the field of music theory in ways that are still being felt today. When I applied for a fellowship at the American Council of Learned Societies in fall 2019, the JSS affair, which I discuss in detail in chapter 4, had not broken—I simply wished to expand on my critical race analysis of American music theory, and I was honored to have been selected as the Susan McClary and Robert Walser Fellow of ACLS for that cycle. The JSS affair—in which certain authors staked out clear white supremacist and antiblack positions with respect to the academic study of music in the United States—proved beyond any reasonable doubt that we, in American music theory, have enormous difficulty in understanding how race has shaped our field, how nonwhiteness has consistently been marginalized, and how the field remains remarkably unjust with respect to race and racial matters.

Inadvertently then, the JSS affair, with all the accompanying actions, open letters, and press coverage, has shaped my work here to some extent. And though I don't discuss it much in this Intro, this affair helps us understand how racist (and sexist) structures operate in music academia, how those structures are focused on stifling dissent, and how they are rooted, to a very large degree, in antiblackness (and misogyny). That is, the more I've thought about the whole JSS affair, the more I've realized that the virulent reaction to my SMT plenary talk was not so much about challenging whiteness as it was about the simple fact that the challenge came from blackness. This plays a significant role in this book. Perhaps most important, despite the antiblack hate and anger that suffuse volume 12, this journal issue has been a great gift to American music theory because it lays bare the racist and sexist structures at the core of our field, so that we might begin the conversation regarding how to dismantle those structures in order to make music theory more welcoming for everyone.

I generally do not shy away from naming names when necessary. Of course, I do so respectfully and collegially, but if someone acts questionably, I will name the person who did so and give the evidence for calling the actions questionable. The most important aspect of identifying the actors by name is simple: accountability. We should all hold ourselves to account, and we cannot do so if we only speak in abstractions. I myself have had to swallow some bitter pills as I think back on my own career and how my actions have upheld some of the false tenets of the whiteness and maleness of the field. Also, as one of only a handful of tenured African American music theorists in the field, naming names, and naming identities, is also necessary in order to contrast the narratives being related. Accordingly, *On Music Theory* is something of an ethnography of American music theory, an ethnographic account of the field from my black perspective.

Notably, virtually no one in the United States will admit to antiblack or racist behavior—think here of the many times that President Donald Trump talked about how "not-racist" he is—so it becomes something of a "they said, they said" situation. But this is, in fact, one of the greatest mythologies of our colorblind American society, the idea that there is nothing worse than being called racist, sexist, or similar things. Sadly, we all can act in any of those discriminatory ways. I myself have acted in antiblack fashion in my life, though it pains me to say it here. All I can do is admit to such acts, confront them, and then vow to be better in the future, that is, hold myself accountable. We must all realize that these adjectives—racist, sexist, antisemitic, Islamophobic, transphobic, ableist, among many others—are not slurs but, rather, useful descriptors for common human behaviors. Turning them into epithets, into almost unspeakable slurs, is a common tactic of white-male frames to fool us into believing that the very discussions on race, gender, Jewishness, sexuality, etc., are the things to be stifled, the problem to be solved. This avoidance tactic has one main goal: to freeze us all into inaction so that the existing white cisgender patriarchy remains in place, unchallenged, as a mythological goal to which we should all aspire. *On Music Theory* rejects such avoidance tactics; instead I offer my clear-eyed approach only in the spirit of scholarly inquisition and betterment for the field.

Following this Intro, *On Music Theory* has six chapters and an Outro, each of which is framed as a discussion "on" some aspect of music and music theory. Chapter 1 examines the definition of music theory and then discusses precedents for race scholarship in the music academy. I then discuss demographic data in the Society for Music Theory and in music theory textbooks. Chapter 2 explores the concepts of whiteness, the west, western civilization, and music's western canon, and how the west only emerged in the nineteenth century as a justification, in large part, for white supremacy to solidify its territorial conquests and power structures across the globe. I also discuss the epistemologies of whiteness, and the fact that we have engaged in a willful knowledge avoidance with respect to the white mythologies that make up this chapter. Chapter 3 unpacks the legacy of Heinrich Schenker, and how our generally unskeptical view of this fervently racist figure has had horrible repercussions in music theory with respect to racial justice and equity. Chapter 4 examines, for the first time from my perspective, the controversy surrounding volume 12 of the *Journal of Schenkerian Studies*, which segues into a discussion of music theory's general antiblackness in chapter 5. Antisemitism in classical music, far more prominent that we generally acknowledge, is the topic of chapter 6, while in the Outro I sum up *On Music Theory* and try to offer some constructive thoughts for the future. Throughout the whole text, and especially in the later chapters, I offer suggestions and recommendations for what we might do to remedy problems in music theory specifically, and to make the academic study of music more welcoming generally. But I hasten to add that *On Music Theory* is not so much a guide for *how* we can change music theory, but for *why we must.*

In *Living a Feminist Life* Sara Ahmed adopts a simple citation policy: she does not cite any white men. Further, she speaks of how "citations can be feminist bricks: they are the materials through which, from which, we create our dwellings."[26] Citations can also be antiracist bricks from which to create our dwellings. In citing authors we grant them legitimacy and authority, potentially turbocharging their worth to the field. Historically, the only authors who get so turbocharged in music theory are white men. Though I don't ban white-male authors from this book altogether, the reader will find that their collective voice has been greatly diminished. I've made a conscious effort to foreground voices that are not both white and male. Further, I've gone quite far outside of music theory sources with this work, and I often cite nonacademic sources as well, such as various news outlets, social-media sources, podcasts, interviews, trade books, and websites, among other such sources. And while music theory is the focus, I draw on other academic fields to make my points, fields such as African American studies, classics, feminist studies, journalism, law, philosophy, and sociology. My expansive and eclectic use of sources for *On Music Theory* remedies the simple fact that, until recently, the only citations that have been considered worthy of inclusion in music-theoretical work were generally those written by white persons, usually men. And, again, some of this book includes case studies in which I myself have played a central role as one of a handful of tenured African American music theorists—thus to an extent my book serves as a testimonial, from a black perspective, of certain events that have happened in the field over the past several years against the backdrop of current political and cultural events in the United States.

There are those who will undoubtedly criticize my work as "blaming white folks." Let me be clear: *On Music Theory* blames no one person, nor

---

26. Sara Ahmed, *Living a Feminist Life* (Duke University Press, 2017), 15–16.

any one race of people. I do often speak of the historic white supremacy of the United States, which, if you take an honest look at the history of our country, is not in question. Yet importantly, white supremacy is not an American invention at all but, rather, a European one. I also note that white persons themselves are the victims of white supremacy in music theory (and the country writ large), in the burdens of supporting the many mythologies of white-male greatness at the expense of everyone else, in maintaining and promoting the godlike status of the Beethovens and the Mozarts in music, all while insisting that it has nothing to do with race or gender, just exceptionalism. Yet I cast no aspersions, throw no stones, assign no guilt, and blame no one actor, with the possible exception of myself, since I acknowledge my own part in the promotion of music theory's historic white supremacy and patriarchy.

Regrettably, in my career I have been a bricklayer in the fortification of music theory's white-male frame. And, over the years, I have laid those bricks happily and willingly. But I now have a different perspective on the field. Does this mean I will now give up my work as a Russianist, which has indeed fallen squarely within the confines of music theory's white-male frame? Of course not. (Nor should anyone else give up a music-theoretical interest because it is both white and male.) But I now do so with a new perspective that actively seeks interaction with nonwhite and nonmale perspectives, which will, in turn, only enrich my work as a Russianist. This is not about casting blame, which, ultimately, is easy. Rather, it's about two things: responsibility and accountability. Every American of any race, white, black, and all others, should think about their own responsibility and accountability regarding our racial reckoning, and we should realize that it has much to do with seniority as well—after all, how much responsibility does a high school student bear for racial injustices in music theory? And yes, white persons, as the beneficiaries of white privilege and entitlement, must especially look at these issues anew and, collectively, take responsibility for past injustice. This has nothing to do with guilt or blame, but with the arduous path forward that we can all travel by accepting some responsibility and accountability for what must now be called our American racial dystopia. As Kimberlé Crenshaw writes, "When it comes to racial reckoning, the future of our country depends not on whether we litigate who among us is guilty *but whether we all see ourselves as responsible.*"[27]

---

27. Kimberlé Crenshaw, "The Panic over Critical Race Theory Is an Attempt to Whitewash U.S. History," *Washington Post*, July 2, 2021 (my italics).

Over the 2020–2021 academic year I gave over sixty invited virtual lectures and, among white friends and colleagues, I noticed what I might call many "deer in headlights." I believe that often white persons in the academic study of music are, let's say, confused about what to make of the rapid changes happening in our music academies, and I think many are wondering what their roles might be in the future or, for that matter, what the role of whiteness will be. I'd like to make two points accordingly. From my side I consider the active participation of white colleagues in our music academies, with respect to restructuring music curricula and the music academies themselves, to be not just desirable, but absolutely necessary, and I for one welcome these colleagues to such discussions with open arms. I'm honored that countless white persons have reached out to me to begin discussions on how we can, collectively, reimagine the academic study of music in the United States and beyond. No, this does not mean that such scholars should be leading the discussions, as they have historically, nor does it mean that those who continue to believe that "music theory has nothing to do with race or gender, and those who point out so-called racist and sexist structures are the actual racists and sexists" should be listened to—they should not, and those facile arguments should be discounted out of hand. But the basic point here is that white persons are essential to the reframing of our music academies, and I think it's important to say so here in my Intro. Second, I'd like to underscore just how much white persons will benefit by letting go of the mythologies of whiteness (and maleness) that still undergird American music theory specifically, and the academic study of music generally.[28] This second point relates to letting go of the "godlike" status, as I mentioned above when I wrote about responsibility, of the select few composers who we have been instructed are the only composers that have really mattered in music's history, the composers of a so-called western canon, another mythology that I unpack in chapter 2.

Of all cities in the United States, New York has the greatest libraries. However, one thing notably altered that simple fact as I wrote this book: the worst pandemic we've seen in modern history. Covid-19 has changed the course of my work in ways I could have never predicted. And though my Kindle reader is exploding and I've bought more hard-copy books for

---

28. For a compelling account of how we can all benefit from letting go of white supremacy's many mythologies, see Heather McGhee, *The Sum of Us: What Racism Costs Everyone and How We Can Prosper Together* (One World, 2021).

delivery than I ever thought I would, there are many books and other materials that have been out of my reach as I've done this work. Specifically, one part of the project that has suffered has been the historical groundwork for some of the topics I raise. If, for example, I want to show music theory's antisemitism in nineteenth-century Europe, which really should not be in doubt when thinking of the Austro-Germanic figures involved, many of the historical accounts—and the letters, diaries, and manuscripts, in English, German, and other European languages—were out of reach because of the pandemic. I had even envisaged, some years ago, a trip to work in certain archives in Germany, Austria, and possibly Russia in order to provide a historical framework for discussing music theory's historic racism, sexism, and antisemitism. So my work has taken a few new turns, focusing more on materials available online, while doing the best I can to provide historical accounts where necessary. I look forward to returning to the history, and the libraries and archives that house it, after the pandemic ends, perhaps with the next project I undertake.

There will be times in this book when I try to show imbalances by discussing the identities of controlling groups in power structures, like an editorial board for a publication or the musical contents of a textbook. In so doing I occasionally needed to make a judgment on, for instance, someone's race or gender, especially when I do not know the individual myself, which is most often the case. When this need arose, I researched individuals online to try to determine the likely identity of the people involved, to see if they themselves have self-identified; otherwise I might ask a third party or, in certain cases, the people themselves. And though I have tried to be as accurate as possible, there are bound to be mistakes, so I apologize, in advance, if I have misrepresented identities in any fashion. It's just that, when discussing race, white power structures have made us all so reticent to have such discussions that we are often shocked when someone brings up another person's racial identity, especially if that person can reasonably qualify as white. This is a tactic of white racial framing, and it is for this reason that I occasionally lean into various identities, to have adult conversations about those things that white men often don't want us to talk about, for fear of losing power and prestige.

In *The Viennese: Splendor, Twilight, and Exile, New York Times* correspondent Paul Hofmann quotes the Dutch conductor and composer Bernard van Beurden and his incisive observation about the Viennese and about Austria: "The Austrian lives in a two-room apartment. One room is bright, friendly, the 'cozy parlor,' well furnished, where he receives his guests. The other room is dark, somber, barred, totally unfathomable."[29] The same could be said of American music theory, or the American academic study of music for that matter, and the apartment in which it dwells. In the friendly room, we music theorists invite guests as we bake a cake, sing songs as someone plays the upright piano, and ring in the new year with friends. And in the twenty-first century, we are fine with celebrating the occasional composer—"Wow, listen to this great string quartet by Florence Price!"—who had hitherto not been considered worthy of this friendly room. However, the dark, dimly lit, "unfathomable" room is where music theory's dreadful secrets hide, where we are frightened to look for fear of what we might see. In this candlelit room, one might find a diary expressing the idea that women, because of their sex, are second-rate composers or cannot lead orchestras; a letter expressing the idea that nonwhite peoples—especially those from Africa—are culturally and biologically inferior to whites; a picture of Adolf Hitler hanging inconspicuously in the corner of the room over the writing desk. To a large extent, *On Music Theory* resides in this dark room and exposes uncomfortable truths. After quoting van Beurden, Hofmann adds: "If the visitors in the friendly parlor are not naive, they will nevertheless soon steal glances of the 'other room,' where the ambivalent Viennese personality also dwells."[30] In *On Music Theory*, I do not ask the reader to "steal a glance" into music theory's "other room." Rather, I ask the reader to enter that room with me and spend actual time there, to live with music theory's dark history, to come to terms with its unpleasantness, and to confront the injustices that have occurred in our history as a result of grim acts in the past. This I do because I am convinced that only by confronting past injustice can we move forward and plot an equitable path for the future of music theory. This I do because I am convinced that, in this fashion, we can make music richer, more meaningful, and more welcoming for everyone.

---

29. Cited in Paul Hofmann, *The Viennese: Splendor, Twilight, and Exile* (Anchor Press, Doubleday, 1988), 1.

30. Hofmann, *The Viennese*, 1.

ONE

On Music Theory, Race, and Racism

All of us know, whether or not we are able to admit it, that mirrors can only lie, that death by drowning is all that awaits one there. It is for this reason that love is so desperately sought and so cunningly avoided. Love takes off the masks that we fear we cannot live without and know we cannot live within.[1]

On May 25, 2020, in Minneapolis, Minnesota, Derek Chauvin, a white police officer, murdered George Floyd, a black civilian, by kneeling on his neck for over nine minutes while Floyd lay on the pavement, hands zip-tied behind his back. Chauvin, smirking for the onlookers who filmed him, remained calm and righteous, never flinching in his belief that it was his right to treat Floyd in this manner. Though this type of murder has been, in US history, not at all uncommon, this twenty-first-century lynching of yet another black body has been somehow unique. More specific, this killing—for which Chauvin was convicted, in April 2021, on all three counts with which he was charged—changed something for white America. Many white persons who had been on the sidelines in our American racial dystopia—in which we BIPOC are told by white structures that things are constantly getting better in a one-way march of racial progress, rather than having those white structures realize that racial progress has always been, in the United States, an ongoing battle between racist thought and antiracist thought—came off the sidelines and took a stand. White music theorists were no exception, as white friends and colleagues in the field acted and committed to confront racism in ways that I personally have never seen in music theory in my more than twenty years in the field.

---

1. James Baldwin, *The Fire Next Time* (Michael Joseph, 1963), 102–3.

The main problem I have noticed as music theory faces its racial past is in how we confront what we see in the mirror as we look at ourselves. Understanding the exclusionist nature of the field is not difficult, and it is also easy to add to the music theory mix a few composers of color and think that this represents a solution to our racial dilemma. However, as Baldwin says in the epigraph to this chapter, all we ever see in that mirror is lies, whether we acknowledge that or not. The lie we are told by music theory, the lie that awaits in the mirror to be seen by the field if it is strong enough to glance, is that the dark secrets of our past are exceptional to our field, and that, by and large, our history has been one of social justice and decency. Of course, this is largely untrue of American music theory, since this is largely untrue of the United States as a country. I often remark that Richard Wagner needed to write a long essay, "Das Judenthum in der Musik" (Jewishness in music) in 1850, published under a pseudonym not insignificantly, in order for us to consider Wagner an antisemite today.[2] I hardly need to point out that, had Wagner not written that and other vile anti-Jewish screeds, we would likely not consider him to be antisemitic today, but his hatred of Jews and Jewishness would have remained. And despite all this, we in music theory, and in classical music generally I hasten to add, have found a way to bracket off Wagner's hatred of Jews, making excuses like "Well, people were much more antisemitic back then" and "Wagner had Jewish friends," all of which allows Wagner to remain in the pantheon of great composers who, as we are told in the academic study of music, are all that matter. Many other composers treated as canonical by music theorists held similar antisemitic beliefs, and, to a large extent, we have whitewashed their antisemitism in order to maintain a facade of exceptionalism, of greatness, all of which, sadly, normalizes and legitimizes antisemitism in the field. And, to finish the Baldwin analogy, not hate but love, and the respect for others that love fosters—love for our fellow musicians, races, ethnicities, and cultures, and the belief that everyone's music and music theory is worthy of academic consideration— will free us from our misconceptions and unmask the true beauty of music theory for all to enjoy.

---

2. See Richard Wagner, *Das Judenthum in der Musik* (Verlagsbuchhandlung von J. J. Weber, 1869). Original published under the pseudonym Karl Freigedank, "Das Judenthum in der Musik," *Neue Zeitschrift für Musik* 17, no. 19 (1850): 101–7 and 17, no. 20 (1850): 109–12.

Defining Music Theory

In the entry entitled "Theory" in *Oxford Music Online*, from 2013, David Carson Berry and Sherman Van Solkema define music theory. Here is the initial paragraph for that long entry:

> An area of study that tends to focus on musical materials per se, in order to explain (and/or offer generalizations about) their various principles and processes. It investigates how these materials function (or, in a more speculative vein, how they might function), so that musical "structure" can be better understood. More broadly, in the United States, music theory refers to an academic discipline with a dual focus on research and pedagogy. Regarding the latter, especially at the undergraduate level (and earlier), theory is often coterminous with a program for teaching a variety of skills, from the rudiments of melody and rhythm, to harmony, counterpoint, and form (along with their attendant "ear training" or aural perception). Related to but standing apart from these fundamentals of praxis are the various research areas of modern theory. . . . It should be noted that music analysis plays a major role in this agenda. Although conceptually separate from theory, in that analysis often focuses on the particulars of a given composition whereas theory considers the broader systems that underlie many such works, in practice the two have a reciprocal relationship.[3]

This seemingly innocuous definition of music theory, one I could have given myself years ago, actually bears many significant traits that point directly to whiteness. Notably, "white" as a descriptor for this type of music theory had never been used until quite recently, with theorists preferring "western" or "European" as preferred descriptors for "music theory," which is intended, in part, to obfuscate race and whiteness in the field. To my mind two terms jump right out: musical materials and function. The idea that music theory deals with musical "materials" points to its reliance on a "notes on the page" formalistic attitude toward the field, and, insofar as classical-music notation is a well-developed system, these materials provide a method for privileging music from Europe, music that has become over time, from a racial standpoint, white. (There are many other global tradi-

---

3. David Carson Berry and Sherman Van Solkema, "Theory," *Oxford Music Online*, 2013.

tions, some with notational systems, some without, that could reasonably be included in music theory so defined here.) In other words, music theory uses the cover of formalism to smuggle in, along with compelling music, ideas about race, both pro-white and antiblack. "Function" was first used by the German music theorist Hugo Riemann (1849–1919) in 1893.[4] Borrowed from mathematics, function became one of the most important ways of discussing chords in the classical system, and therefore in harmony and in harmonic progressions.

Other terms that show the strong penchant for whiteness in this definition for music theory are "harmony," "counterpoint," "form," and "structure." Indeed, harmony, counterpoint, and form are often cited as reasons why western music theory is believed to be more sophisticated and complex than other music theories, which is why we are told that it is most worth our attention. In the introduction to the entry the authors speak of the dominating traditions in late twentieth-century America:

> At the beginning of the 1980s, it could be claimed that the main areas of American theory involved, on the one hand, Schenkerian studies of tonal music and, on the other hand, the investigation of 20th-century music through 12-tone and set theories—a dual emphasis sometimes summarized with the alliteration "Schenker and Sets."[5]

Thus the influence of Heinrich Schenker (1868–1935) is stated early on in this entry, which is significant because of the white supremacist underpinnings of his music theories, which I discuss in depth in chapter 3. In fact, the only names mentioned prior to Schenker in this entry for music theory are two ancient Greeks, Aristoxenus and Pythagoras, both in the introduction, which speaks to the music-theoretical origin mythology of ancient Greece. Pinpointing 1960 as the point at which American music theory broke away from the sibling fields of musicology and ethnomusicology, Berry and Van Solkema highlight the main trends that have shaped the field up until the early twenty-first century. Notably, all the headings in this entry relate directly to what could be called white music-theoretical traditions, such as twelve-tone music, transformational approaches, or theories of form. The

---

4. See Hugo Riemann, *Vereinfachte Harmonielehre, oder Die Lehre von den tonalen Funktionen der Akkorde* (Augener, 1893).

5. Berry and Van Solkema, "Theory."

preceding sections on the eighteenth and nineteenth centuries focus entirely on western traditions.

Of course, *Oxford Music Online*, along with *Die Musik in Geschichte und Gegenwart*, is one of the preeminent music dictionaries in the world.[6] And there are numerous entries for all kinds of global music theories and traditions, many of them captured under headings for nations or ethnicities. But the framing here is very much one of whiteness, in which "theory" in its most basic form is that of the west and of Europe. What this does is create a hierarchy, with music theory as it is considered in its most abstract form, as an "academic discipline with a dual focus on research and pedagogy," as the *Oxford* authors say, on top, and all other subsidiary music theories relegated to other generally non-European and non–North American nations. And when I say "North American" here it's important to add that, in white frameworks, North America usually equates with two and only two countries, Canada and the United States, despite the fact that North America the continent, located entirely in the northern hemisphere of our planet, extends all the way down to the Panama-Colombia border. The reason for this is simple: Canada and the United States are the only majority-white nations in North America. Finally, author representation is also important in this encyclopedia entry. Though there are names in the entry and bibliography that don't represent white men, such as Kofi Agawu, Calvin Grimes, Adele Katz, Jairo Moreno, or Janet Schmalfeldt, the vast majority of the names mentioned—I'd say at least 90%—are of white men. And the two entry authors are white men as well.

I'll end this section by giving a much simpler definition for music theory, one to which I'd like to aspire: "the interpretation, investigation, analysis, pedagogy, and performance of any music from our planet." I struggle with redefining music theory in the twenty-first century in the United States. There is so much racial- and gender-identity baggage in our collective understanding of what American music theory is and what it should be. And so much of this baggage is only now being seen for the first time, though it's been hiding in plain sight ever since the 1960s, when the *Oxford Music Online* authors claimed American music theory began.

---

6. The Soviet Union's six-volume *Музыкальная энциклопедия* (Music encyclopedia) is also worth mentioning here. See Yuri Keldysh, *Музыкальная энциклопедия*, 6 vols. (Sovetskaia Entsiklopediia, 1991). For more on this Russian-language music encyclopedia, see my "Russia's New Grove: Priceless Resource or Propagandistic Rubbish?," in *Music's Intellectual History*, *RILM Perspectives* (2008): 659–70.

How Music Theory Has Dealt with Race in the Past

Much like the country that spawned it, American music theory has trouble acknowledging its racial past. One of the most important aspects of how our field has dealt with race is the simple fact that those who have framed race, who have told the relevant stories, have been, with remarkable consistency, white persons. To tell stories in this fashion is to tell them from a white racial frame. In *The White Racial Frame: Centuries of Racial Framing and Counter-framing*, sociologist Joe Feagin argues that whites have shaped history in the United States by constructing a white racial frame "to rationalize and insure white privilege and dominance over Americans of color."[7] I argue that this frame is very much active in music theory today, with respect to the composers we choose to analyze and teach, and the theorists we tend to study and admire. Feagin defines the white racial frame as

> an overarching white worldview that encompasses a *broad and persisting set of racial stereotypes, prejudices, ideologies, images, interpretations and narratives, emotions, and reactions to language accents, as well as racialized inclinations to discriminate.*[8]

Feagin continues:

> For centuries now, it has been a dominant and foundational frame from which a substantial majority of white Americans—as well as many others accepting or seeking to conform to white norms and perspectives—view our still highly racialized society.[9]

Based on his definition, one may think immediately of negative stereotypes of blacks and question whether they apply to music theory. What I stress at this point, however, is not so much negative black stereotypes as positive white stereotypes or, as Feagin calls them, "pro-white subframe[s],"[10] which are fundamental to music theory and which also spur a "racialized inclination to discriminate." Music theory has many of the prejudices and stereotypes that are part of the white racial frame, most noticeably in how we

---

7. Joe Feagin, *The White Racial Frame: Centuries of Racial Framing and Counter-framing*, 2nd ed. (Routledge, [2009] 2013), x.

8. Feagin, *The White Racial Frame*, 3.

9. Feagin, *The White Racial Frame*, 3.

10. Feagin, *The White Racial Frame*, 10.

privilege the compositional and theoretical work of whites over nonwhites. The subtle ways in which music theory disadvantages BIPOC are harder to grasp, but a penetrating race analysis can reveal some of these disadvantages. Indeed, this pro-white subframe has often resulted in antiblack behavior in the field. Perhaps the most important function of the white racial frame is to keep the system as it is: "One function of the white frame is to justify the great array of privileges and assets held by white Americans as the group at the top of the racial hierarchy."[11] There can be no question that white persons hold the power in music theory—music theory's white racial frame entrenches and institutionalizes that power.

Another paramount aspect to music theory's white racial frame, an aspect that predates academic music's predilection for whiteness, is its male framework, its patriarchy. Men have been discriminating against women far longer than whites have been discriminating against nonwhites, and this simple fact plays a notable role in music theory.[12] In *Elite White Men Ruling: Who, What, When, Where, and How*, Joe Feagin and coauthor Kimberley Ducey identify an "*elite-white-male dominance system*, a complex and oppressive system central to most western societies that now affects much of the planet."[13] One of the biggest problems with how music theory has framed race emanates from the simple fact that those telling the stories are, with remarkable consistency, white men. Feagin and Ducey note that "this elite has historically generated much of the racial, gender, and class framing rationalizing their actions."[14] Thus music theory's stories about race are half-truths at best, and have historically served only to corroborate white-male narratives. What music theory has never had, and what it needs, is sustained critique from various BIPOC and all those who do not identify as cisgender men to uncover how and why music theory remains unjust from racial and gender standpoints.

Thus the two main identities that frame my work in *On Music Theory* are *white* and *male*, the twin pillars of domination in our field. In many ways I approach these two identities from a sociological perspective, in order to

---

11. Feagin, *The White Racial Frame*, 146.

12. Race scholar Ibram X. Kendi places the origins of racist ideas and white supremacy in mid-fifteenth-century Europe and the slave trading of King Alfonso V of Portugal. See Kendi's *Stamped from the Beginning: The Definitive History of Racist Ideas in America* (Nation Books, 2016), chapter 2, "Origins of Racist Ideas."

13. Joe Feagin and Kimberley Ducey, *Elite White Men Ruling: Who, What, When, Where, and How* (Routledge, 2017), 1.

14. Feagin and Ducey, *Elite White Men Ruling*, 2.

show the behind-the-scenes power that they wield. Since its inception in the mid-twentieth century, American music theory has tried to maintain a "notes on the page" distance from the human experience, in which the musical score is paramount and all other avenues of inquiry subordinate. Of course, on the one hand, this was a way of turning attention to formalistic elements in music, to break away from the historically minded sibling field of musicology and prove music's scientific bona fides in an era filled with Cold War scientific explorations.[15] But on the other hand, music theory's break with the human experience allowed it to further enshrine white cis-gender men as those at the top of the heap, those who were allowed to tell music theory's history and its stories, those who reaped the most benefits of a system they contrived for themselves. Feagin and Ducey write:

> We demonstrate that *whiteness* and *maleness* are extraordinarily important social dimensions shaping this elite's personal and collective reality, including their dominant social framing and their decisions flowing from that framing. As we demonstrate, these elite white men have for centuries constituted the group at the top of three major social hierarchies—the capitalistic, sexist, and racial hierarchies. They have long created, maintained, and extended these inegalitarian hierarchies that are imbedded in and shaping all societal institutions. Generally speaking, contemporary social scientists and other social analysts have substantially bypassed an in-depth analysis of the reality and significance of the *white* and *male* aspects of this controlling elite's motivations to act and, thus, the important decisions that result.[16]

Thus whiteness plus maleness has proven to be the most crucial element in my own reframing of music theory, and these are the two most basic identities from which I work. Notably, I do not focus on the socioeconomic aspects of music theory's forms of oppression, the "capitalistic" argument that is part of Feagin and Ducey's work. The reason I do not do so is that I believe that, in so doing, one takes the focus off whiteness, and I have found that redirection to be one of the main goals of white persons in discussions about race. This is not to say that there is not a socioeconomic element to our racial disparities in music theory—there most certainly is. Rather, it is to

---

15. For more on this break see Patrick McCreless, "Music Theory and Historical Awareness," *Music Theory Online* 6, no. 3 (August 2000).

16. Feagin and Ducey, *Elite White Men Ruling*, 4.

bring the conversation back to where it needs to dwell, namely, to race and whiteness. And though my primary focus remains race, I often venture into discussions of gender in relation to race, since race and gender have been tied right at the hip in the history of American patriarchal white supremacy.

While there have been no stand-alone music-theoretical books to deal explicitly with race and whiteness in the field, there are precedents, especially musicological. Here I'm thinking of mainstream, which is to say white, musicology and music theory. The first significant such precedent, to my mind, is Ronald Radano and Philip Bohlman's edited volume *Music and the Racial Imagination* from 2000.[17] A compelling and meaty volume, it represents a deep dive into racial matters in the academic study of music. In the introduction its editors speak of the "specter of race" that "lurks in the house of music," a scrim to our musical performances that has yet to be backlit and thus noticed.[18] To Radano and Bohlman race, for all intents and purposes, has been erased from the larger musical conversation. This notable volume seeks to rectify this erasure. Its twenty-two diverse contributors— whose nine BIPOC authors include Asian, Latinx, and black voices—offer a global outlook on how race and music intersect, and how we might begin to make racial matters part of the conversation in our American music academy.[19] Notably, Radano and Bohlman construct race from a western perspective, which is of course European, historically speaking: "Fundamental to European concepts of race is an opposition between musics that historically participated in the construction of a European canon and those that did not."[20] In 2000, however, even in musicology, which is better at acknowledging race than music theory, there was still a hesitancy to connect this European construction of race to either white supremacy or antiblackness. These latter two terms are now quite common, yet, in certain conservative quarters, still controversial. So *Music and the Racial Imagination*, for all of its

---

17. Ronald Radano and Philip V. Bohlman, eds., *Music and the Racial Imagination* (University of Chicago Press, 2000).

18. Radano and Bohlman, *Music and the Racial Imagination*, 1.

19. In *On Music Theory* I use "Latinx" as the genderless version of Latina (a woman from Latin America, broadly speaking) and Latino (the same for a man). Latinx has caused debates over the past several years insofar as it is seen as an American, English-language, and hegemonic term that is generally not used in the Spanish- and Portuguese-speaking areas where Latinx people largely come from. I use the term to challenge the implicit gender binary of "Latina/Latino," and to show solidarity with gender nonbinary and transgender people in Latin America. For more on this topic, see Fernanda Zamudio-Suarez, "Race on Campus: What Does 'Latinx' Mean?," *Chronicle of Higher Education*, March 16, 2021.

20. Radano and Bohlman, *Music and the Racial Imagination*, 25.

rigor and incisive scholarship, is still representative of an earlier time when a more direct accounting of race and whiteness was still suppressed, or at least unspoken, in the academy.

Another significant musicological precedent is Julie Brown's edited volume *Western Music and Race* from 2007.[21] A compelling contribution, this book is somewhat mistitled since it primarily considers European constructions of race between 1883, the year of Richard Wagner's death, and 1933, the rise of the Third Reich. That is, American conceptions of race are minimized, which is also evidenced by the makeup of the authors: only one BIPOC author, Guthrie P. Ramsey Jr., who is black, among the nineteen names. Thus this volume represents a white racially framed perspective on music and race, which can be called "traditional" in the sense that only white voices, historically, have been amplified in academic music. This is not to downplay the significance of this volume, which includes penetrating scholarship for the fifty years of European history to which it is dedicated. A more appropriate title may have been "Western Music and European Conceptions of Race, 1883–1933." In her introduction, Brown cites the three broad areas of research into race in musicology, ethnomusicology, and music theory: the antisemitic and the "so-called regeneration theories of Wagner," musical and cultural policies of the Nazis, and African American music.[22] She then identifies her volume as bridging the divide between the first two areas, thus minimizing American perspectives on race.

Thomas Christensen's *Stories of Tonality in the Age of François-Joseph Fétis* from 2019 represents a significant foray into race in music theory, which, when it comes to humanistic matters like race, has always played on the back side of the beat when compared to musicology.[23] To be clear, race is only a subsection of his larger project, but notable nevertheless. Part monograph on the history of tonality through a nineteenth-century (primarily) French perspective, part biography of one of tonality's most significant practitioners, Christensen's account of tonality's history, its story, is riveting. And though the book's narrative is to a significant extent historical, it can certainly be called theoretical as well, with musical examples outlining notable points in tonality's history. Because Fétis, later in life, turned to the pseudoscientific race writings of Arthur de Gobineau, Christensen devotes chapter 5 to

21. Julie Brown, ed., *Western Music and Race* (Cambridge University Press, 2007).

22. Brown, *Western Music and Race*, xiv–xv.

23. Thomas Christensen, *Stories of Tonality in the Age of François-Joseph Fétis* (University of Chicago Press, 2019).

racial matters and how they shaped Fétis's thinking late in life. In a powerful part of that chapter, "The Racialization of Tonality," Christensen speaks of Gobineau's impact on Fétis:

> The writings on race of Arthur de Gobineau may be an extreme example of this [racial] bias, with his adulation of the pure blood of the great white Aryan race and his dire warning about racial miscegenation leading to the decline of Western civilization, but they are nonetheless a sobering indicator. All the more sobering is to discover that Fétis owned a copy of Gobineau's notorious tract and evidently made much use of it.[24]

Christensen's focus on Fétis's obsession with the superiority of the "race blanche" represents a significant step forward in music-theoretical race studies. Christensen does an admirable job of tying Fétis's racist thought into his monograph, though he does not speculate as to what this racist thought may have meant for the future of tonality or, more specific, how Fétis's belief in musical white superiority may have impacted the racial development of music theory as a discipline. What Christensen gives us, then, is a model through which we might begin to consider race in music theory's history.

Finally, Brian Hyer's discussion of tonality in *The Cambridge History of Western Music Theory* is worth mentioning as a precedent to my work, since Hyer also discusses Fétis's racial theories in relation to music theory, and especially how racial superiority manifested itself in music.[25] Hyer writes:

> Tonalité was in fact the site of a remarkable number of cultural anxieties, worries about the future of music, but also (and perhaps surprisingly) about race. For Fétis, there was a strong anthropological dimension to tonalité: he believed that different human societies were attracted to different pitch repertoires because of their different mental capacities, which were, moreover, a function of "cerebral conformation." Fétis asserted that primitive (non-Western) societies were limited to simpler scales because of their simpler brain structures, while the more complex psychological organizations of Indo-Europeans permitted them to realize, over historical time, the full

---

24. Christensen, *Stories of Tonality*, 204.
25. Brian Hyer, "Tonality," in *The Cambridge History of Western Music Theory*, ed. Thomas Christensen (Cambridge University Press, [2002] 2008), 726–52.

musical potential of tonalité; his theories were similar in their biological determinism to the racial theories of Gobineau.[26]

From this passage, and from the prior passage about Fétis from Christensen, we can see just how important the racial theories of French pseudoscientist Gobineau were and, especially, his *Essai sur l'inégalité des races humaines* (Essay on the inequality of human races) from 1853–1855.[27] Gobineau's theories on racial subordination were widely read in the nineteenth and early twentieth centuries, and greatly impacted both Fétis and Richard Wagner. Perhaps most important for American music theory, Heinrich Schenker was directly influenced by Gobineau as well. For those outside of music theory, Schenker, who figures prominently in *On Music Theory*, is arguably the most important figure in the history of American music theory, a topic I discuss in detail in chapter 3. And with respect to the pseudo race scientist Gobineau, a simple search for "Gobineau" on *Schenker Documents Online* yields five instances where Schenker referred to Gobineau positively in his diary entries, all from 1918, and Schenker famously refers to Gobineau in "Von der Sendung des deutschen Genies" (The mission of German genius), from *Der Tonwille*, as well.[28] What this all allowed for was "scientific" proof of racial inferiority and superiority in music, which amounted to a calling for musical eugenicists such as Carl Seashore in the early twentieth century in order to maintain and reinforce musical structures that benefited the white men who created those structures.[29]

Hyer speaks of how Fétis sought to advance "Orientalism," the European project to research and catalog those cultures that were not western, but also not African or American, that could pose a threat to Europe, which was, in the nineteenth century, becoming "the West." This project supported many

---

26. Hyer, "Tonality," 748. About this quotation, I would add that, to a black person, it is not at all "surprising" that tonality could cause "cultural anxieties" or "worries" if discussed in terms of race within a white framework.

27. Arthur de Gobineau, *Essai sur l'inégalité des races humaines* (Essay on the inequality of human races), 4 vols. (Paris, 1853–55).

28. Heinrich Schenker, *Der Tonwille: Pamphlets in Witness of the Immutable Laws of Music, Offered to a New Generation of Youth*, trans. Ian Bent, William Drabkin, Joseph Dubiel, Timothy Jackson, Joseph Lubben, and Robert Snarrenberg (Oxford University Press, [1921–23] 2004), vol. 1, 13.

29. See Julia Eklund Koza's *"Destined to Fail": Carl Seashore's World of Eugenics, Psychology, Education, and Music* (University of Michigan Press, 2021). See also Johanna Devaney, "Eugenics and Musical Talent: Exploring Carl Seashore's Work on Talent Testing and Performance," *American Music Review* 48, no. 2 (Spring 2019): 1–6.

half-baked ideas and generalizations about what the Orient was, but key to this European understanding was racial superiority. Hyer writes:

> A strong motive behind these generalizations was the tacit fear that various African and Eastern cultural practices constituted a threat to European notions of social self-identification: in contrast to the modern West, the Orient appeared to European writers as a primitive or even animalistic realm of sexual desire, religious violence, and racial terror. In general, these [nineteenth-century European] writers organized knowledge about the East into cross-cultural comparisons that served to denigrate non-Western others and thus associated the Oriental with marginalized elements in their own societies—the ignorant, backward, degenerate, insane, and the feminine.[30]

This denigration of "non-Western others" was a key component in constructing nineteenth-century "western" mythologies and, with them, racial hierarchies and white supremacy. Hyer accurately points to the simple fact that tonality, as such, was not an impartial music-theoretical construct, unaffected by the social forces that surrounded it. To the contrary, tonality was a tool, an armament in the battle for hearts and minds in nineteenth-century conceptions of music and the academic study thereof. Hyer writes:

> While the essentialization of race in terms of pitch repertoires has since been discredited, the practice remains part of the genealogical heritage of tonality. But the main point here is that the concept of tonality, as an ideological construct, serves to articulate and promote a far from disinterested view of the historical past.[31]

These four works—*Music and the Racial Imagination*, *Western Music and Race*, *Stories of Tonality in the Age of François-Joseph Fétis*, and "Tonality"—represent significant precedents to my own work in how race played out in music theory and in our music academies. But, to be clear, they generally represent a white racially framed view of racial music and musical race. That is, they represent white musicological and white music-theoretical points of view on nonwhite musical matters. Though my own such view is also that of a music academician, it is also a black view. Thus I try, with my

---

30. Hyer, "Tonality," 749.
31. Hyer, "Tonality," 749.

work, to flip the script and view academic music from a race angle, rather than the other way around, as Radano, Bohlman, Brown, Christensen, and Hyer, who are all white themselves, do. And when this script gets flipped and academic music is viewed from a nonwhite perspective, the concept of whiteness naturally comes to the fore as the most powerful element that has shaped the academic study of music in the United States. I don't wish to disparage any of the authors and editors of these notable books; I only wish to point out that in them, for the most part, race is considered from a white perspective, and that comes with its own set of issues. In a sense, the two edited volumes and "Tonality" were a product of their times, when discussions of "white supremacy" and "structural" or "systemic" racism were the exclusive domain of race scholarship and critical race theory. My work here builds on these four precedents in race scholarship in music and gives a black—and generally, I hope, nonwhite—perspective on race in our American music academy.

In looking at two musicological edited volumes with "race" in the title, and two music-theoretical works that dealt specifically with race, I've hardly given a full picture of authors who have tried to unpack how race plays out in the music academy, nor have I tried to. There are many such authors, both white and nonwhite, who have done significant race scholarship—I am only a small part of a much larger conversation, and I stand on the shoulders of so many others who have sought to make the academic study of music more welcoming. Often these authors expand what counts as music theory, such as Sumarsam's "Inner Melody in Javanese Gamelan Music" from 1975, or Willie Anku's "Principles of Rhythm Integration in African Drumming" from 1997.[32] More generally, the great work of *Analytical Approaches to World Music*, along with its several online journals under the general editorship of Lawrence Shuster, has provided venues in which to explore nonwestern ideas in music theory.[33] Michael Tenzer's *Analytical Studies in World Music* from 2006 remains a landmark volume for its time, and the many articles in the now-defunct *Black Music Research Journal* still provide fertile ideas for expanding nonwhite music theory.[34] As the editor of *Gamut: Online Journal of the Music Theory Society of the Mid-Atlantic*, I oversaw the forum "Eth-

32. See Sumarsam, "Inner Melody in Javanese Gamelan Music," *Asian Music* 7, no. 1 (1975): 3–13; and Willie Anku, "Principles of Rhythm Integration in African Drumming," *Black Music Research Journal* 17, no. 2 (Autumn 1997): 211–238.

33. See http://iftawm.org/journal/oldsite

34. See Michael Tenzer, ed., *Analytical Studies in World Music* (Oxford University Press, 2006).

nic Diversity in Music Theory: Voices from the Field," which featured five outstanding pieces that sought to reframe music theory with issues of diversity in mind.[35] New relevant dissertations, such as Zhuqing Hu's "From Ut Re Mi to Fourteen-Tone Temperament: The Global Acoustemologies of an Early Modern Chinese Tuning Reform," and Daniel Walden's "The Politics of Tuning and Temperament: Transnational Exchange and the Production of Music Theory in 19th-Century Europe, Asia, and North America," continue to push music theory in new directions.[36] Bibliographies and new websites abound, and there is a great amount of new material online that seeks to reframe the field.[37] Indeed, there are far too many such works, works that lie outside of white-male music theory, or the academic study of music generally, to list in a paragraph here—I simply wish to acknowledge that there is great work out there, both inside and outside music theory, that seeks to include other music theories apart from where music theory has resided in the United States historically.[38]

35. See Philip Ewell, ed., "Forum: Ethnic Diversity in Music Theory: Voices from the Field," *Gamut: Online Journal of the Music Theory Society of the Mid-Atlantic* 2, no. 1 (2009). The five items were "Inconvenient Truths, and Changes to Believe In: Foreword to the Forum," by Jeannie Ma. Guerrero, "Diversity, Music, Theory, and the Neoliberal Academy," by Sumanth Gopinath, "Diversifying Music Theory," by Youyoung Kang, "In and around Music Theory and the Academy: A Perspective," by Horace J. Maxile Jr., and "On Diversity," by Amy Cimini and Jairo Moreno.

36. See Zhuqing Hu, "From Ut Re Mi to Fourteen-Tone Temperament" (PhD dissertation, University of Chicago, 2019), and Daniel Walden, "The Politics of Tuning and Temperament" (PhD dissertation, Harvard University, 2019).

37. For web resources see *Black Opera Research Network* (blackoperaresearch.net); *Composers of Color Resource Project* (composersofcolor.hcommons.org); *ÆPEX Contemporary Performance* (http://aepexcontemporary.org); *Engaged Music Theory* (engagedmusictheory.com); *Music by Black Composers* (musicbyblackcomposers.org); *Institute for Composer Diversity* (composerdiversity.com); *Expanding the Music Theory Canon* (expandingthemusictheorycanon.com); *Project Spectrum* (projectspectrummusic.com); and Dave Molk and Michelle Ohnona, "Promoting Equity: Developing an Antiracist Music Theory Classroom," *New Music Box*, January 29, 2020 (https://nmbx.newmusicusa.org/promoting-equity-developing-an-antiracist-music-theory-classroom).

38. See also Ellie Hisama, "Getting to Count," *Music Theory Spectrum* 43, no. 2 (2021): 1–15; Tamara Levitz, "The Musicological Elite," *Current Musicology* 102 (2018): 9–80; Matthew Morrison, "Race, Blacksound, and the (Re)making of Musicological Discourse," *Journal of the American Musicological Society* 72, no. 3 (2019): 781–823; and Cora Palfy and Eric Gilson, "The Hidden Curriculum in the Music Theory Classroom," *Journal of Music Theory Pedagogy* 32 (2018): 79–110. Edited volumes: Rachel Lumsden and Jeffrey Swinkin, eds., *The Norton Guide to Teaching Music Theory* (Norton, 2018); Robin D. Moore, ed., *College Music Curricula for a New Century* (Oxford University Press, 2017); and Ronald Radano and

Other works, again both inside and outside music theory, have challenged the whiteness of the field even more directly. For instance, Kofi Agawu's "Tonality as a Colonizing Force in Africa" frames music theory's main subject, tonality, as a force for seizing and maintaining power in colonial empires.[39] Loren Kajikawa, in two articles, "The Possessive Investment in Classical Music: Confronting Legacies of White Supremacy in U.S. Schools and Departments of Music" and "Leaders of the New School? Music Departments, Hip-Hop, and the Challenge of Significant Difference," directly confronts white power in American music academies.[40] Though an ethnomusicologist, Kajikawa addresses the latter article to music theorists while citing the controversy over volume 12 of the *Journal of Schenkerian Studies* that involved me and my music-theoretical scholarship. In the former Kajikawa directly confronts what gets to count as music study in the United States, and how those musics that are not directly linked to whiteness have been shunted to the side. Naomi André's authoritative *Black Opera* not only adds a racial dimension to the production of opera, but also offers a new term, "engaged musicology," to encourage others to not shy away from those aspects of opera, or of academic music, that may be uncomfortable, bringing historical context into dialogue with present-day issues.[41] Finally, Kira Thurman's compelling *Singing Like Germans: Black Musicians in the Land of Bach, Beethoven, and Brahms* maps out the intersection of African Americans, on the one hand, and their explorations in Germany and Europe on the other.[42]

Tejumola Olaniyan, eds., *Audible Empire: Music, Global Politics, Critique* (Duke University Press, 2016). Monographs: Karl Hagstrom Miller, *Segregating Sound: Inventing Folk and Pop Music in the Age of Jim Crow* (Duke University Press, 2010); Ronald Radano, *Lying Up a Nation: Race and Black Music* (University of Chicago Press, 2003); Guthrie P. Ramsey Jr., *Race Music: Black Cultures from Bebop to Hip-Hop* (University of California Press, 2004); Nina Sun Eidsheim, *The Race of Sound: Listening, Timbre, and Vocality in African American Music* (Duke University Press, 2019).

39. Kofi Agawu, "Tonality as a Colonizing Force in Africa," in *Audible Empire: Music, Global Politics, Critique*, ed. Ronald Radano and Tejumola Olaniyan (Duke University Press, 2016), 334–55.

40. Loren Kajikawa, "The Possessive Investment in Classical Music: Confronting Legacies of White Supremacy in U.S. Schools and Departments of Music," in *Seeing Race Again: Countering Colorblindness across the Disciplines*, ed. Kimberlé Williams Crenshaw, Luke Charles Harris, Daniel Martinez HoSang, and George Lipsitz (University of California Press, 2019), 155–74; and "Leaders of the New School? Music Departments, Hip-Hop, and the Challenge of Significant Difference," *Twentieth-Century Music* 18, no. 1 (2020): 45–64.

41. Naomi André, *Black Opera: History, Power, Engagement* (University of Illinois Press, 2018).

42. Kira Thurman, *Singing Like Germans: Black Musicians in the Land of Bach, Beethoven, and Brahms* (Cornell University Press, 2021).

This topic affects me deeply insofar as my own African American father was deeply in love with all things German and would have liked to study in Germany himself had he had the opportunity.

In this section I've given four significant precedents to my work from white authors in order to understand how mainstream academic music has dealt with race historically, and then I've listed many additional works that, in one way or another, endeavor to do some of the same things. I should also mention, if briefly, the long line of black scholars, aside from those I've listed, who have worked with African American musics: music theorists like Dwight Andrews, Horace Boyer, Calvin Grimes, Horace Maxile, Teresa Reed, Jewel Thompson, and Lucius Wyatt; musicologists like A.D. Carson, Eileen Hayes, Travis Jackson, Tammy Kernodle, Emmett Price, Rosita Sands, Eileen Southern, and Josephine Wright; or composers like George Lewis, Guthrie Ramsey, and *countless* others. To an extent such scholars have done work similar to that which I do in the present monograph. Yet, as I alluded to earlier, there has never been, to my mind, a monograph that deals specifically with race, racism, and whiteness in American music theory written by an African American author, so in this sense I believe *On Music Theory* is unique. Nevertheless, I am deeply indebted to all those who came before me or work alongside me who strive for the same goal, namely, making the academic study of music richer and more welcoming for everyone.

Race and Demographic Data in Music Theory

According to the Society for Music Theory's "Annual Report on Membership Demographics" for 2019, 83.7% (977 members) of the society's 1,173 members were white.[43] This number has decreased from a high of 88.6% (957) in 2015, but both of these percentages, which even include student society members, are misleading. By far and away the most important number that needs tracking in this report is tenured full-time professors, and this report does not track "tenure" as a category. The reason tenure is important is simple: tenure equates with power in academia. That is, tenure puts a faculty member in the position to speak their mind without fear of losing their job, which in turn allows that faculty member to build the structures—the curricula, exams, degree programs, ensembles, reading lists, admission and

---

43. Jenine Brown, "Annual Report on Membership Demographics," Society for Music Theory, October 2019, 4–5 (https://societymusictheory.org/sites/default/files/demographics /smt-demographics-report-2019.pdf).

audition requirements, among others—that then become institutionalized in the music academy. By this metric, the situation in the Society for Music Theory and American music theory writ large is much more dire. Allowing for the fact that, most often, associate and full professors have tenure, the report states that 90.6% (173) of associate professors and 96.0% (168) of full professors are white, so that roughly 93.5% of tenured faculty in American music theory are white.[44]

This is the most important number to discuss from the SMT demographic report, since this number represents those who can actually change a curriculum that focuses exclusively on the music or music theories of white men, discontinue entrance/exit or diagnostic exams meant to police and enforce a commitment to whiteness and maleness, or refashion musicianship instrumental requirements beyond piano proficiency. Whereas a tenure-track job may represent a green card—and, before that, admission into a top doctoral program may represent an H-1B visa—tenure represents a passport to full citizenship in the field, with all of the rights and privileges (and, all too often, not so many responsibilities) that come with that citizenship. And even if American music theory is now ready to grant H-1B visas and green cards to a growing number of nonwhite theorists, much like in our country on the whole, the white frame of American music theory is still averse to granting full citizenship to BIPOC—think here of my own battle for tenure at Hunter College that I outlined in the Intro—for the simple reason that, once the number of tenured BIPOC faculty increases, the influence of whiteness will decrease, which is something white frameworks generally don't want, even if this dynamic plays out only in the subconscious, as it often does.

For over twenty-five years, since the formation of the Committee on Diversity in 1995, SMT has been trying to increase racial and ethnic diversity in the society. This has been done through a variety of initiatives, which include but are not limited to forming committees to address demographic

---

44. I'm essentially averaging these two numbers here since it's unclear in the report what the total members are. The reports states that "when making the percentages shown below, totals within each rank excluded the 72 members who left their rank field empty, the 45 members who did preferred to not [sic] provide their race/ethnicity, and the six members for which no data was collected in the race/ethnicity field" (Brown, "Annual Report on Membership Demographics," 9). Because of this unclear sentence, I was unable to calculate the precise percentage of tenured faculty, a number that may only slightly change anyway since it is only on rare occasions that associate and full professors are not tenured (and, for that matter, occasionally assistant professors are, in fact, tenured).

issues; providing grant monies targeting ethnic and racial minority communities; instituting programs for mentoring BIPOC students and scholars; culling demographic data to get a better handle on the issues; convening special sessions, panels, and roundtables on ethnic and racial issues at academic conferences; and diversifying repertoires to include the music of nonwhite composers. It's time to acknowledge that these efforts have failed.

Race and Demographic Data in Music Theory Textbooks

Textbooks are presented as authoritative sources that outline the foundations of a discipline. Instructors and students alike rely on the depth and accuracy of the materials presented in their classrooms; thus textbooks are chosen carefully with respect to past traditions, current trends, and future possibilities. However, when examining contemporary music theory textbooks in the United States, one questions whether the traditions, trends, and possibilities presented truly represent the country for which these textbooks are intended. In fact, over 98% of the musical examples from seven representative textbooks were written by white persons.[45] In pointing this out, I highlight one of the most pressing and current aspects of music theory education in the United States: systemic and structural racism. Music theory, in its presentation of what music is, represents a system that excludes those who are not white. This system, in turn, represents a structure, one of racial exclusionism.[46]

In this section I undertake a brief racial examination of the seven most common undergraduate music theory textbooks. More specific, I look at their musical examples and how they reflect or do not reflect current trends. These textbooks are representative of music theory's white racial frame, which contains many racialized structures that reliably benefit whites while disadvantaging nonwhites. Because whiteness has worked

---

45. I chose these seven textbooks as the most representative based on discussions with textbook publishers and other music theory professors.

46. I undertook this music theory textbook analysis with Megan Lyons in early 2020. The textbook by Burstein/Straus, *Concise Introduction to Tonal Harmony* (Norton, 2020), is now in its second edition, which is not reflected in this analysis. For a more complete version of this work see Philip Ewell and Megan Lyons, "Don't You Cry for Me: A Critical-Race Analysis of Undergraduate Music Theory Textbooks," forthcoming in *Teaching and Learning Difficult Topics in the Music Classroom*. I thank Megan Lyons for her work on this textbook-analysis project.

hand in glove with maleness in shaping the music theory curriculum represented in these textbooks, I'll also consider female composer representation in discussing the racial aspect of these textbooks. Unsurprisingly, the textbooks are overwhelmingly populated with examples written by white men, despite the fact that there are significant examples of women and BIPOC composers going back many centuries, composers who could easily have been included in the academic study of music.[47] This history of exclusionism negatively affects us all, especially our students, who, in my opinion, easily see this racial and gender exclusionism and consider it unjust, and who understand how it only serves to reinforce white-male norms while alienating BIPOC and female students.

Seven textbooks, as seen in table 1.1, account for roughly 96% of the market share of music theory textbooks.[48] Of the 2,930 musical examples presented in the seven textbooks, only 49 (1.67%) were written by nonwhite composers, while 68 (2.32%) of the examples were composed by women.[49] Three textbooks—by Aldwell/Schachter/Cadwallader, Burstein/Straus, and Laitz—contain a total of only 3 examples by nonwhites, while containing a total of 1,319 examples. For these three textbooks, only 0.2% of the examples were written by nonwhites, and these textbooks account for roughly 24% of the market share. These three textbooks also have the fewest examples by women, with a total of 7 examples, for only 0.5% of the total examples.

Of course, a small number of white-male composers account for many of the examples in all textbooks. Table 1.2 shows the percentages for the three most common composers, Johann Sebastian Bach, Ludwig van Beethoven, and Wolfgang Amadeus Mozart. In the textbook by Benward/Saker, for instance, 33% of the examples were by Bach alone, while 46% of its examples were composed by these three composers. In the textbook by Aldwell/Schachter/Cadwallader, exactly half of the musical examples were written by these three composers, while the textbook by Clendinning/Marvin, at 30%,

47. Such as the female composers Hildegard von Bingen (1098–1179) or Barbara Strozzi (1619–1677), or the black composers Vicente Lusitano (c. 1522–c. 1562) or Joseph Bologne (1745–1799).

48. According to Justin Hoffman, senior acquisitions editor at Oxford University Press, formerly of W. W. Norton & Company, Inc. (Justin Hoffman, email correspondence with author, May 24, 2019).

49. With regard to the possible overlap between these two groups, there were six composers who were both nonwhite and female: Chen Yi, L. Viola Kinney, Florence Price, Vicki Sue Robinson, Maymie (also spelled "Mayme") Watts, and Mary Lou Williams.

Table 1.1. Examples by Nonwhite and Women Composers in Seven Common Music Theory Textbooks

Textbook	Market share (%)	Total examples	Examples by nonwhites (N)	(%)	Examples by women (N)	(%)
Aldwell, Schachter, and Cadwallader, 4th ed. (2011)	5	465	0	0	0	0
Benward and Saker, 9th ed. (2015)	13	333	8	2.40	7	2.10
Burstein and Straus, 1st ed. (2016)	11	304	1	0.33	5	1.64
Clendinning and Marvin, 3rd ed. (2016)	25	504	15	2.98	14	2.78
Kostka, Payne, and Almén, 8th ed. (2018)	29	370	10	2.70	10	2.70
Laitz, 4th ed. (2015)	8	550	2	0.36	2	0.36
Roig-Francoli, 2nd ed. (2010)	5	404	13	3.22	30	7.43
Total	96	2,930	49	1.67	68	2.32

Table 1.2. Percentages of Examples by J. S. Bach, Beethoven, and Mozart in Seven Common Music Theory Textbooks

Textbook	Examples by J.S. Bach (%)	Examples by Beethoven (%)	Examples by Mozart (%)	*Total* (%)
Aldwell, Schachter, and Cadwallader, 4th ed. (2011)	20	11	19	50
Benward and Saker, 9th ed. (2015)	33	5	8	46
Burstein and Straus, 1st ed. (2016)	17	12	13	42
Clendinning and Marvin, 3rd ed. (2016)	14	3	13	30
Kostka, Payne, and Almén, 8th ed. (2018)	16	9	14	39
Laitz, 4th ed. (2015)	5	13	14	32
Roig-Francoli, 2nd ed. (2010)	19	7	11	37

Table 1.3. Racial and Gender Makeup of Composers in Seven Common Music Theory Textbooks

Textbook	Market share (%)	Total composers (N)	Nonwhite composers (N)	Nonwhite composers (%)	Women composers (N)	Women composers (%)
Aldwell, Schachter, and Cadwallader, 4th ed. (2011)	5	41	0	0	0	0
Benward and Saker, 9th ed. (2015)	13	90	7	7.78	7	7.78
Burstein and Straus, 1st ed. (2016)	11	51	1	1.96	4	7.84
Clendinning and Marvin 3rd ed. (2016)	25	110	12	10.91	9	8.18
Kostka, Payne, and Almén, 8th ed. (2018)	29	94	10	10.64	3	3.19
Laitz, 4th ed. (2015)	8	90	2	2.22	1	1.11
Roig-Francoli, 2nd ed. (2010)	5	98	6	6.12	17	17.35
Total	96	574	38	6.62	41	7.14

features the lowest usage of these three composers. Clearly, an overwhelming number of examples in the seven textbooks were written by an extremely small group of composers, almost all German speaking, which points to music theory's inability to envision a music-theoretical world beyond a small number of so-called canonic composers or, more generally, beyond whiteness and maleness.

Considering the abundance of examples by white-male composers, it is worth calculating the content of the textbooks by the number of *composers* with respect to race and gender, and not the number of musical examples. Table 1.3 shows that the textbook by Aldwell/Schachter/Cadwallader has the fewest distinct composers, 41, while the textbook by Clendinning/Marvin has the most, 110. The latter textbook also has the greatest number of non-white composers, 12. Also noteworthy is the high number of women composers, 17 (17.35% of total composers) contained in the textbook by Roig-Francoli. Finally, when considering composers and not musical examples, 6.62% of the composers represented in all textbooks are nonwhite, and 7.14% of the composers represented in all texts are women. These are slightly better numbers than those of musical examples, but the excessive amount of attention dedicated to white-male composers does not allow for much of an expansion of composers who do not identify as such.

In a moving piece on the African American composer Florence Price, *New Yorker* music critic Alex Ross touches on our dependence on white-male composers, calling it "lazy":

> The adulation of the master, the genius, the divinely gifted creator all too easily lapses into a cult of the white-male hero, to whom such traits are almost unthinkingly attached. . . . To reduce music history to a pageant of masters is, at bottom, lazy. We stick with the known in order to avoid the hard work of exploring the unknown.[50]

Our dependence on white-male composers is also a result of white racial framing. As a comparison, once textbook authors realized that there were virtually no women composers in our music theory textbooks, they began to include them. In similar fashion, the first solution these authors will consider to solve the racial imbalance will likely be to find more examples by Joseph Bologne, William Grant Still, and Scott Joplin. But stocking our textbooks with musical examples by these black composers is not the sole solution to this problem, which is a result of framing functional tonality as the only organizational force in music worthy of music theory's consideration in the music theory classroom. As the main musical organizational force that emerged from Europe in the seventeenth to nineteenth centuries, functional tonality is also racialized as "white," and a fine example of a racialized structure, which sociologist Eduardo Bonilla-Silva defines as "the totality of the social relations and practices that reinforce white privilege."[51] Thus the problem in our music curricula concerns not only the racial and gender identity of the composers we study, but the music theories behind their music. This distinction between the whiteness of the musics and the whiteness of the music theories is of vital importance insofar as we in music theory can generally only envision one (expanding the repertoire to include nonwhite/nonmale composers) and not the other (studying nonwhite/nonmale music theories).

There are a total of thirty-three nonwhite composers in the six textbooks that feature at least one (Aldwell/Schachter/Cadwallader has none). Table 1.4

---

50. Alex Ross, "The Rediscovery of Florence Price," *New Yorker*, January 29, 2018.

51. Eduardo Bonilla-Silva, *Racism without Racists: Color-Blind Racism and the Persistence of Racial Inequality in America*, 5th ed. (Rowman & Littlefield, [2003] 2018), 9.

shows the race and nationality of these composers. I've shown women composers in bold type. Of these thirty-three composers, only two are not black (African descent)—Chen Yi (Chinese woman, b. 1953) and Toru Takemitsu (Japanese man, 1930–1996), whose examples, one each, appear in the textbook by Clendinning/Marvin. Thus our music theory examples are, from a racial perspective, black and white and virtually nothing else. By focusing all efforts, minimal though they are, to diversify race based solely on blackness, we music theorists entirely marginalize and erase nonblack people of color, which is *extremely* common in the United States. It should go without saying that contributions from all nonblack people of color deserve music theory's consideration at all levels: classrooms, conferences, publications, and the racial/ethnic makeup of governing structures. In the seven most common music theory textbooks, which represent 96% of the market share, only 2 examples from 2,930 total examples were written by AAPI composers, and those two examples appear in just one textbook, which—for the largest continent on the planet, representing some 58% of the world's population—is shameful.[52]

Final Thoughts on "On Music Theory, Race, and Racism"

In an essay in response to the January 6, 2021, insurrection at the US Capitol, Ibram X. Kendi wrote:

> To say that the attack on the U.S. Capitol is not who we are is to say that this is not part of us, not part of our politics, not part of our history. And to say that this is not part of America, American politics, and American history is a bald-faced denial. But the denial is normal. In the aftermath of catastrophes, when have Americans commonly admitted who we are? The heartbeat of America is denial.[53]

As I've worked with race scholarship and applied its ideas to music theory, many have rushed to suggest that the points I make are exceptions to the rule, that music theory, though not without its problems, is not fundamentally white supremacist (or sexist, antisemitic, ableist, transphobic, etc.). But this is denialism, and this denialism will get us nowhere. Just as our political leaders claim about the January 6, 2021, insurrection at the Capitol,

---

52. AAPI refers to Asian American and Pacific Islander.
53. Ibram X. Kendi, "Denial Is the Heartbeat of America," *The Atlantic*, January 11, 2021.

Table 1.4. Nonwhite Composers in Seven Common Music Theory Textbooks (women in **bold**)

Name	Years	Race	Nationality
Adderley, Julian	1928–1975	Black	American
Basie, Count	1904–1984	Black	American
Chen Yi	1953–	Asian	Chinese
Coltrane, John	1926–1967	Black	American
Davis, Hal	1933–1998	Black	American
Davis, Roquel	1932–2004	Black	American
Dett, Nathaniel	1882–1943	Black	Canadian-American
Dozier, Lamont	1941–	Black	American
Ellington, Duke	1899–1974	Black	American
Gordy, Berry	1929–	Black	American
Hampton, Lionel	1908–2002	Black	American
Hendricks, Jon	1921–2017	Black	American
Holland, Brian	1941–	Black	American
Hutch, Willie	1944–2005	Black	American
Johnson, Robert	1911–1938	Black	American
Joplin, Scott	1868–1917	Black	American
Kinney, L. Viola	1890–1945	Black	American
Kynard, Ben	1920–2012	Black	American
Parker, Charlie	1920–1955	Black	American
Pinkard, Maceo	1897–1962	Black	American
Price, Florence	1887–1953	Black	American
Richie, Lionel	1949–	Black	American
Robinson, Smokey	1940–	Black	American
Robinson, Vicki Sue	1954–2000	Black	American
Saint-Georges, Chevalier	1745–1799	Black	French
Silver, Horace	1928–2014	Black	American
Strayhorn, Billy	1915–1967	Black	American
Takemitsu, Toru	1930–1996	Asian	Japanese
Taylor, Billy	1921–2010	Black	American
Watts, Maymie	1926–?	Black	American
West, Bob	?	Black	American
Williams, Mary Lou	1910–1981	Black	American
Wyche, Sid	1922–1983	Black	American

or about an uptick in anti-Asian violence, or any other form of hate in our country, American music theory claims that this similar type of hate "is not who we are," in denialist fashion—I give an extensive example of this toward the end of chapter 5. But I refuse to allow music theory to cleave itself from that which is a key part of America's history. This hate is, in fact, a *significant* part of who we are.

No matter where we look or how we look at it, American music theory is, in part, antiblack. American music theory is, in part, anti-Asian. American music theory is, in part, misogynistic, Islamophobic, antisemitic, anti-LGBTQ+, and ableist, among other forms of hate. American music theory is, in part, all these things for the simple reason that America itself is, in part, all of these things. To deny that music theory is any of these things only guarantees that the field will remain, at least in part, antiblack, anti-Asian, anti-woman, etc., all of which helps to ensure that whiteness and maleness remain the most powerful duo behind the scenes, the magnets to which we've all been taught we must gravitate. I reject this form of music-theoretical gravitation. If 93.5% of people with actual power, with tenure, in music theory are white, if 98.3% of the musical examples from the seven most common undergraduate music theory textbooks were written by white composers—or if a required doctoral History of Music Theory multi-semester seminar sequence focuses on 100% white-male figures, as is often the case—I would ask the reader, how does this *not* represent a white supremacist structure? I believe we can do better, and I believe we must. We in music theory must begin to admit that the hate and anger that have come to the fore in our field recently are not exceptional. We must all take a hard look in James Baldwin's mirror and see the lies for what they are: lies. "This is not what American music theory is" must become "This is, in part, *exactly* what American music theory is." Kendi agrees:

> We must stop the heartbeat of denial and revive America to the thumping beat of truth. The carnage has no chance of stopping until the denial stops. *This is not who we are* must become, in the aftermath of the attack on the U.S. Capitol: *This is precisely who we are. And we are ashamed. And we are aggrieved at what we've done, at how we let this happen. But we will change. We will hold the perpetrators accountable. We will change policy and practices. We will radically root out this problem. It will be painful. But without pain there is no healing.*
>
> And in the end, what will make America true is the willingness of the American people to stare at their national face for the first time, to open the book of their history for the first time, and see themselves for themselves—all the political viciousness, all the political beauty— and finally right the wrongs, or spend the rest of the life of America trying.
>
> This can be who we are.[54]

---

54. Kendi, "Denial Is the Heartbeat."

I'll end this chapter with a vignette. "When you say classical music is racist, you're saying I'm racist, which I resent since I love this music." So read a comment, under the guise of a question, directed to me in a spring 2021 Zoom chat during a Q&A for one of the many invited lectures I was giving at that time. The commentator and would-be questioner, a white woman— she self-identified as such in the chat—seemed to be upset after my talk. She had taken issue with some of the points I had made about colorblind racism in music, and about the myth of race neutrality. This is a common trope— that music, of and by itself, can't be racist because it's just about the "notes on the page"—among defenders of the status quo in the academic study of music. There was just one small problem with the comment from the white woman in the Zoom chat: I've never said that classical music is racist, nor would I.

For the record, I would never say that classical music is not racist either. "Racist" is a tripwire that is best avoided if one wishes to advance the cause of racial and gender justice in our American music academy. I generally avoid the term "critical race theory" for similar reasons. In my many writings on the subject, which probably total over thirty thousand words in various online venues, I have called exactly two people racist. In "Music Theory and the White Racial Frame" I wrote, "Heinrich Schenker was an ardent racist and German nationalist."[55] I'll let the reader decide for themself if that's the case after reading chapter 3 of *On Music Theory*. I would point out that the two reviewers for that article did not correct this statement, nor did the many editors of *Music Theory Online*, in which that article appeared. And, again for the record, I most certainly stand by that statement today. I would also point out that Carl Schachter spoke of Schenker's racism in an article from 2001 and, as far as I recall, there was no controversy over Schachter's use of the word "racism" in relation to Schenker.[56]

Aside from Schenker, the only other person I've called a racist is Philip Ewell. Here's how I put it at the end of "Music Theory's Future" in my six-part blog series, "Confronting Racism and Sexism in American Music Theory":

> In "The Heartbeat of Racism Is Denial," Kendi writes, "Only racists say they are not racist. Only the racist lives by the heartbeat of denial. The antiracist lives by the opposite heartbeat, one that rarely and

55. Philip Ewell, "Music Theory and the White Racial Frame," *Music Theory Online* 26, no. 2 (September 2020), para. 4.1.2.

56. See Schachter, "Elephants, Crocodiles, and Beethoven: Schenker's Politics and the Pedagogy of Schenkerian Analysis," *Theory and Practice* 26 (2001): 4.

irregularly sounds in America—the heartbeat of confession." Anyone who knows me well knows that, to an extent, I confess to being racist. To an extent, I confess to being sexist. To an extent, homophobic, antisemitic, Islamophobic, transphobic, ableist, among others. Regrettably, I am all of these, for I am human. But by reading, listening to, and *hearing* those who know more about these issues than I do, I vow to work at becoming the least racist, sexist, homophobic, antisemitic, Islamophobic, transphobic, and ableist person I can be. I consider this to be a worthy goal. Is this not also a worthy goal for music theory?[57]

Now, am I a racist to the extent that Heinrich Schenker was? I certainly hope not, but that's not really for me to say. I'd prefer to be judged by my actions—talk is cheap, as the saying goes. Ultimately, playing the "racist" card, which inevitably devolves into a silly discussion over semantics, has one primary goal: to shut down conversations about race. The reason this card is played so often by right-wing and conservative voices is because they are overwhelmingly white, and whiteness will stand to lose some power and prestige—not entirely, but some—if American structures and institutions are allowed to change to better reflect the racial will of our country. In other words, it is meant only to confuse and obfuscate the issues so that conversations about race become impossible. But I do believe that, in the academic study of music currently, there are enough rational voices, white, black, and those of all other races, who can clearly see the racial and gender injustice that our white-male and western system of music has wreaked, and I am generally hopeful now that structural changes can be made so that all musics, like all races of humans, can be heard and considered on equal footing, a simple goal to which any true civilization, any true democracy, should aspire.

---

57. See Ibram X. Kendi, "The Heartbeat of Racism Is Denial," *New York Times*, January 13, 2018, and Philip Ewell, "Confronting Racism and Sexism in American Music Theory" (musictheoryswhiteracialframe.com).

TWO

On White Mythologies

Metaphysics—the white mythology which reassembles and reflects the culture of the West: the white man takes his own mythology, Indo-European mythology, his own logos, that is, the mythos of his idiom, for the universal form of that he must still wish to call Reason.[1]

In "Racialized Modernity: An Analytics of White Mythologies," sociologist Barnor Hesse writes, "Modernity is racial. *Whiteness, Christian, the West, Europeanness* comprise a series of racial tropes intimately connected with organicist and universalist metaphors so frequently assumed in various canonical accounts of modernity."[2] Here Hesse speaks of the simple fact that, in basic concepts of the west, and this certainly applies to the academic study of music in the United States, there is an embedded racial aspect that goes unexplored. Hesse posits a "racialized modernity" that seeks to restore to their rightful place ideas about race that were scrubbed from the white mythologies handed down to us all, namely, that is, restore them to discussions about the histories of the west and what those histories mean to contemporary understandings about race. I too wish to make race part of the conversation, and, in my case, I do so in the academic study of music. Accordingly, one must see whiteness, and its many claims of greatness and exceptionalism, for what it is: mythological. I hasten to add that this does not mean that white persons can't be exceptional at what they do: they most certainly can. What I do mean to say is that there is nothing about whiteness

---

1. Jacques Derrida, *Margins of Philosophy* (Harvester Wheatsheaf, 1982), 213. Cited in Barnor Hesse, "Racialized Modernity: An Analytics of White Mythologies," *Ethnic and Racial Studies* 30, no. 4 (2007): 643–44.
2. Hesse, "Racialized Modernity," 643.

of and by itself that makes it more prone to exceptionalism, which has been a main tenet of white supremacy since its beginnings roughly five hundred years ago.

Whiteness

There has never been a consensus with respect to what constitutes whiteness, or what constitutes a human race for that matter. Historian Nell Irvin Painter puts it succinctly in *The History of White People*: "No consensus has ever formed on the number of human races or even on the number of white races. Criteria constantly shift according to individual taste and political need."[3] Further, in her work Painter tracks four "enlargements" of whiteness in American history, from its extremely narrow Anglo-colonial definitions, rooted in Church of England and Protestant Christian theologies, to its current broad definitions that include a great many generally European peoples.[4]

In 1691 the Virginia House of Burgesses passed An Act for Suppressing Outlying Slaves, which was meant to deal primarily with combating runaway slaves. In this legislation was contained what most race scholars cite as the first official use of the word "white" in North America, here written with original British spellings, but clear enough:

And for prevention of that abominable mixture [of races] and spurious issue which hereafter may encrease in this dominion, as well by negroes, mulattoes, and Indians intermarrying with English, or other **white** women, as by their unlawfull accompanying with one another, *Be it enacted by the authoritie aforesaid, and it is hereby enacted*, that for the time to come, whatsoever English or other **white** man or woman being free shall intermarry with a negroe, mulatto, or Indian man or woman bond or free shall within three months after such marriage be banished and removed from this dominion forever, and that the justices of each respective countie within this dominion make it their perticular care, that this act be put in effectuall execution.[5]

---

3. Nell Irvin Painter, *The History of White People* (Norton, 2011), 383.

4. The US Census Bureau currently includes Middle Easterners and North Africans in its definition of white: "White: A person having origins in any of the original peoples of Europe, the Middle East, or North Africa." See "About the Topic of Race," United States Census Bureau (https://www.census.gov/topics/population/race/about.html).

5. See An Act for Suppressing Outlying Slaves, April 1691, *Encyclopedia Virginia*, https://

Clearly, in this passage, which contains the only two instances of "white" in the legislation, the primary concern was keeping the races from mixing. Therefore, this can be seen as the first "anti-miscegenation" law that mentions "white" in North America.[6] These laws were written and rewritten all the way until the US Supreme Court, in *Loving v. Virginia*, struck down all such laws once and for all in 1967. It's also worth pointing out how, in the first instance, whiteness was conjoined with womanhood, by targeting "white women" as those who should not marry nonwhite men, thus acknowledging women as potential repositories of whiteness in a burgeoning white supremacist system.

This brings up the sexual aspect of the maintenance of whiteness in a white supremacist system. In *White Fright: The Sexual Panic at the Heart of America's Racist History*, historian Jane Dailey ties this sexual policing to the civil rights of blacks:

> For more than a century, between emancipation and 1967, African American rights were closely bound, both in law and in the white imagination, to the question of interracial sex and marriage. At every stage of the struggle for civil rights, sex played a central role, even when its significance was left unspoken. Overcoming the conflation of sexual and civil rights was a project of decades and arguably the greatest challenge champions of Black equality faced.[7]

Dailey further speaks of how crucial the laws surrounding interracial sex and marriage were in defining what, exactly, constituted blackness and whiteness in the United States, and how those two categories became utterly intertwined with the concepts of "slave" and "free."

Like many race scholars before her, Dailey discusses how, during Reconstruction, the rise of black political participation forced whites to think of new ways to limit black power. Tying black men's ostensible incapacity to govern politically with their alleged inborn tendency for "predation and fixation on white women," a dual falsehood rose with black electoral power in

---

encyclopediavirginia.org/entries/an-act-for-suppressing-outlying-slaves-1691 (accessed July 5, 2022) (boldface mine).

6. For more on this law and the role that Christianity played in its creation see Rebecca Anne Goetz, *The Baptism of Early Virginia: How Christianity Created Race* (Johns Hopkins University Press, 2012).

7. Jane Dailey, *White Fright: The Sexual Panic at the Heart of America's Racist History* (Basic Books, 2020), 3.

the post–Civil War era.[8] Dailey lays bare just how important it was for white women to play their part in maintaining white supremacy:

> White supremacy depended on a lot of things to work, but at the level of racial reproduction it insisted on white women cooperating in their role as the guardians and repositories of white racial purity. In this role, white women would not—could not—engage in voluntary sexual intercourse with Black men. Under the new conditions of the Jim Crow South, the space for white women's sexual desire constricted almost as quickly as Black men's political power.[9]

Ibram Kendi makes a similar point about how important controlling white women's bodies was to the cause of white supremacy: "White-male interest in lynching Black-male rapists of White women was as much about controlling the sexuality of White women as it was about controlling the sexuality of Black men."[10] I include the first use of "white" and how it was linked to racial purity through limiting sexual interaction among the races generally, and between white women and black men specifically, to show what a white supremacist and racist structure looks like, and to point out how they become institutionalized through legislation. I'd also like to point out just how committed, once the racial hierarchy became set in the eighteenth and nineteenth centuries, white supremacist legislators were to keeping the races apart, something that most certainly played out in the academic study of music in our country as well.

A final simple example of a white (supremacist) and racist structure that became an institution is the very first US naturalization law, from 1790, only three years after the Constitutional Convention. This naturalization law began, "Be it enacted by the Senate and House of Representatives of the United States of America, in Congress assembled, that any Alien, being a free white person," can become a naturalized citizen of the United States. Thus citizenship, with all the rights and privileges it contained, from its very beginnings was conceived of only for white persons. And why "free" whites? Because, in 1790, whites could still be unfree in the United States. This first naturalization law is a perfect example of a racist structure. It's also a perfect example of a white structure, since the law was created of, by, and for white

---

8. Dailey, *White Fright*, 7.
9. Dailey, *White Fright*, 16.
10. Ibram X. Kendi, *How to Be an Antiracist* (One World, 2019), 189.

persons. And because the structure of citizenship becomes, almost immediately, an institution, this is also a racist and a white institution. Importantly, white structures and institutions exist in the academic study of music in the United States. All one has to do is look, and there they are.

White Supremacy

> White supremacy is a belief that in a country where white people are dominant, that's all down to their natural and innate abilities and any effort to change that is an affront to the natural order of things.[11]

In *So You Want to Talk about Race*, Nigerian American writer Ijeoma Oluo writes, "White Supremacy is this [American] nation's oldest pyramid scheme. Even those who have lost everything to the scheme are still hanging in there, waiting for their turn to cash out."[12] Indeed, everyone who has bought into the lie of white greatness—and I include both white and many nonwhite persons here, myself included in the past—are still waiting for their bite at the apple, for their chance to reap the benefits of whiteness. A pyramid scheme is a business model that relies on new members to recruit new members who are willing to make an initial payment. Those at the top of the pyramid do make money, since part of all payments go to them, but the vast majority of people down toward the bottom of the pyramid only lose money, since there is nothing of any value being offered. The mythological belief that whiteness represents something greater than nonwhiteness, while offering nothing of any intrinsic value, has been used to create all matter of stories that "whiteness" can be achieved if one only works hard enough. To be clear, I don't wish to disparage white persons of and by themselves—they, like all others, may or may not be complicit in upholding the tenets of white supremacy. That is, any race can buy into the many mythologies of white supremacy and search for the pot of white gold at the end of the rainbow.

My Black Father's White Supremacy

If events from the past few years have taught us anything it's that white supremacy, or at very least discussions thereof, is on the rise in the United

---

11. John Oliver, *Last Week Tonight*, Season 8, Episode 5, March 14, 2021 (at 30′00″).
12. Ijeoma Oluo, *So You Want to Talk about Race* (Seal Press, 2018), 12.

States. In an article from October 2020, *New York Times* journalist Michael Powell notes, "News aggregators show a vast increase in the use of the term 'white supremacy' (or 'white supremacist') compared with 10 years ago. *The New York Times* itself used the term fewer than 75 times in 2010, but nearly 700 times since the first of this year alone."[13] While extreme, violent versions of white supremacy surely exist, many subtler, softer versions, expressed in the power structures, governing bodies, and cultural preferences of our country, consistently find ways to insert themselves into our otherwise quotidian lives. For instance, when Donald Trump proclaimed in Poland in July 2017, "We write the symphonies," white supremacists took note—white cultures are superior cultures, and it is not only fine to say so out loud, but to take pride in such proclamations, even if they are fictitious.[14]

My African American father, John Ewell (1928–2007), believed in such a subtle yet significant white supremacy. The only cultures he valued were rooted in white, western societies, and he often disparaged nonwestern cultures that, in his view, didn't measure up. John—who graduated Morehouse College alongside Martin Luther King in 1948 and ultimately got a PhD in number theory from the University of California, Los Angeles, in 1966— wore tweed coats already in his late teens, horn-rimmed glasses long before he needed them, and drove a Mercedes he couldn't really afford. He listened only to western classical music, which he felt represented a higher level of humanity. In his defense, he was trying to assimilate, which made sense for blacks wanting to advance in the virulently racist American society of the mid-twentieth century. In *Singing Like Germans: Black Musicians in the Land of Bach, Beethoven, and Brahms*, musicologist Kira Thurman writes, "Some believed that the respectability afforded to art music offered African Americans a way to fight denigration by white people," which is exactly what my father believed.[15] Like many white (and nonwhite) Americans, John himself ultimately bought into a narrative of Joe Feagin's "white racial frame" and its pro-white subframe, which presupposes that white cultures are more valuable than nonwhite ones, and that those white cultures must prevail in the worldwide marketplace of ideas.

My father's heroes were mathematicians such as Leonhard Euler, Carl

---

13. See Michael Powell, "'White Supremacy' Once Meant David Duke and the Klan. Now It Refers to Much More," *New York Times*, October 17, 2020.

14. For more on this episode and the falsehoods therein, see Anthony Tommasini, "Trump Is Wrong if He Thinks Symphonies Are Superior," *New York Times*, July 30, 2017.

15. Kira Thurman, *Singing Like Germans: Black Musicians in the Land of Bach, Beethoven, and Brahms* (Cornell University Press, 2021), 39.

Friedrich Gauss, and Bertrand Russell, and composers such as Wolfgang Amadeus Mozart, Giuseppe Verdi, and Sergei Rachmaninov. John believed, falsely, that by assimilating to white methods and white beliefs—he, as whiteness teaches, would not have labeled those methods and beliefs as "white" but simply "exceptional"—humanity could raise itself up to a mythically higher standard, a white standard, and that that goal was available to all races if they simply tried hard enough. John's assimilationist coup de grâce came in 1960 when he married my Norwegian-immigrant mother, Viola Lavik.

My father, seemingly unaware of the systemic racism and structural disadvantages that African Americans face, scoffed at blacks unwilling or unable to assimilate to American society, blacks who wore what he considered strange clothing, who rapped over beats he did not consider to be music, or who spoke English he considered nonstandard. Yet my father was certainly cognizant of blackness. Nothing made him prouder than when blacks succeeded in activities normally associated with white persons. Thus, his black heroes were athletes like Arthur Ashe, Serena Williams, and Tiger Woods, and musical performers like Kathleen Battle, Jessye Norman, and André Watts.

If there are three concentric circles of white supremacy currently in the United States, with self-proclaimed white supremacist Richard Spencer in the first and Donald Trump in the second, my black father would have fallen in the third circle. In other words, anyone—white, black, or of any other race—can believe in white supremacy in America. As my father's son, I myself have been guilty of similar white supremacist beliefs, beliefs that a mythical European culture, on the whole, is worthier of our attention than other cultures, though never to the extent that my father believed in such myths. Of course, I no longer believe that. With this current work I venture beyond white supremacy's third concentric circle, a theoretical realm of racial equality and justice, one so knowable yet so unknown. I am finally coming to terms with my black father's white supremacy, to say nothing of my own. I hope that anyone who shares his convictions can show the fortitude to do the same.

Western Civilization and Origin Myths

I've long wondered why, in discussions of a western canon in music, which centers of course on Western Europe historically, the Iberian Peninsula has been erased from existence. After all, it represents the westernmost part of continental Europe, but for some reason its composers have virtually never been considered part of music's western canon. To prove my point, I'd ask the reader to name one significant Portuguese composer from, say, the eighteenth or nineteenth centuries. There were many, of course, but they have been entirely glossed over. During the past few years I've concluded that the reason why the Iberian Peninsula has been erased from existence is simple: because that is one place where European nonwhiteness has resided. Amazigh, Arabs, Maghrebis—usually but not always Muslims—and others have been there for centuries. Of course, so have those who over time would become white, but the messy history of whiteness's interaction with nonwhiteness has made it easier to exclude that part of Europe, the westernmost part of the west.

Many scholars have shown that the idea that ancient Greece was the sole progenitor of western civilization is spurious. Nell Irvin Painter writes, "Without a doubt, the sophisticated Egyptian, Phoenician, Minoan, and Persian societies deeply influenced the classical culture of ancient Greece, which some still imagine as the West's pure and unique source."[16] According to classicist Rebecca Futo Kennedy, this idea of Greece as the "unique source" of western civilization has roots in what is sometimes known as the "Greek Miracle," which peaked roughly twenty-five hundred years ago:

> This narrative is rooted in an idea known as the "Greek Miracle," a phrase used to refer to the supposedly unique flowering of arts, philosophy, and science between the sixth and fourth centuries BCE in Greece and western Anatolia (modern Turkey), a "miracle" that is dated to coincide, not coincidentally, with the rise and fall of Athenian democracy. It is a myth that gets trotted out frequently . . . by those who may be (un)consciously trying to continue to hide the field's racism and misogyny behind a sanitized story of (white, male, Euro-American) greatness.[17]

And, by being silent about mythologies of greatness, Kennedy suggests that we essentially abet those who would want to tie white supremacy to the west. She adds that "by our silences we provide cover for continuing to be sexist, racist, and classist under cover of the greatness of 'Western Civilization.'"[18]

---

16. Painter, *History of White People*, x.

17. Rebecca Futo Kennedy, "We Condone It by Our Silence: Confronting Classics' Complicity in White Supremacy," *Eidolon*, May 11, 2017 (https://eidolon.pub/we-condone-it-by-our-silence-bea76fb59b21).

18. Kennedy, "We Condone It."

Kwame Anthony Appiah writes that western civilization "is at best the source of a great deal of confusion, at worst an obstacle to facing some of the great political challenges of our time. . . . I believe western civilisation is not at all a good idea, and western culture is no improvement."[19] Appiah shows how the concepts of western civilization and western culture are nineteenth-century constructs. For my purposes here, it's paramount to understand that the idea of a western canon in music is, similarly, a nineteenth-century human construct meant, in very large part, to secure and enshrine white-male dominance in the academic study of music. Rebecca Futo Kennedy writes that the term "western civilization" doesn't appear in the literature before the 1840s.[20] Kennedy also writes that the term was invented in order to bind together people on three continents—Europe, North America, and Australia—who shared the same beliefs in settler colonialism, Christianity (preferably Protestant), and whiteness. And, most important, she says, "The concept of 'western civ' itself doesn't emerge until the late 19th century. And when it does, it is explicitly white supremacist."[21]

But the seeds of western civilization as the unique child of ancient Greece and Rome were certainly planted before the late nineteenth century. The philosopher Georg Wilhelm Friedrich Hegel famously told his students in Nuremberg in 1809, "The foundation of higher study must be and remain Greek literature in the first place, Roman in the second."[22] So this project of creating the west was well under way going back, in reality, for centuries in European history. And, at the same time, the denigration of Africa and blackness was paramount. For example, with respect to Africa and its black inhabitants, Hegel said:

> The peculiarly African character is difficult to comprehend, for the very reason that in reference to it, we must quite give up the principle which naturally accompanies all *our* ideas—the category of Univer-

19. Kwame Anthony Appiah, "There Is No Such Thing as Western Civilisation," *The Guardian*, November 9, 2016. See also his *Lines of Descent: W. E. B. Du Bois and the Emergence of Identity* (Harvard University Press, 2014), and *The Lies That Bind: Rethinking Identity* (Liveright, 2018).

20. Rebecca Futo Kennedy, "On the History of 'Western Civilization,' Part 1," *Classics at the Intersections* blog (https://rfkclassics.blogspot.com/2019/04/on-history-of-western-civiliz ation-part.html).

21. Kennedy, "On the History."

22. G. W. F. Hegel, "On Classical Studies," in *On Christianity: Early Theological Writings*, trans. T. M. Knox and Richard Kroner (Chicago: University of Chicago Press, 1948), 324. Cited in Appiah, *The Lies That Bind*, 196.

sality. In Negro life the characteristic point is the fact that consciousness has not yet attained to the realization of any substantial objective
existence—as for example, God, or Law—in which the interest of
man's volition is involved and in which he realizes his own being.
This distinction between himself as an individual and the universality
of his essential being, the African in the uniform, undeveloped one-
ness of his existence has not yet attained; so that the Knowledge of
an absolute Being, an Other and a Higher than his individual self, is
entirely wanting. The Negro, as already observed, exhibits the natural
man in his completely wild and untamed state. We must lay aside all
thought of reverence and morality—all that we call feeling—if we
would rightly comprehend him; there is nothing harmonious with
humanity to be found in this type of character.[23]

The "our" to which Hegel refers to here is not the "west" but, rather,
Europe, and not all of Europe to be sure. These lines, written not long
before his death in 1831, provide something of an intellectual framework
for the antiblackness that underpins a white supremacist system. If, as
Hegel argues, the "Negro" has not attained "objective existence," with religion ("God") or systems of justice ("Law"), then it makes perfect sense
that one need not treat a black person as a human and an equal. It would
be hard to put into words Hegel's impact on nineteenth-century philosophical thought, which gave rise to the concept of the west later in that
century. Hegel also underscored that key aspect in the creation of the western mythology, namely, ancient Greek (and, to a lesser extent, Roman)
provenance. In his discussion of this western myth creation, Appiah traces
it back to the European late Middle Ages:

> So from the late Middle Ages through Hegel until now [2018], people
> have thought of the best in the culture of Greece and Rome as a Euro-
> pean inheritance, passed on like a precious golden nugget, dug out
> of the earth by the Greeks, and transferred, when the Roman Empire
> conquered them, to Rome, where it got a good polish. Eventually, it
> was partitioned among the Flemish and Florentine courts and the
> Venetian Republic in the Renaissance, its fragments passing through
> cities such as Avignon, Paris, Amsterdam, Weimar, Edinburgh, and

23. Georg Wilhelm Friedrich Hegel, *The Philosophy of History*, trans. J. Sibree (Batoche
Books, 2001), 110–11.

London, and finally reunited in the academies of Europe and the
United States.[24]

Perhaps the most significant historian to take on the origin myths of
western civilization was Martin Bernal in *Black Athena*.[25] In three dense
volumes Bernal forms two models for Greek history, namely, what he calls
the "European" or "Aryan" model, and the "Levantine" or "Ancient" model.
Bernal also argues that the European model, that of the "western civilization" narrative, originated only in the early nineteenth century, and that the
true roots of ancient Greek culture originated with Egyptian and Phoenician (Semitic) precedents.[26] In the first volume of *Black Athena*, *The Afroasiatic Roots of Classical Civilization*, Bernal links some of the mythologies of
the European model to the racism that was part and parcel of the erection
of white supremacist structures in Europe. Ultimately, he suggests that we
should replace the European model with the Ancient model, one which
accepts the fact that Egypt colonized Greece long before Socrates came
along, a history that the ancient Greeks themselves acknowledged. This he
urges because the newer European, or Aryan, model was based on racist
thought and white supremacy:

> If I am right in urging the overthrow of the Aryan Model and its
> replacement by the Revised Ancient one, it will be necessary not only
> to rethink the fundamental bases of "Western Civilization," but also
> to recognize the penetration of racism and "continental chauvinism"
> into all our historiography or philosophy of writing history. The
> Ancient Model had no major "internal" deficiencies, or weaknesses
> in explanatory power. It was overthrown for external reasons. For
> 18th- and 19th-century Romantics and racists it was simply intoler-
> able for Greece, which was seen not merely as the epitome of Europe
> but also as its pure childhood, to have been the result of the mixture
> of Native Europeans and colonizing Africans and Semites. Therefore
> the Ancient Model had to be overthrown and replaced by something
> more acceptable.[27]

---

24. Appiah, *The Lies That Bind*, 196.

25. Martin Bernal, *Black Athena: The Afroasiatic Roots of Classical Civilization*, 3 vols. (Rutgers University Press, 1987).

26. Bernal, *Black Athena*, vol. 1, 1.

27. Bernal, *Black Athena*, vol. 1, 2. (I note that this entire passage was italicized in the
original.)

Here Bernal touches on, possibly, the most important aspect of the western civilization myth: that in creating the origin myth of an ancient precedent to western greatness, the mixture of races was not only undesirable, but impossible, since the purity of the "white race" had to be maintained in eighteenth- and nineteenth-century Europe in building the many mythologies of white supremacy. In other words, the Ancient model—in which the ancient Greeks themselves acknowledged their debt to ancient Egypt, and which had been common knowledge before the eighteenth century—had to be "overthrown" if, in fact, the racial purity of whiteness were to be maintained, and unsullied. And with this line of thought "western civilization," and with it the western canon in music, was born.

In an instance of "racialized modernity," to use Barnor Hesse's term, Bernal shows that the creation of the European/Aryan model of ancient Greece served as a perfect mythology to sustain and justify not just western greatness, but its violent excursions across the globe and its rapacious lust for colonies outside of Europe. If Europe and its racial whiteness were to be put forth as superior, it would need a story to sell this superiority, and the European/Aryan model of ancient Greece provided just that. Musicians were quick to follow suit with their own promotion of white-male greatness in the realm of music composition and music history, with its western canon of music theory and history. For those Europeans who wished to promote white supremacy as a structural force in society, Bernal notes:

> The paradigm of "races" that were intrinsically unequal in physical and mental endowment was applied to all human studies, but especially to history. It was now considered undesirable, if not disastrous, for races to mix. To be creative, a civilization needed to be "racially pure."[28]

One problem loomed especially large in creating a new narrative of ancient Greece as progenitor of the west: the fact that there were so many riches, architectural wonders, and proof of great civilizations in Egypt—that is, in Africa—and the idea that it was entirely possible that nonwhite people had had a hand in creating that greatness. Notably, western historians, usually but not always white, are quick to point out that ancient Greeks and Egyptians did not speak of human races in terms of "white" and "black," but that's not the point here. Rather, I underscore that nineteenth-

---

28. Bernal, *Black Athena*, vol. 1, 29.

and twentieth-century historians severed ancient Egypt from the narratives of the west precisely because Africans were considered to be black in contemporaneous racial theories of the nineteenth and twentieth centuries. In other words, it doesn't matter that the ancients didn't recognize "white" and "black" races: nineteenth-century white supremacists did, and they simply mapped "white" and "black" onto ancient peoples to create the appearance of racially pure societies to undergird their relatively new white supremacist system.

This narrative of Egyptian greatness, and therefore of African greatness and African exceptionalism, was at great odds with how blacks were being treated by Europeans across the globe, especially in the nineteenth century as theories of racial superiority and inferiority intensified—with chattel slaves generally being the most inferior of all races, at times referred to as the "slave race" in the nineteenth-century United States. Bernal writes:

> If Europeans were treating Blacks as badly as they did throughout the 19th century, Blacks had to be turned into animals or, at best, subhumans; the noble Caucasian was incapable of treating other full humans in such ways. This inversion sets the scene for the racial and main aspect of the "Egyptian problem": *If it had been scientifically "proved" that Blacks were biologically incapable of civilization, how could one explain Ancient Egypt—which was inconveniently placed on the African continent? There were two, or rather, three solutions. The first was to deny that the Ancient Egyptians were black; the second was to deny that the Ancient Egyptians had created a "true" civilization; the third was to make doubly sure by denying both. The last has been preferred by most 19th- and 20th-century historians.*[29]

---

29. Bernal, *Black Athena*, vol. 1, 241. We can all find solace in the move away from the word "Caucasian," which Bernal uses in this quotation, to signify a white person, a word given to us by the German physician and anthropologist Johann Friedrich Blumenbach in the late eighteenth century. His 1775 doctoral dissertation at the University of Göttingen, "De generis humani varietate nativa" (On the natural variety of humankind), which went through many revisions in his lifetime, ultimately defined five racial groups for human races: American, Caucasian, Ethiopian, Malayan, and Mongolian. The best and most beautiful race, to Blumenbach, was of course the Caucasian, based on his belief that people from Georgia, in the Caucasus mountains between the Black and Caspian Seas, and European whites stemmed from the Georgian Caucasians—which was utter nonsense of course. (For more on Blumenbach and his classifications, see Painter, *History of White People*, chapter 6.) As a humorous aside, when I lived in Russia in the early 1990s as a cello student at the St. Petersburg Conservatory of Music, I needed to find an apartment, so I went to the classifieds and

Indeed, on a recent trip to the Brooklyn Museum, which has a notable Egyptian collection, I snapped a photo of one plaque that contextualized some of the exhibit. It read, in part:

> The ancient Egyptians were an African people who first appeared in the Nile Valley by 4,500 B.C.E. and created a distinctive culture. Egyptologists no longer maintain the false hypothesis that lighter-skinned outsiders created Egyptian culture.
>
> Nineteenth- and early twentieth-century historians largely interpreted the archaeological evidence on the African continent through a racist filter that rejected the notion that Africans could create a high-civilization. Today Egyptologists have data that clearly shows that Egyptian culture was invented by indigenous people in southern Egypt and spread toward the Mediterranean Sea about 3,000 B.C.E.[30]

It's common knowledge that ancient Egyptians, Greeks, and Romans did not think of themselves in terms of black or white races, but, again, that's not the point here. The point is that those Europeans who created white supremacy in the sixteenth to nineteenth centuries did think in those terms, and they essentially were assigning white and black races retroactively to the ancients in order to provide a history, a story, of whiteness's greatness.

Unsurprisingly, Martin Bernal's landmark *Black Athena* caused immediate controversy. Perhaps the most ardent defender of the divine provenance of the ancient Greeks was classicist Mary Lefkowitz, who wrote a monograph, *Not Out of Africa: How "Afrocentrism" Became an Excuse to Teach Myth as History*, and coedited a volume, *"Black Athena" Revisited*, devoted, in very

---

started looking. In Russia, and especially in St. Petersburg, лица кавказской национальности (Caucasian nationalities) were, and still are, often called черные люди (black people), since the skin color of Caucasians—not just Georgians, but Abkhazis, Armenians, Azerbaijanis, Chechens, Dagestanis, Ingush, and Ossetians, among others—is often darker than Slavic Russians. Importantly, the word for "black" (черный) in Russian is quite a bad word for people, something akin to "Negro" or "colored" in the United States. As I looked through the classifieds for an apartment I kept coming across the following: лица кавказской национальности не беспокоятся, which means "Caucasians need not apply." Having myself twice been denied apartments in New York City in the early 1990s because I'm black, I couldn't help but laugh at this wording, even if it was still darker-skinned people who were being discriminated against.

30. Edward Bleiberg (curator of Egyptian art) and Yekaterina Barbash (associate curator of Egyptian Art), wall text for "Ancient Egypt: An African Culture," *Ancient Egyptian Art*, Long-Term Installation, Egyptian Galleries, Third Floor, Morris A. and Meyer Schapiro Wing, Brooklyn Museum, Brooklyn, New York. Visited most recently on June 8, 2022.

large part, to refuting Bernal's historical account of the ancients.[31] I find it telling that Lefkowitz adds teaching "myth as history" in the subtitle of her monograph, since teaching the ancient Greeks is so often exactly that. Think here of the almost certainly false story of Pythagoras at the black-smith's shop, which I discuss below. We in music theory have created an entire mythology of Pythagoras and those hammers at the shop, and some-how it seems perfectly fine to treat this story as authoritative, if not factual, and not mythological, which it almost certainly was.

This brings up the largest problem with Lefkowitz's counterarguments, which are counterarguments consistently heard when someone wisely ques-tions the issue of race and gender in historical accounts of white-male excep-tionalism, an exceptionalism never described as such of course. In a 2018 piece, "Black Athena, White Power: Are We Paying the Price for Classics' Response to Bernal?" classicist Denise Eileen McCoskey puts it better than I can:

> Leaving aside the personalities and general climate surrounding *Black Athena*, it is Lefkowitz's main premise regarding historical inquiry that I want to call out, since it is one too many classicists still endorse today: namely, that Afrocentrism pursued readings of the ancient world based in emotion, bias, and the need to build "self-esteem," while Classics, tightly wrapped in the mantle of "objectivity," rigor-ously sought the "truth."[32]

This spot-on criticism of Lefkowitz resonates deeply with me since so many in conservative quarters of music theory have criticized my own "Afro-centric" work combining race scholarship with music theory as emotional and biased, while their own arguments are to be considered reasoned and objective. But this is one of the most effective tactics in the promotion of our white-male frame, namely, painting the person questioning why our racialized and gendered structures exist as an emotional and unhinged critic—I myself have been called an antisemite, charlatan, dumbass, moron, and nitwit, among many other slurs, on social media and in unsolicited

---

31. See Mary Lefkowitz, *Not Out of Africa: How "Afrocentrism" Became an Excuse to Teach Myth as History* (Basic Books, 1997), and Mary Lefkowitz and Guy MacLean Rogers, eds., *Black Athena Revisited* (University of North Carolina Press, 1996).

32. Denise Eileen McCoskey, "Black Athena, White Power: Are We Paying the Price for Classics' Response to Bernal?," *Eidolon*, November 15, 2018 (https://eidolon.pub/black-athe na-white-power-6bd1899a46f2).

communications—while those who defend the status quo are heroes of the natural order of things, and of the truth. McCoskey continues:

> Such a dichotomy—that "emotional" people of color politicize history, while "reasonable" white people seek objective fact—was patently false in the 1980s, even as it became a staple in the arsenal of arguments defending the exclusionary practices of many disciplines. Needless to say, the notion that white people are somehow more conditioned for "objectivity" when it comes to historical thought is painfully false when set against the backdrop of white supremacy's renewed nostalgia for the classical world.[33]

Painfully false indeed! This history—one might call it a father-knows-best paternalism in which white men rightfully proclaim and lead while others listen and follow—is as old as our country itself. Is it any wonder that there are still those in music theory who would believe that white men are somehow more inclined toward an unknowable "objectivity," other people toward a known emotionality?

The debate over western civilization in the field of classics spilled onto a national stage in January 2019, at the annual conference of the Society for Classical Studies, which took place in San Diego, California. The debate happened during the Q&A session in a panel entitled "The Future of Classics" and featured, primarily, Sara Bond, an associate professor of history at the University of Iowa, Dan-el Padilla Peralta, an associate professor of classics at Princeton University, and Mary Frances Williams, an independent scholar living in California.[34] The main controversy happened when Williams said to Padilla Peralta, who is black, "I believe in merit. I don't look at the color of the author. You [Padilla Peralta] may have got your job because you're black, but I prefer to think you got your job because of merit."[35] Sociologist Eduardo Bonilla-Silva classifies this as a microaggression, that is,

33. McCoskey, "Black Athena, White Power."

34. The session was chaired by Stephen Hinds (University of Washington), included an address by Helen Cullyer (executive director of the Society for Classical Studies), and a panel that included Bond, Padilla Peralta, and Joy Connolly (then of the CUNY Graduate Center, currently president of the American Council of Learned Societies).

35. Cited in Rachel Poser, "He Wants to Save Classics from Whiteness. Can the Field Survive?," *New York Times*, February 2, 2021. For the complete exchange at the Q&A, see "SCS Annual Meeting (2019): 'The Future of Classics' Unedited Full Panel," https://youtu.be/lcJZCVemn-4, at 45'00".

when "one implies that a minority is unqualified for a job or admission to school and is only present because of affirmative action."[36] I can say firsthand that, as a black person who went to Stanford University as an undergraduate and Yale University for graduate school, and got a tenure-track job at the University of Tennessee out of graduate school, I have been told to my face more than once that my success was due to the fact that I'm black and, behind my back, it's undoubtedly been said countless times again. More generally, since the rise of colorblindness in the 1960s in the United States, it's become quite hard for whiteness to witness blackness's success and not immediately think that, at least in part, that success is due to the person's blackness and not based primarily on merit, as is the case with whiteness. This falsehood is rooted not only in antiblackness but also, more importantly, in whiteness's inability to see the many structural and institutional advantages it has enjoyed over the centuries in America, advantages that continue right up to this day.

But here I wish to highlight the origin myths of western civilization, since they were part of the controversy surrounding "The Future of Classics." In a follow-up piece that appeared in the politically conservative online publication *Quillette*, Mary Frances Williams outlined the main points that she was trying to make—here are the first two:

1. It is important to stand up for Classics as a discipline, and promote it as the political, literary, historical, philosophical, rhetorical, and artistic foundation of Western Civilization, and the basis of European history, tradition, culture, and religion. It gave us the concepts of liberty, equality, and democracy, which we should teach and promote. We should not apologize for our field.
2. It is important to go back to teaching undergraduates about the great classical authors—Cicero, the Athenian dramatists, Homer,

---

36. Eduardo Bonilla-Silva, *Racism without Racists: Color-Blind Racism and the Persistence of Racial Inequality in America*, 5th ed. (Rowman & Littlefield, [2003] 2018), 28. Here's how Padilla-Peralta responded at the Q&A, after Frances Williams interrupted him: "I did not interrupt you once, so you are going to let me talk. You are going to let someone who has been historically marginalized from the production of knowledge in classics talk. And here's what I have to say about the vision of Classics that you outline. If that is in fact the vision that affirms you in your white supremacy, I want nothing to do with it. I hope the field dies that you've outlined and that it dies as swiftly as possible. And I hope, I fervently hope, that those of you in the room will take stock in consideration of what has happened here." See "SCS Annual Meeting (2019)," https://youtu.be/lcJZCVemn-4, at 49′10″.

Demosthenes, the Greek and Roman historians, Plato, and
Aristotle—in English translation in introductory courses.[37]

This is a great example of a master universalist western narrative often
given by white racial frames to justify their existence. These points completely erase from existence nonwhiteness: the many nonwhite peoples—
Amazigh, Arabs, Dagestanis, Maghrebis, Mongols, Romani, Sámi, Tatars,
Turks, among many others—who inhabited Europe for centuries and, in
some cases, millennia, who have always been in Europe, and who have
contributed to Europeanism; the many nonwhite religions that have been
part of Europe; and the many nonwhite authors and intellectuals who have
played a significant role in that continent's history. Perhaps most important,
Williams highlights the greatness of western civilization, the foundation for
European history, the basis for liberty, equality, and democracy. That certain
trends in the history of Europe dealt with liberty, equality, and the voice of
the people is not in question. But to state openly that western civilization
"gave us the concepts of liberty, equality, and democracy," is entirely misleading, since those concepts are ultimately of the entire world's making,
and not only from France, England, and Germany, which is really what is
being said. Williams is not a well-published author, but her beliefs are not at
all uncommon in our institutions of higher education. And in the academic
study of music, we are pointedly behind classics, as we have not yet begun to
unpack the damage that "the west" and our western canon have done.

Over the past several years, and especially since the August 2017 "Unite
the Right" rally in Charlottesville, Virginia, in which white supremacists
used ancient Greek and Roman tropes and symbols as proof of white superiority, classics has pushed back hard against those who would use the field as
proof of white greatness. Bold authors such as Sarah Emily Bond, Rebecca
Futo Kennedy, Denise Eileen McCoskey, and Dan-el Padilla Peralta have
done great work to reframe the common twentieth-century narratives surrounding western civilization's starting with the Greeks and the many con-
comitant mythologies linking western civilization to white-male greatness.[38]

---

37. Mary Frances Williams, "How I Was Kicked Out of the Society for Classical Studies
Annual Meeting," Quillette.com, February 26, 2019 (https://quillette.com/2019/02/26/how
-i-was-kicked-out-of-the-society-for-classical-studies-annual-meeting).

38. Both Bond and Kennedy maintain long bibliographies containing the most recent
literature that reframes these false narratives from a racial-justice standpoint. See Kennedy's
"Classics at the Intersections: Race/Ethnicity Bibliography" (https://rfkclassics.blogspot.com
/p/bibliography-for-race-and-ethnicity-in.html), and Bond's "History from Below: Hold My

Indeed, the American Society for Classical Studies itself, founded in 1869 and the preeminent society in the field, reflected this latest thinking in reaction to the misappropriation of classics by white supremacists when it released a statement in November 2016 that spoke of the field's roots spanning three continents, "from India to Britain and from Germany to Ethiopia," and that "Classical Studies today belongs to all of humanity."[39] It concluded:

> For this reason, the Society strongly supports efforts to include all groups among those who study and teach the ancient world, and to encourage understanding of antiquity by all. It vigorously and unequivocally opposes any attempt to distort the diverse realities of the Greek and Roman world by enlisting the Classics in the service of ideologies of exclusion, whether based on race, color, national origin, gender, or any other criterion. As scholars and teachers, we condemn the use of the texts, ideals, and images of the Greek and Roman world to promote racism or a view of the Classical world as the unique inheritance of a falsely-imagined and narrowly-conceived western civilization.[40]

I suppose a relevant question after reading this quotation would be "falsely-imagined and narrowly-conceived" by whom? A conservative reading might be "by white supremacists," I suppose. However, I'd argue that this narrow make-believe reading of western civilization is, in fact, imagined by virtually all in our academies and institutions of higher learning to one extent or another, and then promoted as fact. But either way, if our preeminent American society for classics can acknowledge this shortcoming, certainly we in music theory can do the same with respect to our western canon, a canon that itself is most certainly both falsely imagined and narrowly conceived.

Mead: A Bibliography for Historians Hitting Back at White Supremacy" (https://sarahemi lybond.com/2017/09/10/hold-my-mead-a-bibliography-for-historians-hitting-back-at-white -supremacy).

39. Helen Cullyer, "Public Statement from the SCS Board of Directors," Society for Classical Studies, November 28, 2016 (https://classicalstudies.org/scs-news/public-statement-scs -board-directors).

40. Cullyer, "Public Statement."

The Western Canon in Music

To see how all this played out in music, I'll turn to the most famous historical textbook, the same one that I used as an undergraduate music major at Stanford University in the late 1980s, *A History of Western Music*, by Donald J. Grout.[41] Notably, when W. W. Norton published Grout's significant historical text in 1960, far and away the most commonly assigned in the late twentieth century in the United States and still widely used today, the Cold War was in full swing.[42] On her blog, in a Google *n*-gram, Rebecca Futo Kennedy shows that, in roughly 1960, the term "western civilization" peaked in its usage in the United States, reflecting both the Cold War—with the Soviet Union's purported opposition to "the west"—and the Civil Rights movement.[43] In my discussion I'll cite the fourth, seventh, and tenth editions of *A History of Western Music*, from 1988, 2006, and 2019, respectively. The fourth, which added the Yale music theorist Claude Palisca as coauthor, was very much like the previous three editions. In the preface, Palisca commented briefly on "western": "The word *Western* in our title reflects the realization that the musical system of western Europe and the Americas is but one of several among the civilizations of the world."[44] Thus in 1988 there was an awareness of global musical traditions and of the fact that this textbook represented only a certain part of that tradition, but it's clear that "western" was an agreed-upon synonym for "Europe and the Americas." It goes without saying that there was no acknowledgment of the history of the west as a mythological human construct, only about one hundred years old in 1960, meant to sustain and promote white supremacy. There could not have been, since all discussions of this mythological aspect of the west were actively suppressed in mid-twentieth-century America, especially as white supremacy was collapsing under its own weight.

Right off the bat, in chapter 1, "The State of Music at the End of the Ancient World," Grout and Palisca begin with the Roman Empire in the

---

41. Donald J. Grout, *A History of Western Music* (Norton, 1960).

42. For more on the twentieth-century history of music history textbooks in the United States, see chapter 1, "Cosmopolitan and Provincial: American Musical Historiography," from Richard Crawford's *The American Musical Landscape* (University of California Press, 1993).

43. Kennedy, "On the History."

44. Donald J. Grout and Claude Palisca, *A History of Western Music*, 4th ed. (Norton, 1988), ix.

fifth century, highlighting the "Christian era."[45] Of course Christian theology played an enormous part in creating the many mythologies of the west, and Grout and Palisca emphasize this further in the very first heading of chapter 1, "The Greek Heritage":

> The history of Western art music properly begins with the music of the Christian Church. But all through the Middle Ages and even to the present time artists and intellectuals have continually turned back to Greece and Rome for instruction, for correction, and for inspiration in their several fields of work. This has been true in music.[46]

With these words, and this textbook, the origin myths of ancient Greece in music were solidified. It's worth pointing out how explicitly Grout and Palisca tie "western art music" to the Christian church, a church that obviously didn't exist in ancient Greece. Here the authors are splitting the difference: western music began with the Christian church, but it also didn't, because it began with ancient Greece. Of course there were many musical traditions that predated those of the Christian church, both secular and sacred, but they have been erased from "western" history. But Grout and Palisca were not at all exceptional in this erasure. It was, in fact, the story of mid-twentieth-century America.

Cutting to the 2019 tenth edition, with Indiana University musicologist J. Peter Burkholder as an additional coauthor (since the seventh edition in 2005), many changes are notable.[47] There is much to admire in this newest edition. There are more compositions from women and BIPOC, generally, and different genres such as jazz and popular. There is an impressive editorial advisory board of twenty scholars, and the depth of research and knowledge is formidable. Still, the outlines from Grout's original text are ever present in this newest edition, and the pitfalls still the same.

The first chapter, "Music in Antiquity," now has preliminaries to the section "Music in Ancient Greece," including "The Earliest Music," "Music in Ancient Mesopotamia," and "Other Civilizations."[48] These additions, which do break out of the typical western narrative of ancient Greek roots, are wel-

45. Grout and Palisca, *History of Western Music*, 1.
46. Grout and Palisca, *History of Western Music*, 2.
47. See Donald J Grout, Claude Palisca, and J. Peter Burkholder, *A History of Western Music*, 10th ed. (Norton, 2019).
48. Grout and Palisca, *History of Western Music*, 5–9.

come, but the text turns to ancient Greece almost immediately, with "Music in Ancient Greece" on page 9 in chapter 1, which indicates its true heritage. The most problematic section, in my opinion, is that which immediately precedes "Music in Antiquity" in chapter 1. I'll quote at length here, since there is so much of "western civilization" contained herein:

> The culture of Europe and the Americas—known as Western culture to distinguish it from the traditional cultures of Asia—has deep roots in the civilizations of antiquity. Our agriculture, writing, cities, and systems of trade derive from the ancient Near East. Our mathematics, calendar, astronomy, and medicine grew from Mesopotamian, Egyptian, Greek, and Roman sources. Our philosophy is founded on Plato and Aristotle. Our primary religions, Christianity and Judaism, arose in the ancient Near East and were influenced by Greek thought. Our literature grew out of Greek and Latin traditions and drew on ancient myth and scripture. Our artists imitated ancient sculpture and architecture. From medieval empires to modern democracies, governments have looked to Greece and Rome for examples.
>
> The music of Western culture, known as Western music, also has roots in antiquity, from the scales we use to the functions music serves. The strongest direct influence comes through Greek writings, which became the foundation for European views of music.[49]

I'm made uncomfortable by many points in this long quotation: the notion of pitting the west against Asia as some kind of antipode, to the total erasure of Africa and the precolonial Americas; the problematic belief that our philosophy "is founded on Plato and Aristotle," or that our literature came from Greek and Latin traditions; or that the west does not include Islam, which has been part of Europe since that religion's founding in the seventh century CE, to say nothing of other European non-Abrahamic religions. But most troubling to me is the incessant use of the first-person plural pronouns, "our" and "we." I myself was born in Long Beach, California, to an African American dad and a Norwegian mom, and I've lived four years in Canada, seven in Russia, and the rest of my life in the United States. I could therefore reasonably be called a "westerner"—I'm writing in English, after all—yet I see very little of myself in this long quotation. In other words, I strongly disagree with the "our" and the "we." What about those tens of

---

49. Grout and Palisca, *History of Western Music*, 4.

millions of US citizens and permanent residents whose connections to any alleged west are more distant than mine? And what about those millions of US citizens who were here long before Europeans began arriving roughly five hundred years ago? I now write from Brooklyn, New York, which is the historic territory of the Lenape and Canarsee peoples, who were forcibly displaced by Dutch settlers in the 1620s. Yet these peoples are still here, they always were, and they should be honored. I strongly doubt that they would see the "our" and "we" in this long quotation. In hindsight, this particular quotation could have been preceded with a simple clause: "As whiteness and maleness have taught us over roughly (but not more than) 150 years, the culture of Europe and the Americas . . ."

All of which is to say that the history of western music is based on a lie. And that lie, of a western civilization going back to the ancient Greeks but not a day further, is, for all intents and purposes, deeply rooted in white supremacy. Other fields, like classics, as I've shown, have done a far better job than we have in academic music in interrogating their histories from a racial perspective. Art and art history have also done a much better job than we have in music.[50] In American music studies, discussions about race have been systematically ignored or obscured, and it's high time we begin those discussions. For all its outstanding scholarship, what this newest version of *A History of Western Music* does, as most such works do, is adapt the western mythology to new twenty-first-century realities on the ground. What this means is to engage in additive DEI activities, adding women and BIPOC figures, for instance, or other nonclassical genres of music and still other global musics that become known as "nonwestern" or "world music," and acknowledge the changing nature of the field. At the end of the tenth edition, in a section entitled "The Future of Western Music," Burkholder writes, "The popularity of fusions, mashups, mixtures, and blends in recent [twenty-first century] years is only the latest manifestation of a long-standing trait in the Western tradition: combining multiple influences to create something new."[51] True, western music, such as it is, adapts. But what it does not do, what it can never do, is reveal the truth about itself, namely, that there is no such thing as the west and there never has been.

It seems the team behind *A History of Western Music* discussed the use of

---

50. See, for example, "Using Photography to Tell Stories about Race," *New York Times*, December 6, 2017, by art curator and historian Maurice Berger, who died at the age of sixty-three in March 2020 from complications due to Covid-19.

51. Grout, Palisca, and Burkholder, *A History of Western Music*, 1009.

the first-person plural with which I take issue above. Here's how the long passage already quoted read in the seventh edition, from 2006, with differences noted in **bold type** (from the 2006 version) and ~~strikethrough text~~ (from the 2019 version):

> **European culture** ~~The culture of Europe and the Americas—known as Western culture to distinguish it from the traditional cultures of Asia—~~has deep roots in the civilizations of antiquity. **Its** ~~Our~~ agriculture, writing, cities, and systems of trade derive from the ancient Near East. **Its** ~~Our~~ mathematics, calendar, astronomy, and medicine grew from Mesopotamian, Egyptian, Greek, and Roman sources. **Its** ~~Our~~ philosophy is founded on Plato and Aristotle. **Its** ~~Our~~ primary religions, Christianity and Judaism, arose in the ancient Near East and were influenced by Greek thought. **Its** ~~Our~~ literature grew out of Greek and Latin traditions and drew on ancient myth and scripture. **Its** ~~Our~~ artists imitated ancient sculpture and architecture. From medieval empires to modern democracies, governments have looked to Greece and Rome for examples.
>
> **Western music also has roots in antiquity, from concepts such as notes, intervals, and scales to ideas about how music affects emotions and character.** ~~The music of Western culture, known as Western music, also has roots in antiquity, from the scales we use to the functions music serves.~~ The strongest direct influence comes through Greek writings, which became the foundation for European views of music.

I don't have at my disposal all ten editions of *A History of Western Music*, but clearly the motion has been from a more distant third-person view of western music as "European," with "its" traditions, to a more personal first-person account of "our" music, culture, and traditions, in which "we" Americans take part.[52] I would have thought the motion would be the other way around from 2006 to 2019, but Burkholder and his editorial advisers settled on making the story of western music more American, more personal. Note specifically how "European culture" became "the culture of Europe and the Americas—known as Western culture to distinguish it from the traditional cultures of Asia." This amounts to a doubling down on the western-culture

---

52. I understand that this textbook is used widely outside of the United States as well, but its primary market is still the United States.

and western-canon mythologies, which by 2019 had already been called into question in certain academic fields that could reasonably be said to have been based on white-male European models, such as the academic study of music in the United States. But the lineage of the three editions—from Grout and Palisca's emphasis on western music's roots in the "Christian Church," to the "European" view of this music with "its" traditions, to "western music" as "our" "American" music—actually adumbrates the larger narrative that certain European and American historians have written over many decades prior to *A History of Western Music*. In the fourth and final lecture, "Culture," from his lecture series "Mistaken Identities: Creed, Country, Color, Culture," for the BBC *Reith Lectures* in New York City in 2016, Kwame Anthony Appiah said: "European and American debates today about whether Western culture is fundamentally Christian inherit . . . a genealogy in which 'Christendom' was replaced by 'Europe' and then by the idea of 'the West.'"[53] In this sense, *A History of Western Music* tracks this larger narrative quite nicely.

In *The Lies That Bind*, Appiah writes:

> In each of my five test cases [religion, nation, race, class, and culture], we fall into an error I'll describe in the first chapter: of supposing that at the core of each identity there is some deep similarity that binds people of that identity together. Not true, I say; not true over and over again. . . . Yet these errors are also central to the way identities unite us today. We need to reform them because, at their best, they make it possible for groups, large and small, to do things together. They are the lies that bind.[54]

But as Appiah says, western civilization "is at best the source of a great deal of confusion, at worst an obstacle to facing some of the great political challenges of our time," so there is a conundrum here.[55] Are there positive elements to a western identity, elements that may bring people closer together and unite us? Possibly, if thinking about the United States on the whole, as one nation among the other 194 on earth, nations with which the United States must compete. But without a reckoning about its beginnings as a pillar of white supremacy, "western civilization" and its musical child, the

---

53. Kwame Anthony Appiah, "Mistaken Identities: Creed, Country, Color, Culture," *The Reith Lectures* (BBC Radio 4, 2016), https://www.bbc.co.uk/programmes/b080twcz

54. Appiah, *The Lies That Bind*, xvi.

55. Appiah, "There Is No Such Thing."

western canon, have done far more harm than good, and it's now time to move beyond this particular mythology to a more just musical world.

To be clear, *A History of Western Music* is not alone; it simply gives an account of the west from a musical perspective, as so many other historical accounts in other fields, as well as in music itself, do. And it does so in compelling fashion. These critiques are not easy to give, but my criticism is ultimately not about any one person in particular. Rather, I'm criticizing the entire enterprise of the academic study of music in the United States, one in which we still largely believe in the existence of a mythical west, its civilization, and its canon, a concept that has been and continues to be used as a tool of oppression. Finally, I should note here that I myself could have written such a textbook some years ago—though much more poorly, to be fair to Grout, Palisca, and Burkholder—since I held the same beliefs about academic music. This is how we were all taught in the twentieth century, and there wasn't much room for deviation.

One crucial aspect of teaching western music history has been the denial of potential greatness in other musics. In "Is Western Art Music Superior?" ethnomusicologist Judith Becker shows that this denial is tantamount to musical colonialism. She begins with two emblematic quotations—one from Nicolas Ruwet, one from Harold Powers—that state unequivocally that western music is more "complex" than nonwestern music, the implication being that it is, consequently, superior.[56] In building her case, Becker cites the three main tenets that have been used to allegedly prove this superiority: (1) that western music is based on natural acoustical laws, such as the overtone series, which shows a link between man and nature, (2) that this music is more complex than nonwestern musics, with its tonal hierarchies and developed harmonic syntax, and (3) that western music is more expressive, and therefore more meaningful, than other musics of the world.[57] She concludes:

No one, I think, denies that Western art music has a foundation in the natural world, is very complex, and is deeply meaningful to its musicians and audiences. The problem lies in denying these attributes to other peoples' music. Because we often cannot perceive it,

---

56. Judith Becker, "Is Western Art Music Superior?," *Musical Quarterly* 72, no. 3 (1986): 341.

57. Becker, "Is Western Art Music Superior?," 341–42.

we deny naturalness, great complexity, and meaningfulness to other musical systems. Despite all protestations to the contrary, to deny equivalences in all three pillars of belief—that is, naturalness, complexity and meaningfulness, to the musical systems of others—is ultimately to imply that they are not as developed as we are. The doctrine of the superiority of Western music is the musicological version of colonialism.[58]

For a textbook example of the denial of complexity and meaningfulness of nonwestern musics I'll briefly cite Fred Lerdahl's "Cognitive Constraints on Compositional Systems," in which he explores "the relationship between composing and listening."[59] Lerdahl defines the difference between "complexity" (a positive value) and "complicatedness" (a neutral value), and explains that complexity makes for a richer and better music than complicatedness does. He then writes, with respect to complexity in music, "Balinese gamelan falls short with respect to its primitive pitch space. Rock music fails on grounds of insufficient complexity. Much contemporary music pursues complicatedness as compensation for a lack of complexity."[60] Thus, as Judith Becker states, the denial of "complexity" has been a key element not only in proving the superiority of "western art music," but in denying the complexity and meaningfulness (and humanity I might add) of both nonwestern and nonclassical musics.

The situation in music theory is quite similar to that in musicology. The 2002 *Cambridge History of Western Music Theory*, edited by Thomas Christensen, is instructive. Unlike *A History of Western Music*, Christensen's volume is not a textbook but, rather, a "resource for scholars and students."[61] Its thirty-one essays by eminent scholars in the field do an admirable job of giving the key moments in music theory's western narrative, a narrative that Christensen himself acknowledges is anfractuous and unclear: "Does such a discipline actually exist? Is 'music theory' ultimately an intelligible

58. Becker, "Is Western Art Music Superior?," 342.

59. Fred Lerdahl, "Cognitive Constraints on Compositional Systems," in *Generative Processes in Music: The Psychology of Performance, Improvisation, and Composition*, ed. John A. Sloboda (Oxford University Press, 2000), 231–59. Reprint from Oxford Scholarship Online (2012), 1.

60. Lerdahl, "Cognitive Constraints," 24.

61. Thomas Christensen, ed., *The Cambridge History of Western Music Theory* (Cambridge University Press, [2002] 2008), 16.

and meaningful historical subject?"[62] Indeed, music theory's history in its western sense is vast and complicated, and even deciding what should be included and unpacked is a herculean task. In his introduction to the volume Christensen says:

> If there is one unifying theme to the stories that emerge from all these chapters, perhaps, it is in the perplexing and never-ending dilemmas music theory engenders: a discipline that seems to stand apart from practice yet is inextricably tied to that practice; a discipline that claims to transcend history yet is through and through historical. Ultimately, I believe, none of these tensions can be—or should be—resolved. Rather, each can be seen as helping to provide the energy and impetus of the music-theoretical enterprise. For theory is not just a set of observational tools; these tools also tell us something about those who use them."[63]

Indeed they do! And those who have used these western music-theoretical tools over roughly 150 years have been white people, usually men. As far as I can tell, all thirty-three authors in the volume are white, and I imagine virtually all the "tools" were created by white persons as well. That is, music theory's tools "tell us something about those who use them."

I often speak of the many "nonwestern" music-theoretical traditions that have been erased by whiteness, and Christensen too acknowledges these "distinguished non-Western traditions of music theorizing" that will not be part of his volume, since it was clearly beyond the purview of his work. In his introduction, he does a great job in unpacking "music theory" and its many intricacies and idiosyncrasies for the reader. But one would hope that in *The Cambridge History of Western Music Theory*, both "music theory" *and* "western" would be unpacked, but "western" is left more or less untouched. It's time we music theorists seriously interrogate the west, its narratives, epistemologies, and mythologies. I certainly don't blame Christensen for not doing a deep dive into the history of "western" and how it was used as a tool of oppression in the creation of white supremacy. In the late twentieth century, western mythologies going back to the ancient Greeks were so set in stone that it really didn't make any sense to question them to begin with (but Martin Bernal, who was a white man, certainly did, to his great credit).

---

62. Christensen, *Cambridge History*, 2.
63. Christensen, *Cambridge History*, 21.

The west was the west, and that was that. The east was the "Orient," among many other things in this narrative, but this mythical east was problematic right from the beginning, perhaps the most basic reason being that there was no nonwhite supremacist system being built that would or could somehow counter what was being built in the purported west. To put this another way, the east was presented as a foil to the west, and not something deserving of the same level of scholarly attention in and of itself in western countries, however defined.

One clear western music-theoretical mythology is that of Pythagoras and his trip to the blacksmith's shop. The story goes that, observing hammers of six, eight, nine, and twelve pounds being struck, Pythagoras intuited the octave, fifth, and fourth with the vibrating ratios 2:1, 3:2, and 4:3. Christensen himself invokes this particular mythology, though not as such, in his introduction.[64] In another contribution to the volume, Calvin Bower speaks explicitly about the power of this particular Pythagorean mythology:

> The roots of this myth so fundamental to the history of Western musical thought are buried within ancient values and archetypes that can never be fully fathomed. The empirical data offered in the myth is wholly specious, for hammers of comparable weights would not sound the musical intervals presented in the story. However, the myths and dreams of a civilization are judged not by their empirical truth or falsity, but by the expression of intellectual and spiritual complexes they reveal within a culture.[65]

So much about our western mythologies "can never be fully fathomed." But this is, at least in part, the point: keeping parts of the narratives of greatness unknown, and not knowable, in order to create an element of faith in the whole enterprise of white-male exceptionalism. I would be stunned if anything like the story of Pythagoras actually happened, but again that's the point. Those who want to believe can continue believing knowing that there is nothing I can do to disprove that belief. When I hear of Pythagoras at the blacksmith's shop I immediately think of virgin births, Noah's Ark, and creationism. The truth or falsity is not the point here but, rather, the "intellectual and spiritual complexes" that these myths and dreams "reveal within

---

64. Christensen, *Cambridge History*, 22.

65. Calvin M. Bower, "The Transmission of Ancient Music Theory into the Middle Ages," in Christensen, *Cambridge History*, 143.

a culture." And, with dogged consistency, these western myths and dreams had two identities, namely, white and male.

One of the most exciting aspects of contemporary music studies in the United States is the freedom that comes with letting go of the many mythologies of a musical "western canon."[66] From Paul Henry Lang's *Music in Western Civilization* (1941) to Richard Taruskin's *Oxford History of Western Music* (2005), we could all stand to interrogate the history of "the west" and its ties to the history of white supremacy.[67] This will unnerve some, especially senior colleagues who have invested so much in these mythologies. But their scholarship and focus on Beethoven et al. does not make the mythologies any less false. To be clear, I have great love for Beethoven et al.; I know that I'll always enjoy listening to, and playing, their compositions, and I'm happy to make their work part of my classes in the future. And I have great respect and admiration for the scholars who have written about so-called canonic composers; I myself have done so in my career as well. But understanding how and why we have put these composers into an otherworldly category, all in the service of patriarchy and white supremacy—and consequently letting go of the mythologies we have historically been taught, often by white men themselves, notably—is ultimately both rewarding and emancipating.

In general, I no longer use the term "western canon" to describe music that is historically from Austria/Germany, France, and possibly Italy for the most part, and more historically tied to these three territories the further you go back in time in this western narrative. I also avoid the term "European" to describe this music, since the complete erasure of the vast majority of Europe—which extends from Portugal to the Caspian Sea on its southern extremes, and up to the northern Ural Mountains in its northeast corner— has been presumed in our musical concept of "Europe." To say nothing of the northwest corner of Europe, Norway, and the Sámi, formerly known as Laplanders, the northwestern European peoples who are not considered to be white yet have been part of Europe for millennia. It should go without saying that there are numerous BIPOC groups that have inhabited Europe for many centuries and, yes, millennia, which is one reason why "European" and "west" are such problematic terms for what is really being discussed: a nineteenth- and twentieth-century version of whiteness.

66. For a discussion of western operatic mythologies, see Olivia Giovetti, "Origin Myths: The Middle Eastern Heritage of Opera," *Van Magazine*, April 4, 2019 (https://van-magazine .com/mag/origin-myths).

67. See Paul Henry Lang, *Music in Western Civilization* (Norton, 1941), and Richard Taruskin, *The Oxford History of Western Music*, 5 vols. (Oxford University Press, 2005).

I tend to use the word "classical" for this music, while I realize that "classical" is also used for certain Indian, Iranian, and other musical traditions. Most often, I now use geographical locations—"In this piece, written in 1720 in Köthen, a city in what is now Germany, Johann Sebastian Bach used a set of dances, a suite, as the form for the piece"—to discuss classical music.[68] This may sound silly to a professional musicologist, but it sets the stage for our undergraduates and properly frames the composer and work. And I avoid the constituent parts, "west" and "canon," for similar reasons. "Western civilization" has already, for the most part, gone the way of the covered wagon in academic circles, and I believe that will happen with the musical western canon as well.

One Example of How the Western Canon Discriminates

In 2020 I had an article published in *Music Theory Spectrum* on the music of Nikolai Rimsky-Korsakov, "On Rimsky-Korsakov's False (Hexatonic) Progressions outside the Limits of a Tonality."[69] One of the two anonymous reviewers had recommended rejection. Fortunately, the editor had the good sense to go to third and fourth reviewers—the other initial reviewer was far more positive—who ultimately recommended publication. I was particularly struck by one passage in the rejection:

> To me, the part of the paper needing the most rethinking is the attempt to use its evidence to establish a claim of Rimsky-Korsakov's greatness as a composer. . . . Few *Spectrum* readers will buy the claim that Rimsky-Korsakov's use of some device or other, at some particular historical time, is all the ticket that he needs to gain admission to the cemetery of great composers.[70]

There's one main problem with this passage—I never attempted to "use evidence to establish a claim of Rimsky-Korsakov's greatness as a composer."

---

68. And I also used full names, like Johann Sebastian Bach instead of J. S. Bach or, simply, Bach. See Chris White, "Beethoven Has a First Name: It's Time to 'fullname' All Composers in Classical Music," Slate.com, October 24, 2020 (https://slate.com/culture/2020/10/fullname-famous-composers-racism-sexism.html).

69. Philip Ewell, "On Rimsky-Korsakov's False (Hexatonic) Progressions outside the Limits of a Tonality," *Music Theory Spectrum* 42 (2020): 122–42.

70. Anonymous *Music Theory Spectrum* review.

I consider Rimsky-Korsakov to be a compelling composer, and I quite like his music. (I'd say exactly the same thing, but not more, about Johannes Brahms, by the way.) And it should surprise no one that in Russia Rimsky-Korsakov is something of a national hero, on par with any so-called western canonic composer. Here's what I wrote at the end of the abstract as a goal for the paper: "Ultimately, I aim to enrich the discourse on Rimsky-Korsakov the teacher, writer, and composer, beyond the typical Western narrative of Rimsky-Korsakov as, primarily, the teacher of Igor Stravinsky."[71]

This reviewer, clearly, believes deeply in the idea of a western canon and that Rimsky-Korsakov is not part of it. The reviewer also believes that, through evidence, probably "scientific," one can "establish" a composer's "greatness." But in our American white-male western canon, there is no amount of evidence that could possibly establish Rimsky-Korsakov's greatness, and that is in fact the point of music theory's white-male frame—policing and enforcing who gets to be called great. The reviewer writes that there exists a "cemetery of great composers," one to which we should all bow presumably, and to which one can "gain admission." Does anyone really doubt who makes up that cemetery? That cemetery was set at twelve composers by Heinrich Schenker nearly a century ago, and what we've done in music theory is work from that list of twelve—which included Domenico Scarlatti, let us not forget, but not Igor Stravinsky, Pyotr Tchaikovsky, or Richard Wagner—and expand it with our mythologies of white-male greatness as necessary. So we can begin to think of composers such as Claude Debussy, Béla Bartók, and Arnold Schoenberg.

Perhaps the biggest irony about this reviewer—whose cemetery is no doubt filled with white men who mostly spoke German—is the fact that Rimsky-Korsakov was both white and male, though as a Russian Slav and Eastern Orthodox, he would probably not have been considered white during his lifetime, neither in Europe nor in the United States. Finally, this episode highlights the injustice in the so-called doubly blind academic peer review in music theory, in which reviewers who believe in a false idea of "greatness," hidden behind a cloak of anonymity, can systematically include a given set of ideas and repertoires while excluding that which does not comport with that same set of ideas and repertoires. In other words, I believe that part of the reason that this reviewer recommended rejection is because the reviewer believes Rimsky-Korsakov is not as deserving of our attention

71. Ewell, "Rimsky-Korsakov's False (Hexatonic) Progressions," 122. This was obviously still when I used "western" in my writing.

as typical canonic western composers. And through this process of gatekeeping, we have a radically exclusionist racial and gender framework of American music theory, in which the epistemic core of our field is still devoted to composers who were white men who mostly spoke German.

But we ask the wrong question if we ask whether we can consider a given composer who is outside the "western canon" alongside those few who are truly on the inside. Of course we can. A classic thesis topic among graduate students concerns finding a composer outside of the purported western canon and then arguing for that composer's ascent into the mythology: "In my paper I will show that [composer's name] has been undervalued and underperformed and deserves more of our scholarly attention." If only we all realized that no amount of effort, of handwringing, will get that composer into the canon—because that's not how white men set up the canon in the nineteenth century. That white-male structure is set, and there can only be gradations of levels below those at the very top of the structure, which is occupied by Ludwig van Beethoven and, possibly, Wolfgang Amadeus Mozart. We should instead be working to dismantle the godlike status of such canonic composers, which, ultimately, no one else can ever reach—this is the point of the white supremacist structure in fact, such that all outside composers, like Rimsky-Korsakov and countless others, can only look in from the outside, only dream of admittance to the pantheon of greatness, the cemetery of great composers. The idea that admittance is theoretically possible, yet practically impossible, is the key feature of this system. By the way, I've just described a crucial aspect of a pyramid scheme.

How the Western Canon Creates Racist Policies:
The Foreign-Language Requirement

Ibram Kendi writes, "A racist idea is any idea that suggests one racial group is inferior or superior to another racial group in any way," while "a racist policy is any measure that produces or sustains racial inequity between racial groups."[72] Music theory's belief in and promotion of the western canon has created racist policies in our music curricula, and a perfect example of this is in the foreign-language requirement common in most music theory graduate programs.

Historically, American music theory has recognized five (and only five)

---

72. Kendi, *How to Be an Antiracist*, 18–19.

foreign languages to fulfill graduate language-proficiency requirements: ancient Greek, Latin, Italian, French, and German. These five languages precisely track the western white mythologies that I've outlined in this chapter. In most US graduate music theory programs, competency in one or more of these languages has been required in order to graduate. In top-down fashion, remaining languages are othered such that, if a student wants to use a different language to satisfy the language requirement, some kind of dispensation must be granted—I was given such a dispensation for Russian as a graduate student at Yale University in the 1990s—so as to keep the structure of the five official languages intact. The requirement to be able to translate into English one or more of these five languages is a racist policy born of the racist idea that white persons are superior to BIPOC, a racist idea that is in fact the backbone of our musical western canon. American music theory's white racial frame believes that the only foreign (i.e., non-English) music-theoretical works worth studying were written in these five languages. It should go without saying that there are music-theoretical works worth studying written in foreign languages other than these five, and that they can be representative of other long-standing rich music theory traditions, both inside and outside of the European continent.

This language requirement is sometimes obfuscated by underscoring the ability to "translate into idiomatic English," thereby stressing not only the student's ability to understand the original language, but also the need to render it in idiomatic English. But this ability need not be tested by translation; writing idiomatic English is already a requirement for US graduate programs. The requirement is also sometimes obfuscated by removing the descriptors, "German" for instance, from in front of "language requirement," such that, in theory, any foreign language will count. Thus the "German language requirement" becomes, simply, the "language requirement." But the five original languages will still be privileged, so this is obfuscating and not an antiracist policy solution. Why will they still be privileged? Because the entire enterprise is already tilted toward the five main languages. The excerpts for translation have already been chosen, and the faculty who will grade them already identified. In certain cases stipends are provided specifically for studying those five languages. Arrangements have been secured between foreign-language departments and music departments. Existing research areas of certain faculty get emphasized and, consequently, dissertations and theses develop along those research areas and amplify the five languages yet again. In fact, removing the word "German" from in front of "language requirement" is actually *more* racist than leaving it in, insofar as obfuscating the whiteness of racist structures is always a primary goal of whiteness, and I can think of no better way to obfuscate the racism of this requirement than removing the word "German" from in front of "language requirement." I often say that having graduate *music* students prove proficiency in German would be like requiring graduate students in German to pass a clarinet-performance proficiency exam. Sure, there's a lot of great clarinet music out there, but one does not need to play the clarinet to get a doctorate in German languages and literature, just as one certainly doesn't need to know German to get a doctorate in music theory.

The entire institution of this language requirement centers around the western narrative that we have all been taught, and this requirement represents a racist policy, that is, it "produces and sustains racial inequity between racial groups." It does this by, in no uncertain terms, telling BIPOC scholars that the music theories of the places they or their ancestors may have come from are not as important as European music theories, the music theories of the mythical white race. It goes without saying that *all* of the texts written in those five languages—by figures such as Aristoxenus (c. 375–335 BCE), Boethius (c. 477–524 CE), Gioseffo Zarlino (1517–1590), Jean-Philippe Rameau (1683–1764), and Hugo Riemann (1849–1919), for example—that graduate students are supposed to be conversant with, were, in fact, written by people who either would have considered themselves white, as in the eighteenth through twentieth centuries, or who would have been considered white by others in the western narrative, like the ancient Greeks or Romans. Defenders of the status quo might point out that there is new research in German or French that our students should also be conversant with, but nine times out of ten this new research was written by white persons about white persons, so there's nothing there that actually combats the racism so deeply embedded in the language requirement. It's also worth pointing out that fully 100% of those white people whose foreign-language texts American music theory has deemed worthy of knowing in our history were also cisgender men, which means that the foreign-language requirement is also a sexist policy. Consequently, I'm of the opinion that the foreign-language requirement common in graduate music theory programs be eliminated. Those who disagree with me will insist that this requirement is not a racist policy, that it is, in fact, a *race-neutral* policy (as well as a gender-neutral policy). But such policies don't exist, and it's actually pretty easy to see how the foreign-language requirement, now normally only focusing on German and French, and possibly Italian, produces or sustains inequity between racial groups. Sure, anyone, irrespective of one's race (or gender), can learn German, but the fact that virtually all the texts that we are meant to read were written by white (male) persons should be all the proof we need to show that this is most certainly not a race- (or gender-) neutral policy, and should therefore be eliminated.[73]

Epistemological Ignorance

In order to believe these western mythologies in which ancient Greece served as the sole progenitor of a purported western culture that, in turn, reached an alleged apex in artistic, cultural, and moral thought in Europe in roughly the seventeenth to nineteenth centuries, one must come to new decisions about history, and the epistemology that dictated how it was written. In other words, if, as was so often said and written during and after the Enlightenment, all humans were created equal, how could we justify the horrors of chattel slavery, for example? In "Epistemological Ignorance," philosopher Charles Mills explains how four Enlightenment social-contract theorists—Thomas Hobbes, Immanuel Kant, John Locke, and Jean-Jacques Rousseau—began, ostensibly, with the egalitarian starting point of moral and epistemic equality among all people.[74] This was supposed to represent a move away from the premodern feudal European paradigm of nobility and the divine right of kings, to a more just version of equality. But, as Mills points out, this break between an illiberal premodernity and a liberal modernity was quite partial indeed, and never complete. He shows how both white women and people of color, the latter of whom were essentially unnoticed as such in ancient and medieval thought, were subordinated in Enlightenment thought:

> People of color, a category largely marginal to ancient and medieval thought (except in the Christian iconography of the "Monstrous Races"), enter the global Euro-polity as natural subordinates, conquered by the expansionist Euro-empires that are also integral to

---

73. I hesitate to even point out the technological justification for eliminating these graduate language requirements, namely, translation websites such as "Google translate," which can do basic translations better than most students who've passed language-proficiency exams.

74. Charles W. Mills, "Epistemological Ignorance," in *Fifty Concepts for a Critical Phenomenology*, ed. Gail Weiss, Ann V. Murphy, and Gayle Salamon (Northwestern University Press, 2019), 108. Ibram X. Kendi also traces this type of inequality back to the Enlightenment. See his *How to Be an Antiracist*, 90.

modernity (Hobbes's and Locke's incompetent Native Americans, unable to leave the state of nature on their own or appropriate it efficiently; Rousseau's feckless "savages"; Kant's biological racial hierarchy of Europeans–Asians–Africans–Amerindians).

Rather than an unqualified egalitarian liberalism, then, what we actually have is a bourgeois, patriarchal, and racial/imperial liberalism, where the supposedly generic "men" are propertied, male, and white. It is their moral status that is equalized; it is their cognitions that are recognized; it is their selves and the polities which privilege them that determine what can be "known."[75]

Thus what can be "known" is defined by white, propertied men. Their "moral status" was "equalized" in the sense that, in premodernity, white propertied men could easily be any number of rungs below the nobility or the church, while with modernity such men became "equals." And it is precisely these white men who, in the nineteenth century, when our American music institutions were beginning—like the New York Philharmonic in 1842, the Metropolitan Opera in 1883, the Peabody Institute in 1857, the New England Conservatory in 1867, and the Yale School of Music in 1894—defined what was meant to be studied and performed in these institutions. In other words, what was proper to "know."

Mills continues:

If in premodernity the overtly subordinated, denied even the pretensions to equality, could simply be ignored, now—in an epoch nominally marked by a commitment to equal rights, equal cognitive powers, and equal political consent—those excluded by an inferiority at least facially in tension with supposedly egalitarian and universalist pronouncements *must be actively denied* "knowings" that contradict the established order. Knowing thyself, knowing thy society, would mean coming to "know" one's identity as a victim of an oppressive classist/patriarchal/white-supremacist socio-political order. But such truths cannot be *known* if the system is to preserve itself.[76]

Here Mills shows that, in order for a white supremacist system to exist, certain knowledge must be actively suppressed. Thus my entire discussion

---

75. Mills, "Epistemological Ignorance," 109.
76. Mills, "Epistemological Ignorance," 109.

about a western civilization or canon, in which I give evidence that it is a recent phenomenon intended to provide a backdrop to white supremacist colonial narratives that justified the horrific violence that colonization entailed, must be suppressed at all costs. The very survival of the white (and male) supremacist enterprise depends on it, depends on promoting and teaching ignorance. One can easily understand why teaching African American slaves to read and write was generally against the law in antebellum America. Is it any surprise, then, that my own explorations into the racial and gender history of music theory have met with such hostile reactions in certain conservative and senior quarters of the field? In fact, allowing such counternarratives as mine to land and, possibly, have an effect represents an existential crisis to the field as defined by those conservative (largely, though not exclusively, white-male) quarters. But I am a relative newbie to all of this, having immersed myself in these narratives only beginning about seven years ago. In fact, these counternarratives have always existed, and white-male supremacy has, with remarkable effectiveness and verve, crushed these counternarratives so that the west, and, with it, whiteness and maleness, reigns supreme. To be transparent about these histories would be a death knell to white supremacy and the west. Mills adds:

> Particularly in states pretending to be liberal, whether Western or Western-implanted, which do claim to uphold transparency as a norm, actual transparency would be fatal. What is required instead is a structural opacity denying its actual identity, predicated, in Miranda Fricker's terminology, on a "principled" testimonial and hermeneutical injustice to dangerous "knowers": the systemic refusal of credibility to their potentially antisystemic claims and conceptual frameworks. Given the actual class, gender, and racial hierarchies of nominally inclusive and egalitarian liberal democracies, an epistemology of knowledge-seeking must simultaneously constitute itself as an epistemology of knowledge-avoidance: an epistemology of ignorance. *Knowing as a general cognitive ideal will thus require, whenever necessary, knowing to not-know.*[77]

---

77. Mills, "Epistemological Ignorance," 109–10. The source he cites by Miranda Fricker is her *Epistemic Injustice: Power and the Ethics of Knowing* (New York: Oxford University Press, 2007).

I would like to self-identify here as a "dangerous 'knower,'" a purveyor
of "antisystemic claims and conceptual frameworks." In this sense I consider
myself an antiracist killjoy very much in the vein of feminist writer Sara
Ahmed and her notion of the "feminist killjoy," one who consistently points
out racial and gender injustices in society by killing the joy of those who
would wish to take credit for antiracist or antisexist action—like forming a
diversity committee in an academic society, for instance—without even realizing that those actions are anything but antiracist or antisexist.[78] American
music theory's unremitting promulgation of "the west" and its self-professed
superiority is, in fact, a joint effort on the part of music-theoretical power of
"knowing to not-know." In other words, certain knowledge must actively be
avoided if one is to remain faithful to the basic tenets of white-male music-
theoretical superiority.[79]

A perfect example of "knowing to not-know" in American music theory
is Heinrich Schenker and his manifest racism. We American music theorists
decided long ago that to promote and sustain Schenkerian thought would
require engaging in an "epistemology of knowledge-avoidance" with respect
to Schenker's racism (and his sexism by the way) in order to keep the whole
Schenkerian vessel afloat. And it must be said that music theory has done
so with incredible vim, skill, and efficacy over many decades now. Because I
have directly challenged the entire Schenkerian enterprise, I have been called
at times a "dangerous" thinker on social media and elsewhere, which I take
as a point of pride. I suppose I am dangerous to someone who wishes to
keep the Beethovens and Mozarts—or the Shakespeares, Michelangelos, or
Hegels for that matter—on their hallowed hilltop rather than seeing them
simply become one part of a much larger narrative that includes all peoples
of the world, which will ultimately only enrich and benefit everyone, including white persons themselves, I hasten to add. And with respect to Schenker,
my unvarnished account of his demonstrable horribleness, which I explain
in detail in the following chapter, shatters the hagiographic picture that our
white racial frame has painted about the man for nearly a century now,
which is why my account has at times been either dismissed or met with
extreme vitriol. Or, as Ta-Nehisi Coates puts it in his own unvarnished his-

78. For more on Sara Ahmed and the feminist killjoy, see feministkilljoys.com
79. For more on the concept of epistemological ignorance in philosophy, see Charles
Mills, *The Racial Contract* (Cornell University Press, 1997), 18. See also Shannon Sullivan
and Nancy Tuana, eds., *Race and Epistemologies of Ignorance* (State University of New York
Press, 2007).

tory of our American racial tragedy, "The history breaks the myth. And so the history is ignored, and fictions are weaved into our art and politics that dress villainy in martyrdom and transform banditry into chivalry."[80]

Final Thoughts on "On White Mythologies"

I am not a classicist, nor am I a philosopher, sociologist, or anthropologist, and my discussions of white mythologies, western civilization, the western canon, and epistemological ignorance will certainly draw scrutiny. As well they should. And as surely as I welcome collegial and respectful criticism of my work, certain points are not in question. First, ancient Egypt preceded ancient Greece by thousands of years and, as is well known, the ancient Greeks cited Egyptian influence themselves. Second, while ancient Greek writings have been studied since they were first written down beginning roughly twenty-five hundred years ago, the human construct of "western civilization" emerged only in the mid-to-late nineteenth century. Third, at that time European intellectual thought reified racial hierarchies to justify the many colonial horrors taking place around the world while making sure that those hierarchies fit the narratives of Christian theology (God's will) and European philosophy. Of course, the main driving force behind the reification of racial hierarchies was white supremacy, which justified, to the white mind, the power that it had seized by whatever means necessary. Fourth, significant musicians took these hierarchies and applied them to music. For example, Richard Wagner and François-Joseph Fétis were influenced by the fictitious race science of the French aristocrat Arthur de Gobineau and his four-volume *Essai sur l'inégalité des races humaines* (Essay on the inequality of human races), published 1853–1855. Heinrich Schenker clearly drew inspiration from Gobineau's work when he said, "For peace will not come to mankind until *inequality*, the principle of all creation, becomes an axiom in the intercourse of nations and individuals."[81] And, as I already mentioned, Schenker makes five references to Gobineau's writings in his diaries, as well

---

80. Ta-Nehisi Coates, *We Were Eight Years in Power* (One World, 2018), 64.
81. Heinrich Schenker, *Piano Sonata in C Minor, Op. 111*, in *Beethoven's Last Piano Sonatas: An Edition with Elucidation*, trans. and ed. John Rothgeb (Oxford University Press, 2015), vol. 3, 23 n. 13. See, especially, "Literature" on companion website http://fdslive.oup.com/www.oup.com/uscompanion/us/static/companion.websites/9780199914180/C_minor_Op_111_Web.pdf (italics mine.)

as in "The Mission of the German Genius."[82] Fifth, and finally, significant music historians have pinned the beginning of our musical western canon to two entities, namely, the Christian church and ancient Greece. I hardly need to point out that this canon is therefore the child of western civilization, not its parent.

I *am* an American music theorist with a deep and abiding sense that American music theory, and the academic study of music writ large, is fundamentally unjust from racial and gender standpoints. The many mythologies outlined above have convinced large swaths of the United States that Ludwig van Beethoven was the greatest composer, William Shakespeare the greatest writer, Michelangelo the greatest sculptor, and George Washington the greatest statesperson the world has ever known. This is not to say, and it has never been to say, that these white men were *bad* at what they did. Not at all—they were significant men who deserve attention. But it is to say that, because of America's historical white supremacy and patriarchy, virtually all voices that were not both white and male have been ignored, shunted to the side, which has made a field like music theory extremely exclusionist in nature. This, in turn, has greatly impoverished what we do. Understanding this will allow us to engage with composers and musicians who were not both white and male *on equal terms* with those who were, which is something we should have been doing all along. The spate of recent activity in not just DEI but, especially, antiracism and antisexism gives me hope that the future of music theory, and of the academic study of music, is bright.

---

82. Heinrich Schenker, *Der Tonwille: Pamphlets in Witness of the Immutable Laws of Music, Offered to a New Generation of Youth*, trans. Ian Bent, William Drabkin, Joseph Dubiel, Timothy Jackson, Joseph Lubben, and Robert Snarrenberg (Oxford University Press, [1921–23] 2004), vol. 1, 13.

THREE

On Heinrich Schenker and His Legacy

The dominant racial frame has sharply defined inferior and superior racial groups and authoritatively rationalized and structured the great and continuing racial inequalities of this [American] society. In a whitewashing process, and most especially today, this dominant framing has shoved aside, ignored, or treated as incidental numerous racial issues, including the realities of persisting racial discrimination and racial inequality.[1]

It would be hard to overstate Heinrich Schenker's influence on American music theory. Whether one specifically studies Schenker and Schenkerian analysis, tonal music generally, popular music, or post-tonal topics, Schenker in many ways represents our shared model of what it means to be a music theorist. If Beethoven is our exemplar of a music composer, Schenker is our exemplar of a music theorist. After all, his is the only named theory routinely required in music theory graduate programs.[2] And with respect

---

1. Joe Feagin, *The White Racial Frame: Centuries of Racial Framing and Counter-framing*, 2nd ed. (Routledge, [2009] 2013), 22. Much of this chapter is contained in section 4, "Schenkerian Theory as a Racialized Structure of the White Racial Frame," from my article "Music Theory and the White Racial Frame," *Music Theory Online* 26, no. 2 (September 2020), though there are significant changes throughout.

2. It's difficult to say exactly which doctoral music theory programs in the United States and Canada still require Schenkerian analysis, since curricula are constantly shifting, but the last time I checked, in early 2020, with the help of CUNY Graduate Center student Michèle Duguay (who's now an assistant professor at Indiana University), at least one course in Schenkerian analysis was required at the Cincinnati Conservatory of Music, the CUNY Graduate Center, Florida State University, Indiana University, McGill University, University of Michigan, Temple University, and the University of British Columbia. Adding graduate classes coded as "tonal analysis," which are often, in fact, classes in Schenkerian analysis, such

to the many mythologies of white-male greatness in the western canon of music, Heinrich Schenker and his legacy have done more to perpetuate, reinforce, and enshrine those mythologies than anything else in American music theory.

Heinrich Schenker was an ardent racist and German nationalist. However, no one has clearly linked his repugnant views on people to his music theories. I endeavor to do that in this chapter. In doing so, I follow the express admonition of Schenker himself, who argued explicitly that his views on race and music were to be considered together in his overall view of the world. In a larger sense, I argue that Schenkerian theory is an institutionalized racialized structure—a crucial part of music theory's white racial frame—that exists to benefit members of the dominant white race of music theory.

For those who know nothing about Schenkerian analysis, I think the best way to briefly explain it is through an analogy. Almost twenty years ago, when my wife and I lived in Tennessee, we wanted to do some landscaping in our large backyard, so we invited a landscape architect to give us a bid. Showing us a sample project, the architect pulled out a large, probably one square meter, booklet that had thin sheets of translucent paper bound on one side and stacked one over the other. That project had five levels of detail. As we looked at all five overlaid sheets, we could see all the details that a former client had wanted: hardscaping with a fire pit, fencing, shrubbery and two small trees, an irrigation system, and a lighting system. The architect told us that each sheet represented an option to the buyer. Lift the top sheet and, voilà, the lighting system was gone (and the cost was reduced accordingly). You don't need an irrigation system? Another sheet was lifted off. You'll plant your own vegetation? The middle sheet not needed. And once there was only one sheet left, it represented the hardscaping, that which was the starting point for the work (and the least expensive cost to the buyer).

In short, Heinrich Schenker did similar work with music compositions in the classical tonal style by graphing out the most important details on sheets of musical staff paper, though he did not stack pages one on top of the other. Rather, he lined up background, middle ground, and foreground graphs vertically on a single page. He called the different sheets of paper

programs included the University of Chicago, Eastman School of Music, University of North Texas, and Northwestern University. In addition, "proseminars" are often encouraged, and if the faculty member's specialty is Schenkerian analysis, then that is the class taken by music theory graduate students.

from my landscaping analogy "layers," with the most detailed five-page version the "foreground," the three-page version the "middle ground," and the one-page, most basic landscape the "background." Schenker felt that all pieces of music that were truly great would exhibit the same "fundamental structure," that is, the same most basic form of the landscape's background. (And, admittedly, my analogy breaks down here, since not everyone would say that the hardscaping, for instance, is most important to their backyard, but the layered aspect of the analogy is sound.) Schenker would graph a previously composed piece of music, say, a symphony by Johannes Brahms, onto staff paper and identify the background structure that, in terms of tonality, manifested itself in a harmonic motion from I (tonic) to V (dominant) back to I (tonic), which happened under a long-range descending diatonic scale or part of a scale. His method of analyzing classical music was taken by certain disciples from Vienna, Austria, to the United States, beginning in the 1930s, and it has become the main method for analyzing tonal music in American music theory over many decades now.[3]

In telling the story of Heinrich Schenker and his legacy, music theory's white-male frame has been consistent with its unwritten guidelines:

1. If possible, don't mention Schenker's racism and, if confronted about it, feign ignorance.
2. When dealing directly with Schenker's racism, erect an impenetrable barrier between Schenker's reprehensible views on race, sexuality, and nationality on the one hand, and his views on music and musical structure on the other.
3. Invoke Schenker's Jewishness as a mitigating factor for his repulsive beliefs, thus creating a victim narrative, and use softened language—"troubled," "antidemocratic," "nationalist," "unfortunate," but never "racist"—to describe the man.
4. Contextualize his repulsiveness as par for the course in Schenker's milieu, early twentieth-century Europe, thus further mitigating Schenker's reprehensibility.
5. Fortify the impenetrable barrier between Schenker's heinous views on people, on the one hand, and his useful views on music on the other.

---

3. For more on the American history of Schenkerism see David Berry, "Hans Weisse and the Dawn of American Schenkerism," *Journal of Musicology* 20, no. 1 (2003): 104–56.

When I gave a plenary talk at the Society for Music Theory in November 2019, I deviated significantly from these five points. I never mentioned the fact that Schenker was Jewish, for example, and I suggested quite explicitly that his racism most certainly permeated his musical ideas and that the barrier between them had been erected by whiteness and maleness in order to further the cause of whiteness and maleness. The reason why this was such apostasy was simple: if it can be shown that Schenker's views on people can be linked to his views on musical structure, it becomes harder to maintain the Schenkerian enterprise as a whole.

One of music theory's greatest feats is its ability to sever its own past from the present. If some historical aspect of a theory is unseemly or unsavory, we typically bury it and move on. What, after all, do political, social, and cultural attitudes have to do with the content of someone's underlying music-theoretical thought? Thus, we have a figure like Heinrich Schenker, whose writings get whitewashed for general consumption. In discussing the historical/theoretical divide often cited in music-theoretical circles, Thomas Christensen writes:

If we . . . consider solely the theoretical "content" of some past theory, we are presuming that this content can be extracted from—and rationally analyzed outside of—its historical and biographical contexts. Theories, simply put, make normative claims that are temporally immutable.[4]

The logic behind the transcendent "immutability" of music theories allows the white racial frame to overlook the racialized structures that reliably benefit whites over nonwhites. (To be clear, Christensen is arguing against this timeless interpretation in his work.) This is also the logic behind colorblind racism, which lets music theory accomplish two things: it makes it seem that music theory is above being racial or racist, while at the same time it keeps in place the racialized structures that benefit whites over nonwhites. To put this another way, to consider these theories ahistorically is to surgically remove all traces of racism, insofar as racist strains do nothing to advance the theories in question, all of which allows the white-racial-frame

---

4. Thomas Christensen, "Music Theory and Its Histories," in *Music Theory and the Exploration of the Past*, ed. Christopher Hatch and David W. Bernstein (University of Chicago Press, 1993), 9.

music theorist to reside in a music-theoretical witness protection program, never to be held accountable with respect to the difficult questions concerning race and whiteness.

Joe Feagin makes a point about German sociologist Max Weber (1864–1920), Schenker's contemporary, that rings true for Schenker and how we music theorists deal with him:

> Take the example of Max Weber, who died in the early twentieth century but has had a great impact on Western social science ever since. Like other social scientists of his era, he held to the tenets of blatant biological racism, a view that infected his historical and geo-political arguments, yet one that almost never gets critically discussed in textbooks and empirical analyses that to this day use his analytical concepts.[5]

Similarly, Schenker also believed in biological racism, a point that either goes unstated or gets glossed over in virtually every historical account. And, as with Weber, Schenker's racist views "infected" his music-theoretical "arguments," as I show below. Feagin continues, "Since the time of Weber, many Western social scientists accent European superiority in modernity."[6] Clearly, this is the model music theorists have followed as well, the accenting of "European superiority in modernity" in our choice of repertoires to study and methods to teach.

Another contemporary of Schenker, the color-theorist Johannes Itten (1888–1967), is worth mentioning. As University of Texas design historian Carma Gorman told me in an email after one of my talks in November 2020, Itten's "ideas are still being taught as gospel in first-year art and design foundations courses across the U.S.A., even though his theories are a) one hundred years old, b) demonstrably false, and c) overtly racist."[7] Gorman points out that in one of his foundational works, *The Elements of Color*, origi-nally published in German in 1961 as *Kunst der Farbe*, Itten speaks about the "aura" and the "different subjective color types" for different people under the heading "Subjective Timbre":

---

5. Feagin, *The White Racial Frame*, 6.
6. Feagin, *The White Racial Frame*, 6.
7. Carma Gorman, email exchange with the author, November 11, 2020. I use this and the following email quotation with Gorman's permission.

Light blond types with blue eyes and pink [i.e., white] skin incline towards very pure colors, often with a great many clearly distinguished color qualities. Contrast of hue is the basic feature. Depending on the forcefulness of the individual, the colors may be more or less luminous.

A very different type is represented by people with black hair, dark skin, and dark eyes, for whom black plays an important part in the harmony.[8]

Itten's linking of race with artistic color immediately invokes the notion of "racial purity" that coursed through the veins of so many white persons in the early to mid-twentieth century. Turning to the education of students, Itten writes of the subjective color combinations that will help the students discover themselves. Yet in speaking of the "subjective forms and colors" of students, he notes that it is important "to teach the general objective rules of form and color":

The blond type should be assigned such subjects as Springtime, Kindergarten, Baptism, Festival of Bright Flowers, Garden at Morning. Nature subjects should be vivid, without lightdark contrasts.

Good assignments for a dark type would be Night, Light in a Dark Room, Autumn Storm, Burial, Grief, The Blues, etc. Nature Studies can be done in charcoal or black and white pigments.[9]

Thus, objectively speaking, whiteness should be assigned studies that feature, for instance, springtime, baptisms, and festivals, while darkness (one presumes blackness here) should be assigned storms, burials, and grief—to Itten, this was the natural order of things. What is remarkable is not so much that such a figure as Itten existed but, rather, how influential he was and *continues to be up to today*, just like Heinrich Schenker. Take one instance of a current hagiography, from 2019, as an example: *Johannes Itten* in the Hirmer series Great Masters in Art.[10]

Notably, Gorman believes, as do I, that figures like Itten and Schenker

8. Johannes Itten, *The Elements of Color*, ed. Faber Birren, trans. Ernst van Hagen (Van Nostrand Reinhold, 1970), 24. Originally published as *Kunst der Farbe* (Otto Maier Verlag, 1961).

9. Itten, *The Elements of Color*, 24–25.

10. Christoph Wagner, *Johannes Itten*, Great Masters in Art (Hirmer, 2019).

were often chosen to represent their fields not *despite* their racism but, in fact, *because* of it. The Ittens and the Schenkers—and the Max Webers and countless others—grew out of the western tradition, a tradition that was not even one hundred years old by the mid-twentieth century, let's not forget, that sought "scientific" evidence to promote the greatness of white men, while erasing from existence all others. Gorman further speculated:

> One reason why art and design programs have continued to teach first-year students the ethnocentric, elitist, racist, and sexist "elements and principles" (or "laws") of color, composition, and typography that white-male bigots cooked up more than a century ago is because these theories about "good design" are the most effective (legal) means they have of communicating to women and students of color that they are (still) not welcome in the field. (Dedicating 90% to 100% of a survey textbook's prose and illustrations to the work of white males is also a pretty effective, and entirely legal, way of signaling to women and people of color that they will never be "great" and never really belong.)[11]

The same reasoning could be made about American music theory, since our field, like art and design programs, has been extremely unwelcoming to those who do not identify as white cisgender men. The brief textbook example that Gorman gives closely mirrors my own analysis of music theory textbooks, as well as my brief discussion of *A History of Western Music*. I'd make one point to push back against what Gorman writes, however. I'm not convinced that to teach design or music exclusively through the work of white men is "entirely legal," as she says. Think here of the 1964 Civil Rights Act or the 1972 Title IX legislation. Or, if you prefer a constitutional reading, think of the Fourteenth Amendment to the US Constitution, which guarantees both due process (which we've obviously never undertaken in music theory) and equal protection of law to all citizens. Were I a graduate student today, I'd strongly consider questioning the legality of a field that is taught from an entirely white-male point of view. Food for thought anyway.

---

11. Carma Gorman, email exchange with the author, January 28, 2021.

Schenker's Racism

Schenker's German nationalism is well known:

> Only one thing can be of service: recognition of the truth! It is time that Germans freed themselves from the illusion that all men and all nations are equal. . . . Let Germans be alive to the superior quality of their human propagating soil (*Menschenhumus*).[12]

Schenker also believed in the inequality of peoples: "For peace will not come to mankind until inequality, the principle of all creation, becomes an axiom in the intercourse of nations and individuals."[13]

But I wish to focus on Schenker's racism, which has the most relevance to music theory's white frame. Schenker was highly cognizant of race and often mentions it in his plentiful writings on politics, culture, nationhood, music, and art. In *Schenker Documents Online*, a simple search for the word "race" yields fifty-seven results, nearly all by Schenker about human races.[14] Schenker regularly uses the term "race" (*Rasse*), as well as "white" (*weiß*), and "black" (*schwarz*) as modifiers for human races. He speaks of "less able or more primitive races"[15] and "wild and half wild peoples."[16] He speaks of whiteness

---

12. Heinrich Schenker, *Der Tonwille: Pamphlets in Witness of the Immutable Laws of Music, Offered to a New Generation of Youth*, trans. Ian Bent, William Drabkin, Joseph Dubiel, Timothy Jackson, Joseph Lubben, and Robert Snarrenberg (Oxford University Press, [1921–23] 2004), vol. 1, 17.

13. Heinrich Schenker, *Piano Sonata in C Minor, Op. 111*, in *Beethoven's Last Piano Sonatas: An Edition with Elucidation*, trans and ed. John Rothgeb (Oxford University Press, 2015), vol. 3, 23 n.13. See, especially, "Literature" on the companion website http://fdslive.oup.com/www.oup.com/uscompanion/us/static/companion.websites/9780199914180/C_minor_Op _111_Web.pdf

14. Ian Bent, William Drabkin, et al. n.d., *Schenker Documents Online*, http://www.schen kerdocumentsonline.org/index.html. *Schenker Documents Online* (hereafter *SDO*) is an online database of his correspondence, diaries, and lesson notes that were previously unpublished, with transcriptions of the original German, translations into English, and various explanatory annotations.

15. Heinrich Schenker, *Piano Sonata in C Minor*, online "Literature" supplement, 21 n. 13.

16. *SDO*, OJ 1/15, September 8, 1914, transcr. Marko Deisinger, trans. William Drabkin. In relation to "inferior races" Schenker says, "Let me not be misunderstood: Even the babbling of a child, the first awkward sentences, certainly have a captivating charm, as do Arabic, Japanese, and Turkish songs. But in the first case our joys are derived from the child itself and the wonderful miracle of a human being in its development; in the second, our curiosity is aroused by the foreign peoples and their peculiarities" (Schenker, *Counterpoint*, vol. 1, 28).

in relation to the "animal" Japanese, that the "white race" will need to adapt in order to "annihilate" the Japanese "animals."[17] About Slavs—from which the word "slave" derives, since so many Slavs were taken as slaves into Europe in the history of European slavery—Schenker poured more scorn, writing about the "Slavic half-breed": "There will be no peace on earth until . . . the German race crushes the Slavs on the grounds of superiority."[18]

Citing "musically inferior races," he dismisses the possibility that other cultures could possibly have any music theoretical systems at all when he writes, "How can anyone dare to suggest that we look to musically inferior races and nations for allegedly new systems, when in fact they have no systems at all!"[19] This quotation points to another unexplored aspect of Heinrich Schenker the man, namely, his incuriosity. To make such a dumb statement—that other musics of the world "have no systems at all!," every bit as untrue in 1910 when he wrote it as it is today and, obviously, as it ever was—and so emphatically no less, throws the entire enterprise of Schenkerian studies into question in my opinion. If Schenker could make such a fallacious and subscholarly claim about music theoretical systems, and try to pass it off as genuine scholarship, how many other of his music-theoretical claims could or should be called into question?

About blacks Schenker had the lowest of opinions. When speaking about self-governance, Schenker said about blacks, incredulously, "Even negroes proclaim that they want to govern themselves because they, too, can achieve it,"[20] thus acknowledging his belief that blacks, incapable of self-governance, are the lowest form of human being—in fact, subhuman in Schenker's understanding. Recall here, by the way, my discussion based on Martin Bernal in chapter 2 about how the "Aryan/European" narrative of civilization erases the existence of ancient Egypt to maintain the falsehood that ancient Greece was untouched by blackness. Clearly, Schenker is espousing the western narrative, with ancient Greek (white) roots, with respect to self-governance, a narrative that was concretized when he commented on black governance in the early twentieth century.

Schenker disparages the music of blacks, namely, "negro music" and jazz,[21] as well as negro spirituals, claiming that they were a "completely falsi-

---

17. *SDO*, OJ 1/15, August 20, 1914, transcr. Marko Deisinger, trans. William Drabkin.

18. *SDO*, OJ 1/15, July 26, 1914, transcr. Marko Deisinger, trans. William Drabkin.

19. Heinrich Schenker, *Counterpoint: A Translation of Kontrapunkt by Heinrich Schenker*, ed. John Rothgeb (Schirmer Books, [1910 and 1922] 2001), vol. 1, 28.

20. *SDO*, DLA 59.930/10, transcr. Ian Bent and Lee Rothfarb, trans. Lee Rothfarb.

21. Heinrich Schenker, *The Masterwork in Music*, trans. Ian Bent, Alfred Clayton, and Derrick Puffett, ed. William Drabkin (Dover Publications, [1930] 2014), vol. 3, 77.

fied, dishonest expropriation of European music."[22] It seems that Schenker liked these spirituals inasmuch as he compared them to European music. But instead of according blacks and blackness a measure of integrity or artistic beauty, he reduces this particular black genre—the spiritual—to thievery, stripping it of its humanity and implying that blacks were incapable of producing good music on their own, which, in turn, bespeaks his hatred of blackness. Finally, when speaking of the low levels of current music-history education, Schenker writes that "the historians educate their students mostly to the level of a kind of music-salon-Tyrolean, music-negro."[23]

One point rarely made in Schenker studies concerns his views against the intermarrying of races, which led to the "mongrelization" that was a mainstay of biological race science of the nineteenth and twentieth centuries. Yet there can be no doubt that Schenker was against racial mixing. He says, "'Race' is good, 'inbreeding' of race, however, is murky."[24] In "Von der Sendung des deutschen Genies" (The mission of German genius), from *Der Tonwille*, Schenker expressed horror at the mixing of races in "Senegalese marriage relationships"[25] and "intermarrying black racial stock with . . . a French mother."[26] This is of paramount importance because white-frame authors, on the rare occasion that they deal with the topic, have generally tried to call Schenker's racism cultural, and not biological,[27] insofar as linking Schenker to biological racism would ally him with some extremely unsavory eugenicist figures in the late nineteenth and early twentieth centuries. In other words, by calling Schenker's racism cultural instead of what it was, biological, the white racial frame seeks to shield Schenker from unwanted criticism.

Schenker's reference to the Senegalese reflects his intense rejection of the aftereffects of the Versailles Treaty that ended World War I. Senegal was a French colony, and many black troops fought for France in that war. What Schenker especially objected to was the stationing of these black troops in

22. *SDO*, OJ 4/4, January 1931, transcr. Marko Deisinger, trans. William Drabkin.
23. Heinrich Schenker, *Piano Sonata in C Minor*, online "Literature" supplement, 12.
24. *SDO*, OJ 89/7, [2], transcr. and trans. John Rothgeb and Heribert Esser.
25. Schenker, *Der Tonwille*, vol. 1, 5 and, specifically, 5 n. 15.
26. Schenker, *Der Tonwille*, 18.
27. See, for example, Nicholas Cook, *The Schenker Project: Culture, Race, and Music Theory in Fin-de-Siècle Vienna* (Oxford University Press, 2007), and Carl Schachter, "Elephants, Crocodiles, and Beethoven: Schenker's Politics and the Pedagogy of Schenkerian Analysis," *Theory and Practice* 26 (2001): 4–5.

occupied German territory.[28] Schenker wrote: "The [European] peoples have been shamed, disgraced, and, in the words of the Old Testament, 'been made to stink.' . . . Europe, even more so after the Franco-Senegalese business, needs purifying, in body and spirit."[29] Schenker continues:

> Is it not the League of Nations that also, for example, placed the filthy French in such oafish control of Germany's Saarland, and permitted in the regions occupied by them the ignominy of its black troops— the advance party of its genitalitis [i.e., inflamed genitals], of the flesh of its flesh, of the cannibal spirit of its spirit.[30]

My point here is simple: there exists an antiblack racism to Schenker's writings that remains unexplored, and this racism has infected, and become integral to, the white racial frame of music theory. And, as I wrote earlier, if there's anything worse than the erasure of blackness in American history, it's the erasure of antiblackness, and Schenker's antiblackness has most certainly been erased in music theory's history. In this last quotation, note the homoerotic fetishization and objectification of the black male body, in speaking of the genitals and "flesh of its flesh," that was common in late nineteenth- and early twentieth-century Europe and that represents a further dehumanizing of blacks. Such fetishization and objectification of the black body were also mainstays of biological racism, of course. Schenker's linkage of blacks with cannibalism, promoting the vile stereotype of the "African savage," should only be understood as a grotesque pathology, one that so often infused white, western pseudobiological writings on race. Even though Schenker glorified Germans over all others, there exists a strong white supremacist element to his theories about both race and music in light of his antiblack racism. After all, it is well known that Schenker allowed two non-Germans—Domenico Scarlatti (an Italian) and Frédéric Chopin (a Pole)—into his pantheon of "genius" composers.[31]

---

28. Schenker, *Der Tonwille*, 7 n. 40.

29. Schenker, *Der Tonwille*, 7.

30. Schenker, *Der Tonwille*, 15–16. The use of "genitalitis" here references not simply the genitals, but "inflamed" genitals, suggesting a genital disease or condition particular to black persons. Otherwise, "genitals" is *die Genitalien* in German, and a cognate. I thank Carma Gorman for pointing this out to me.

31. Schenker had strong connections to Poland through his childhood in Galicia and his early Polish schooling, which likely made it easier for him to accept Chopin into his pantheon of genius. For more on Schenker's Polish connections, see Martin Eybl, "Heinrich Schenker's

Whitewashing Schenker

Schenker's racist and German-nationalist beliefs presented a dilemma for those who edited and promoted Schenker's works and translated them into English. To solve the problem, Schenker's offensive writings were simply cast aside as unimportant or whitewashed for general consumption. Recall what Feagin said in the epigraph to this chapter: "In a whitewashing process . . . this dominant framing has shoved aside, ignored, or treated as incidental numerous racial issues, including the realities of persisting racial discrimination and racial inequality."[32] To understand how this whitewashing takes place, I begin with the prefatory material to the 1979 translation of *Der freie Satz*, by Ernst Oster.[33] In his "Preface to the English Edition," Oster mentions that Oswald Jonas, in an earlier German edition, omitted several passages of *Der freie Satz* "that have no bearing on the musical content of the work,"[34] while Oster himself wrote of his own translation, "I felt it best to omit several additional passages of a very general, sometimes semiphilosophical nature here; these omissions are not expressly indicated."[35] In his "Introduction to the English Edition," Allen Forte wrote about Schenker's various offensive material, "Almost none of the material bears substantive relation to the musical concepts that [Schenker] developed during his lifetime and, from that standpoint, can be disregarded."[36]

In the preface to his edition of Schenker's *Kontrapunkt*, John Rothgeb says:

> We urge the reader to recognize that however much Schenker may have regarded his musical precepts as an integral part of a unified world-view, they are, in fact, *not at all logically dependent on any of his extramusical speculations.* Indeed, no broader philosophical context is necessary—or even relevant—to their understanding.[37]

Identities as a German and a Jew," *Musicologica Austriaca: Journal for Austrian Music Studies,* September 21, 2018 (http://www.musau.org/parts/neue-article-page/view/54).

32. Feagin, *The White Racial Frame,* 22

33. Suzannah Clark also discusses this whitewashing process in "The Politics of the Urlinie in Schenker's 'Der Tonwille' and 'Der freie Satz,'" review article of Matthew Brown's *Explaining Tonality: Schenkerian Analysis and Beyond, Journal of the Royal Musical Association* 132, no. 1 (2007): 141–64.

34. Heinrich Schenker, *Der freie Satz,* trans. and ed. Ernst Oster (Longman, [1935] 1979), xiii.

35. Schenker, *Der freie Satz,* xiii.

36. Schenker, *Der freie Satz,* xviii.

37. Schenker, *Counterpoint,* vol. 1, xiv (italics mine).

In stating that Schenker's music theories are "not at all logically dependent on" his "extramusical speculations," that is, his racism, Rothgeb takes a stance diametrically opposed to my own. Rothgeb is not only saying that Schenker was himself incorrect when he asserted that his musical views were "an integral part of a unified world-view," but also implying that it would be irresponsible for us to examine this subject further.

In another example of how the white frame whitewashes Schenker, William Benjamin dismisses Schenker's racism, saying that his "apparent racism was an emotional reflex which stood in contradiction to his personal belief system."[38] So, in Benjamin's extraordinary interpretation, Schenker was not only not racist, but perhaps even a closet humanist and egalitarian. A more extreme revision of Schenker's horribleness one could scarcely conjure.

Nicholas Cook offers humor as a possible reason for Schenker's disgusting language. After a quote from Schenker about "tension spans" in music being better than a "blood test" as an attribute of the German race in Beethoven, Cook says: "In fact, I assume that the idea of employing music theory as a new and more scientific test of racial purity is an example of Schenker's rather heavy, and sometimes dark, humour."[39] Much later on in the text, sensing that this excuse may be met with dismay, Cook writes:

If the explanation I offered there, that Schenker is making a joke, is not convincing, then perhaps another might be that the strangeness of the remark is a symptom of a thought Schenker represses rather than articulates: that Ludwig van Beethoven could perhaps have been the German genius he was because foreign blood flowed in his veins.[40]

And here we have another excuse, further proof of the lengths to which music theory's white racial frame has gone to whitewash Schenker. The only thing that seems to be completely off the table is simply calling Schenker the zealous racist he was. Finally, Cook, in a parenthetical comment, makes it clear that he believes linking Schenker's racism to his musical theories is unhelpful when he speaks about Schenker's "authoritarian impulse that is expressed in the many hierarchies which make up Schenker's worldview (it is tempting but I think *not very helpful* to draw the obvious parallel with

38. William Benjamin, "Schenker's Theory and the Future of Music," review of Schenker's *Der Freie Satz, Journal of Music Theory* 25, no. 1 (1981): 157.

39. Cook, *The Schenker Project*, 148. See also Schachter, "Elephants, Crocodiles, and Beethoven," 17 n. 22.

40. Cook, *The Schenker Project*, 238. Beethoven was both German and Flemish.

his music theory)."[41] What Cook means to say here is that it is unhelpful insofar as it calls attention to race—that is, *unhelpful to music theory's white racial frame*. I, however, happen to think it is extremely helpful, in terms of understanding how we deal with race in music theory, to draw this "obvious parallel."

William Rothstein also whitewashes Schenker's offensive language. With respect to *Der freie Satz*'s appendix 4, which contains many reprehensible statements, Rothstein says:

> The inclusion or exclusion of that appendix was a matter of intense controversy behind the scenes when *Free Composition* was about to be published. Those who argued for its omission were generally those most loyal to Schenker, who feared for the public reaction to his supposed indiscretions, and who most partook of the defensive mentality associated with the émigré group of orthodox disciples. They feared, apparently, that the core of Schenker's thought might be discredited along with his peripheral ramblings.[42]

There is nothing "supposed" about Schenker's "indiscretions"; Schenker was a fervent German nationalist whose racist convictions lay at the very heart of his theories on people and on music. As further proof, I cite Schenker's letter in praise of Adolf Hitler, a letter he wrote to his pupil Felix-Eberhard von Cube in May 1933, four months *after* Hitler's rise to the German chancellery. Here is what Schenker said:

> Hitler's historical service, of having got rid of Marxism, is something that posterity (including the French, English, and all those who have profited from transgressing against Germany) will celebrate with no less gratitude than the great deeds of the greatest Germans! If only the man were born to music who would similarly get rid of the musical Marxists; that would require that the masses were more in touch with our intrinsically eccentric art, which is something that, however, is and must remain a contradiction in terms. "Art" and "the masses" have never belonged together and never will belong together. And where would one find the huge

---

41. Cook, *The Schenker Project*, 153 (italics mine).
42. William Rothstein, "The Americanization of Heinrich Schenker," *In Theory Only* 9, no. 1 (1986): 8.

numbers of musical "brownshirts" that would be needed to hunt down the musical Marxists?[43]

Schenker's praise of Hitler should be unsurprising to anyone who knows Schenker's writings intimately. What is remarkable, however, is how successfully music theory's white racial frame suppresses such information, casting it aside as unimportant, about a figure who remains so foundational to our field.[44] The history of Schenkerian apologia—in which white persons severed Schenker's racist convictions from his music theories in order to promote Schenkerism—is difficult, emotionally, to recount. In the United States, the country most responsible for advancing Schenker's ideas, we are so often told of our democratic ideals, of our exceptionalism, that we have a hard time acknowledging our virulent racist past, as if it were somehow un-American. Such a sentiment led Rothstein to say about Schenker's beliefs, "Let us identify those [German nationalist] elements that clash most spectacularly with the American mind."[45] In point of fact, there is not much of a clash at all. Schenker's racist thinking is quite in line with American views on race in the 1920s, 1930s, 1940s, and beyond. That is, Schenker's racism is easily subsumed into music theory's white racial frame—they exist quite naturally in symbiotic fashion.[46]

---

43. *SDO*, OJ 5/7a, [46], formerly vC46, transcr. and trans. William Drabkin.

44. At the expense of overcontextualizing Schenker, which is something I generally criticize in *On Music Theory*, it's worth pointing out that there were many Jews who supported Hitler, for the same reasons that Schenker mentions, before the late 1930s, when it became painfully clear that to be a Jew in Hitler's Germany was extremely dangerous. For instance, there was an organization in the early years of Nazi Germany called Verband nationaldeutscher Juden (Association of German National Jews), a conservative, antidemocratic group that embraced Nazism and saw this as a path toward the assimilation of Jews into German society, Jews who apparently didn't take seriously Hitler's antisemitic statements (rather, they saw it as pandering to *das Volk*, i.e., the masses, for political support). This association disbanded in 1935, the year of Schenker's death.

45. Rothstein, "Americanization of Heinrich Schenker," 7.

46. In *Mein Kampf* Adolf Hitler himself said: "At present there exists one State which manifests at least some modest attempts that show a better appreciation of how things ought to be done in this [racial citizenship] matter. It is not, however, in our model German Republic but in the U.S.A. that efforts are made to conform at least partly to the counsels of commonsense. By refusing immigrants to enter there if they are in a bad state of health, and by excluding certain races from the right to become naturalized as citizens, they have begun to introduce principles similar to those on which we wish to ground the People's State." Adolf Hitler, *Mein Kampf*, trans. James Murphy (Hurst and Blackett, [1925] 1939), 340. Indeed, as Michael Mann has pointed out, many of Schenker's writings "could well have come from

I wish to recouple this severed link between Schenker's hierarchical beliefs about music and his hierarchical beliefs about people. I know someone else who would wish to recouple this severed link, someone who would vociferously disapprove of the decoupling of Schenker's racism from the basic tenets of his music theory, someone for whom Schenker's racist beliefs were anything but "peripheral ramblings," and that person is Heinrich Schenker himself. In numerous writings, he insisted that his views on racial and national hierarchies were key to his beliefs on life and on music. William Drabkin acknowledges as much:

In both his published writings and private communications, Schenker decried the mixing of politics with music. . . . Yet the notion of hierarchy, of a strict ordering of the tones of a composition, is so thoroughly consistent with his deeply conservative outlook on life and culture that *it is difficult to uncouple his theory entirely from two of his most consistently expressed ideological stances*: (1) the centrality of the German people in European culture, underscored by their preeminence in music, and (2) the steady decline of culture and political order in Europe since the late eighteenth century, ultimately resulting in the complete demise of musical art by the beginning of the twentieth century.[47]

There can be no question that our white racial frame has "shoved aside, ignored, or treated as incidental"[48] Schenker's racism. It has done so to keep in place racialized systems that benefit whites and whiteness.

---

the pen of the Führer himself." Michael Mann, "Schenker's Contribution to Music Theory," *Music Review* 10 (1949): 9. For more on the strong links between American racism and Nazi ideology, see Alex Ross, "How American Racism Influenced Hitler," *New Yorker*, April 23, 2018. As a final example of these links and of just how prevalent racist and German nationalist thought was in pre–World War II America, the period in which Schenkerism began in the United States, see Marshall Curry's short video documentary of a 1939 pro-Nazi rally at Madison Square Garden, "When 20,000 American Nazis Descended upon New York City," *The Atlantic*, October 10, 2017 (https://www.theatlantic.com/video/index/542499/marshall -curry-nazi-rally-madison-square-garden-1939).

47. William Drabkin, "Heinrich Schenker," in *The Cambridge History of Western Music Theory*, ed. Thomas Christensen (Cambridge University Press, [2002] 2008), 815 (italics mine).

48. Feagin, *The White Racial Frame*, 22.

Reframing Schenker

To my knowledge, the first English-language author to call out Schenker's racism, and to use that term specifically, was Carl Schachter: "Schenker was by no means free from racism."[49] This is no strong condemnation, to be sure, but his work stands out nevertheless as a rare attempt to *reframe* the overarching white-frame narrative on Schenker. Unlike Cook, whose monograph on Schenker was published six years after Schachter's article, Schachter acknowledges that a study comparing Schenker's "hierarchical world view" with his "hierarchical theory of [musical] levels" could be fruitful, saying, "Tracing such a relationship is not necessarily invalid."[50] This is precisely what I do below. Schachter agrees that Schenker's views on people affected his music theory, and that Schenker intended them to be considered as one. When asked by Joseph Straus whether Schenker's "dreadful politics" impacted his theoretical work, Schachter answered: "Of course they related to his theoretical work."[51] Further, Schachter says:

> Schenker himself obviously believed that his political fulminations and his musical ideas belonged together, that both were armaments, as it were, in a cultural struggle that would eventually lead to a regeneration both of music and of the society at large in the German-speaking world.[52]

Schachter concedes that Schenker is hardly the first to think of tonal music hierarchically. However, it is one thing to consider hierarchical structures in music, on the one hand, yet something entirely different to suggest—as Schenker does when he says that only the "German genius" is capable of producing musical masterworks—that such hierarchies are reflective of hierarchies of human races, on the other. There can be no question that for Schenker, the concept of "genius" was associated with whiteness to some degree. What our white racial frame suppresses is how Schenkerian theory and Schenkerism glorify whiteness at the expense of nonwhiteness. All of this is intimately related to the white frame, which "over centuries of operation . . . has encompassed both a strong positive orientation to whites

---

49. Schachter, "Elephants, Crocodiles, and Beethoven," 4.
50. Schachter, "Elephants, Crocodiles, and Beethoven," 13.
51. Carl Schachter, *Unfoldings: Essays in Schenkerian Theory and Analysis*, ed. Joseph N. Straus (Oxford University Press, 1999), 11.
52. Schachter, "Elephants, Crocodiles, and Beethoven," 3–4.

and whiteness (a pro-white subframe) and a strong negative orientation to racial 'others' who are exploited and oppressed (anti-others subframes)."[53] Schachter's reframing is not unproblematic. For instance, he is mistaken when he says that "Schenker, when invoking German superiority, never speaks of . . . the mongrelization produced by racial mixing . . . or any of the concepts of so-called racial science."[54] As I mentioned above, Schenker most certainly did speak out against racial mixing, which of course was a mainstay of biological race science. Again, this speaks to our white racial framing of Schenker's racism as cultural, not biological, in order to mitigate his racism.

The author who has done the most to reframe Schenker's racism is Martin Eybl in *Ideologie und Methode zum ideengeschichtlichen Kontext von Schenkers Musiktheorie*.[55] Indeed, in "Elephants, Crocodiles, and Beethoven," Carl Schachter cites Eybl's *Ideologie und Methode* as an inspiration in his own effort to reframe Schenker's legacy.[56] For his part, Eybl challenges those who seek to separate Schenker from his racist past:

That Schenker's worldview has nothing to do with his music theory represents an equally vague preconception as the assertion that his worldview of and by itself makes his [music] theory obsolete. If an analysis of Schenker's ideological background demonstrated that his music theory is ideologically self-sufficient, then this would assure an unproven (and difficult to prove) basis for the strategy pursued by some of Schenker's students and disciples to silently ignore his polemics and messianic tendencies.[57]

---

53. Feagin, *The White Racial Frame*, 10.

54. Schachter, "Elephants, Crocodiles, and Beethoven," 4–5. In fairness to Schachter, the relevant material that I cite, from *Schenker Documents Online*, was not available to him when he wrote his article in 2001. Nor was the English translation of "Von der Sendung des deutschen Genies" from *Der Tonwille*, which came out in 2004. One presumes, however, that the German version of *Tonwille* was available to Schachter in 2001, a version in which Schenker expresses his horror at interracial marriages between blacks and whites.

55. Martin Eybl, *Ideologie und Methode Zum ideengeschichtlichen Kontext von Schenkers Musiktheorie* (Hans Schneider, 1995).

56. Schachter, "Elephants, Crocodiles, and Beethoven," 4.

57. Eybl, *Ideologie und Methode*, 12. My translation from the German, which reads, "Dass Schenkers Weltanschauung mit seiner Musiktheorie nichts zu tun habe, stellt ein ebenso vages Vorurteil dar wie die Behauptung, sein Weltbild allein schon mache seine Lehre obsolet. Stellt sich bei der Untersuchung von Schenkers ideologischem Hintergrund heraus, dass seine Musiktheorie ideologisch autark ist, böte dies die nie bewiesene (und schwer beweisbare) Grundlage für die Strategie mancher Schüler und Nachfolger Schenkers, dessen Polemiken

This is precisely what our white racial frame has done: silently ignored Schenker's "polemics and messianic tendencies." At this point, in a footnote, Eybl mentions Cook, Forte, Jonas, Oster, and Rothstein as authors who have sought to make this break with Schenker's work and claim that Schenker's music theory is "ideologically self-sufficient." This "break" represents the "impenetrable barrier" that I mentioned at the beginning of this chapter. Perhaps more important, Eybl acknowledges Schenker's racism forthrightly. In a section entitled "Hierarchie der Völker" (Hierarchy of peoples), Eybl builds a case for Schenker's racism: "Given his postulate of racial inequality, racism is not fundamentally alien to the hierarchical structure of Schenker's worldview; references to Africans in the French army testify to this."[58]

Eybl is unafraid to speak of the Nazi implications of Schenker's prose. He specifically calls into question Schenker's invocation of *Menschenhumus*,[59] and how this term was used by Nazis to invoke German white supremacy. In a section entitled "Genie und Masse" (Genius and the masses), Eybl says, while quoting terms from Schenker,

The term *Menschenhumus* is based on the idea that Germanism unequivocally constitutes the best natural condition for the development of geniuses: in *Menschenhumus* of the highest category the "German genius" is manifest. . . . Anyone who considers the term *Menschenhumus* to be a simple translation of the burdened conceptual pair of blood and soil is ignoring the pseudoscientific bases of national-socialist racism and its predecessors.[60]

But this is, in fact, one of the main goals of the white racial frame—to ignore facts if those facts contravene or damage the impact of a given racialized structure of the white frame. Schenker invokes *Menschenhumus* as a scientific basis for German superiority in music. We must not now or ever

und messianische Anwandlungen stillschweigend zu übergehen."
58. Eybl, 20. My translation: "Mit seinem Postulat von der Ungleichheit der Rassen ist der Rassismus der hierarchischen Struktur von Schenkers Weltbild nicht grundsätzlich fremd; Hinweise auf Afrikaner in der französischen Armee legen davon Zeugnis ab."
59. Translated as "human propagating soil" by Ian Bent in Schenker, *Der Tonwille*, 17.
60. Eybl, *Ideologie und Methode*, 25. My translation: "Dem Ausdruch 'Menschenhumus' liegt die Vorstellung zugrunde, das Deutschtum bilde ein für alle Mal die besten natürlichen Voraussetzungen für die Entwicklung von Genies: im 'überlegenen Wert seines Menschenhumus' erweist sich das 'deutsche Genie'. . . . Wer den Terminus 'Menschenhumus' für die blosse Übersetzung des belasteten Begriffspaars Blut und Boden hält, ignoriert die pseudowissenschaftliche Grundlegung des nationalsozialistischen Rassismus und seiner Vorläufer."

cast aside such important information, especially about a figure who remains so central to our field.

Though Eybl goes farther than anyone else to impugn Schenker for his repulsive thoughts on various peoples, he still allows for the idea that those thoughts did not penetrate Schenker's music theory:

> Schenker's worldview is based on rankings—it is hierarchically struc-
> tured. . . . And on every one of his three levels Schenker rejects forms
> of egalitarian thought. Schenker regards the weakening of these stati-
> cally conceived hierarchies as the fundamental problem of his time.
> Their reconstruction is the goal of the cultural war that he pursued
> through journalistic and pedagogical means. The degree to which the
> strict hierarchy of his life's philosophy spilled over to his teachings on
> music must remain undetermined for now.[61]

Eybl published that in 1995. I believe the time has come to rigorously examine to what extent Schenker's views on race align with his views on music.

How Schenker's Racism Affects His Music Theory

How exactly Schenker's racism seeped into his musical theories is a question ripe for exploration. The easiest entry point is the language he uses in
discussing his rigidly hierarchical beliefs as they applied to both race and
music. Wayne Alpern has shown how utterly dependent Schenker was on
his law studies when he crafted his music theories.[62] Schenker was equally

---

61. Eybl, *Ideologie und Methode*, 29. Schenker's "three levels" refer to the background, middle ground, and foreground of musical structure, which I explained at the beginning of this
chapter. My translation: "Schenkers Weltbild liegen Rangordnungen zugrunde, es ist hierar-
chisch strukturiert. . . . Und auf jeder der drei Ebenen erteilt Schenker den Formen egalitären
Denkens eine Absage. Die Verletzung der statisch gedachten Rangordnungen hält Schenker
für das Grundübel seiner Gegenwart. Ihre Wiederherstellung ist das Ziel des Kulturkriegs,
den er mit publizistischen und pädagogischen Mitteln führte. Die Frage, ob und inwieweit
nun die strenge Hierarchie seiner Weltanschauung in Schenkers Lehre vom musikalischen
Zusammenhang einfloss, muss vorläufig offen bleiben."

62. See Wayne Alpern, "Music Theory as a Mode of Law: The Case of Heinrich Schenker,
Esq.," *Cardozo Law Review* 20 (1999): 1459–511; see also Alpern, "The Triad of the True,
the Good, and the Beautiful: Schenker's Moralization of Music and His Legal Studies with
Robert Zimmermann and Georg Jellinek," in *Essays from the Fourth International Schenker
Symposium*, ed. L. Poundie Burstein, Lynne Rogers, and Karen M. Bottge (Georg Olms Ver-
lag, 2013), vol. 2, 7–48.

dependent on his legal views when writing about race. His prose was infused with legal thinking when he wrote of the "laws of nature" as they relate to both humans and tones. Schenker views compositions as living organisms: "I should like to stress in particular the biological factor in the life of tones. We should get used to the idea that tones have lives of their own."[63] Thus, to Schenker, music was the manifestation of biological life as represented in the laws of nature.

As with the inequality of races, Schenker believed in the inequality of tones. Compare the following two passages, one concerning people, the other music:

But let the German mind also gather the courage to report: it is not true that all men are equal, since it is, rather, out of the question that the incapable ever become able; that which applies to individuals surely must apply to nations and peoples as well.[64]

It is therefore a contradiction to maintain, for example, that all scale tones between "C" and "c" have real independence or, to use a current but certainly musically unsuitable expression, "equal rights."[65]

This is a clear example of how Schenker's thinking about the inequality of human races can relate to the inequality of musical tones, and how his thinking about racial inequality manifests itself in his musical theories. In short, neither racial classes nor pitch classes are equal in Schenker's theories, and he uses the same language to express these beliefs.

Schenker often relates music to the human body and living organisms: "It should have been evident long ago that the same principle applies both to a musical organism and to the human body: it grows outward from within."[66] And insofar as "musical coherence can be achieved only through the fundamental structure in the background and its transformations in the middleground and foreground,"[67] Schenker implies that blacks are inferior because only the white German genius, with superior *Menschenhumus*, is capable of producing the background that Schenker speaks of. In other words, blacks are not capable of producing the same level of artistry and beauty that whites

---

63. Heinrich Schenker, *Harmony*, trans. Elisabeth Mann Borgese, ed. Oswald Jonas (University of Chicago Press, [1906] 1954), xxv.

64. Schenker, *Piano Sonata in C Minor*, online "Literature" supplement, 21 n. 13.

65. Schenker, *Der freie Satz*, 13 n. 3.

66. Schenker, *Der freie Satz*, 6.

67. Schenker, *Der freie Satz*, 6.

are capable of. Such genius cannot be black insofar as blacks represented a race inferior to whites, who were uniquely qualified to produce works of genius. And among whites, Germans, with their superior *Menschenhumus*, were the best at producing such beauty. Nicolas Cook calls this Schenker's "theory of genius":

> Schenker's theory of music, as it emerges from his later writings, is not actually a theory of music at all: it is a theory of genius, or of mastery in music. It is concerned with the relationship between foreground and background; and since it is only the genius who can penetrate to the background, the theory has no application to the works of the non-genius.[68]

And, according to Schenker, the genius cannot be black insofar as blacks represented a race inferior to Germans. Finally, like me, *New Yorker* critic Alex Ross agrees that "genius" is problematic from a racial perspective:

> The danger of the word "genius" is that it implies an almost biological category—an innately superior being, a superhero. It is probably no accident that the category of "genius," an obsession of the nineteenth century, coincided with the emergence of the pseudoscience of race, which held that certain peoples were genetically fitter than others.[69]

When Schenker writes, in disbelief, "Even negroes proclaim that they want to govern themselves because they, too, can achieve it," he is clearly stating that he does not believe that blacks are capable of self-governance. In other words, blacks must be governed and, inasmuch as he wrote this in 1922, when virtually all of Africa was under white colonial rule, what Schenker is implying is that blacks must be governed by whites. In his music-theoretical work, Schenker makes analogous points. He says, when writing of the fundamental line (*Urlinie*, represented by "diatony"): "In accord with its origin, it [diatony] simultaneously governs the whole contrapuntal structure, including the bass arpeggiation and the passing tones."[70] About the scale degrees of the fundamental structure, Schenker writes, "The scale-

68. Nicholas Cook, "Schenker's Theory of Music as Ethics," *Journal of Musicology* 7, no. 4 (1989): 423.
69. Alex Ross, "Antonio Salieri's Revenge," *New Yorker*, May 27, 2019.
70. Schenker, *Der freie Satz*, 11.

degrees of the fundamental structure have decisive control over the middle-ground and foreground."[71] About how the fundamental structure (*Ursatz*) controls everything, Schenker says, "We must remember that all growth (every continuation, direction, or improvement) finds its fulfillment only through the control of the fundamental structure and its transformations."[72] Schenker believed that the fundamental structure must "govern" and "control" the middle-ground and foreground elements of the music composition. Similarly, Schenker believed that blacks must be governed and controlled by whites. Indeed, Schenker's hierarchical beliefs on race are so intimately connected with his hierarchical views on music that one wonders which motivated which. Insofar as many of his reprehensible statements on race occurred after the publication of *Harmonielehre* in 1906 and *Kontrapunkt* in 1910 and 1922, one could argue that his views on music drove, reified, and even inspired his views on race. But without question, the two belong together—they are inseparable.

The linking of Schenker's racism with his music theories is necessarily speculative—this is obviously my interpretation. Further, I do not wish to imply that everything in Schenker's music theories can or must be related to race. His music theories are complicated, come from many sources, and can be interpreted in many ways. My more modest claim is that race, racism, and white supremacy are, in fact, significant parts of Schenker's music theories, and parts that we should consider in how we approach the man and his ideas. Of course, Schenker's insistence that his ideas were all representative of a unified worldview is perhaps the best proof that his views on race are part of his views on music, and vice versa. Schenker believed that his views on people and his views on music "belonged together," as Carl Schachter says.[73] Given this simple fact, relating Schenker's music theories to his racism makes perfect sense.

Schenker's Sexism

In this chapter I've underscored Heinrich Schenker's importance to music theory and how his racism negatively affects our field from a race perspective. But, probably unsurprisingly, Schenker believed in the inferiority of

---

71. Schenker, *Der freie Satz*, 111.
72. Schenker, *Der freie Satz*, 18.
73. Schachter, "Elephants, Crocodiles, and Beethoven," 3.

women and the superiority of men as well. Here's a brief example of what Schenker wrote about women:

> Despite their mutual dependency—in terms of necessity of existence, they remain equal!—the man ranks above the woman, the producer is superior to the merchant or the laborer, the head prevails over the foot, the coachman is more than the wheel of the wagon he steers, the genius means more than the people who represent merely the soil from which he springs.[74]

"The man ranks above the woman," says Schenker, whose sexism also remains underexplored in music theory. Of course, as in any white supremacist system, there is a certain equality for women insofar as white women are, quite literally, the repositories of whiteness and of white men. (This, incidentally, is why there was consistently such a sexual panic surrounding the mixing of the races in the history of the United States, and in the history of white supremacy.) In our field the white-male frame whitewashes sexism much the same way it whitewashes racism. In order for those who do not identify as cisgender men to be successful in music theory, they must adhere to and prop up music theory's male frame in the same way that BIPOC must adhere to and prop up the white frame. Promoting whiteness and maleness while maintaining the dual myths of race and gender neutrality is key to one's success in music theory. Surely W. E. B. Du Bois realized this about race in 1934 when he wrote, in *Black Reconstruction*, "We shall never have a science of history until we have in our colleges men who regard the truth as more important than the defense of the white race, and who will not deliberately encourage students to gather thesis material in order to support a prejudice or buttress a lie."[75] Similarly, we will never have a true science of music theory's history until we have a reckoning with music theory's historical roots in white supremacy and patriarchy.

Teaching Schenker

I do not suggest that we stop teaching Schenkerian analysis, or that scholars should cease their work thereon—there are of course many significant

---

74. Schenker, *Counterpoint*, vol. 1, xix.
75. W. E. B. Du Bois, *Black Reconstruction* (Harcourt, Brace and Company, 1935), 725.

scholarly inquiries in this area of research. I've often been asked why I still support Schenkerian analysis, in the field or in the classroom. Aside from the simple fact that there are many inspiring scholars who are connected to Schenkerism in one fashion or another, scholars who in no way themselves evince Schenker's horrific racism, there is another subtle reason: such work allows for deeper conversations about difficult topics. In "Gaslight of the Gods: Why I Still Play Michael Jackson and R. Kelly for My Students," William Cheng explains why he still generally presents the work of problematic figures to his students, saying that engaging with such figures "is not so different from feeling uncomfortable and trapped in a relationship with a problematic partner," adding that "our vulnerability to charismatic music [or music theories I'd add] offers a key to understanding our vulnerability to charismatic people, institutions, and ideologies more broadly."[76] The one caveat I'd add here is that no student, at any level, should ever be *required* to study Schenkerian theory; rather, I believe it should continue to be offered as an option to those students who wish to engage with Schenker and Schenkerism.

But given the racism within the theory, we who teach Schenkerian techniques are confronted with an ethical and intellectual dilemma. Philosopher Laurie Shrage makes a useful analogous point when speaking about her field's antisemitism:

> When the anti-Semitic views of great thinkers such as Kant, Voltaire or Hume (or Hegel, Schopenhauer, Heidegger and Wittgenstein, for that matter) are exposed, one typical response is to question whether these prejudices are integral to their important works and ideas. But this may be the wrong question. A better question is: Should those who teach their works and ideas in the 21st century share them without mentioning the harmful stereotypes these thinkers helped to legitimize?[77]

I wholeheartedly agree. Clearly, philosophers have whitewashed the antisemitism of their important figures in much the same way we have whitewashed Schenker's racism, or other racialized structures of our white racial frame for

76. William Cheng, "Gaslight of the Gods: Why I Still Play Michael Jackson and R. Kelly for My Students," *Chronicle of Higher Education*, September 15, 2019.

77. Laurie Shrage, "Confronting Philosophy's Anti-Semitism," *New York Times*, March 18, 2019.

that matter. I believe that, at a minimum, we must present Schenker's work to our students in full view of his racist beliefs and let our students decide what to do with that information. Overall, the study of Schenker and his music theories has "helped to legitimize harmful stereotypes" about blacks and other BIPOC, and women as well—we music theorists can no longer simply ignore this fact.

Final Thoughts on "On Heinrich Schenker and His Legacy"

Schenker is but one figure in a long history of racialized thought in music theory, a line of thought that remains underexplored. His racism is seen through a western lens that distorts and sanitizes racist behavior, often in service of fictitious science. In *The Invention of Race in the European Middle Ages*, Geraldine Heng writes:

> Like many a theoretical discourse, race theory is predicated on an unexamined narrative of temporality in the West: a *grand récit* that reifies modernity as *telos* and origin, and that, once installed, entrenches the delivery of a paradigmatic chronology of racial time through mechanisms of intellectual replication pervasive in the Western academy, and circulated globally. This global circulation project is not without its detractors, but the replication of its paradigmatic chronology is extraordinarily persistent.[78]

This unexamined chronology of racial time and, with it, how we understand race in music theory remain "extraordinarily persistent" precisely because of how we frame race in our field. Schenker's views on race were extreme, to be sure, but he was certainly not alone. Hugo Riemann, Arnold Schoenberg, Anton Webern, and many others on whose theories we rely all believed in German—and almost certainly white—superiority. François-Joseph Fétis, who spent enormous amounts of time trying to prove the racial superiority of "civilized" whites through phrenological and biological race pseudoscience, believed that "uncivilized people . . . are unable to understand rapports of tones because of the inferiority of their cerebral conformation."[79]

---

78. Geraldine Heng, *The Invention of Race in the European Middle Ages* (Cambridge University Press, 2018), 20.
79. Rosalie Schellhous, "Fétis's 'Tonality' as a Metaphysical Principle: Hypothesis for a New Science," *Music Theory Spectrum* 13, no. 2 (1991): 234.

Fétis is important because he was extremely influential in the nineteenth century and beyond, and because he so clearly *racialized* music theory. In race and modernity studies, there are approaches that seek to link the pseudoscientific race studies of authors like Fétis to racial aspects of modernity. About such approaches, sociologist Barnor Hesse writes that they "analyse the logic of race in the ideas of modern western philosophers; particularly how Enlightenment derived thought framed inegalitarian theories of race as part of modern scientistic and humanistic discourse."[80] In this fashion, racist thoughts and theories—a "paradigmatic chronology of racial time," as Geraldine Heng writes—were subsumed under the rubric of humanistic discourse, another instance of white racial framing. In fact, much of how we understand race in the United States is part of a global "western" understanding of race that is, in fact, written by white persons. It is therefore unsurprising that white Schenker scholars do not point out the racialized aspects of the man and his work in the same way I do as a nonwhite. And it is exactly these nonwhite perspectives on race that are ignored or glossed over in global race theory, as described by Heng, who, it should be noted, is a BIPOC scholar.

Fétis's and Schenker's delusions of grandeur are worth noting, since they evince an overt mythological connection to music theory that is usually not so explicit. Of course, music theory's mythologies, as any mythology, are meant to create narratives that are immune to criticism, narratives that are meant to be taken on faith: think here, once again, of the almost certainly apocryphal story of Pythagoras at the blacksmith's shop. Both Fétis and Schenker claimed to have had supernatural revelations about their contributions, which speaks to the unchecked mythologization in our white-male frame that elevates our key figures to an irreproachable level. That is, by making the tools of music theory divine, white men further immunize those tools and their inventors from racial criticism. So, though "Fétis claimed that the idea of 'tonalité' came to him as a revelation under a tree in the Bois de Boulogne on a warm spring afternoon in 1831,"[81] Alexandre-Étienne Choron actually coined the term some twenty-one years prior.[82] So Fétis was either uninformed or he was lying. Schenker also had similar godlike tendencies: "Inasmuch as all religious experience, and all branches of philosophy and science press for the shortest formulae, a similar urge led me to con-

80. Barnor Hesse, "Racialized Modernity: An Analytics of White Mythologies," *Ethnic and Racial Studies* 30, no. 4 (2007): 644.
81. Bryan Hyer, "Tonality," in Christensen, *Cambridge History*, 729.
82. Hyer, "Tonality," 726ff.

ceive . . . tonal composition only out of the nucleus of the *Ursatz* as the first *Auskomponierung* of the fundamental chord (tonality); I was given a vision of the *Urlinie*, I did not invent it."[83] The only thing missing from Schenker's testimony here is a claim that he was given this vision while sitting under a tree, which seems to be a common trope in white-male mythologies. It should go without saying that Fétis had no "revelation" about tonality, nor was Schenker "given a vision" of the *Urlinie*. We must never let such mythological megalomaniacal claims go unchecked in our field.

It would be hard to name anyone who has had a greater impact on what we do than Schenker. It is easy to point to Richard Wagner as another significant figure who had repulsive beliefs, amply expressed in his various antisemitic writings. But, unlike Schenker, we do not hold up Wagner as someone through whose *theories* we might understand tonal music. In other words, if one studies music theory in the United States, Wagner's racism is optional, while Schenker's is not. Several of the undergraduate music theory textbooks that I cite in chapter 1 draw significantly on Schenker's theories— from the very beginning, we teach Schenkerian thought. And, try though some might, it is no longer possible to cleave Schenker's racism from his music theories and simply say, as was so often said in the twentieth century, that Schenker's musical theories have nothing to do with race.

Finally, earlier in this section I pointed out, via Carl Schachter, that Schenker was far from the first music theorist to posit hierarchical structures in music.[84] I myself freely acknowledge the existence of hierarchies in nature and in music, and pointing them out can be a useful exercise—hierarchical thinking is not the problem, and I don't wish to suggest that, because of his hierarchical thinking, Schenker's music theories were flawed. Boleslav Yavorsky (1877–1942), Schenker's contemporary, also contrived a universal theory of music that featured hierarchies.[85] The problem with Schenker and his theories is that his firm belief that there were only twelve "genius" composers— one of whom was Domenico Scarlatti, let us not forget—coupled with his intense belief in a racial hierarchy with whites at the top and blacks at the bottom *as part of his unified worldview*, has promoted the mythology of white (male) musical greatness at the expense of all other musicians, whether

---

83. Sylvan Kalib, "Thirteen Essays from the Three Yearbooks 'Das Meisterwerk in der Musik' by Heinrich Schenker: An Annotated Translation," 2 vols. (PhD dissertation, Northwestern University, 1973), vol. 2, 218.

84. See Schachter, "Elephants, Crocodiles, and Beethoven," 13.

85. For more on Yavorsky's theories, see my "On the Russian Concept of Lād, 1830–1945," *Music Theory Online* 25, no. 4 (December 2019).

American music theory acknowledges this or not. In teaching Schenker without attention to this mythology, we in music theory have created hostile environments for those who do not identify as white cisgender men, or those scholars, of any identity, who wish to work with composers and musicians who were not white cisgender men. And by pointing this out I'm breaking the barrier that, over many decades, was erected by music theory's white racial frame between Schenker's racial hierarchies, on the one hand, and his musical hierarchies on the other, a barrier to which Schenker himself would have objected insofar as he believed these two hierarchies belonged together in his unified view of the world.[86]

Epilogue to Schenker and His Legacy

The recurring refrain from those who disregard and rationalize [Dr.] Seuss' racism is, "he was a product of his time." . . . However, not all White people "of his time" engaged in overt racism, or used their platforms to disseminate racist narratives and images nationally, and globally, as he did. There are White people throughout history, and of his generation, who actively resisted racism and risked their lives and careers to stand up against it. Minimizing, erasing, or not acknowledging Seuss' racial transgressions across his entire publishing career deny the very real historical impact they had on people of color and the way

---

86. For another example of an early twentieth-century musician who believed deeply in white supremacy and clearly linked musical theories to racial theories, look no further than the American pianist and composer John Powell, who drew on Germanism—he traveled to Vienna to study piano and composition at the turn of the century—for his virulent form of American racism. See Errollyn Wallen, "A Racist Music," BBC Radio 3, *Sunday Feature*, November 24, 2019, in which I am one of the featured interviewees. In "Unequal Temperament: The Somatic Acoustics of Racial Difference in the Symphonic Music of John Powell," Lester Feder unpacks the depths to which white supremacy suffused Powell's music, and how, like Schenker, Powell himself insisted that his white supremacist beliefs belonged together with his racist beliefs, and that to separate them would require "a willful act of deafness, not only to his compositions but to the words in which he described them." Feder, "Unequal Temperament," *Black Music Research Journal* 28, no. 1 (Spring 2008): 52. Finally, Feder stresses the importance of the German tradition to an American white supremacist like Powell, which comports with the story of Schenker's American beginnings in the 1930s and 1940s: "Powell's white supremacist political language constructed widely accepted criteria by which an individual's humanity was judged; Powell's musical language constructed the same criteria by drawing upon the values of humanity and subhumanity inherent in the Germanic musical tradition" (52).

that they continue to influence culture, education, and children's views of people of color.[87]

Much has been made about the March 2021 decision by Dr. Seuss Enterprises to stop licensing for and publication of six titles by Theodore "Dr. Seuss" Geisel.[88] The decision by the group that controls his legacy was immediately drawn into the cancel-culture vortex of right-wing media, despite the fact that the only ones doing the canceling were those who controlled the rights to do so, and not any teachers, schools, or universities, the usual targets of right-wing academic hate. The quotation above makes two points. The first is that the dismissal of a historical figure's racism denies the "very real historical impact" that such racism has had on BIPOC over the years. However, I think the other point is more crucial: the insistence that Dr. Seuss was simply "a product of his time"—something said recurrently about Heinrich Schenker in music theory's white framing—since this implicates countless white men in a purportedly racist children's book publication enterprise when, in fact, there were many white men (and women) who fought against such racism in the mid- to late twentieth century.

Dr. Seuss's racism pales in comparison to that of Heinrich Schenker. I think one of the worst things about our treatment of Schenker lies in a simple fact of omission, as with Dr. Seuss. Schenker was Jewish, and he was also a product of his times; therefore, the logic goes, other early twentieth-century Jews held the same or similar horrific racist beliefs that Schenker held, but this was and is largely untrue. Jews, like any other group of people on our planet, have widely varying racial beliefs that run the gamut from hardcore racist to hardcore antiracist. But without clarifying Schenker's racism against the backdrop of worldwide Judaism, we run the risk of implying that Schenker's racist beliefs were somehow normative for Jews in the early twentieth century. Which Schenkerian scholar has stated clearly that Schenker's virulent racism was, in fact, rare among Jews of his time? To my mind, no music theorist in our white racial frame has done so since to do so would contravene the many mythologies of white-male greatness in American music theory, damage the entire Schenkerian enterprise, and lay bare the racial biases and hierarchies of the field. In point of fact, nineteenth- and

---

87. Katie Ishizuka and Ramón Stephens, "The Cat Is Out of the Bag: Orientalism, Anti-blackness, and White Supremacy in Dr. Seuss's Children's Books," *Research on Diversity in Youth Literature* 1, no. 2 (2019), Article 4, p. 35.

88. Jenny Gross, "6 Dr. Seuss Books Will No Longer Be Published over Offensive Images," *New York Times*, March 4, 2021.

twentieth-century Jews showed remarkable strength and resiliency in the face of unspeakable horrors, and, on the whole, their commitments to social and racial justice have been, over time, vibrant and indisputable. But this simple fact, to our great misfortune and to our collective shame, gets lost in the totally incomplete picture we paint of Heinrich Schenker and his legacy.

Saving Schenker from himself is American music theory's most popular national pastime. Barrels of ink have been spent in an effort to make this reprehensible figure palatable to our field, and when someone has had the good sense to point out how Schenker has helped create an environment in which women and BIPOC face hostility and hatred, the campaigns to discredit and stifle those perspectives are swift and unrelenting. Rewriting history is never easy, but several factors have made rewriting Schenker easier than it otherwise might seem.

In a gripping account of her own grandfather's Nazi past, Sylvia Foti unpacks history's revisionism with respect to her home country of Lithuania.[89] Her grandfather, Jonas Noreika, was executed by the Soviets in 1947 and is presently considered something of a national hero in Lithuania. Foti's research led her down a dark path in which she discovered that, contrary to Lithuanian lore, her grandfather collaborated with the Nazis and was responsible for the deaths of thousands of Lithuanian Jews. Of course, as her country came under Soviet power after World War II, such atrocities were swept under the rug, frozen out of official accounts of Lithuania's past— only stories of anti-Soviet atrocities were allowed. In fact, her father, in 1933, had written *Raise Your Head, Lithuanian*, "Lithuania's equivalent of *Mein Kampf*," as Foti noted.[90] Yet for all his pro-Nazi efforts he was sent to a Nazi concentration camp, not for trying to save Jews, but for stymieing efforts to recruit SS soldiers. For uncovering the truth about her own grandfather, Foti has been vilified in the Lithuanian community in her hometown of Chicago, as well as in Lithuania itself.

In a telling passage, a passage that can relate directly to Schenkerian revisionist history and to music theory's consistent whitewashing of Schenker's transgressions, Foti writes of a four-part process that occurs in creating a national hero out of a complicated figure like her grandfather. First, one must shift all blame to the Nazis. This, of course, is easy, since the Nazis and their ideologies were so manifestly vile, deeply steeped in conspiratorial

---

89. Silvia Foti, "No More Lies. My Grandfather Was a Nazi," *New York Times*, January 27, 2021.

90. Foti, "No More Lies."

thinking and horrific violence. But with respect to Schenker, what of his own Nazi sympathies, so clearly apparent in his 1933 letter in praise of Adolf Hitler, which I cited above? In fact, Schenker believed deeply in the Nazi's anti-communist and anti-Marxist agenda, and he believed in many similarly Nazi-tinged, German, post–World War I mythologies that gave rise to the Nazis and their campaigns of German national grievance and greatness. Indeed, Schenker was known to express antisemitic statements, as when he wrote in his diary in 1923, "The Jews top the list as Germany's enemies."[91] As painful as it might be to confront this part of Schenker's past, it is precisely these moments that might give rise to real progress with respect to racial justice in music theory.[92]

Second, Foti says that one must "create a victim narrative." I hardly need to point out that countless authors have created such a narrative around Heinrich Schenker, using his Jewishness as a shield to protect Schenker from unwanted criticism. Third, one must "discredit counternarratives," which is precisely how certain quarters in music theory have treated my appraisal of Schenker and his legacy. Leaning into this discrediting by turning the person who challenges how we have treated Schenker and his legacy into a racist or antisemite is a key component of transforming someone like Schenker into a sympathetic figure and, in extreme instances, something of a hero. But discrediting counternarratives by discrediting the author is common for those who take a stand against bigotry and hatred if it disrupts the natural (white male) order of things. Ibram Kendi agrees: "People seeking to discredit books are aggressively striving to discredit authors, knowing for many people there's no separating the author from the book (or project). It is unfortunate, but that's the reality for authors, especially authors writing against bigotry and writing for equity and justice."[93]

The fourth and final step in rehabilitating problematic figures, according to Foti, is refusing to accept the idea that two or more contradictory truths about the figure can exist at the same time. So, on the one hand, Schenker was a significant, influential, and prolific music theorist and musician who greatly impacted how we have interpreted music in the twentieth and

---

91. *SDO*, OJ 14/45, [22], transcr. Marko Deisinger, trans. Scott Witmer.

92. For an account of two other Jewish intellectuals, the lawyer Erich Kaufmann and the historian Ernst Kantorowicz, who were even more committed to Nazism than Schenker, see James Q. Whitman, *Hitler's American Model: The United States and the Making of Nazi Race Law* (Princeton University Press, 2017), 41–42 and 175 n. 105.

93. "Ibram X. Kendi Likes to Read at Bedtime," *New York Times*, "By the Book" series, February 25, 2021.

twenty-first centuries in the United States. Yet, on the other, through Schenker's manifest racism and sexism, music theory has created a subfield, Schenkerian theory, in which BIPOC and those who do not identify as cisgender men face hostility and hatred, insofar as Schenkerian theory is a racialized and gendered structure that values the work of white cisgender men above all others, and a structure that is still usually required coursework in graduate music theory programs. This refusal to accept these contradictory truths about Schenker usually results in bothsidesing the issue—pointing out that Schenker, had he lived long enough, would have perished in a Nazi concentration camp, or that Schenker's repulsive beliefs were not uncommon in Vienna in the early twentieth century—with the primary goal of obfuscation. Indeed, this hardened refusal to understand how Schenker's legacy has resulted in racial and gender injustice in American music theory has been a significant impediment to making our field more just and more welcoming. Shining a light on such injustice remains a primary goal of *On Music Theory*.

FOUR

On Volume 12 of the
Journal of Schenkerian Studies

Why is it my talking about race has caused you to lose your mind?[1]

On June 24, 2020, I had a Zoom conversation with a dear friend in the field. We were discussing antiracist actions we might try to take in music theory in light of our American racial reckoning from summer 2020. George Floyd had just been murdered a month before our conversation, and protests were raging throughout the country. Toward the end of our call my friend asked if I had seen the recent issue, volume 12, of the *Journal of Schenkerian Studies*, published by the University of North Texas Press, which included a "symposium" of responses to the plenary talk I had given at the Society for Music Theory in November 2019. I said I had not seen the issue, so my friend sent me a screenshot of the table of contents, noting that "it looks pretty bad." Little did we know at the time that this journal issue would change the course of American music theory, and music theory in other parts of the world, in ways the field had never seen before.

White Stories, Black Histories, My Testimony

As of the summer of 2021, one year after publication, if you log on to the website for the *Journal of Schenkerian Studies*, there are eleven volumes listed,

---

1. Black accountant Dorothy Brown commenting on white-male reactions to her book *The Whiteness of Wealth: How the Tax System Impoverishes Black Americans—and How We Can Fix It.* "The Whiteness of Wealth with Dorothy A. Brown," *Why Is This Happening, with Chris Hayes* podcast (at 37'44").

volumes 1–11; volume 12 has been erased from the site, with not even so much as a footnote referring to the controversial nature of that issue of the journal.[2] As I wrote in my Intro, if there's anything worse than the erasure of blackness in American history, it's the erasure of antiblackness, and the erasure of volume 12 from the JSS website is, in fact, a grand music-theoretical erasure of antiblackness. When whiteness tells the stories of our American racial past, it consistently gives skewed accounts and, in extreme instances, erases racial injustice from existence—think here of the Tulsa race massacre in 1921, which whiteness effectively erased from American history for nearly one hundred years.[3] Then, as is so often the case in the United States, these white stories get memorialized as *history*, as an accurate "objective" retelling of events that can then be taught to and enshrined in the American mind. Yet when blackness tells its version of the story, blackness is told by whiteness that that version is biased, emotional, embellished, and not rooted in fact. We blacks are told by whiteness that our history is inaccurate and divisive, that we are "storytelling" in a "Gather round the campfire, children" fashion. And most important in our American racial fantasy, blackness's narratives of events must remain stories, and never be considered histories, which would puncture the bubble of whiteness's greatness and nobility.

In some languages, "story" and "history" are rendered by the same word, as in French (*histoire*) or Russian (*история*). That is, stories and histories are two sides of the same coin. I'll let the reader decide for themself whether I'm telling stories or writing histories in *On Music Theory*, or in this chapter on volume 12 for that matter, but in either case, my testimony here is, in my opinion, of the utmost importance, perhaps the most significant part of my book. In other words, if I don't write my testimony on volume 12 in this chapter, we risk the possibility of losing the gist of the entire narrative, the possibility of letting whiteness, once again, come out on top in its retelling of events in which the egregiousness of a particular racist action gets sanded down, whitewashed, and repackaged for general consumption. I refuse to let this happen. Not on my watch.

It makes perfect sense to me why music theory would want to move on

2. See https://digital.library.unt.edu/explore/collections/JSCS

3. On May 31 and June 1, 1921, white mobs attacked and massacred roughly three hundred black residents in the Greenwood District in Tulsa, Oklahoma, an area known as "Black Wall Street," because of its relative affluence. In point of fact, however, there were *dozens* of white-on-black race massacres across the country in post–World War I America in 1919, a period that became known as "Red Summer." For more on the Tulsa massacre see Mike Hale, "Telling the Story of the Tulsa Massacre," *New York Times*, May 30, 2021.

from volume 12. It's uncomfortable to see some of the racism that is part of American music theory so out in the open for the whole world to see—it's much easier to move on, think about the positive things, and highlight how our field is improving. Yet if we lapse into a state of denialism, if we have no accurate account from a nonwhite perspective of what volume 12 represented, we cannot fix music theory's racial problems since we won't even know of their existence. In one sense, this chapter represents the response to the volume 12 symposium authors that I was not allowed to give. But I actually think of it in much larger and more important terms. I think of it as a testimony, my testimony, on all the events of summer 2020 and beyond in music theory, events that included not only the publication of volume 12 but many reactions to that volume, some of which I discuss in detail below. Thus this chapter is written, in very large part, for the sake of posterity. Ultimately, it is imperative to see volume 12 and its aftermath for what it truly is: the greatest gift to American music theory that we've ever seen, since because of the manifest racism of the journal issue and of many reactions to it, we can begin to have the frank conversations we need to have in order to make substantive changes to our field. If I don't give this testimony, this black history, we might *all* lose this once-in-a-lifetime opportunity, this gift to us all, a beacon of hope to make American music theory more welcoming for everyone.

Background

So much has been written about the JSS affair that it's difficult to even comment on it now.[4] I should say up front that, in my opinion, the main driving force behind volume 12 was antiblackness. In other words, the aggressive symposium authors were not so much responding to what they believed was being attacked, whiteness—here represented by Heinrich Schenker's American legacy—but, rather, to what was doing the alleged attacking, blackness. Of course, to call my nine-minute discussion of Heinrich Schenker in my SMT plenary talk on November 9, 2019, an "attack," as it has been widely called by conservative scholars and in conservative media outlets, is white racial framing. It was not an attack, but a discussion of how whitewashing Schenker's demonstrable racism has negatively affected our field from a racial-justice perspective, much like my discussion of Heinrich Schenker in

---

4. For samples of some of the media attention that this issue has garnered see the "Media" tab on my website, philipewell.com, a tab that didn't exist prior to summer 2020.

chapter 3 of *On Music Theory*.[5] More broadly, my twenty-two-minute plenary talk was actually a challenge to the field of music theory to listen to, and
hear, what a black scholar and blackness were saying about structural racism
in the field and how we might address it. Sure, Schenker loomed large, but
my arguments, then and now, are much larger than any one person.

As I will show below, volume 12 was full of rage, and I believe that that
rage simply would not have happened if I were white, since whiteness will
always see the equality and humanity in whiteness, even if it forcefully disagrees with a given position that whiteness has taken. What set whiteness off
in my case was my blackness, and my cri de coeur to be treated as an equal.
Emory University African American studies professor Carol Anderson calls
this "white rage":

> The trigger for white rage, inevitably, is black advancement. It is not
> the mere presence of black people that is the problem; rather, it is
> blackness with ambition, with drive, with purpose, with aspirations,
> and with demands for full and equal citizenship. It is blackness that
> refuses to accept subjugation, to give up.[6]

Black advancement triggers white rage, which drove publication of volume
12 in my opinion. And as Anderson says, it's not the mere presence of blackness that is the problem. The problem here was that I, a black person, had
been given a platform, a microphone, with which to make my case about
structural racism in music theory.

I think I may have heard some murmurings about responses to my SMT
talk in fall 2019, but the first official word I got was with everyone else, when
JSS issued a call for papers on the SMT-Announce listserv on December 31,
2019, with a quick, three-week turnaround submission deadline of January
20, 2020, which immediately indicated the nature of volume 12 as something out of the ordinary (calls for published papers usually happen many
months or even more than a year before a deadline).[7] Also significant, these

---

5. For a literal transcript of my November 2019 SMT plenary talk, see Ewell, "Music
Theory's White Racial Frame," *Music Theory Spectrum* 43 (2021): 1–6. I'll use this transcript
in further citations of the talk.

6. Carol Anderson, *White Rage: The Unspoken Truth of Our Racial Divide* (Bloomsbury,
2016), 3.

7. See the call for papers as "Exhibit 6" in Jincheng Du, Francisco Guzman, John Ishiyama, Matthew Lemberger-Truelove, and Jennifer Wallach, *Ad Hoc Panel Review: Report of
Review of Conception and Production of Vol. 12 of the* Journal of Schenkerian Studies, November 25, 2020.

responses were not peer reviewed, which is the industry standard for academic publication.[8] I also thought it was strange that the call linked to my personal website for the PowerPoint slides I had used, as well as my personal Vimeo channel, on which I had uploaded the video of my plenary talk, which further proves how involved my material was in this process from which I was being excluded.[9] What would have happened if I had simply removed those sources from my personal website?

Of course, it was also strange that responses to my talk would be solicited without inviting me to participate in any capacity, but it wasn't my place to invite myself since, as I've said in many public lectures, "I shouldn't have to request an invitation to a party thrown in my honor." In my opinion, the reason I was not invited is simple: I'm black and, in the history of our country, whiteness is quite uninterested in hearing from blackness or considering its opinion, even if that blackness is the focal point of a given issue. Perhaps oddest of all: this symposium was in response to an approximately twenty-two-minute talk, not to a written article. In all my more than twenty-five years in academia, I have never heard of a symposium of written articles responding to a short talk which, by its very nature, represents a work in progress—this, quite simply, never happens.

Because of the unusual nature of volume 12, the University of North Texas, which houses the *Journal of Schenkerian Studies*, launched an investigation into the issue and, on November 25, 2020, published its findings, which found significant problems with the editorial management and review process. Among many inadequacies was the absence of outside peer review for the fifteen essays in response to my SMT plenary talk, which is standard for a symposium like this. Another problem was that the editorial advisers for JSS, Timothy Jackson and Stephen Slottow, never considered inviting me to respond to the response essays in the journal, which is also standard. Quoting from the investigation:

> The panel asked the editors (Dr. [Benjamin] Graf and Mr. [Levi] Walls) and the editorial advisors (Drs. [Timothy] Jackson and [Stephen] Slottow) why Dr. Ewell was not invited to respond to the contributions in Volume 12, and whether that had been considered. All of them replied that inviting Dr. Ewell had not been considered until controversy arose concerning the volume in the summer of

---

8. Du et al. *Ad Hoc Panel Review*, 7.

9. Du et al., *Ad Hoc Panel Review*, Exhibit 6. I have since removed the slides and the video of my plenary talk from my website, though I still have them on file of course.

2020. Only then did the idea emerge that perhaps Dr. Ewell could be invited to respond in Volume 13. However, that was not part of the original plan and was only considered as an option once the controversy over the contents of Volume 12 escalated.[10]

This revelation—which shows how completely uninterested JSS was in hearing from blackness after my brief nine-minute discussion of Schenkerism at the SMT plenary—shows antiblackness in its truest form, in the notion that blackness need not be heard from, that blackness is not worthy of consideration, even when that blackness was precisely the target of the antiblack behavior that caused the very escalation cited. There's also the simple notion of shoring up whiteness, the protection of white "genius" against what JSS viewed as an "attack." The beauty of the JSS issue is that under no circumstance can whiteness claim that race had nothing to do with this, which is what normally happens when race is not specifically mentioned. Their discussion about having me respond in that journal is ultimately a sad commentary on the deep-seated antiblackness of music theory and of academia. But this is, in fact, the essence of antiblackness: the inability to see blackness's humanity, and the accompanying dismissal of black voices from the narratives told, from the histories written. Or, as journalist Ta-Nehisi Coates says, "The essence of American racism is disrespect," and, in the final analysis, volume 12 was disrespectful of blackness.[11]

For an example of a proper music-theoretical symposium, with an academic article, invited authors responding to that article, and a final response from the initial author, I'd recommend looking at the symposium surrounding Richard Taruskin's "Catching Up with Rimsky-Korsakov" in *Music Theory Spectrum* from 2011.[12] In this case, Taruskin's ever-provocative work was answered by eight eminent theorists—Kofi Agawu, Robert Gjerdingen, Marianne Kielian-Gilbert, Lynne Rogers, Dmitri Tymoczko, Pieter van den Toorn, Arnold Whittall, and Lawrence Zbikowski—to which Taruskin responded in turn. This is the type of scholarship, the type of collegiality, that we all expect from our field. Even if we disagree, we can still follow the basic rules of the road, which is exactly what the *Spectrum* editor, Severine Neff, did.[13] It would have been inconceivable not to invite Taruskin to

10. Du et al., *Ad Hoc Panel Review*, 9.
11. Ta-Nehisi Coates, "The Case for Reparations," *The Atlantic*, June 2014.
12. See Richard Taruskin, "Catching Up with Rimsky-Korsakov," *Music Theory Spectrum* 33, no. 2 (Fall 2011): 169–85, and the rest of the symposium on pages 186–229.
13. I checked with Neff to ask if these submissions were all peer reviewed and she confirmed that they were. Severine Neff, email correspondence with author, September 6, 2021.

respond to his critics in such a symposium. But again, I believe the reason for this treatment is simple. Taruskin was white and was therefore accorded all of the privileges that whiteness gets in academic scholarship.

Though I was never invited to participate in the JSS symposium, I did hear from two faculty at the University of North Texas during the process. On January 15, 2020, under the subject heading "citations for your SMT slides," Stephen Slottow, who is a music theory professor at UNT, emailed me to ask for citations, since they weren't on the slides he was looking at. There seemed to have been an urgency to his request, as he asked me to provide this material "as soon as possible, if it is not too inconvenient." On the same day, I responded that there was a separate bibliography for my talk on my website, and I directed him to the proper area so that he could find it. Then, on January 24, 2020, under the subject heading "JSS responses," Ellen Bakulina, who was a music theory professor at UNT at the time (she has since moved on to McGill University), emailed me to ask if I had any questions about the responses and to say that, if I did, I could direct them to Professors Slottow and Jackson. She had CCed Stephen Slottow on this email, and there were no attachments. On the same day, I responded to Bakulina, "Nope, no questions Ellen. Best, Phil." I do not know why Bakulina sent that email, or if anyone suggested to her that she send it. Aside from these two emails, I never received any other communication from UNT or JSS about the ensuing publication of volume 12.[14]

By my count, exactly five of the fifteen symposium respondents were what I'll call here "good faith" authors, that is, they are authors who responded to the call for papers and turned out compelling pieces that responded to the points I was making in only three weeks. Those authors are Richard Beaudoin, Suzannah Clark, Stephen Lett, Rich Pellegrin, and Christopher Segall. It's extremely important to disambiguate these five authors from the other ten, who seemed to be coordinating their efforts before the call for papers went out. In fact, two of the five good-faith authors, Richard Beaudoin and Christopher Segall, sent me their contributions for commentary before sub-

---

14. On January 14, 2021, Timothy Jackson filed a lawsuit in a Texas federal court against twenty-six named defendants: eight members of the UNT Board of Regents in their official capacity, seventeen faculty members in Jackson's own division, and one PhD student and teaching fellow. Because of the ongoing nature of this court case, I will not comment on it. Two sources that outline the court case are Colleen Flaherty, "Countering Allegations of Racism—in Court," *Inside Higher Education*, January 28, 2021 (https://www.insidehigher ed.com/news/2021/01/28/professor-counters-allegations-racism-court), and Olivia Giovetti and Jeffrey Arlo Brown, "Music, in Theory," *Van Magazine*, January 28, 2021 (https://van-magazine.com/mag/schenker-lawsuit/).

mitting, which I happily gave. All five of these good-faith authors reached out to me after publication of volume 12 to express their dismay over how their work was being included in such a strange unscholarly endeavor, and to disavow the gist of volume 12. None of the other ten authors did. I will not comment further on these five good-faith authors and their submissions.

The remaining ten core authors, in my opinion, were not responding to the call for papers and were of two types, eight invited authors and two inviting authors, Timothy Jackson and Stephen Slottow, who coordinated volume 12 as the "editorial advisory board."[15] I suspect that these ten authors, to one extent or another, were coordinating their efforts behind the scenes—both Jack Boss and Timothy Jackson included cross references in their essays, indicating that they had read other contributions to the symposium—and either knew or should have known that this was the case. I note here that I've heard from several scholars who were asked to submit a response to volume 12 but declined, since they sensed the unscholarly nature of the symposium. Finally, it is clear from the *Ad Hoc Panel Review* investigation into publication of volume 12 that Timothy Jackson was leading the effort to publish the symposium of responses to my SMT plenary talk: "According to the editors [Benjamin Graf and Levi Walls], as well as to Dr. [Stephen] Slottow, Dr. Jackson 'took the lead' on this [symposium] section."[16]

Racism in Volume 12

Broadly speaking there are two types of racism coursing through the pages of volume 12: assimilationist and antiblack. Of course there is a great deal of overlap between the two, in statements like "Blacks need to raise themselves up," "Black fathers need to take responsibility for their children," and "Black people need to wear standard clothing and mainstream hairstyles."[17] The antiblackness in such statements should be clear to the readers—we never speak of policing the hairstyles of whiteness, for instance—but the assimilationist aspect is slightly harder to grasp, the idea that there is another

---

15. Du et al., *Ad Hoc Panel Review*, 5.

16. Du et al., *Ad Hoc Panel Review*, 5–6.

17. For a brilliant take on whiteness's obsession with black hair, see John Oliver's *Last Week Tonight*, Season 8, Episode 11. On the same see also Karen Han, "John Oliver Teaches Fellow White People What They Need to Know about Black Hair," *Brow Beat*, Slate.com, May 10, 2021 (https://slate.com/culture/2021/05/john-oliver-black-hair-last-week-tonight-video.html).

higher level of existence to which blacks should aspire, and that that existence belongs to one race in particular in the United States: whiteness. To be
clear, we blacks do not need to raise ourselves up to any mythically higher
plane of existence insofar as we blacks are already on the same level as all
other races, and neither inferior nor superior; we black fathers take exactly
the same responsibility for our children as all other races of fathers in the
history of our country, despite what any "academic study" may have alleged;
and we blacks should have the freedom to wear our clothes and hairstyles as
we please, without any fear of discrimination or recrimination.

But there are differences between assimilationism and antiblackness as
well. Sometimes sentiments are purely antiblack, as in Elijah Anderson's concept of the "nigger moment," which I cited in my Intro. This "putting blackness in its place" has nothing to do with assimilationism. Rather, it is meant
to denigrate and demean blackness and to let blackness know that whiteness
is in control. On the other hand, a good example of assimilationism that is
not necessarily antiblack is in the concept of the "model minority," so often
directed at Asians and Asian Americans. But even in the model-minority
mythology, there is an underhanded antiblackness at play, since blackness
is considered to be the lowest and most degraded form of humanity in our
American version of white supremacy. University of Wisconsin English professor Leslie Bow challenges the myth of the model minority and how it can
represent antiblackness, on the one hand, and American exceptionalism on
the other:

> At one level, the hailing [of the model minority] represents the equiv-
> alent of "I love your people"—your work ethic, your belief in edu-
> cation, your self-discipline, your yummy food—and this is largely
> understood not to be "about" Asian Americans as much as a slap
> in the face to African Americans and Latinos. On another level, the
> "model minority" construct is a reflection of American narcissism, a
> screen for those idealized virtues, those "excellences," that are both
> unattainable and intrinsic to national self-fashioning.[18]

Thus the artificial raising of one minority racial group over others is
meant, in part, to further dehumanize blackness (and brownness) in the

---

18. Leslie Bow, "Difference without Grievance: Asian Americans as the 'Almost' Minority,"
in *Written/Unwritten: Diversity and the Hidden Truths of Tenure*, ed. Patricia Matthew (University of North Carolina Press, 2016), 71–72.

United States, in another effort by whiteness to tell black and Latinx persons, "Why can't you be more like this other group, since they are almost just like us white persons?" But, to be clear, whiteness does not consider Asian-ness, or AAPI-ness, to be the equal of whiteness. In this sense the model minority myth serves to reinforce the whiteness of American institutions. Also, Bow calls out American narcissism in that it highlights the "excellences" of the Asian model minority while somehow implying that those same excellences are representative of the whiteness to which all races should aspire. But still, assimilationist racism is not, of and by itself, antiblack, and it's important to keep this distinction in mind.

In the United States, in which our version of white supremacy is so intimately linked with antiblackness, there is almost always an undercurrent of antiblackness in expressions of assimilationist racism. One would have to leave our country and look at, for example, a country like Myanmar to understand an assimilationism void of antiblackness. Myanmar, which only gained independence from the United Kingdom in 1948, experienced all forms of assimilationism while under colonial rule, and those assimilationist ideas still run strong: that the far-off country of Great Britain, and the whiteness associated with that country, represents a higher plane of existence over local peoples such as the Bamar or Rohingya. I traveled to Myanmar in 2018 and I was struck by how deep assimilationism stills runs in that country. As I marveled at the hundreds of ancient Buddhist temples in and around Bagan, some quite massive and dating back to the ninth century CE, I experienced a cognitive dissonance thinking about what was happening in England in the ninth century and then about the present-day assimilationism in Myanmar. But colonialism and white supremacy are powerful forces in many parts of the world. I offer this example, however, merely to highlight that the assimilationist racism in Myanmar is essentially void of antiblackness, and it's important to understand the differences and similarities between antiblack racism and assimilationist racism.

Music Theory's Assimilationism

Because so much of the racism in volume 12 is assimilationist, I'll delve into this topic before discussing the ten core responses. I'll draw on race scholar Ibram Kendi's tripartite history of racist ideas in the United States, namely, segregationism, assimilationism, and antiracism. In Example 4.1 I've included three quotations defining the terms "segregationist," "assimilationist," and "antiracist." Most important is the simple belief that assimilationism equates with racism in Kendi's paradigm. He says, "Assimilationist ideas are racist ideas. Assimilationists can position any racial group as the superior standard that another racial group should be measuring themselves against, the benchmark they should be trying to reach. Assimilationists typically position White people as the superior standard."[19] It should therefore go without saying that, of the three, only antiracism is acceptable.

Any race can fit into any one of the three circles shown in Example 4.1. Yes, there were BIPOC who believed in segregationism and even white supremacy, though their numbers are *far* lower than the American history we've officially been taught in our schools. More important, there are countless significant white antiracist figures and scholars, especially in the late twentieth and twenty-first centuries. However, in the history of racist ideas in the United States, black persons had what Kendi—using language inspired by W. E. B. Du Bois's "double consciousness"—calls a "dueling consciousness" between assimilationist and antiracist ideas. I'll remind the reader that my African American father was stuck in the assimilationist circle, though he didn't even realize it himself. And while my black father was a committed assimilationist, my white mother was a staunch antiracist, and it was from her that I myself learned what true antiracism looked like long before that term entered my vocabulary.

However, with respect to white people, Kendi says that, historically,

white people have their own dueling consciousness, between the segregationist and the assimilationist: the slave trader and the missionary, the proslavery exploiter and the antislavery civilizer, the eugenicist and the melting pot-ter, the mass incarcerator and the mass developer, the Blue Lives Matter and the All Lives Matter, the not-racist nationalist and the not-racist American. Assimilationist ideas and segregationist ideas are the two types of racist ideas, the duel within racist thought. White assimilationist ideas challenge segregationist ideas that claim people of color are incapable of development, incapable of reaching the superior standard, incapable of becoming White and therefore fully human. Assimilationists believe that people of color can, in fact, be developed, become fully human, just like White people.[20]

---

19. Kendi, *How to Be an Antiracist* (One World, 2019), 29.
20. Kendi, *How to Be an Antiracist*, 30.

Segregationism

Segregationist: "One who is expressing the racist idea that a permanently inferior racial group can never be developed and is supporting policy that segregates away that racial group" (Kendi, *How To Be An Antiracist*, 24).

Assimilationism

Assimilationist: "One who is expressing the racist idea that a racial group is culturally or behaviorally inferior and is supporting cultural or behavioral enrichment programs to develop that racial group" (Kendi, *How To Be An Antiracist*, 24).

Antiracism

Antiracist: "One who is expressing the idea that racial groups are equals and none needs developing, and is supporting policy that reduces racial inequity" (Kendi, *How To Be An Antiracist*, 24).

Example 4.1. Ibram Kendi, tripartite history of racist ideas in the United States

The historical duel of racist ideas in America that was so common among white people in our history has yet to be fully understood in the United States. The African people brought to America in chains, or the indigenous people who were already here when Europeans began arriving in significant numbers in the sixteenth and seventeenth centuries, were not incapable of being civilized, nor were they capable of rising to the level of whites. The simple fact is that *there was never anything wrong with Africans or Native Americans to begin with.* The mythology that there was something wrong with them is perhaps the most durable and heart-wrenching legacy of racism that remains for us all—black persons, white persons, and those of all other races—to unravel in the United States. Indeed, certain authors in the volume 12 symposium show that this particular mythology of racial superiority and inferiority is still very much alive and well in American music studies.

With respect to how music is taught in the United States, the academic study of music started in the nineteenth century with segregationism. Think here of our major music institutions, like the New York Philharmonic, which only admitted its first black musician, violinist Sanford Allen, in 1962, 120 years after its founding in 1842. Or New York's Metropolitan Opera, which only staged its first opera by an African American in 2021 despite the fact that blacks have been composing operas going back at least to John Thomas Douglass's three-act *Virginia's Ball,* which premiered in New York City at the Stuyvesant Institute in 1868, fifteen years before the Metropolitan Opera was founded in 1883.[21] And whereas occasionally music conservatories were open to blacks in the nineteenth century—such as the New England Conservatory, which opened its doors in 1867 and graduated its first African American, Rachel M. Washington (voice) in 1872—most others were closed to blacks.

In "A Message of Inclusion, A History of Exclusion: Racial Injustice at the Peabody Institute," violinist Sarah Thomas catalogs the common American story of racial exclusion, in this case at one of our oldest and most pres-

---

21. The Metropolitan Opera staged *Fire Shut Up in My Bones,* by black composer Terrance Blanchard, in the fall of 2021, making it the first opera by an African American composer staged at the Met. Douglass, born of a slave mother in 1847, was a virtuoso violinist who taught David Mannes, after whom the Mannes School of Music in New York City is named, in the 1870s. In his 1938 autobiography Mannes speaks admiringly about Douglass, and how he would have wished to play in a professional orchestra. Mannes writes, about Douglass, "He tried to enter a symphony orchestra in this country, but those doors were closed to a colored man." See Mannes, *Music Is My Faith* (Norton, 1938), 39.

tigious conservatories.[22] It took Peabody nearly a century after its founding in 1857 to admit its first black student, Paul Brent (piano), in 1949, and there was great controversy with his admittance. Though racial exclusion was rarely written into school charters, it was generally accepted in segregated American educational institutions. Responding to Brent's application to Peabody, its president, William Marbury, wrote to the board of directors in July 1949, "We are brought face to face with the issue whether to modify our long-standing rule against the admission of negro students," thus putting in writing that which was only unofficial policy at the time.[23] Once the issue was put to a vote, only one board member, Douglas Gordon, openly opposed admitting Brent. In his letter to President Marbury about admitting Brent, Gordon wrote:

It seems to me that it would be a great mistake to change the present policy. In our climate the presence of negroes can to some be extremely offensive. Notwithstanding this, to others their presence together with whites at school, etc., is [illegible] in the South going to lead to such a mixed race as can see [sic] in Sicily or Brazil,—not a very edifying spectacle.[24]

One presumes that the "some" to which Gordon refers are "some white people," who find the "presence of negroes" to be "extremely offensive." Further, "others," and one presumes "other white persons" here, may be scared that having blacks "at school" could lead to a "mixed race," as in "Sicily or Brazil," which would not be "edifying." This is all surely an abhorrent view, and today one might like to think that such views were, in fact, exceptional among whites in the early to mid-twentieth century. Unfortunately, this is simply not true. For example, about the second coming of the Ku Klux Klan in the 1920s, historian Linda Gordon writes: "Most important, the 1920s Klan's program was embraced by millions who were not members, *possibly even a majority of Americans.* Far from appearing disreputable or extreme in its ideology, the 1920s Klan seemed ordinary and respectable to

22. Sarah Thomas, "A Message of Inclusion, a History of Exclusion: Racial Injustice at the Peabody Institute," Hugh Hawkins Research Fellowship for the Study of Hopkins History, MA thesis, John Hopkins University, 2019.
23. Thomas, "A Message of Inclusion," 21.
24. Thomas, "A Message of Inclusion," 71. Thomas transcribed this quote from a handwritten letter, thus the illegibility.

its contemporaries."[25] No, such abhorrent views about blacks among whites in the early to mid-twentieth century were not at all exceptional. More likely, they were, in fact, the norm.

On the point of admitting Paul Brent to Peabody, there was otherwise great reluctance among the other board members, as evidenced by another response to President Marbury, this one by board member J. Hall Pleasants: "I feel that there is an hysterical element in the way the negro question, especially in its racial aspects, is being rushed at the present time, and that under the guise of racial equality, things are going too fast."[26] Slowing down racial progress is a common trope among white persons in the history of the United States, a slowing down often referred to as "incrementalism" or "gradualism." Finally, the board members expressed that they could only admit Brent as an exception to their unwritten rule against admitting black students—rather than openly get rid of racial barriers—and he would only be so admitted if he were deemed "extremely talented" at his audition, which meant that a higher bar for admittance was being established for Brent as a black applicant.[27] We blacks often say that we have to be twice as good as our white counterparts in order to get half the credit. I feel that often white persons either reject this view outright or have trouble understanding it. With the case of Paul Brent, we have proof that he was being held to a higher standard than the typical white applicants to Peabody—sadly, being held to a higher standard still applies today to many BIPOC (and women and other marginalized groups as well) in any number of arenas in the United States.

Difficult though it may be to acknowledge, our American music institutions were founded on the very same segregationist ideas that made up the entire fabric of nineteenth-century America. However, when Jim Crow racism became untenable and collapsed under its own weight by the 1960s, all American music institutions, for the most part, migrated to assimilationism. Official and legal American segregationism was established as "separate but equal" in 1896 by the US Supreme Court in *Plessy v. Ferguson* and was only undone in 1954 when that court overruled *Plessy* in *Brown v. Board of Education.* Thus it was actually quite natural for music conservatories and institutions to reflect the ongoing racial segregation of the country writ large up until the second half of the twentieth century. With *Brown,* and the civil rights legislation of the 1960s, assimilationism became the norm, and, sadly,

---

25. Linda Gordon, *The Second Coming of the KKK: The Ku Klux Klan of the 1920s and the American Political Tradition* (Liveright Publishing, 2017), 3 (italics mine).

26. Thomas, "A Message of Inclusion," 70.

27. Thomas, "A Message of Inclusion," 20, 22, 57, and 69.

this assimilationism is where our music institutions still reside: none is truly antiracist.

Though we can see racial disparities, we have not yet begun to grapple with the segregationist and, more important, the assimilationist racist history of how we have taught music in our conservatories and schools of music in the United States. I'm often asked how we can be antiracist in academic music in the United States, and my first answer will always be that *we cannot understand what antiracism in academic music will look like in the future until we understand what racism in academic music looked like in the past.* This is not to say that it's impossible to solve some of today's problems without unearthing the past. Rather, I'm suggesting that, because we know virtually nothing about how racism has played out in the structures and institutions of the academic study of music, we can't understand what musical antiracism will look like today—it is not possible to combat something you do not understand or, in many cases, even acknowledge. True antiracist work in the field, like that of Sarah Thomas on racial exclusionism at Peabody, lies in unearthing past racist activities, many of which are, in fact, assimilationist activities, if not segregationist. We must research the past, in depth, in order to come to a better understanding of how our musical institutions were created in order to benefit white cisgender men while disadvantaging all others to one extent or another. This research is demanding, and can be exhausting, but this is where the best solutions actually reside, and the change that this work can affect will be rewarding and emancipating for everyone, thus making the academic study of music more welcoming.

The Ten Core JSS Response Authors

Remarkably, it seems that these ten white-male authors were unaware, well into the process of publishing volume 12, that I had submitted an approximately eighteen-thousand-word article on music theory's white racial frame to *Music Theory Online* in June 2019, before I had even given my SMT plenary talk. And if they were aware of my long article, I suspect that they dismissed it as insignificant and not worth waiting for. It's clear to me that JSS's poor due diligence speaks to their one-sidedness in framing what they viewed as an attack on a sacred figure, Heinrich Schenker. Also remarkably, the volume 12 symposium was not peer reviewed, as symposia in academic journals normally are.

The short introduction to the symposium is instructive:

The *Journal of Schenkerian Studies* is proud to publish the following responses to Philip Ewell's SMT 2019 plenary paper, "Music Theory's White Racial Frame." As the editors of an academic journal whose mission it is to encourage the exchange of ideas, we are pleased that these responses express a variety of thoughts and perspectives. Informed debate is the essence of scholarly inquiry, and a field or methodology, such as music theory, stands to prosper by interrogating and critiquing itself. The *Journal of Schenkerian Studies* holds no official stance regarding the issues addressed by the following symposium. We consider ourselves to be—first and foremost—an emissary of the music theory community; we are glad to serve this role through the publication of these responses.[28]

I imagine that, once the editors realized that their efforts might be seen as one-sided, they issued the call for papers with the three-week deadline, in order to get the "variety of thoughts and perspectives" mentioned above. I note that the "exchange of ideas" and "informed debate" never actually happened, since the person to whom they were responding was not invited to participate. Instead, in my opinion, ten authors, led it seems by Timothy Jackson and Stephen Slottow, sought to cast aspersions on me and my research. In what follows I'll offer some views on these ten responses to my plenary talk, outlining especially the assimilationism and antiblackness that drove publication of volume 12.

David Beach: "Schenker—Racism—Context"

I have to be honest: I'm flummoxed that the "context" argument is still rolled out in relation to Schenker and his racism. To say that Schenker's horribleness has been overcontextualized would be a massive understatement, and surely Schenkerians must realize that these hackneyed arguments don't hold up any longer. Nevertheless, before my plenary talk, discussions of Schenker and his legacy were shrouded in multiple layers of nuance, complexity, and context, and expressed in euphemisms and coded language. In "Fuck Nuance," sociologist Kieran Healy speaks of the obfuscation that this context, and overcontextualization, often entails, an obfuscation that is crucial to music theory's white-male frame's desire to sustain and promote Schen-

---

28. Introduction, "Symposium on Philip Ewell's SMT 2019 Plenary Paper, 'Music Theory's White Racial Frame,'" *Journal of Schenkerian Studies* 12 (2020): 125.

kerism, an obfuscation that is the ultimate goal of Beach's "Schenker—
Racism—Context." Healy says, "By calling for a theory to be more comprehensive, or for an explanation to include additional dimensions, or for a
concept to become more flexible and multifaceted, we paradoxically end up
with less clarity. We lose information by adding detail."[29] But the confusion
that comes with such nuance, such context, is often actually the point.

I'll make four points about Beach's response. First, I'd like to point out
what I read as the determined and unquestioning nature of his belief in
white-male greatness, in phrases like "the great works of European art music
of the eighteenth and nineteenth centuries," or "the music of the great
masters."[30] After that last one, Beach adds, parenthetically and sardonically,
"(indeed a group of white guys!)," thereby acknowledging the racial and
gender exclusionism of the field.[31] Given this baseline, a baseline that is
rooted in the many mythologies of our western musical canon that I outlined in chapter 2, it becomes easier to see how Beach seems to believe that
Schenker's transgressions are worth excusing. But such is the case with any
mythology of greatness, that the narratives told are worth the excuses made,
faith more important than skepticism.

Second, I'd point out Beach's euphemistic language when speaking of
Schenker's racism. Citing Schenker's remarkably disgusting "Mission of the
German Genius," Beach says that it "contains much *unfortunate rhetoric*."[32]
I'd refer the reader back to my chapter 3, in which I outline some of this
"unfortunate rhetoric," such as Schenker's expression of horror about mixing
"black racial stock" with a French mother, lest white racial purity be sullied;
that Germans should embrace the "superior quality of their human propagating soil"; or that Europe must be "purified" of the stink of blackness,
represented by black Senegalese troops stationed in Germany after World
War I, with their "inflamed genitals" and "cannibal spirit." But for whom,
exactly, is Schenker's rhetoric "unfortunate"? I'd say only for those who wish
to sweep it under the rug in order to maintain the racialized and gendered
structure that is Schenkerian theory. But, to be clear, this rhetoric was not
unfortunate to Schenker—it simply represented the truth in his eyes. Nor is
it unfortunate to me since, because of Schenker's prolixity concerning such
rhetoric, pointing out Schenker's repugnance is like shooting fish in a barrel.
Yet using the word "racist" to describe someone who was so demonstrably

---

29. Kieran Healy, "Fuck Nuance," *Sociological Theory* 35, no. 2 (2017): 122.
30. David Beach, "Schenker—Racism—Context," *Journal of Schenkerian Studies* 12 (2020): 127.
31. Beach, "Schenker—Racism—Context," 127.
32. Beach, "Schenker—Racism—Context," 127 (italics mine).

racist is something music theory's white racial frame simply cannot coun-
tenance if it might somehow contravene the narratives of exceptionalism
that we've all been taught, the narratives Beach parrots with his language of
"great works of European art music" and "the great masters."

Third, Beach writes, "He [Ewell] states that Schenker's anti-black racism
informed his [Schenker's] theory," and comes to the conclusion that "this is
simply not correct."[33] Here's how I actually put it: "When reading Schenker's
music-theoretical works anew from a critical-race perspective, it is actually
quite easy to see his racism in his music theories," and "Here we begin to
see how Schenker's racism pervaded his music theories."[34] So I spoke of a
general racism and not specifically "antiblack" racism. That is, Beach added
"antiblack" to his criticism of my work, focusing on the one point he himself is likely thinking about, and putting that word into my mouth. In fact,
Beach's addition of "antiblack" is antiblack itself, since it seeks to drive a
wedge between various minoritized groups, a common tactic of white racial
framing. In other words, if it can be shown that my criticism is of Schenker's
antiblackness, rather than of his general racism, it might become easier for
other nonwhite racial groups to support Schenker and dismiss my claim.
But the larger point to make here is that the eminent Schenkerian Carl
Schachter would agree with me, and not with Beach. As I noted in chapter
3, Schachter believed that comparing Schenker's hierarchical worldview with
his hierarchical music theories "is not necessarily invalid."[35] Further, when
asked by Joseph Straus whether Schenker's "dreadful politics" impacted his
music-theoretical work, Schachter answered: "Of course they related to his
theoretical work."[36] Schachter's agreement with me on this simple, but significant, point refutes this part of Beach's argument.

Fourth, and most controversially, Beach wrote:

My suggestion to Philip Ewell is that he stop complaining about us
white guys and publish some sophisticated analytical graphs of works
by black composers. I, for one, would welcome into the analytical
canon works by both black and women composers.[37]

---

33. Beach, "Schenker—Racism—Context," 127.
34. Ewell, "Music Theory's White Racial Frame," 4.
35. Schachter, "Elephants, Crocodiles, and Beethoven: Schenker's Politics and the Pedagogy of Schenkerian Analysis," *Theory and Practice* 26 (2001): 13.
36. Carl Schachter, *Unfoldings: Essays in Schenkerian Theory and Analysis*, ed. Joseph N.
Straus (Oxford University Press [1999]), 11.
37. Beach, "Schenker—Racism—Context," 128.

This comment is, at once, both antiblack and assimilationist. It is also sexist. Feminist philosopher Kate Manne takes sexism

> to be the theoretical and ideological branch of patriarchy: the beliefs, ideas, and assumptions that serve to rationalize and naturalize patriarchal norms and expectations—including a gendered division of labor, and men's dominance over women in areas of traditionally male power and authority.[38]

In his suggestion, Beach acknowledges that there are no works by women composers in the canon, that he would "welcome" such works in the canon, and that in order to do so one must "publish some sophisticated [Schenkerian] analytical graphs" of works by women composers. This is commonly known as gatekeeping. In other words, in order for women to enter the canon, they must get a (white) male stamp of approval. Beach's comment is sexist insofar as he has rationalized and naturalized the patriarchal norms and expectations of music theory—recall his pointing out that the "great masters" were "indeed a group of white guys!"—while exerting his traditional role of male power and authority. Beach's beliefs represent the theoretical and ideological branch of patriarchy and are therefore sexist. Finally, it seems Beach has taken this personally in speaking about "us" white guys—as either representative of the ten core authors or, perhaps, of senior music theorists generally—which speaks to a defensiveness that is quite common in white racial frames.

This controversial comment prompted Beach to issue what is commonly referred to in politics as a "non-apology apology" to me. This came on the listserv for the Society for Music Theory on August 12, 2020, via the music theorist Su Yin Mak, with the subject heading, "RESPONSE TO THE MUSIC THEORY COMMUNITY":

> I write to apologize to those whom I have offended by my comments in the recently released volume 12 of the *Journal of Schenkerian Studies*. First, let me say that I stand behind my observation that it was Schenker's concept of structural levels in music that influenced his judgement of music of other cultures and of contemporary music, not the other way around. But I never meant to imply that I condone this view. I most definitely do not. Indeed, I welcome applications of Schenkerian and other analytical approaches to diversified reper-

---

38. Kate Manne, *Entitled: How Male Privilege Hurts Women* (Crown Publishers, 2020), 8.

toires, although I recognize I may not be the best placed to do so personally. Second, I want to apologize for my comment to Philip Ewell about "leaving us white guys alone." At the time it was written it was intended as tongue-in cheek, not to be taken as seriously. But it is easy to see how it was found offensive in that it seems to confirm the "white racial frame" addressed by Ewell in his plenary session. Since that time the situation has became [*sic*] further charged by subsequent appalling public events and the understandable surge of calls to action in the "Black Lives Matter" movement, which I wholeheartedly support. Again, my apologies to the SMT Board and the Music Theory Community for the offense caused.

I note that Beach did not apologize to me. He apologized for the comment he made to me, but the apology went to the "SMT Board" and the "Music Theory Community," so this is, as I said, a non-apology apology. The performative allyship in Beach's citation of Black Lives Matter signifies that Beach is what I call an "ally in name only," or AINO, since he would likely not agree with the types of structural changes that I would call for in the academic study of music yet wishes to state his support for Black Lives Matter. Understanding when someone is an AINO and not a true ally is key in the struggle for justice in academic music, since one wastes time engaging with AINOs, time better spent on other things.

Jack Boss, "Response to P. Ewell"

In debating, it often happens that one can take the premises used by one's opponent to arrive at a certain conclusion, and use them to reach exactly the opposite conclusion. In the case we are discussing here, it seems as if Philip Ewell has portrayed Heinrich Schenker as arguing from the premise that musical works of genius build themselves out from an Ursatz through diminution, and reaching the conclusion that Black musicians cannot produce works of genius. And Ewell seems to be calling on present-day music theorists to throw out not only what he understands to be Schenker's conclusion (which, whether Schenker believed it or not, is surely an erroneous one, deserving of censure) but also the premise that leads to it (the Ursatz can help us identify works of genius).[39]

---

39. Jack Boss, "Response to P. Ewell," *Journal of Schenkerian Studies* 12 (2020): 133.

So begins Jack Boss's response, a true head-scratcher, to my SMT plenary talk. I had to check the transcript of my talk to see if I had said anything resembling what Boss outlines above. I had not. I'd point out how Boss suggests I'm an "opponent," and not a colleague—for the record, I do not consider Boss, or any of the other nine core volume 12 authors, opponents; rather, I consider them colleagues. But most disturbing is Boss's complete mischaracterization of my talk. No, I never argued "from the premise that musical works of genius build themselves out from an Ursatz through diminution." In fact, I never said the words "genius," "diminution," or "Ursatz" a single time in my talk. And no, I never called "on present-day music theorists to throw out" Schenker's "premise" that "the Ursatz can help us identify works of genius." Though I feel I'm sounding like a broken record, I'll state once again the main points of my talk as it relates to Heinrich Schenker and his legacy: Schenkerian theory and analysis, a racialized (and gendered, not insignificantly, though I did not make this point in my talk) structure of music theory's white racial frame, benefits whiteness while disadvantaging nonwhiteness. Further, I stated that, because our white racial frame has consistently whitewashed Schenker's racism, this results in colorblind racism, which seeks to stall or stop explicit discussions about race or racism, all of which creates hostile environments for those who do not identify as white, which, in turn and in part, accounts for the stark racial imbalances, and racial injustices, we currently see in music theory.

I also never stated explicitly, in my talk, my belief that Schenker believed that blacks were incapable of producing works of genius, though I certainly believe so and did, in fact, make such a statement in my long article on which I based my plenary talk, and I touched on it in chapter 3 as well. Here's how I put it in the article (but not in my plenary address, to which Boss was allegedly responding):

> Schenker often relates music to the human body and living organisms: "It should have been evident long ago that the same principle applies both to a musical organism and to the human body: it grows outward from within." And insofar as "musical coherence can be achieved only through the fundamental structure in the background and its transformations in the middleground and foreground," Schenker implies that blacks are inferior because only the white German genius, with superior *Menschenhumus* [human propagating soil], is capable of pro-

ducing the background that Schenker speaks of. In other words, to Schenker, blacks are not capable of producing the same level of artistry and beauty that whites are capable of.[40]

But Boss is unwilling to acknowledge that Schenker believed that blacks were incapable of producing works of genius by casting doubt on this notion when he writes parenthetically, in the quotation above, "(which, whether Schenker believed it or not, is surely an erroneous one, deserving of censure)." Does Boss actually think that Schenker may have believed that blacks *could* produce works of genius on the same level as "the great masters" such as Beethoven or Mozart? Boss's casting of doubt on something that, on its face, sounds absurd—of course Schenker never believed that blacks were so capable—represents yet another instance of whitewashing Schenker. Framing is everything here, and it's clear from this quotation that music theory's white racial frame cannot even admit the most basic aspects of Schenker's racism, which ultimately *has a negative impact on us all,* including on white persons themselves.

From here Boss offers an analysis of a piece by the African American pianist Art Tatum. Boss seeks to prove that, using Schenkerian analysis, blacks were, indeed, capable of producing works of genius. Boss writes:

> Tim Jackson has already shown (pp. 157–166) that Schenker's attitude toward Black musicians was more nuanced than what Ewell asserts, changing over time as Schenker himself matured. So my response will focus instead on the possibility, perhaps even the necessity during our present time, of using the premises of Schenkerian analysis to lead to the opposite conclusion; that Black musicians did indeed produce works of genius, works which ornamented their structures in new and fascinating ways, and are worthy of our study.[41]

As I show below, Timothy Jackson's response contains arguably the most aggressive assimilationist and antiblack sentiments, yet Boss seems to have no problem with them in his citation of Jackson's essay. This cross reference

---

40. Ewell, "Music Theory and the White Racial Frame," *Music Theory Online* 26, no. 2 (2020): para. 4.5.3. The two quotations in this passage are from Heinrich Schenker, *Der freie Satz*, trans. and ed. Ernst Oster (Longman Publishers, [1935] 1979), 6.
41. Boss, "Response to P. Ewell," 133.

146 · ON MUSIC THEORY

also underscores that at least some of the ten core authors were sharing their work with each other in what appears to be a coordinated effort.

In analyzing a solo piano improvisation by black African American pianist Art Tatum, Boss's response has a subtler layer of antiblackness that's worth examining. When stating that blacks, too, produced works of genius, Boss evokes the false presumption that nonwhite musics are generally inferior to music of the white western canon. Let me be clear here. Music of the white western canon is not superior to any other music in the world, nor is it inferior. Music of the white western canon—itself a mythological human construct meant, in very large part, to enshrine white-male dominance in the academic study of music in the United States—is on exactly the same level as all other musics, in the same way that all races of humans are on the same level. In applying Schenkerian tools to the music of Tatum, Boss seeks to "elevate" or "uplift" that music to the level of a mythically superior white music.[42] This harmful fallacious mindset believes that *only in certain cases* can nonwhite music rise to the level of canonical so-called masterpieces. This again is the mindset of the assimilationist, the civilizer. This subtler form of antiblackness, and of white supremacy, is possibly even more pernicious than other overt forms found in volume 12, since it can be harder to identify and understand. I'll remind the reader that this subtler form of white supremacy is precisely the form *that my African American father believed in,* as I outlined in chapter 2. I will return to this particular aspect of assimilationist racism, the false notion that applying white-male methodologies to black music somehow elevates or uplifts that music to a higher level, in chapter 5.

On July 27, 2020, Boss too issued a non-apology apology to me, on Facebook. Boss wrote:

> I've become aware in the last couple of days that my contribution to the recent *Journal of Schenkerian Studies* was offensive to some of you. My apologies to those I offended. I meant it in the spirit of celebrating the work of Black musicians, which I understood as an anti-racist activity, and finding a way for Schenkerian analysis to contribute to that, but I see now that it could be interpreted as an attempt to strengthen the "white racial frame" in music theory.

---

42. The notion of "racial uplift" has a time-honored tradition in the United States and in American music. See Lawrence Schenbeck, *Racial Uplift and American Music, 1878–1943* (University Press of Mississippi, 2012).

I advocated for the publication of Philip Ewell's most recent MTO article, and I do plan to study it in greater depth this summer, in preparation to discuss it with one of my fall classes. I hope to learn from my students, and from many of you, as I prepare for and lead my classes. I'm willing to listen to you and have constructive discussions. If you would like to talk with me, I would welcome that; on Facebook or PM.[43]

Such non-apology apologies are legion in politics—"Mistakes were made, and if I've offended anyone, I apologize"—but they're not so common in music theory. In my opinion, the inability of Jack Boss or David Beach to offer an unequivocal apology stems from their belief that I don't deserve an apology. In other words, I believe it was a bridge too far for them to simply say, "I apologize to Philip Ewell." This inability to see the humanity in blackness and to address it directly is, simply put, antiblack.

On August 5, 2020, Boss sent me a long email explaining his reaction to his first reading of my lengthy article on white framing that had just appeared in *Music Theory Online* in June 2020. His email was thoughtful and conciliatory. On the same day I responded to Boss with my own long, thoughtful (I hope) email. One point I underscored, since he had raised it in his Facebook message, was that there was absolutely *nothing*, currently, about American music theory that is "antiracist," which is something that we collectively are only now beginning to understand. Nevertheless, I wish to thank Boss for his email and his self-reflection, which, as I know myself, is not easy for mid-career or senior scholars, in any field. Of the ten core authors from volume 12, Boss is the only one who reached out to me directly like this after publication of my article, and it's important to note so here. Finally, I also note that Boss was the only one of the ten core authors to sign the summer 2020 "Open Letter on Antiracist Actions within SMT," a letter I discuss below.

Charles Burkhart, "Response to Philip Ewell"

Burkhart's response is two hundred words long, written in one paragraph. He says that my talk contained "two main points": (1) that we could reduce

---

43. I responded directly to Boss on Facebook shortly after his non-apology apology and he did, in fact, finally apologize to me, using my name. I regret sending that Facebook response to Boss, since blackness should not have to request apologies—such apologies are insincere by their very nature.

a common undergraduate music theory sequence "from four to two years," and (2) that "Schenker's racism infects his music theory."[44] To the first point . . . huh? I did mention, in my conclusion, that we should consider trimming a four-*semester* classical music theory sequence to two semesters in order to add two new semesters of nonwestern, or other, music theory—so two years to one of classical music theory—but that was hardly the first take-away from my talk. To the second point, sure, but I note that this does erase the other approximately 60% of the talk when I was not discussing Heinrich Schenker. I give credit to Burkhardt for acknowledging "Schenker's racism," however, without qualification.[45] Burkhardt concludes his paragraph by saying, "Are we therefore to pauperize ourselves—to throw out [Schenker's] better ideas—the ones that have vastly enriched the field of music theory? If not, what is the point in dwelling on [Schenker's] faults at such length? Why this animus?"[46] If the reader reads my long article, I don't think they'll find much animus in there, but I'll let them decide. Yet with respect to Burkhardt's question of why we should dwell on Schenker's faults, the answer is simple: because in 2020 I was one of only two black associate professors in the entire roughly twelve-hundred-member Society for Music Theory, which comes, in part, as a result of not examining Schenker's legacy.[47] Burkhardt's charge of animus is part and parcel of the "blame the victim" mentality when whiteness combines with maleness in American history, which is a strategy that is often directed at me when I speak openly about race in music theory. Indeed, white narratives of the "angry black man" have been a key component of white racial framing in our country for centuries.

Allen Cadwallader, "A Response to Philip Ewell"

"Hierarchies are not about equality and inequality."[48] What a stunning statement from Allen Cadwallader in his response to me. Here's how the dic-

---

44. Charles Burkhart, "Response to Philip Ewell," *Journal of Schenkerian Studies* 12 (2020): 135 or 136 (the issue is mispaginated, and Burkhardt's paragraph is on either 135 or 136, depending on whether one counts from the end or the beginning).

45. Burkhart, "Response to Philip Ewell," 135 or 136.

46. Burkhart, "Response to Philip Ewell," 135 or 136.

47. According to SMT's 2019 demographic report. See Jenine Brown, "Annual Report on Membership Demographics," Society for Music Theory, October 2019, 9 (https://societymusictheory.org/sites/default/files/demographics/smt-demographics-report-2019.pdf). Also, in August 2021 I was promoted to full professor at Hunter College.

48. Allen Cadwallader, "A Response to Philip Ewell," *Journal of Schenkerian Studies* 12 (2020): 137.

tionary on my computer defines "hierarchy": "a system or organization in which people or groups are ranked one above the other according to status or authority." This sure seems to have a lot to do with inequality to me. And, without question, the racial hierarchy of America's historic white supremacy was precisely about inequality, with white persons at the top and all other nonwhite groups below in the hierarchy in varying degrees of inequality when compared to whites.

In response to my suggestion that "Schenker's racism pervaded his music theories," Cadwallader writes in a footnote, "This conclusion is ludicrous and suggests that Professor Ewell is not at all well versed in theories of functional common practice tonality."[49] So by simply suggesting that Schenker's racism is reflected in his music theories, Cadwallader concludes that my knowledge of common-practice tonality is suspect, my over thirty published music theory articles be damned. I believe this statement is antiblack, and not assimilationist, that is, there is nothing in this statement that is trying to say that, if only Ewell tried harder, he could raise himself to the level of whiteness and properly understand "theories of functional common practice tonality."

At the end of his response, Cadwallader tries to end on a high note.

In 2020, almost exactly 100 years after the term *Urlinie* [a fundamental melodic descent] appeared in print, music theorists and pedagogues have the means and perspective to focus on the good, not the bad, and to broaden substantially our musical vistas to include women and people of color. It need not be Either/Or. I have spent my entire career involved with Schenker's work, mostly with his theories and his analyses alone, marveling at the musical insights they can reveal about a certain repertoire. Let us expand that repertoire and celebrate diversity in scholarship and in the classroom. But let's not set aside the countless musical ideas and analytical techniques Schenker bequeathed to posterity.

This statement is assimilationist. Let's just think about the good, not the bad, and help women and BIPOC see the true beauty of Heinrich Schenker and his musical (but certainly not racial) theories. There is no shortage of irony in Cadwallader's desire to "celebrate diversity in scholarship and in the classroom," since Schenkerian analysis applied to other non-white-

---

49. Cadwallader, "Response to Philip Ewell," 137 n. 2.

male composers still keeps the white supremacy, and the patriarchy, of the system intact. This relates to the distinction between DEI and antiracism that I outlined in the Intro: "celebrating diversity" in the music theory class-room by adding women and BIPOC composers does nothing to disrupt the white supremacist patriarchal underpinnings of the field. What Cadwallader appears to be taking issue with is my *antiracist* scholarship, in which I show how and why those women and BIPOC composers were excluded to begin with. I do agree that "it need not be Either/Or." I state quite clearly, toward the end of my long article, my desire that Schenkerian analysis survive in the twenty-first century, which I still desire.[50] But my desire is quite different from Cadwallader's no doubt.

On June 29, 2020, with the subject heading "From Allen Cadwallader," I received the following email:

> First, let me say what an idiot I think you are. You obviously can't do theory and analysis, so you make a career out of pitting blacks against whites. Your only hope of making a name is to "right" some injustice. Your ilk is if you can't do, then find some social injustice to talk about.
>
> Let's meet, in the forum of your choice. Pick your piece and let's have an analysis symposium. Talk to me about counterpoint, harmony, linear analysis; you are inept at all of these.
>
> Allen Cadwallader[51]

Talk about animus! I'm an inept idiot who obviously doesn't understand the-ory and analysis. This is, in my opinion, unbridled antiblackness, precisely the kind of antiblackness that courses through the veins of, regrettably, too many people in our country, especially white people. Cadwallader's charge that I am "pitting blacks against whites" is a common white-framing tac-tic, to rile up those who advocate for colorblindness knowing full well that colorblindness keeps America's racial hierarchy intact. To be clear, I'm not pitting any race of people against any other race. Rather, I am exposing how white framing works in the field of American music theory—Cadwallader's email proves precisely how this white framing works better than, possibly, anything that I myself have written.

---

50. See Ewell, "Music Theory and the White Racial Frame," para. 8.1.

51. Roughly eight hours later Cadwallader followed this up with a tepid apology, "My apologies. It's been a tough time." In neither email could Cadwallader bring himself to type a salutation, that is, he couldn't bring himself to "say my name."

This form of antiblackness is not limited to conservative whites. Rather, this type of antiblackness runs the gamut from liberal to conservative. I don't know Cadwallader's politics, but university music professors tend to be Democrats, and self-proclaimed liberals or moderates, who are actually some of the greatest impediments to racial progress in our country. Martin Luther King put it best in his "Letter from a Birmingham Jail" from 1963:

> I must confess that over the past few years I have been gravely disappointed with the white moderate. I have almost reached the regrettable conclusion that the Negro's great stumbling block in his stride toward freedom is not the White Citizen's Counciler or the Ku Klux Klanner, but the white moderate, who is more devoted to "order" than to justice; who prefers a negative peace which is the absence of tension to a positive peace which is the presence of justice; who constantly says: "I agree with you in the goal you seek, but I cannot agree with your methods of direct action"; who paternalistically believes he can set the timetable for another man's freedom; who lives by a mythical concept of time and who constantly advises the Negro to wait for a "more convenient season." Shallow understanding from people of good will is more frustrating than absolute misunderstanding from people of ill will. Lukewarm acceptance is much more bewildering than outright rejection.[52]

If nothing else, volume 12 proves that music theory has a "shallow understanding" of matters about race in American music theory, and has, at best, shown a "lukewarm acceptance" of black composers, theorists, performers, and scholars throughout American musical history. No amount of spin can disprove this simple fact. I believe it's fair to say that all ten of the volume 12 respondents that I'm discussing here could be considered "white moderates" as King describes them. Finally, I'd point out that many music theorists, especially senior theorists, agree with the goal I seek—making music more welcoming for everyone—but "cannot agree with [my] methods of direct action," as King states.

On February 25, 2021, my colleague Megan Lavengood posted to Twitter two of three nasty emails that she received from Allen Cadwallader in relation to a blog post she had written in July 2020 in support of my work and

---

52. Martin Luther King, "Letter from a Birmingham Jail," 1963 (https://www.africa.upe nn.edu/Articles_Gen/Letter_Birmingham.html).

how volume 12 had proved the points I was making.[53] Cadwallader called
Lavengood a "know nothing" who was "hiding behind issues of social justice" and stated that he was "tired of all this bullshit" and that Lavengood
was a "fraud." I relay this story here to convey just how deep run the hate
and anger of entitled white men. It seems that Cadwallader simply can't con-
ceive of a music theory outside of his narrow world of Heinrich Schenker,
of "counterpoint, harmony, and linear analysis," and that any attempt to
confront racial or social justice in the field is "bullshit."

Finally, on March 31, 2021, Cadwallader sent me the following email:

Good afternoon Philip,

My, you have certainly had much more than your 15 minutes of fame.
I will put nothing more in print about my feelings about all of this,
because we all know the kind of tactics you engage in: post everything
on the internet, even personal communications. What I am suggesting
is an open debate, on zoom, or whatever. Let's talk about REAL music
theory chops and what they mean in today's society. If you are willing.
Respond. I'll meet you anyplace, anytime.

Allen Cadwallader[54]

For someone wishing to "put nothing more in print," Cadwallader certainly puts a lot more in print! Considering the emails to Lavengood and
me, Cadwallader is not only engaging in what I believe to be misogynistic
and antiblack behavior, but also intense bullying. To my mind, his school-
yard antics—what amounts to "meet me behind the shed at noon!"—sound
a lot more like a spoiled and entitled teenager, and certainly not a retired
music professor. I shared this email on Twitter, and again here, since it's
important to see the kind of racist and sexist behavior that ensues when
toxic forms of whiteness and maleness combine in American society. That is,
I shared this email not to shame Cadwallader but to hold him *accountable*,
as I hold myself accountable for my actions. To be clear, the combination
of whiteness and maleness is not always toxic. But in a country such as
ours, in which whiteness and maleness have been by far and away the most
important keys to gaining power, those two identities, when combined, have

---

53. See the Twitter thread (https://twitter.com/meganlavengood/status/1364910504930
590724).

54. I've since blocked Cadwallader's email from my account.

created the most common forms of identity toxicity—with the dual institutions of white supremacy and patriarchy—which is something we must all confront and combat, since social justice runs straight through those who feel entitled to that power and privilege by virtue of their race and gender.

Nicholas Cook, "Response to Philip Ewell"

Cook's response is one of the milder responses of the ten, and he focuses on the two citations from my talk in which I claim he whitewashes Schenker's racism. I stand by that claim, I should state right here at the outset. The first point to make is that Cook, like all ten core authors, is treating my nine-minute discussion of Schenker as if that's all the work that I'd ever done on the topic. Cook's monograph *The Schenker Project*, which won SMT's "Wallace Berry" Outstanding Publication Award in 2010, is a fine piece of scholarship worthy of consideration, and I read it eagerly and thoroughly some years ago as I worked on this project. Why, then, am I to be judged by a nine-minute oral discussion of Schenker, and not by academic written publications? More to the point, why did Cook not think to write to me—I met him in the mid-1990s at Yale University, so there's a personal relationship he could have drawn on—to see if, in fact, I had done no work on the topic beyond my nine-minute outline of Schenkerism at the SMT plenary? This, in fact, is the only overt antiblackness that I'd cite on Cook's part, namely, the inability to treat me as an equal colleague, worthy of sending a simple email to get to the bottom of the matter, instead of buying into the general antiblackness that drove publication of volume 12.

In my talk I suggested that Cook's claim that Schenker was only joking when he wrote the disgusting things he wrote amounted to whitewashing Schenker. Cook replied that this was "downright misleading" since he was referring to a single instance when Schenker commented on Beethoven.[55] But it seems that Cook himself also considers this claim of "humor" to be misleading since, as I pointed out in chapter 3, much later on in his book, Cook cites this "humor" excuse for Schenker's racism as possibly "not convincing":

> If the explanation I offered there, that Schenker is making a joke, is not convincing, then perhaps another might be that the strangeness of the remark is a symptom of a thought Schenker represses rather

---

55. Nicholas Cook, "Response to Philip Ewell," *Journal of Schenkerian Studies* 12 (2020): 154. See also "Whitewashing Schenker" in chapter 3 for my discussion of this episode.

than articulates: that Ludwig van Beethoven could perhaps have been the German genius he was because foreign blood flowed in his veins.[56]

So Cook himself admits that his suggestion of humor was, at very least, tenuous, and possibly suspect—I'm simply pointing out here that which Cook himself suggests. And, as I said earlier, this also shows the lengths to which music theory's white racial frame goes to sanitize Schenker's horribleness in order to keep in place the racialized and gendered structure that is Schenkerian theory.

Cook disagrees that Schenker was a biological racist and instead insists on cultural racism, citing the volume by Philip Bohlman and Ronald Radano that I discussed in chapter 1: "Actually, it would be very peculiar if Schenker was a biological racist, since that would negate the legitimacy of his own position in relation to the German musical culture of which he saw himself as the only true guardian."[57] Since the passage that Cook quotes from Bohlman/Radano cites "music played by Jews," it seems Cook is suggesting that Jews could not be biologically racist. But this is not true. Any person of any race, including many nonwhites, can believe in the tenets of biological racism—sadly, that simple fact is still true today. Schenker's frequent linkage of music to the human body and biology—that's biological. And Schenker's citation of the white German's *Menschenhumus*, his (no genderneutral language required here) superior "human propagating soil," that's biological racism. Schenker's horror at the thought of "intermarrying black racial stock with . . . a French mother,"[58] that's biological racism. Schenker's belief that "'Race' is good, 'inbreeding' of race, however, is murky,"[59] that's biological racism. Schenker's homoerotic fetishization and objectification of the black male body, that's biological racism. And Schenker's praise of the most notorious biologically racist madman the world has ever known, Adolf Hitler—that's biological racism. To be clear, Cook is correct that Schenker was a cultural racist, that "Schenker believed in some form of cultural

---

56. Nicholas Cook, *The Schenker Project: Culture, Race, and Music Theory in Fin-de-Siècle Vienna* (Oxford University Press, 2007), 238. Beethoven was both German and Flemish.

57. Cook, "Response to Philip Ewell," 154. Cook does not include a footnote citation, but I presume it's the volume by Bohlman/Radano that I discussed in chapter 1.

58. Heinrich Schenker, *Der Tonwille: Pamphlets in Witness of the Immutable Laws of Music, Offered to a New Generation of Youth*, trans. Ian Bent, William Drabkin, Joseph Dubiel, Timothy Jackson, Joseph Lubben, and Robert Snarrenberg (Oxford University Press, [1921–23] 2004), vol. 1, 18.

59. *SDO*, OJ 89/7, [2], transcr. and trans. John Rothgeb and Heribert Esser.

evolutionary theory, implying that white people represent a higher stage of human development than the 'more primitive races' to which he referred," as he puts it in his response to my SMT talk.[60]

But cultural and biological racism are not mutually exclusive. To put it bluntly, and admittedly too crudely, biological racists are all culturally racist too, while cultural racists are generally not biologically racist. To a large extent, this represents the distinction between segregationism (biological racism) and assimilationism (cultural racism)—think here once again of Kendi's tripartite division of racist ideas in America. But ultimately there is, in fact, a vast spectrum of varying degrees of racism. Were there biological racists more committed to its tenets than Schenker? Without a doubt. But this doesn't mean that Schenker did not hold biologically racist viewpoints—he most certainly did.

In the introduction to *Der freie Satz*, Schenker wrote:

> Since the linear progression, as I have described it, is one of the main elements of voice-leading, *music is accessible to all races and creeds alike*. He who masters such progressions in a creative sense, or learns to master them, produces art which is genuine and great.[61]

In his response Cook cites this passage, as have other Schenkerians, as proof of Schenker's belief in cultural racism, his belief in assimilationism, and that any human being can rise to the highest level of humanity, that of German (white) men. And I can't argue that Schenker's statement here isn't assimilationist, or that it is segregationist. What's fascinating to me, however, is how effectively almost all the virulent biologically racist statements by Schenker have been swept under the rug by our white-male frame. Schenker wrote this statement toward the end of his life. Had he changed over time? Possibly. But even then, one can't simply erase the past as if it never happened. Also, do you know what else Schenker wrote toward the end of his life? His praise of Adolf Hitler, in May 1933, four months after Hitler ascended to the German chancellery and less than two years before Schenker's death in January 1935.

Cook's final point, in his final paragraph, concerns my omission of Schenker's Jewishness from my plenary talk. Ever since Schenkerism became a thing in the United States his proponents have used Schenker's Jewish-

---

60. Cook, "Response to Philip Ewell," 154.
61. Schenker, *Der freie Satz*, xxiii (my italics).

ness as a shield against unwanted criticism, thus creating the "victim narrative" that I discussed at the end of chapter 3, a narrative that allowed music theory's white racial frame to turn a reprehensible figure like Schenker into a more palatable figure and, in extreme circumstances, something of a hero. But Jews, like all other peoples on our planet, can run the gamut from completely awesome to, well, less than awesome. Ultimately, to single out Jews as a group for special treatment is antisemitic, a topic to which I'll return in chapter 6. Finally, at the beginning of chapter 3 I gave five unwritten guidelines that our white-male frame has adhered to when dealing with Schenker's ugliness, the third guideline of which was to "invoke Schenker's Jewishness as a mitigating factor for his repulsive beliefs"—this is precisely what Cook does in the final paragraph of his JSS response to me.[62]

Timothy Jackson, "A Preliminary Response to Ewell"

"While I have not personally encountered racism and sexism in academia, I am sure that it is still a problem."[63] I agree with this comment from Timothy Jackson: racism and sexism are most certainly still a problem in academia. He wrote this in 2009, in a personal and moving essay published in *Music Theory Online* about clinical depression in the academy. I can't know if something has changed for Jackson in the intervening twelve years—if he believes that racism and sexism are no longer problematic—but I appreciate the candor nevertheless.

Much has been made of Jackson's response to my SMT plenary talk. The extremely aggressive tone and the numerous antiblack and assimilationist statements evince not academic scholarship but what I believe to be the expression of personal grievances and rage that I've never seen before in an academic music theory publication. That I am the target of that rage is obvious to me, but my broader goal here is to underscore the most egregious examples of assimilationism and antiblackness, since they help to explain not just the driving forces behind volume 12 but, more important, some of the common beliefs held by American music theory itself, difficult though that may be to acknowledge for some in the field.

Jackson's essay is replete with all the mythological white-male narratives of greatness that have constituted the academic study of music in the

---

62. Cook, "Response to Philip Ewell," 154–55.
63. Timothy Jackson, "Escaping from a Black Hole: Facing Depression in Academia," *Music Theory Online* 15, nos. 3 and 4 (August 2009): para. 20.

United States since the nineteenth century. He acknowledges that Schenker would have objected to removing his racist language from his music-theoretical work, but then fortifies what I've called the "impenetrable barrier" between Schenker's racism and his music theories, which music theory's white racial frame, it must now be said, considers a red line that cannot be crossed. Jackson says, "Ewell argues, probably correctly, that Schenker would have objected [to separating musical from extramusical language]. However, it is indeed possible—even desirable—to separate the technical musical-analytical aspects of Schenker's theory from most of his philosophical, political, and aesthetic claims, which also mutated considerably over time."[64] Well, of course it's "desirable" if you wish to keep in place a racialized and gendered structure, Schenkerian theory, that was created of, by, and for white cisgender men in order to benefit themselves while disadvantaging all others. This desirability is actually my point.

I consider Jackson's now infamous charge of "black antisemitism" to be the most antiblack statement in all of volume 12. Jackson writes:

Ewell's scapegoating of Schenker, Schenkerians, and Schenkerian analysis occurs in the much larger context of Black-on-Jew attacks in the United States. . . . Ewell's denunciation of Schenker and Schenkerians may be seen as part and parcel of the much broader current of Black anti-Semitism.[65]

The idea that American blacks are somehow more prone to antisemitism than other racial groups is, by any measure, an antiblack statement, meant to drive a wedge between blacks and Jews, two groups that have been historically marginalized and minoritized in American history and are arguably the most logical allies of all, with our shared painful experiences of seizures of property, forced relocations, forced labor, and unspeakable violence and horror. Ultimately, there is but a single culprit in the promotion of both antisemitism and antiblackness in the United States: the patriarchal white supremacy on which our country is based, a supremacy that has been, without question, the greatest perpetrator of both antisemitic and antiblack violence, in the United States and beyond.[66]

---

64. Timothy Jackson, "A Preliminary Response to Ewell," *Journal of Schenkerian Studies* 12 (2020): 161.

65. Jackson, "A Preliminary Response to Ewell," 162.

66. It is well known that, along with Jews, their primary target, the Nazis slaughtered blacks, especially mixed-race blacks, in their maniacal quest for racial purity, but it is much

158 · ON MUSIC THEORY

To be clear, black antisemitism has nothing to do with assimilationist racism—this is pure antiblackness, which is all too common in our country. Jackson cites pieces by three authors—Lee Sigelman, Ruth Wisse, and Henry Louis Gates Jr.—to back his claim of black antisemitism, but he never specifies what it is, exactly, about African Americans that makes them more prone to antisemitism, which is what he seems to be suggesting in my opinion.[67] Of course blacks can certainly be antisemitic like anyone else, but the sad truth of the matter is that the United States of America, and not black America by itself, is antisemitic, and antisemitic to a much larger extent than US officials would ever care to admit. To make such a broad invidious claim about a group of people, African Americans, who make up roughly 14% of the United States population, some forty-five million people, is not only antiblack, it's subscholarly in the sense that blacks are not monolithic—what about black Jews, for instance—and to make a sweeping "black antisemitism" statement shows none of the nuance that sound scholarship requires.

From the most antiblack statement in all of volume 12, I now pivot to what I consider to be the most assimilationist statement in the JSS symposium. Jackson wrote:

> Of course, I understand full well that Ewell only attacks Schenker as a pretext to introduce his main argument: that liberalism is a racist conspiracy to deny rights to "people of color." He is uninterested in bringing Blacks up to "standard" so they can compete.[68]

To state the obvious, the "standard" to which Jackson refers is a white standard, and blacks are clearly substandard in his opinion. But I do believe that he thinks that, if properly trained and mentored, blacks can raise themselves up to a mythically higher white standard, a standard that is likely not mythical to Jackson. This is precisely the assimilationist racism that Ibram Kendi has outlined, the same assimilationism I wrote about earlier in this chapter. To be clear, this statement is both assimilationist *and* antiblack, since the nonwhite persons Jackson is targeting are black persons. But the gist is the idea that blacks must raise themselves up and assimilate and that I, Philip

---

less known that Jews at times suffered the same fate as blacks in the United States, such as the lynching of the Jew Leo Frank in Georgia in 1915. See Jacob Bogage, "Leo Frank Was Lynched for a Murder He Didn't Commit. Now Neo-Nazis Are Trying to Rewrite History," *Washington Post*, May 22, 2017.

67. Jackson, "A Preliminary Response to Ewell," 162 n. 5.

68. Jackson, "A Preliminary Response to Ewell," 163.

Ewell, am uninterested in doing so. I suppose Jackson is correct in one sense: I am uninterested in raising blacks up to standard, but that's only because I believe that blacks are already on the same standard as all other races of peoples, and therefore don't need any raising to begin with. In other words, my position is antiracist, while Jackson's is rigidly assimilationist. Or, as Ibram Kendi wrote in an essay in *The Atlantic*, "To believe in racial hierarchy, to say that something is wrong with a racial group, is to express racist ideas."[69] Jackson's comment is a textbook example of a racist idea.

While this assimilationist position is ugly and has been much cited, I think the following passage from Jackson's article is even more telling of the assimilationism in American music theory. In other words, American music theory might wince at "bringing blacks up to standard" but might find the following assimilationist statement more palatable, yet it is actually every bit as ugly in my opinion. Jackson writes:

> I would like to propose that genuine solutions lie elsewhere, especially by the African American Community establishing different priorities, by addressing the deficiency of background in classical music caused by few opportunities for serious training, and by the removal of systemic barriers in American society at large. As I see it, a fundamental reason for the paucity of African American women and men in the field of music theory is that few grow up in homes where classical music is profoundly valued, and therefore they lack the necessary background. To master classical performance practice on any instrument, to achieve musical literacy, and theoretical competence, one must begin intensive training when very young. Therefore, parents must provide their children with lessons and insist upon regular practice from an early age. Low socio-economic status does not preclude any racial group from doing so; poverty does not prevent setting priorities; it is not *solely* a matter of money.[70]

This passage, though not as blatantly appalling as the previous two, contains an assimilationism and antiblackness that is, possibly, more pernicious, since this passage contains the type of rhetoric that has resonated with tens of millions of Americans, usually but not always white, who insist that blacks themselves should be blamed, at least in part, for their unfortunate

---

69. Ibram X. Kendi, "Our New Postracial Myth," *The Atlantic*, June 22, 2021.
70. Jackson, "A Preliminary Response to Ewell," 164.

plight in life, rather than blaming the laws and policies that have actually caused that plight. It also seems to presume that all black persons are of a low socioeconomic status, which is also problematic. This passage sounds like something that could have been written in the 1970s—or possibly in the 1980s, during Ronald Reagan's presidency with its white supremacist dog whistles of "welfare queens" and "states' rights"—when whiteness frequently admonished blackness to "set different priorities," as Jackson puts it, and strive for a mythical whiteness. But to see such a passage in an academic music theory journal in 2020 is truly astounding. To be clear, there is nothing about "profoundly valuing classical music" that makes anyone better (or worse), more civilized, or more sophisticated than anyone else. If someone profoundly values classical music, that's fine, but it only means that they profoundly value classical music, and nothing more. Lastly, shifting the racial conversation to "socio-economic status" is one of the oldest tricks in the book for a white-assimilationist (i.e., not segregationist) frame. In short, it's *never* about race. It simply can't be.

A final antiblack example from Jackson's essay shows the intense hierarchy of his racialized thinking, a hierarchy that is in fact representative of American music theory writ large. Jackson writes:

> As for Black composers, they have had to overcome unbelievable prejudice and hardships, yet there have been many talented and technically competent Black composers in the past hundred years. We can certainly listen to their music with pleasure, even if they are not "supreme geniuses" on the level of the very greatest classical composers. One of the cruelest things in Ewell's agenda is his concomitant dismissal of the works of Black classical composers as irrelevant. They are the people who suffer the most from ideologues. That is racism.[71]

I've never "dismissed" the works of black composers, but Jackson seems to think so nevertheless without any evidence to support his claim.[72] This leads him to conclude that my views amount to the "racism" of an "ideologue." If shifting racial conversations to "socio-economic status" is one

---

71. Jackson, "Preliminary Response to Ewell," 165.

72. See my "Erasing Colorasure in American Music Theory, and Confronting Demons from Our Past" (RILM's *Bibliolore* blog series, March 25, 2021). See also my "New Music Theory" (May 1, 2020) from my six-part blog series "Confronting Racism and Sexism in American Music Theory," which outlines many significant African American composers and, by the way, was available to Jackson before volume 12 was published.

of the oldest tricks in the white-framing playbook, accusing a black race scholar who points out racist structures of "racism" is the absolute oldest. Otherwise, this quotation is antiblack, and not assimilationist, since Jackson is simply placing black composers on a lower level than white composers, without the opportunity for black composers to "rise up" to be considered on the same level as white "supreme geniuses"—this hierarchy is set, or "immutable," to use a word that appears often to describe music theories. Considering the last three quotations by Jackson, which contain clear examples of assimilationist and antiblack racism, it's worth citing once again Ibram Kendi's brilliant words about such forms of racism: "Assimilationist ideas are racist ideas. Assimilationists can position any racial group as the superior standard that another racial group should be measuring themselves against, the benchmark they should be trying to reach. Assimilationists typically position White people as the superior standard."[73] In my opinion, it goes without saying here that, to Jackson, white persons represent the superior standard in music, and blacks should "establish different priorities" and strive for whiteness. I can think of no quotations in the modern history of music theory that so clearly display the assimilationist and antiblack racism of the field.

However, to be fair to Timothy Jackson, in this final quotation he only wrote down that which many senior figures in music theory, and in academic music, actually believe—I have heard similar sentiments, in one fashion or another, expressed many times over the years. In the antiblack fallacy of white supremacy, music of the white western canon is still thought to be superior to other nonwhite musics of the world. Many have tried to cleave themselves from the egregious antiblack statements that appear in Jackson's response, and in the other antiblack responses in volume 12 for that matter, but this particular comment about the "supreme genius" of the white-male western canon actually represents deep-seated beliefs held by the field of American music theory itself since its inception in the 1960s. That is, Jackson's musical beliefs—in which black composers, though "competent," are not considered as great or exceptional as the "supreme geniuses" of the white-male western canon—are not at all uncommon among senior, or simply conservative, music theorists, musicians, and music pedagogues in our American music institutions. To argue otherwise would be less than candid.

Since my SMT plenary I've become online friends with Texas A&M Distinguished Professor of Sociology Joe Feagin, because it's his concept of the

---

73. Kendi, *How to Be an Antiracist*, 29.

"white racial frame" that I applied to music theory. We've exchanged many emails and have looked at and edited each other's work. On February 14, 2021, Feagin emailed me the following note: "Hi. This fellow keeps sending me his analyses about the arguments over Schenker, and just now insults to you. . . . Who is he? Hope all is well, Joe."[74] "This fellow" turned out to be Timothy Jackson. Feagin had forwarded one of the emails from Jackson, which Jackson had sent from a Gmail account, in which Jackson insulted me, strained to show how I was misusing Feagin's concept of the white racial frame, and underscored Schenker's Jewishness. Jackson was also promoting Michael Powell's *New York Times* article about volume 12, an article I will discuss in detail below, since Jackson believed that that article accurately promoted his views about the events surrounding the journal issue. Finally, Jackson emphasized just how dangerous my fallacious views were and how I was twisting historical facts in the service of contemporary ideologies.[75]

From friends and colleagues as far away as Czech Republic, Italy, and the United Kingdom—and from *many* friends and colleagues in the United States and Canada—I have heard how Timothy Jackson has contacted them to plead his case. What that case is exactly is hard to say, but two things are clear: Jackson is defending himself (which is fine) and presumably insulting me (which is not). I believe Jackson's many apparent efforts to discredit me represent an aggressive form of antiblackness that knows no rhyme, knows no reason. What Jackson can never do, it seems, is address the extreme anti-black and assimilationist statements he made in his own essay. How many others from whom I have not heard has Jackson contacted to trash talk me? In what other venues? In what other documentation? To state the obvious: I've never even come close to "attacking" Timothy Jackson in any way, shape, or form. Until *after* the publication of volume 12, I had never once mentioned his name in print, or out of print for that matter, since I'm uninterested in his scholarship.

It is as if Jackson somehow considers himself Schenker's earthly representative, and an attack on Schenker is an attack on Jackson. But again, I never attacked Schenker either but, rather, I showed how music theory's treatment of Schenker and his legacy has resulted in racial injustice, something that volume 12 proved beyond any reasonable doubt—in soccer this is known as

---

74. Joe Feagin, email exchange with author, February 14, 2021. I use this email exchange, and one more exchange cited below, with Feagin's permission.

75. On December 28, 2021, Feagin forwarded to me another long email from Jackson with many more insults about me and my work. I think that Feagin is simply trashing Jackson's emails at this point.

an "own goal," in which a defensive player accidentally scores a goal for the other team. As Buddhists, Christians, or Muslims may take offense if they think that someone has offended Siddhartha, Jesus Christ, or the Prophet Muhammad, there are those in our field who similarly take offense if, in their opinion, someone has offended Heinrich Schenker, which, frankly, frightens me. The unquestioning godlike reverence that Schenker has garnered only indicates an unhealthy state of affairs for the field. There should be no godlike figures in music theory whatsoever, and the fact that there are means that we have serious work to do. It will surprise no one when I point out that the only reason that we have allowed this to happen is because of the many western mythologies, deeply rooted in white supremacy and patriarchy, of white-male greatness that we have been required to learn, required to sustain, and required to promote in order to be successful in the field. Only by letting go of these mythologies can we ensure that there will never be another godlike figure in our field, whose presence and promotion have created countless injustices in American music theory.

Boyd Pomeroy, "Schenker, Schenkerian Theory, Ideology, and Today's Music Theory Curricula"

Finally, one of the ten core authors wrote something with which I agree unequivocally: "Schenker was a deeply flawed and conflicted character whose virulently nationalist and racist views are unpalatable by any standards."[76] But aside from this true statement, there is little of merit in Boyd Pomeroy's response. He begins by suggesting that, by admitting Domenico Scarlatti and Frédéric Chopin into his pantheon, Schenker could not have "been motivated primarily by racism,"[77] as if Schenker would have placed Italians or Poles on the same racial hierarchical level as the Senegalese blacks he so loved to denigrate. The distinction here is between race and nation, and to conflate the two is both confusing (which I presume is the intent here) and unscholarly insofar as this distinction is so basic and uncomplicated. Not a great beginning to an academic response.

Pomeroy claims that I am "squarely at odds" with a list of prominent Schenkerians, "including Nicholas Cook, Allen Forte, Robert Morgan, Ernst Oster, John Rothgeb, William Rothstein, and Carl Schachter."[78] There

---

76. Boyd Pomeroy, "Schenker, Schenkerian Theory, Ideology, and Today's Music Theory Curricula," *Journal of Schenkerian Studies* 12 (2020): 179.

77. Pomeroy, "Schenker," 179.

78. Pomeroy, "Schenker," 179.

are two things to note here: I've never mentioned my former teacher Robert Morgan in any of my writings on Schenker, or any of my writings at all as far as I can recall—maybe I am at odds with Morgan, but I certainly haven't suggested so (Pomeroy could have contacted Morgan to find out whether Morgan agrees with this).[79] Second, I disagree that Carl Schachter's views and my own are at odds, as I've already stated. Of course we have our differences, but I'm greatly impressed with Schachter's late work on Schenker, the first English-language attempt to reframe the white-frame narrative on Schenker. The last time I spoke with Carl on the phone, in November 2020, we didn't talk about this—I had called him to thank him for being such a great mentor to me early in my career, since I hadn't talked with him in a couple years—but I've always appreciated his candor on Schenker's racism.

The tone of Pomeroy's response is condescending. My work is "flimsy," "naïve analogizing," and "out-of-context cherry picking."[80] Pomeroy suggests that I would "unceremoniously demote Schenker" and throw "out the analytical baby with the nationalist/racist bathwater."[81] Even if Pomeroy were responding to an academic article, his prose would be unseemly. But, to once again state the obvious, Pomeroy was responding to a nine-minute oral presentation on Schenker and his legacy, part of a larger twenty-two-minute talk that outlined many things aside from Schenker. Who could possibly have given, in nine minutes, the type of detail and nuance that Pomeroy or the other nine core authors seemed to have wanted? The answer is obvious: absolutely no one.

Finally, Pomeroy suggests that we ask ourselves "why Schenkerian thinking has come to dominate so much undergraduate pedagogy."[82] He then goes on to answer what, to him, is a rhetorical question. The reason, of course, is that Schenkerian theory is so vast, so great, and so rich that it's something to be held in awe, and certainly not questioned, since "it actually works best for the very musical phenomena the theory curriculum concerns itself with (. . . melody, harmony, rhythm and meter, phrase structure, form)."[83] But

---

79. Morgan died on November 17, 2021, aged 87. Rest in peace Bob.

80. Pomeroy, "Schenker," 179–80.

81. Pomeroy, "Schenker," 179–80. Whenever I hear white men speak of "not tossing out the baby with the bathwater," which is code for not allowing a white-male space to become less white and/or less male, I always respond, tongue only half planted in cheek, "What's the race of the baby in your metaphor?" I think I know the answer.

82. Pomeroy, "Schenker," 181.

83. Pomeroy, "Schenker," 181.

now that the dust surrounding volume 12 has settled, another answer has emerged as most likely: Schenkerian theory, to a large extent, has risen to the top of the field and dominated because, as a racialized and gendered structure meant to benefit white men while disadvantaging all others, the white men who have promoted it and now defend it, such as the main authors of volume 12, continue to enjoy privileges that those who are not white (cisgender) men do not enjoy, privileges to which these white men feel entitled.

Stephen Slottow, "An Initial Response to Philip Ewell"

Slottow homes right in on my claim that Schenker's racism permeates his music theories, tracing a relationship that Carl Schachter said was "not invalid." I'll point out again that Schenker himself would have agreed with me, since his racial theories and musical theories were part of his unified view of the world. But, somewhat surprisingly, Slottow also agrees: "I agree that Schenker's views on politics and race inform his music theory."[84] So that makes four of us, Schenker, Schachter, Ewell, and Slottow, I suppose—this number will undoubtedly continue to grow.

The most basic problem with Slottow's response is the most basic one of all: that he is treating my nine-minute presentation as if it were a long academic article, and part of some kind of colloquy or true symposium. One could listen to any nine-minute, roughly one-thousand-word oral presentation on any topic and find it lacking in depth, nuance, find it "flimsy" or undercooked. That these ten authors could respond as they did to a nine-minute oral presentation, as if it were the first and last work I had ever done on the topic, only points to a lazy due-diligence process.

Otherwise, Slottow's response is one of the more tepid responses, whose antiblackness is linked to the overall treatment I received in the symposium for which he was one of two editorial advisers, and whose assimilationism is linked to the idea that we should, ultimately, sever Schenker's racism from his music theories, that it's all evolving, and then more nuance and context. In this fashion, Schenkerian theory and analysis is available to everyone, in assimilationist fashion, and there is nothing in the musical theory itself, per se, that is racist or white supremacist. That is, Schenkerian theory is race neutral.

---

84. Stephen Slottow, "An Initial Response to Philip Ewell," *Journal of Schenkerian Studies* 12 (2020): 189.

Barry Wiener, "Philip Ewell's White Racial Frame"

I had never heard of Barry Wiener before volume 12, and it's still unclear to me what his connection to music theory is. But from the incipient paragraph it's obvious that his is not a very serious response. According to Wiener, in my plenary talk I made a "series of accusations" and my "complaint began with Schenkerian theory and ended as a condemnation of Western culture."[85] I would respectfully respond that I was neither accusing nor complaining, nor condemning for that matter, and that I was simply trying to show how music theory's white racial frame manifests itself so that we can try to make the field more welcoming for everyone. Wiener also writes, "He [Ewell] also describes Schenker as 'a white German racist.'"[86] One would hope that, if an author is going to make such an attribution, "white German racist," in an academic scholarly journal, the editors would check the quotation for accuracy. In fact, I never said that Heinrich Schenker was "white" or "German" in my SMT plenary talk, so Wiener is putting those words in my mouth.[87] I'll leave my comments on Wiener's response at that.

[Anonymous], "Response to Ewell"

The anonymous authorship of this response prohibits my comments directly to this author's response. The one thing I'll point out is that I'll consider this person to be a white man until proven otherwise, and I have referred to him as such on Zoom calls and other live conversations (and no one has corrected me). I believe we must not allow anyone's identity privileges and entitlements to hide behind such anonymity, especially in scholarly writing.

Reactions to the JSS Affair

The reactions to the JSS affair, which came from all around the world, were something to behold. I heard from countless commentators, at this point numbering in the thousands, who sent me notes via email, text, social media, handwritten letters, voice messages, or other channels. The vast

85. Barry Wiener, "Philip Ewell's White Racial Frame," *Journal of Schenkerian Studies* 12 (2020): 195.

86. Wiener, "Philip Ewell's White Racial Frame," 195.

87. Again, for a transcript of my SMT plenary, see Ewell, "Music Theory's White Racial Frame."

majority of these comments were in support of me and the positions I had taken. Occasionally, they were not. No less surprising was the official media response. Stories ran in *The Conversation*, the *Dallas Observer*, Fox News, *Inside Higher Education*, National Public Radio, the *National Review*, the *New York Times*, the *New Yorker*, *Van Magazine*, and *Die Zeit*, among many other news outlets.[88] #SchenkerGate began trending on social media, and a Wikipedia page detailed the JSS "controversy."[89] I heard from as far away as Australia, Benin, China, Ecuador, Israel, Mexico, and many European countries. I gave invited lectures, panels, and interviews in Brazil, Canada, China, Germany, Ireland, South Africa, United Arab Emirates, the United Kingdom, and over one hundred places in the United States. This collective worldwide response to volume 12 was astounding.

The reactions from academia and music theory were no less astounding. The official statement from the Society for Music Theory, from July 28, 2020, read:

The Executive Board of the Society for Music Theory condemns the anti-Black statements and personal ad hominem attacks on Philip Ewell perpetuated in several essays included in the "Symposium on Philip Ewell's 2019 SMT Plenary Paper" published by the *Journal of Schenkerian Studies*. The conception and execution of this symposium failed to meet the ethical, professional, and scholarly standards of our discipline. Some contributions violate our Society's policies on harassment and ethics. As reported by participants, the journal's advisory board did not subject submissions to the normal processes of peer review, published an anonymously authored contribution, and did not invite Ewell to respond in a symposium of essays that discussed his own work. Such behaviors are silencing, designed to exclude and to replicate a culture of whiteness. These are examples of professional misconduct, which in this case enables overtly racist behavior. We humbly acknowledge that we have much work to do to dismantle the whiteness and systemic racism that deeply shape our discipline. The Executive Board is committed to making material interventions to foster anti-racism and support BIPOC scholars in our field, and is meeting without delay to determine further actions.[90]

88. I again mention here that links to some of these sources can be found on the "Media" tab of my website, philipewell.com

89. See https://en.wikipedia.org/wiki/Journal_of_Schenkerian_Studies

90. See the SMT statement here: https://societymusictheory.org/announcement/executi

I'm particularly touched that the authors of this statement, mostly white themselves, could see that, as with volume 12, "such behaviors are silencing, designed to exclude and to replicate a culture of whiteness," and that "we have much work to do to dismantle the whiteness and systemic racism that deeply shape our discipline." That's exactly right.

Yale University, my doctoral alma mater, wrote that they "reject and condemn the racist and personal attacks on Prof. Ewell."[91] Notably, Yale's statement pointed out how there were no people of color and only one woman among the respondents, and how the symposium only proved the point I made in my article that music theory's white frame seeks to maintain the status quo generally, and shield Schenker from unwanted criticism specifically. The University of Toronto adopted language similar to SMT's statement and added, "We acknowledge that North American music theory urgently needs to reckon with its racist, anti-black, white supremacist roots in order to evolve and grow."[92] The Music Theory Society of New York State, MTS-NYS, made a similar statement, and an "Open Letter on Antiracist Actions within SMT," ultimately signed by more than nine hundred people from around the world, was drafted and addressed to the Society for Music Theory.[93] Here's the opening paragraph of the letter:

> At the Plenary Session of the Society for Music Theory's 2019 meeting, Philip Ewell, Yayoi Uno Everett, Ellie Hisama, and Joseph Straus powerfully demonstrated how systemic racism, sexism, and ableism animate musical discourse. They spoke not only with candor and wisdom, but also with exceptional courage. The *Journal of Schenkerian Studies*, in Volume 12, has just published a number of vitriolic

---

ve-board-response-journal-schenkerian-studies-vol-12-2020-07. The authors, the leadership of SMT at the time, were President Patricia Hall, Past President Robert Hatten, and Inessa Bazayev, Anna Gawboy, Julian Hook, Gretchen Horlacher, Jennifer Iverson, Jocelyn Neal, Nancy Yunhwa Rao, Philip Stoecker, and Leigh VanHandel.

91. See the Yale statement here: https://yalemusic.yale.edu/news/statement-support-phil ip-ewell

92. See the University of Toronto statement here: https://theory.music.utoronto.ca/statem ent-jss-symposium-philip-ewell-plenary/

93. See the MTSNYS statement (https://mtsnys.org/mtsnys-statement-in-support-of-phil -ewell/) and the SMT open letter, Edward Klorman et al., "Open Letter on Antiracist Actions within SMT" (https://docs.google.com/document/d/1pne06DbjDt-ume06JMtc5fljpbLDk MZgw3mRFOrRepE/edit?fbclid=IwAR29N3iAKX9mQybqTy4NOhtZw8LKU84yQ2qdqz eBCoJzho6n-8j4gIXjywg).

responses to a single aspect of one presentation—under the pretense of scholarly debate, no less—and the ensuing scandal has diverted our field's focus from the structural critiques made in the plenary. The journal's violation of academic standards of peer review, its singling out of Prof. Ewell while denying him a chance to respond, and the language of many of its essays constitute anti-Black racism. These actions provide further evidence of the structural force of white supremacy in our discipline. While this episode is the most recent, and perhaps the most illustrative, the treatment Prof. Ewell received from the *Journal of Schenkerian Studies* is only the latest instance of systemic racism that marginalized Society members have faced for many years.[94]

I encourage the reader to read this extraordinary document in its entirety, since it contains the type of clear-eyed direct antiracist language that is missing from our field all too often. We have much work to do, but statements like these lay the groundwork for change, which gives me hope for the future.

Finally, I should mention the bold statement made by the graduate students in music at the University of North Texas in support of me and my scholarship, and the follow-up similar statement made by certain music faculty in support of me and of those students.[95] At the time of writing, there is a lawsuit in Texas concerning these issues and, as I have mentioned in a footnote, I am withholding commentary because of the ongoing nature of that suit. I can simply say here, however, how humbled I was and am by those courageous efforts in support of me and my scholarship, and I thank all the parties involved for those efforts.

The "European" Response

One of the most remarkable responses to the entire JSS affair came in the form of a European "Open Letter on Schenker's Racism and Its Reception in the United States," from September 28, 2020. I call this letter "European" since most of the signatories reside in Europe and, in the first line of the letter, they write, "The undersigned, European (and non-European) music

---

94. Klorman et al., "Open Letter."

95. The statements by both the UNT graduate students and the UNT music faculty can be found as Exhibits 3 and 4 in Du et al., *Ad Hoc Panel Review*.

theorists, music analysts and music historians."[96] So as to not bury the lede, the best aspect of this letter, remarkably antiblack in its own right, is that it shows that the racism that was contained in volume 12, and therefore in American music theory, is not limited to the United States. One thing that I've emphasized overall with my race scholarship in music is that white supremacy was and is very much a worldwide project, and that it originated in Europe, not in the United States. As a binational person myself, Norwegian and African American, who has lived for seven years in Russia, traveled to most European countries, and knows five European languages to varying degrees of fluency, I know firsthand that the racism that is part of the academic study of music in the United States is most certainly part of the academic study of music in Europe and in other places where white supremacy has been operative as a result of colonialism and colonial conquests. The European response supports this point.

By my count there are forty-seven signatories to this letter, who appear at the bottom of the letter. The main author seems to be Nicolas Meeùs, who is a white man and professor emeritus at Sorbonne University. I see only three authors who signed from the United States: Joel Galand (Florida International University), Rob Haskins (University of New Hampshire), and Dmitry Rachmanov (California State University, Northridge). Otherwise the authors come from in and around Europe. I begin with the most stunning statement of all from the European letter: "We were unable to identify any anti-Black statement (unless in quotations from Schenker's own texts), nor any attack against Philip Ewell *the man* (which is the meaning of *ad hominem*) in this *JSS* volume."[97] Three things stick out: the remarkable condescension of explaining what "ad hominem" means; the fact that, in volume 12, no one actually quoted Schenker's own horrific racist texts as the Europeans claim; and, most astonishingly, that the forty-seven signatories "were unable to identify any anti-Black statement . . . nor any attack against Philip Ewell" in volume 12. This European response truly deserves its own case study in how whiteness dismisses the views and opinions of nonwhiteness in white supremacist structures like those found in the United States and the European countries in which most of these signatories reside. Ultimately, it's a sad commentary on just how much work remains for those in the academic study of music in order to confront the structural whiteness of

---

96. Nicolas Meeùs et al., "Open Letter on Schenker's Racism and Its Reception in the United States," September 28, 2020 (https://heinrichschenker.wordpress.com/open-letter-on-schenkers-racism-and-its-reception-in-the-united-states/).

97. Meeùs et al., "Open Letter."

what we do, here in the United States, in Europe, and surely in other places where white supremacy is operative.

The Europeans framed the JSS affair as a debate, a "dispute" in their opinion, between me and Timothy Jackson. They write that they "have been made aware of the dispute between Prof. Philip Ewell and members of the American Society for Music Theory (SMT) on the one hand, the *Journal of Schenkerian Studies* (*JSS*) and Prof. Timothy Jackson on the other hand." To be clear, *there has never been a debate or dispute between me and Timothy Jackson.* I bear no ill will toward Jackson, or toward the other authors of volume 12, and not even toward Allen Cadwallader, who wrote those horrible personal emails to me that I have cited. To frame this as a debate is to try to obfuscate the assimilationism and antiblackness in music theory in order to sustain and reinforce the white (male) structures of the field, all while framing racist reactions as legitimate self-defense.

The Europeans say that they understand my points about the "lack of diversity" in the academic study of music in the United States, adding that "such problems cannot be discussed in the same terms in Europe." No, I say, *such problems can be discussed in strikingly similar terms in Europe.* They add that the "whiteness in American music theory . . . remains beyond [their] competence," as if European music theory is somehow not white-centric and rooted in white supremacy. With my own strong ties to Europe and having had countless conversations about precisely these types of issues with Europeans over many years, I can say that their viewpoint that Europe is somehow better or simply different from the United States when it comes to racial matters is used quite effectively to stifle and suppress conversations about European racism. To be clear, there is far more *convergence* between Europe and the United States when it comes to racism, racialized structures, and white supremacy than there is *divergence*; after all, I'm writing in the English language, need I point out? The common denominator here is the European invention of white supremacy, whose most influential non-European national proponent has been, over time, the United States of America. We must not let Europeans off the hook simply because George Floyd was murdered in Minneapolis and not Munich.

As with volume 12, the Europeans too saw my nine-minute discussion of Schenker's legacy as an "attack" on Schenker—a common white mischaracterization about blacks who seek equality—whose racism they concede is not doubt:

> There is no question that Schenker and [François-Joseph] Fétis stated this sentiment [the racist idea that whites are superior to people of

color] a century or two ago, but we fail to understand how and why modern American music theory could and should still be based on such old-fashioned ideas. . . . He [Ewell] may fail to realize, however, that Schenker's nationalism and possible racism have been discussed many times in the last forty years.

If the Europeans don't understand "how" contemporary American music theory (and contemporary European music theory as well) is based on "such old-fashioned ideas" as those of Fétis and Schenker, then they clearly have a poor understanding of how systemic racism works. If they can't understand "why," then they have a poor understanding of how white privilege and white entitlement work. If they are asking whether American music theory "could" or "should" be based on white racial framing, the answers are "Yes, it could," and "No, it shouldn't." Further, they contradict themselves in the same paragraph. If "there is no question" that Schenker expressed racist "sentiments," how is it that Schenker's racism is only "possible," as if it's still in question? To suggest that Schenker's racism is only "possible" is to soft-pedal the point or, as I said in my SMT plenary talk, to "whitewash" Schenker's racism. Clearly, whitewashing Schenker's racism is not limited to the United States. Their claim that I "may fail to realize" that Schenker's nationalism and "possible" racism have been "discussed many times in the last forty years" only means that they too failed to read my approximately eighteen-thousand-word article on white racial framing, in which I cite some of that work and which was available to them before their letter was published. Once again, this is poor due diligence, which, ironically, is what the Europeans accused me of when suggesting that I "may fail to realize" that there has been scholarship concerning Schenker's racism.

Like volume 12, this European response is a gift to us all, since it proves that antiblackness is not an American phenomenon only, and it opens up a space for discussion of important issues beyond our own borders. In their response the Europeans upbraid the "Open Letter on Antiracist Actions within SMT" explicitly and, it seems, the Society for Music Theory implicitly. Notably, there were only forty-seven signatories to their open letter, while the open letter to SMT garnered more than nine hundred. Those are numbers I can live with.

A final point about the European response relates to how they try to express their desire for an honest scholarly debate around these issues, issues that they clearly have trouble understanding. "The debate was replaced by censorship," they say, adding:

We very much regret that his keynote address and the JSS symposium that followed did not spur to the general debate for which we believe the time has come. We urge the SMT and the UNT to reconsider the matter and to open a much necessary worldwide debate, to which we are eager to participate.

This call for a debate is a sentiment that I've seen expressed many times by senior white men in the field—some have expressed it to me directly—but this sentiment is disingenuous. In my opinion, they do not seek honest debate but, rather, a platform to double, triple, and quadruple down on the many white mythologies that constitute their views on music theory. (Think here of Allen Cadwallader's emails to me in which he was churlishly demanding a "symposium" and "open debate" about "counterpoint, harmony, and linear analysis.") Importantly, in this case debate was not replaced by censorship at all, as they say. What happened was that SMT, and many others, condemned the antiblack and assimilationist racism that drove publication of volume 12, which actually should be pretty easy to do when reading volume 12 in good faith. In other words, I don't see volume 12 as a debate; it was never intended as such, and to retroactively assign the desire for honest debate to what was, on its face, an exercise in antiblackness is to force the whole matter onto the Procrustean bed of music theory's white racial frame.[98] In a recent piece on the controversies surrounding critical race theory, Kimberlé Crenshaw puts it better than I can:

> Those who want to expand our nation's literacy about our racial past and those who wish it to remain illegible to all but a determined few do agree on one thing: that examining our history has consequences. The disagreement becomes volatile when those who embrace America's promises ask that we take up the truths of our history, while critics claim it is only patriotic to perpetuate a lie. . . . Theirs is not a debate about ideas but rather an attempt—on behalf of the racially inequitable status quo—to shut down debate altogether.[99]

---

98. If the reader will allow for my citation of the rogue blacksmith Procrustes, from ancient Greek mythology, which I criticized earlier—good mythologies provide many useful sayings, after all.

99. Crenshaw, "The Panic over Critical Race Theory Is an Attempt to Whitewash U.S. History," *Washington Post*, July 2, 2021.

I suspect that what the Europeans are actually seeking is a forum to continue to obfuscate issues surrounding race in music theory, which is what volume 12 itself also was in large part. I wrote early on in *On Music Theory*, "For the record, white supremacy and patriarchy do not merit consideration as legitimate structures in a just, civil, and democratic society," which is true not only for societies but for music theory as well, and what such would-be debaters actually want is to wrap up the colorblind racism of the field in a new blanket and present it as the most "reasonable" version of events, of the future, while assuring everyone that their version of music theory is not in any way racist—it's simply the most exceptional and the most worthy of our attention. And these would-be debaters clearly are uninterested in my arguments about the white framing of the field, as evidenced in their open letter. Taken together, this amounts to paternalism, the "father knows best" aspect of white supremacy that dismisses the views of BIPOC scholars out of hand and that some senior colleagues in the field still promote. But, to give credit where credit is due, over nine hundred scholars—the majority of whom were white, not insignificantly, and many of whom were senior in rank—signed the open letter to SMT, so I have hope for music theory, at least as it's practiced in the United States. And lastly, if the Europeans (with the three American signatories) "were unable to identify any anti-Black statement . . . nor any attack against Philip Ewell" in volume 12, they clearly have much more to learn about racial matters and how race plays out in music theory, and I for one do not intend to waste any time "debating" them.

Bothsidesing Volume 12 at the New York Times

On September 25, 2020, *New York Times* journalist Michael Powell emailed me to ask for an interview concerning the issues related to volume 12. He informed me that he was working on a story about my "speech on classical music theory and white supremacy," and whether Timothy Jackson "should face any consequences for his essay" in volume 12. Powell mentioned that he had already spoken with Jackson at length, and he now wanted to talk with me. In my SMT plenary I had, in fact, only mentioned "white supremacy" twice: once in quoted material from Eduardo Bonilla-Silva, and once in relation to my father, and the idea that my dad would have denied that his beliefs about European exceptionalism could have in any way been associated with "white supremacy."[100] My talk was not about white supremacy but,

---

100. See Ewell, "Music Theory's White Racial Frame," 1 and 2.

rather, about music theory's white racial frame, so I could already tell that Powell was reading something into my work and framing it from a perspective different from my own. But the fact that he had interviewed Jackson and now wanted to interview me was all the proof I needed to know that the essence of his piece was going to be bothsidesing volume 12 in order to cast doubt on the latent, and not so latent, white supremacy contained therein, and to recast the journal issue as legitimate debate and a legitimate attempt at self-defense. On September 26, 2020, I wrote back to Powell respectfully declining his request for an interview.

I have given many interviews since summer 2020, but I have been steadfast in my refusal to engage in bothsidesing volume 12. And I have noted many times that to do so would amount to taking part in my own dehumanization, which I will never do—my humanity is not up for debate. Incidentally, I take this language directly from African American birder Christian Cooper, who, on May 25, 2020—the same day that police officer Derek Chauvin murdered George Floyd in Minneapolis, Minnesota, by the way—was wrongly accused of threatening white dog walker Amy Cooper in New York's Central Park, in two phone calls that Amy Cooper made to 911.[101] When asked about why he kept filming Cooper's 911 call rather than simply walking away, Christian Cooper spoke of how he wanted a record of the event and didn't want to give in to the time-honored tradition of white women falsely accusing black men of improprieties, adding, "I am pretty adamant about not being a participant in my own dehumanization."[102]

Entering a dispute or a debate *after* publication of volume 12, which is what Powell was asking me to do, would very much play into the hands of the white framing of the entire issue. In other words, to bothsides volume 12 would help the ten core authors of volume 12 enormously, since it would take the focus off the assimilationist and antiblack racism that filled the pages of the journal issue. Additionally, by engaging in a dialogue or debate post factum, it would contravene the core authors' antiblack belief that my black voice need not be heard in their one-sided account of my nine-minute plenary discussion of Schenker and his legacy. But as I've written numerous times already, there was never any debate to begin with, and I certainly won't be part of creating one ex nihilo in order to serve the cause of assimilationist and antiblack racism. Finally, it's worth pointing out here that, at the time

101. Sarah Maslin Nir, "How 2 Lives Collided in Central Park, Rattling the Nation," *New York Times*, June 14, 2020.

102. Sarah Maslin Nir, "White Woman Is Fired after Calling Police on Black Man in Central Park," *New York Times*, May 26, 2020.

of its publication, I had vowed not to read the volume 12 symposium since I could see its antiblack nature rather easily. Clearly, I ultimately read all entries, but I did so *on my own terms*, without hastily responding to something that was so sloppy and precipitous as volume 12 was to begin with. In so doing, I've exerted an agency not often afforded to blackness, an agency that whiteness generally does not expect from blackness.

Powell's piece, "Obscure Musicology Journal Sparks Battles over Race and Free Speech," comes from a time-honored tradition of white men soft-pedaling and obfuscating racism in the mainstream media, and the *New York Times*, of which I'm a daily reader as a New Yorker, is no exception.[103] At issue is the simple notion of objectivity and the mistaken belief that it is attainable when, in fact, it is not. In *The View from Somewhere: Undoing the Myth of Journalistic Objectivity*, journalist Lewis Raven Wallace writes that news outlets

> adopted "objectivity" first as an aspiration, but they transformed it too quickly into a bludgeon, a weapon to regulate who gets to tell stories. And as journalism professionalized, "objectivity" was defined by the bosses, the people in management (usually white men) who generally sought to maintain the status quo. It quickly became a tool for gatekeeping.[104]

Wallace adds that "predominantly white and male journalists in the 1920s and '30s used 'objectivity' to seek authority, to prove their right to tell the truth."[105] There can be no question that, in music theory, white men have used this same false notion of objectivity to seek authority to prove their right to tell the truth about the field. Wallace's work is especially poignant for me because he is a transgender man and, as such, faced enormous discrimination in journalism and ultimately lost his job at National Public Radio's *Marketplace* because he refused to bothsides transgender issues. That is, like me, he refused to debate his own humanity. Wallace has done great work in showing how there is no such thing as "neutrality" and "objectivity" in reporting, and that we must always call out those who claim that there are such things insofar as they often serve as a cover for discriminatory activity.

---

103. Michael Powell, "Obscure Musicology Journal Sparks Battles over Race and Free Speech," *New York Times*, February 14, 2021.
104. Lewis Raven Wallace, *The View from Somewhere: Undoing the Myth of Journalistic Objectivity* (University of Chicago Press, 2019), 63.
105. Wallace, *View from Somewhere*, 65.

As for the *New York Times*, Wallace cites how the *Times* characterized the black female journalist Ida B. Wells in the late nineteenth century as she sought to tell the truth about black lynchings in the South, namely, that the black men who were lynched were virtually never guilty of any crimes at all. In 1894 a *Times* editorial stated that Ida B. Wells is "a slanderous and nasty-minded mulattress, who does not scruple to represent the victims of black brutes in the South as willing victims."[106] So in the late nineteenth century no bothsidesing was required at all—just pure unbridled antiblackness, and this from what was, then and now, arguably our nation's most esteemed journalistic news source, the *New York Times*.

Such news sources are now coming to terms with the history of structural racism in the reporting on their pages, so there is some hope here. For instance, in December 2020 the *Kansas City Star* ran a long piece outlining the injustices it has wreaked against blacks over its 140-year history.[107] And in an editorial from September 2020 entitled "An Examination of the *Times*' Failures on Race, Our Apology and a Path Forward," the *Los Angeles Times* did the same.[108] These apologies from major mainstream news sources give me hope that we Americans can begin to make substantive change to our policies, structures, and institutions. And they also show that such sources, still mainly run by white men, can self-reflect and try to change course. In fact, over the last couple decades there have been a steady wave of apologies from many mainstream American news outlets. *New York Times* journalist Brent Staples notes:

> The apology movement [in the white press] is historically resonant on several counts. It offers a timely validation of the besieged academic discipline known as critical race theory—by showing that what news organizations once presented as "fair" and "objective" journalism was in fact freighted with the racist stereotypes that had been deployed to justify slavery. It lays out how the white press alienated generations of African Americans—many of whom still view the leading news outlets of the United States as part of a hostile "white media."[109]

---

106. Cited in Wallace, *View from Somewhere*, 49.

107. Mike Fannin, "The Truth in Black and White: An Apology from The Kansas City Star," *Kansas City Star*, December 20, 2020.

108. "Editorial: An Examination of the *Times*' Failures on Race, Our Apology and a Path Forward," *Los Angeles Times*, September 27, 2020.

109. Brent Staples, "How the White Press Wrote Off Black America," *New York Times*, July 10, 2021.

However, an antiblack bias in white media outlets still thrives in our country, and Michael Powell's piece on my work and volume 12 of the *Journal of Schenkerian Studies* is a textbook example of how this bias manifests itself in the twenty-first century. Powell writes of Jackson sympathetically, noting that Jackson was the grandson of Jewish émigrés and that he had lost many relatives in the Holocaust. He notes that Jackson has a singular passion, to search out "lost works by Jewish composers hounded and killed by the Nazis."[110] Powell speaks of Schenker's greatness as well, "a towering Jewish intellect credited with stripping music to its essence in search of an internal language," tracking the narrative of western greatness so crucial to sustaining a figure like Schenker.[111] Volume 12 was without question a blowup in the field of music theory, but to Powell, Jackson is a "tenured music theory professor," while I am a "cellist and scholar of Russian classical music," which lends a misleading air of legitimacy to Jackson's music-theoretical arguments while delegitimizing my own. To state the obvious, I am primarily a tenured music theory professor just like Jackson—a simple fact stated prominently at the top of the landing page of philipewell.com—but that's not how Powell framed it, which I imagine was intentional.[112]

But the best proof that Powell's main goal is to bothsides volume 12 is his omission of the most assimilationist racist statement in the whole issue, namely, Jackson's belief that blacks must be "brought up to standard so that they can compete." Powell's omission of this statement uncovers his true intent: to cast doubt on the racism contained in volume 12 and frame it as a legitimate attempt at self-defense. Notably, Powell leans hard into the most *antiblack* racist statement however, the idea that I am somehow representative of a "black antisemitism." Powell writes:

> Professor Jackson's essay was barbed. Schenker, he wrote, was no privileged white man. Rather he was a Jew in prewar Germany, the definition of the persecuted other. The Nazis destroyed much of his work and his wife perished in a concentration camp.
>
> Professor Jackson then took an incendiary turn. He wrote that Professor Ewell had scapegoated Schenker within "the much larger context of Black-on-Jew attacks in the United States" and that his

---

110. Powell, "Obscure Musicology Journal."

111. Powell, "Obscure Musicology Journal."

112. Powell, "Obscure Musicology Journal." My PhD in music theory is from Yale University, while Jackson's is from the CUNY Graduate Center, where I am on faculty, incidentally, though not when Jackson studied there.

"denunciation of Schenker and Schenkerians may be seen as part and parcel of the much broader current of Black anti-Semitism." He wrote that such phenomena "currently manifest themselves in myriad ways, including the pattern of violence against Jews, the obnoxious lyrics of some hip-hop songs, etc."[113]

By highlighting the most *antiblack* statement in volume 12, while omitting the most *assimilationist*, Powell is pushing a white narrative, a white "objective" perspective, of the entire affair. The reason for this is that it is easier for mainstream America to buy into antiblackness (black antisemitism) than it is for America to buy into assimilationism (bringing blacks up to standard). That is, I suspect more Americans will adhere to a black antisemitism, which they can then use against blacks, than they will adhere to the concept of raising blacks up to standard, which is such a common assimilationist (and antiblack) notion that many may not even see as racist at first glance. And it is for this reason that, in my opinion, Powell highlights Jewish issues in his piece and omits "bringing blacks up to standard" altogether. To be clear, black people certainly can be antisemitic just like anyone else, including Jews themselves. But to suggest that there is something about blackness that makes it more prone to antisemitism is to make an antiblack statement. There are antisemitic African Americans because there are antisemitic Americans, and the United States has been, over time, antisemitic because of the white supremacy and white nationalism that has shaped its history.

Powell writes, "They [JSS] called for essays and published every submission. Five essays stoutly defended Professor Ewell; most of the remaining 10 essays took strong issue."[114] Here Powell omits the distinction between the five authors who were responding to a call for papers and the ten core invited/inviting authors, which I imagine he knew from his interview with Jackson. In other words, he puts all fifteen essays on the same level, when in fact it's paramount to separate the five good-faith authors from the other ten. Finally, Powell cites Jackson's desire to "increase funding" for black musicians and "demolish 'institutionalized racist barriers,'" but fails to mention Jackson's paternalistic belief that blacks should "establish different priorities" to effectually aspire to whiteness.[115]

---

113. Powell, "Obscure Musicology Journal."
114. Powell, "Obscure Musicology Journal."
115. Powell, "Obscure Musicology Journal."

Powell calls the statement made by the graduate students at the University of North Texas in support of me and my work and condemnation of volume 12 an "unsigned manifesto."[116] To call this statement a manifesto is a remarkable revision—read the statement and decide for yourself. Powell gives voice to Jackson's belief that "everything has become exceedingly polarized and the Twitter mob is like a quasi-fascist police state."[117] I've not read or watched his many commentaries on and in right-wing news outlets, but I've heard that Jackson often speaks of the Twitter mob, and so-called wokeness and cancel culture, all typical right-wing talking points. What Powell did not do in his interview with Jackson, at least as it appears in his *Times* article, is ask basic questions about Jackson's antiblack and assimilationist beliefs, questions like why Jackson believes blacks need to be brought up to standard, and what that standard is exactly; why black composers are not "supreme geniuses" like those of the white-male "western" canon; why blacks should "establish different priorities," and what exactly those misguided black priorities are; what it means to "profoundly value classical music" and why doing so is, one presumes, a good thing; or what "black antisemitism" and "Black-on-Jew" attacks are exactly, and why it seems blacks are more prone to such behavior than others.

Powell cites the conservative lawyer for Foundation for Individual Rights in Education, Samantha Harris, as an authority, without mentioning the right-wing bias of that foundation. Harris actually wrote an article on the volume 12 controversy for the *National Review*, which also takes the white perspective of obfuscation and self-defense and generally supports Jackson's views.[118] But one expects such an account from the right-wing *National Review*, which conservative icon William F. Buckley founded in 1955. Harris writes that academic debates are best undertaken in academic journals, with which I agree, but that censorship of ideas is wrong, with which I also agree. But what happens when an academic venue, in this case JSS, is used to

---

116. Powell, "Obscure Musicology Journal." To see the statement itself, see Du et al., *Ad Hoc Panel Review*, Exhibit 3.

117. Powell, "Obscure Musicology Journal."

118. Samantha Harris, "At the University of North Texas, the Mob Comes Calling for a Music Theorist," *Nationalreview.com*, July 31, 2020 (https://www.nationalreview.com/20 20/07/at-the-university-of-north-texas-the-mob-comes-calling-for-a-music-theorist). Harris never contacted me for an interview for her piece, but her colleague, Zachary Evans, did, and on August 18, 2020, Evans interviewed me for the *National Review* for a possible follow-up piece. A couple of weeks later Evans emailed me back informing me that they were not going to publish a follow-up story on volume 12. (Zach, if you're reading this, my offer to continue our conversation over a beer in Manhattan still stands.)

promote various versions of assimilationism and antiblackness, in unusual, precipitous, and sloppy fashion, and a university, in this case the University of North Texas, has to place its stamp of approval thereon? Are there no cases in which censorship or condemnation is appropriate?

It's worth citing another instance of Powell's bothsidesing of racial issues in our country, from another of his articles that I cited earlier in chapter 2, "'White Supremacy' Once Meant David Duke and the Klan. Now It Refers to Much More."[119] Here Powell calls the term "white supremacy" contentious in the United States, and, without question, he is correct. There are tens of millions of Americans, usually but not always white, for whom "white supremacy" is utter taboo. Powell highlights this in the article and speaks of how, nevertheless, the term is becoming more common, which is also correct. The bothsidesing occurs when he begins to paint the controversy as extending to black Americans: "But some Black scholars, businessmen and activists—on the right and the left—balk at the phrase."[120] Powell is not incorrect, but framing "white supremacy" as controversial among black Americans is misleading. There is, in my opinion, a consensus among twenty-first-century blacks—and not just with icons like Ta-Nehisi Coates and Ibram X. Kendi (whom Powell cites) and Nikole Hannah-Jones (whom he doesn't), but with countless others, myself included—that the terms "white," "whiteness," and "white supremacy" are not only fine to use, but totally necessary to try to come to terms with America's racial past. Indeed, the term "white" to represent a human race was used ad nauseam by whites themselves in court rulings, legislation, guidelines, laws, and all other forms of official and unofficial documentation, from 1691 (as I cited in chapter 2) right up until today, and especially in the nineteenth and early twentieth centuries.

Of course there will be blacks who take issue with "white supremacy" today—think here of figures like Supreme Court justice Clarence Thomas or Senator Tim Scott of South Carolina, two blacks who most certainly would not support the widespread use of "white supremacy"—and Powell works hard to find black-academic voices who support this side of the issue for his article. But for every one such voice I imagine I could find ten if not twenty black Americans who would take the consensus side among blacks, that it's not only okay to speak of our white supremacist past, but necessary.

---

119. Michael Powell, "'White Supremacy' Once Meant David Duke and the Klan," *New York Times*, October 17, 2020.

120. Powell, "White Supremacy."

Indeed, with approximately forty-five million to choose from, one could find a black person who will say anything. The National Basketball Association's Kyrie Irving believes the earth is flat, and I'm sure you could find other such blacks, but I'm pretty sure the consensus is round and not flat.[121] (I look forward to Powell's piece about this: "Spherical or Planar? Black Americans Debate Earth's Shape.")

A final point about this particular piece. Much has been made recently of the Tulsa race massacre that occurred in May and June 1921, and one of the most important aspects of the many stories that came out was how, immediately, white officials in Tulsa scrambled to call the massacre, in which roughly three hundred blacks were slaughtered, a "riot," which would frame what happened from a white perspective and mitigate some of the murders as "self-defense." It's only been in the past ten to twenty years that consensus has been achieved *outside* of the black community that what happened was no riot, but a massacre, and blacks had to fight the better part of a century to prove that simple fact, that there was no two-sided "riot," but a one-sided massacre. It won't surprise the reader to learn how Powell framed this massacre: "Then World War I ended, and a wave of falling wages, anxiety and racism among the white citizens of Tulsa led to a *riot* in 1921."[122] In addition to "riot," he mentions World War I, falling wages, and anxiety among whites, again, as mitigating factors, which is just icing on the bothsidesing cake of white American historical journalistic revisionism.

Ultimately, we must all see Powell's piece in the *New York Times* about volume 12 for what it truly is: an attempt to use journalistic "objectivity" to obfuscate the assimilationist and antiblack racism that ran through volume 12 in order to frame it, instead, as a legitimate attempt at self-defense. I don't know who contacted whom to begin this work, whether Timothy Jackson contacted Powell or vice versa, but it's clear that they had similar goals. The simple fact that Jackson promoted Powell's *Times* piece in his email to Joe Feagin, which I cited earlier, is further proof that Jackson was pleased with Powell's work, as it accomplished its goal of casting a smokescreen on the racism in volume 12 and generating confusion about the core issues. To see this from another angle, Powell's piece is another attempt to create debate

121. See Mike Chiari, "Kyrie Irving Explains Flat Earth Stance, Says There Is No Real Picture of Planet," *Bleacherreport.com*, November 1, 2017 (https://bleacherreport.com/articles/2741935-kyrie-irving-explains-flat-earth-stance-says-there-is-no-real-picture-of-earth).

122. Powell, "White Supremacy," (my italics).

where there was none, and it seems that Powell, like certain other white men who have weighed in on volume 12, cannot comprehend the racism in the journal issue. Yet they seem to have no problem in citing "reverse racism" in such cases.[123] But this is the history of our country: white men in power setting policies to benefit themselves at the expense of all others, and then crying foul when a BIPOC or female figure has the temerity to expose the racial and gender injustice that the white-male policies created.[124]

Whimpathetic Reactions to Volume 12

I define "whimpathy" as the intense sympathy and empathy that whiteness garners when it acts in racist or antiblack fashion. To put this another way, whimpathy is the flip side of antiblackness.[125] Think here of the countless

---

123. To be fair to Powell, he does not allege "reverse racism" in his article on volume 12.

124. To be clear, crying foul is not the exclusive domain of white men. For a black-male example of such a cry, see John McWhorter, "Is Music Theory Really #SoWhite?," *It Bears Mentioning* Substack newsletter, February 16, 2021 (https://johnmcwhorter.substack.com/p/is-music-theory-really-sowhite), as well as his "Stay Woke. The Right Can Be Illiberal, Too," *New York Times*, January 25, 2022. In the former McWhorter calls Powell's *New York Times* piece on volume 12 of the *Journal of Schenkerian Studies* "exquisitely fair," while in the latter he calls my recent music theoretical work "flawed," though he offers no reasoning whatsoever to explain how, exactly, it is flawed. See also McWhorter's *Woke Racism: How a New Religion Has Betrayed Black America* (Portfolio/Penguin, 2021), in which he outlines his case that the new American focus on antiracism can be called a religion, and its main proponents—Ta-Nehisi Coates, Nikole Hannah-Jones, and Ibram Kendi for instance—its clergy. McWhorter is a regular contributor to the *New York Times* opinion section, and an associate professor of linguistics at Columbia University. Unsurprisingly, I disagree with the main outlines of McWhorter's arguments, which focus heavily on current hot-button issues while diminishing historical facts. For instance, he supports standardized testing and criticizes antiracist efforts to do away with it insofar as such tests were often rooted in racial segregationism. (For example, see Thomas Russell, "'Keep Negroes Out of Most Classes Where There Are a Large Number of Girls': The Unseen Power of the Ku Klux Klan and Standardized Testing at the University of Texas, 1899–1999," *SSRN Electronic Journal*, April 5, 2010.) McWhorter never seems to adequately address the centuries-long history of racism in our country and the present-day ramifications of that history, as the work of Coates, Hannah-Jones, or Kendi—or of McWhorter's *Times* colleagues Charles Blow, Jamelle Bouie, or Brent Staples for that matter—does. For what it's worth, I consider McWhorter a reasonable essayist and a talented linguist, but not a very good historian (and an awful music theorist).

125. Whimpathy is the twin sibling of sociologist Joe Feagin's "pro-white subframe" of America's white racial frame, which I mentioned earlier. Others simply call whimpathy "white empathy." See Ngofeen Mputubwele and Britta Greene, "Ukraine, War Refugees, and the Problem of White Empathy," *New Yorker Radio Hour*, May 6, 2022.

times that whiteness (often white women) wrongly accused blackness (often black men) of sexual improprieties in the history of our country, improprieties that at times resulted in severe punishment, up to and including public vigilante executions, that is, lynchings. I offer this neologism based on Kate Manne's useful concept of "himpathy," which is "the way powerful and privileged boys and men who commit acts of sexual violence or engage in other misogynistic behavior often receive sympathy and concern over their female victims."[126] The same could be said of the way privileged whites who commit acts of violence receive sympathy and concern over their BIPOC victims. For a textbook example of such a privileged white, look no further than the case of Kyle Rittenhouse, the seventeen-year-old young white man who was acquitted of murder charges after fatally shooting two men in Kenosha, Wisconsin, on August 25, 2020, during a social-justice protest.[127] I don't think anyone in their right mind would suggest that Kyle Rittenhouse would have been acquitted if he were black, and this simple fact is whimpathy (and, in this case, himpathy as well) in action.

I have received many comments, emails, and notes that evince a strong whimpathy toward Timothy Jackson, as well as toward volume 12 on the whole. I'll give one long example here since it's so important to understand how powerful white persons who behave badly can garner so much sympathy from society simply because of their whiteness. If the Senate confirmation hearings of Supreme Court justice Brett Kavanaugh were an exercise in himpathy, many of the pleadings I've received over this past year concerning volume 12 would qualify as exercises in whimpathy.[128] Unsurprisingly, the following long email, which I received on August 13, 2020, was written by a white man, a self-identified former professional orchestral musician who left music to take up a career in finance. He began this unsolicited email, to which I never responded and with the subject heading "A note of support and an appeal," with a long exposition of his own past, and how important he considers my recent work in race scholarship with respect to music theory. I'll quote the rest of the email at length here, since this note is so representative of many similar whimpathetic (and himpathetic) notes I've received in support of Jackson and volume 12:

---

126. Manne, *Entitled*, 5. Ellie Hisama has an entire section on "himpathy" in music theory in "Getting to Count," *Music Theory Spectrum* 43, no. 2 (2021): 5–9.

127. For various articles on the Rittenhouse case see https://www.nytimes.com/news-eve nt/kyle-rittenhouse-trial

128. To read about the himpathy surrounding the Kavanaugh hearings see Kate Manne, "Brett Kavanaugh and America's 'Himpathy' Reckoning," *New York Times*, September 26, 2018.

Just as you [Ewell] maintain it is not necessary to "cancel" Schenker in order to teach music theory or achieve racial progress in classical music education, it should not be necessary to do so to Timothy Jackson. His reaction, though offensive, was made from a place of deep personal hurt ("triggering," if you will), because he has had his entire life's work called into question. But if the fight for racial equity and justice cannot be constructive and empathetic rather than destructive and punitive, it cannot win.

When our actions feed right into the disturbing narratives proffered by Donald Trump, who said, "One of their political weapons is 'Cancel Culture'—driving people from their jobs, shaming dissenters, and demanding total submission from anyone who disagrees," we should examine if we are helping our cause or hurting it, regardless of its righteousness. Despite how frightening we may find him and his followers, they do exist and they believe what he tells them. In this case he is the proverbial stopped clock.

You are not responsible for the UNT graduate students' demand letter, or the SMT open letter that received such a large number of signatories. If only those letters did not call for Dr. Jackson's removal from his position, we would not be in this position. Your explicit support for those letters means you tacitly approve of the "canceling" of Dr. Jackson, an action seemingly fueled less by racial justice than personal vindictiveness for the way the Journal was published and its contents. This makes you no better than he in this matter, except you benefit from a massive wave of anti-racist hammers in search of a nail. And despite your own privileges of tenure and access to all the same scholarly and popular outlets as him, a much larger audience, and most importantly, the comfort of knowing your work is important and justified, you still acquiesce to the darkest anti-racist impulses of your allies in higher education, many of whom possess the institutional station to affect these changes without the ugliness of "cleaning house."

My appeal is for you to publicly renounce the calls for the ruination of Dr. Timothy Jackson's career as demanded in the UNT graduate student and SMT open letters, and to regain the core message of your plenary and writings on racism in music theory. The progress we seek in racial equality in music must be constructive and inclusive, and allow for the inevitable "white fragility" to express itself before joining the discussion. To view this as a zero-sum game with winners and losers, or worse, an Orwellian campaign to root out and punish wrongthink is to play right into the political forces which seek to minimize the effects of racism today and mischaracterize its activists as radicals intent on overthrowing America.

Your message is too important to allow this distraction to continue. Despite how valorous it may seem in the cause of social justice, the accusation that this is a cancel mob brings with it an unfortunate element of truth. If "silence is violence" with regard to anti-racism, *es muß sein* [it must be] for cancel culture. You have the power to make things right. You must call them off.

Goodness, where to begin. I am guilty of a "personal vindictiveness" toward Jackson, which makes me "no better than he in this matter." I enjoy the "privileges of tenure and access to all the same scholarly and popular outlets" as Jackson, yet I "acquiesce to the darkest anti-racist impulses of [my] allies in higher education." I doubt that Jackson or any other white-male tenured music theory professor had to undergo a two-year tenure battle simply because of the color of their skin—nor should they of course—as I outlined in my Intro. I would add that my "access to all the same scholarly and popular outlets" is nowhere near what it is for Jackson, or for any other white-male tenured theorist. This is because music theory is generally antiblack; that is, because I'm black I do not have the same access to music theory outlets that white theorists do. Conservative figures will insist that's not the case—"Music theory is colorblind and race neutral!"—but, with respect, they are incorrect, as I'll show in chapter 5.

To this commentator it would seem that not only is my humanity very much up for debate, he would actually place the blame for any troubles that Timothy Jackson may be undergoing squarely on my shoulders, at least in part. In other words, I am to blame for volume 12 and the controversy it provoked. He accuses me of wanting to "cancel" Jackson, but, I have to be honest, I have no idea of what that means and, more to the point, no one really does. "Cancel culture" is a tool of the Right to, once again, confuse and obfuscate racism (and sexism, and transphobia, and Islamophobia, etc.), to blur the lines of what is, in fact, a fairly straightforward, if unusual, case of antiblackness. In a textbook example of whimpathy, Jackson felt a "deep personal hurt," which, I suppose, somehow mitigates his antiblack and assimilationist statements to this commentator, and for which I bear responsibility again, at least in part. In dismissing music theory's exclusionism he writes that the "progress we seek in racial equality in music must be constructive and inclusive, and allow for the inevitable 'white fragility' to express itself before joining the discussion," which is also a textbook example of whimpathy. Finally, when he writes, "But if the fight for racial equity and justice cannot be constructive and empathetic rather than destructive and punitive, it cannot win," he engages in a bait-and-switch by implying that we should not focus on volume 12 but look elsewhere to work for racial justice, which amounts to both mansplaining and whitesplaining the issue of racial justice. If white men truly held the key to racial justice in our country, we would not be facing the utter racial dystopia we currently have.

I did sign the open letter to SMT, as did more than nine hundred others, but that letter did not "call for Dr. Jackson's removal from his position"—it never mentioned Jackson's name at all—so I'm not sure what this commentator is talking about. As far as I know, Jackson remains a tenured full professor and his job is not in jeopardy. And I did thank the graduate students at the University of North Texas on social media for their statement, precisely because they had offered an explicit apology to me therein. The commentator tries to ally himself with me by speaking in the first-person plural—"our actions" and "how frightening we may find" Trump and his followers (how does he know I'm not a Trump supporter?)—but, at the same time, I am vindictive and privileged. Ultimately, he calls on me to somehow save Jackson from himself, to "publicly renounce the calls for the ruination of Dr. Timothy Jackson's career." But nobody pressured Jackson to publish volume 12 as far as I know—he did that himself, with Stephen Slottow.

What this long email shows, as so many other communications I've received, is that when whiteness combines with maleness, it becomes exceedingly difficult to see things clearly from a racial or gender point of view. Sometimes the comments I receive are curt, like the YouTube commentator who wrote cryptically and threateningly in a comment on my YouTube channel, also in August 2020, "You need to leave Timothy Jackson alone Ewell," again, as if I had done something to Jackson.[129] But the commentator whose long email I have quoted was writing from a good or, let's say, better place—I don't wish to unduly disparage him—but even so he just couldn't help himself from offending blackness. Even with purportedly good intentions, his antiblackness shone through. I've received countless such correspondences, virtually all from white men as far as I can discern, and the message is always the same: I am somehow to blame for what happened with volume 12, and I need to take ownership of it and stop pressing the issue.

---

129. See the comment on my YouTube channel here: https://www.youtube.com/watch?v=GL2rql0EMKw&lc=UgxKRl1J0n-_4NlCxGZ4AaABAg

But it goes without saying that, until this current chapter, I haven't been pressing the issue with volume 12 in my writings—that's ultimately just a diversion to my much larger project, which is to press the issue about racial and gender injustice in American music theory and in the academic study of music in order to make them more welcoming for all.

"JSS Is Not SMT"

"The *Journal of Schenkerian Studies* is not the Society for Music Theory." So commented one senior American music theorist in the Q&A of one of the many virtual talks I gave over the 2020–2021 academic year. Volume 12 was so egregious in its antiblackness that it makes perfect sense for music theory writ large to try to cleave itself from the volume. And so it did. At the end of chapter 1 I quoted an article by Ibram Kendi that's worth recalling here. After outlining the many US politicians who claimed, after the January 6 white supremacist insurrection at the US Capitol, that that action was "un-American" and "not who we are," Kendi wrote:

> To say that the attack on the U.S. Capitol is not who we are is to say that this is not part of us, not part of our politics, not part of our history. And to say that this is not part of America, American politics, and American history is a bald-faced denial. But the denial is normal. In the aftermath of catastrophes, when have Americans commonly admitted who we are? The heartbeat of America is denial.[130]

Volume 12 was no Capitol insurrection, to be sure, but the strains of denialism that white persons engaged in after its publication are drawn from the same source. They come from turning away from the truth and denying the ugliness of our past. To say that "this is not who we are" is to engage in denialism, to engage in a revisionist American history that white frameworks portray all too often. JSS is not SMT . . . really? I imagine that most of the volume 12 core authors are members of SMT, or at very least were in the past. David Beach, who taught at the Eastman School of Music for years, is professor emeritus at the University of Toronto, and he was the dean of the Faculty of Music from 1996 to 2004 and, as such, undoubtedly

---

130. Ibram X. Kendi, "Denial Is the Heartbeat of America," *The Atlantic*, January 11, 2021.

had enormous control over the structures and curricula there. Jack Boss is professor of music theory and composition at the University of Oregon and is the *current* chair of SMT's Publications Committee. Allen Cadwallader taught for many years at the Oberlin College Conservatory of Music, and he coauthored a widely used textbook, *Analysis of Tonal Music: A Schenkerian Approach*, with David Gagne.[131] Timothy Jackson is not just a professor, but holds the title of "Distinguished University Research Professor of Music Theory" at the University of North Texas College of Music. Boyd Pomeroy is a professor of music at the Fred Fox School of Music at the University of Arizona, and Stephen Slottow is an associate professor of music theory at the University of North Texas College of Music. Joel Galand, who signed the European open letter in support of volume 12, has taught music theory at Yale University and the Eastman School of Music, and is currently an associate professor of music theory at Florida International University's School of Music. And Rob Haskins, who also signed the European letter, is a professor of musicology and department chair for music at the University of New Hampshire. These music professors are *deeply* involved in American music theory at all levels, and surely have been involved with SMT over the years, and to say that they are "not who we are" would be quite inaccurate. They are, in part, *exactly* who we are, and we must all acknowledge that if we are to make meaningful changes for the better in music theory.

In my opinion, we music theorists, especially we senior music theorists, must all take some responsibility for our current state of affairs with respect to race, for the fact that nearly 94% of tenured music theory faculty in the United States are white persons, for the fact that over 98% of the musical examples in our music theory textbooks were written by white persons, and for the fact that the required History of Music Theory multi-semester track in graduate school commonly features 100% white-male figures. I take partial responsibility for this state of affairs and I vow to work at changing it. Moreover, though it may sound strange to the reader, I take some responsibility for volume 12 as well—not in any direct sense of course but, rather, in the sense that I have been involved with music theory for over twenty-five years in the United States, and some of my actions during this time have helped to create the environment in which volume 12 could have even been envisioned and published in the first place. Or, as I wrote in my

---

131. See Allen Cadwallader and David Gagne, *Analysis of Tonal Music: A Schenkerian Approach*, 3rd ed. (Oxford University Press, 2010).

Intro, "Regrettably, in my career I have been a bricklayer in the fortification of music theory's white-male frame. And, over the years, I have laid those bricks happily and willingly." One of my very first published articles was in volume 1 of the *Journal of Schenkerian Studies*, the inaugural issue, for example.[132] If we senior music theorists cannot collectively acknowledge that, at least in part, we all bear some responsibility for how we got to where we are, I see no hope for the future.

Final Thoughts on "On Volume 12 of the *Journal of Schenkerian Studies*"

In a June 2021 piece in the *Atlantic*, Ibram Kendi wrote:

> This is a precarious time. There are people tired of quarantining their racist beliefs, anxious about being held accountable by "wokeism" and "cancel culture," yearning to get back to the normality of blaming Black inferiority for racial inequity. The believers are going after these [antiracist] people with disinformation. They are putting words in the mouths of Black Lives Matter activists, critical race theorists, the writers of the 1619 Project, and anti-racist intellectuals—and attacking the words they put in our mouths.[133]

It would be impossible for me to catalog all the times that moderate or conservative figures, both inside and outside of academic music, have put words into my mouth and then attacked those very same words. No, I've never said that I hate Beethoven (I quite like his music in fact). No, I've never said that Heinrich Schenker was white (as a Jew in early twentieth-century Vienna he most certainly would never have been considered as such). And no, I've never said that music theory or classical music is racist, which is probably the most common misquotation attributed to me (as I've already written, I generally avoid the tripwire word "racist" in my work, though I have repeatedly said that American music theory and, by extension, classical music in

---

132. See Ewell, "Scriabin's Dominant: The Evolution of a Harmonic Style," *Journal of Schenkerian Studies* 1 (2006): 118–48. To my knowledge, the only commentator to note this fact was, unsurprisingly, Michael Powell in his *New York Times* piece.

133. Ibram X. Kendi, "Our New Postracial Myth," *The Atlantic*, June 22, 2021.

the United States, is deeply rooted in America's historic white supremacy, which is more a statement of fact than an open question). In a most basic sense, the volume 12 symposium represented an official eighty-nine-page jeremiad—at least with respect to the ten core authors' essays—of putting words into my mouth, and then attacking those very same words. In my short November 2019 SMT plenary address, to which volume 12 ostensibly responded, I essentially made a simple plea: let's please all have an adult conversation about race and racism in American music theory. With volume 12, American music theory, at least in the important subfield of Schenkerian analysis, answered my plea: over our dead bodies.

Ultimately, it's paramount to see volume 12 of the *Journal of Schenkerian Studies* for what it truly is: the greatest gift that American music theory has ever received, as I wrote at the beginning of this chapter. Because of volume 12, no one can reasonably claim that race, racialized structures, or racism have nothing to do with American music theory, and from here, the hard work begins. Volume 12 proved that our status quo is unhealthy and unsustainable. It's not without trepidation that I mention colleagues, like the ten core volume 12 authors or the signatories of the European open letter, in a negative light. But it's important to consider just how much power such senior white-male colleagues wield, and how often we are inclined and even expected to excuse their bad behavior in himpathetic and whimpathetic fashion. The amount of power that such senior white-male faculty have and have had is enormous, and, most important, they have all been involved, as such senior faculty always are, in formulating the music curricula at their respective institutions and setting the policies by which music majors, undergraduate and graduate, must abide.

We make a grave mistake if we think that the extreme positions represented by several authors in volume 12 of the *Journal of Schenkerian Studies* are exceptional to, or are on the fringe of, American music theory. What we must now understand is that virtually every music program in the United States was founded on the very same white-male assimilationist and anti-black models that were so clearly articulated in this journal issue. Indeed, perhaps the most unfortunate aspect of this entire affair is how it reduced my arguments to one figure, Heinrich Schenker, when, in fact, my arguments extend far beyond this one person and his legacy. In this sense, Schenker has become a straw man in order to deflect from my extended arguments, since defending Schenker from unwanted criticism is something that music theory's white racial frame has done so skillfully for many decades now.[134] Notably, there were thirteen more minutes of my SMT plenary talk, some 60% of the material I presented that day, that volume 12 never addressed. But I've addressed the non-Schenker aspects of my talk in the other chapters of *On Music Theory*. Schenker is but one piece of a much larger puzzle.

One of the most shameful aspects of the JSS affair is how graduate students were pulled into the vortex of a so-called cancel culture and what should have always remained a matter for tenured faculty to decide. I'm a big boy and I can handle the pressure, but to witness the treatment that certain graduate students have endured because of the volume 12 controversy is truly awful. Graduate school is not a democracy, and graduate students come to study with faculty to learn, to explore, and shouldn't have to defend themselves *from* faculty during their studies. Another shameful aspect is how the ten core authors did such damage to the subfield of Schenkerian analysis. Conservative voices will blame me no doubt, and, again, I can handle that pressure, that injustice, but the damage that volume 12 wreaked has potentially destroyed the field for younger scholars, younger Schenkerians who were interested in Schenkerian thought, scholars who may now have to alter course as a result. A final shameful aspect is how the five good-faith authors, as well as three other authors—John Koslovsky, Bryan Parkhurst, and Nicholas Stoia, who wrote stand-alone articles that appeared in volume 12—had their legitimate research hijacked by the racism of volume 12. Publishing academic scholarship is hard enough as it is, and these eight good-faith authors deserve to have their research appear in an honest venue so that they can use it to further their careers. Volume 12 essentially erased their scholarship from existence, erased those line items from their CVs, which is wrong.

Commenting on the recent assaults on critical race theory and the idea that it is somehow un-American, Kimberlé Crenshaw wrote:

> The hysteria about this putatively un-American inquiry is possible in part because Americans are not often taught about the policies and practices through which racism has shaped our nation. Nor do we

---

134. Loren Kajikawa makes exactly this point in "Leaders of the New School? Music Departments, Hip-Hop, and the Challenge of Significant Difference," *Twentieth-Century Music* 18, no. 1 (2020): 50.

typically teach that racist aggression against reform has been repeatedly legitimized as self-defense—an embodiment of an enduring
claim that anti-racism is racism against White people.[135]

The essence of volume 12 was "racist aggression against reform" that was, in
the European open letter, the *New York Times*, and countless other media
outlets, "repeatedly legitimized as self-defense." Once we accept that simple
truth and allow it to sink in, the reimagining, the restructuring, the healing
can begin.

---

135. Crenshaw, "Panic over Critical Race Theory."

FIVE

On Music Theory's Antiblackness

There is, quite plainly, a war against black people in this country. We will be tolerated if we do not speak, do not challenge, and appear grateful for everything we have, grateful that our lives are not worse. Our successes are treated as opportunities given and not earned. We do not have the right to address injustices or imbalances, regardless of their historical and statistical obviousness, and when we do the campaigns to smother, discredit, and ignore our perspectives are immediate and unrelenting.[1]

On July 4, 2020, as a wave of protests over racial injustice swept the United States, four Princeton University faculty drafted an open letter to the Princeton president, provost, and leadership, a letter demanding action and change that more than three hundred Princeton faculty and staff ultimately signed. The first paragraph reads:

Anti-Blackness is foundational to America. It plays a role in where we live and where we are welcome. It influences the level of healthcare we receive. It determines the degree of risk we are assumed to pose in contexts from retail to lending and beyond. It informs the expectations and tactics of law-enforcement. Anti-Black racism has hamstrung our political process. It is rampant in even our most "progressive" communities. And it plays a powerful role at institutions like Princeton, despite declared values of diversity and inclusion.[2]

1. Howard Bryant, *Full Dissidence: Notes from an Uneven Playing Field* (Beacon Press, 2020), 188.
2. See Brett Tomlinson, "Faculty Members Propose an Anti-racism Agenda," *Princeton Alumni Weekly*, July 13, 2020 (https://paw.princeton.edu/article/faculty-members-propose-an ti-racism-agenda). The four faculty who drafted the letter were Tracy K. Smith, the Roger S.

Antiblackness is also foundational to American music theory, hard though that might be for the reader to bear. It is a theoretical impossibility that America's historic antiblackness is not manifested in some capacity in America's historic music theory. Uncovering some of these manifestations is a key element of this chapter.

Making a difficult topic even harder, some of music theory's antiblackness has involved me, though I have tried to be as unbiased as possible when discussing antiblackness directed at myself. But, as with volume 12, I need to tell some of these personal stories so that they are out in the open and memorialized, since only by confronting our problems can we ever hope to solve them. My goal here is simple and straightforward: to make music and music theory more welcoming for everyone.

The Society for Music Theory's Outstanding Publication Awards

Prologue

I wrote the following section in summer 2021, and there have been some changes to these SMT awards since then. In the February 2022 SMT news-letter, President Michael Buchler announced that the newly enacted "Pres-idential Award" for BIPOC figures in music theory, an award I criticize below, was paused because of a possible "'othering' effect."[3] I agree with this sentiment, and I commend SMT for this step in the right direction. In a white racial frame, "othering" is a euphemism for "anti-BIPOC," which his-torically is most strongly represented in America's antiblackness, and for this reason I include this critique in chapter 5. Further, the fall 2021 Outstand-ing Publication awardees, not represented in my calculations below because of the timing of *On Music Theory*, consisted of three BIPOC persons out of eight awardees, and the Presidential Award was not granted at all. Most important, the language explaining the award, which I cite in this section, has been removed from the Society for Music Theory's website, and the fol-lowing language now stands in its place: "The Presidential Award is on pause for 2022 while the Board reconsiders its scope and definition."[4]

Berlind '52 Professor in the Humanities, chair of the Lewis Center for the Arts and former US poet laureate; Jenny E. Greene, professor of astrophysical sciences; Dan-el Padilla Peralta, associate professor of classics; and Andrew Cole, professor of English and director of the Gauss Seminars in Criticism.

3. See Michael Buchler, "From the President," *SMT Newsletter* 45, no. 1 (February 2022).

4. See https://societymusictheory.org/grants/publications

I do not know why this change took place, but I willingly and happily acknowledge it here. But as I wrote at the beginning of chapter 4 when I cited the fact that volume 12 of JSS had disappeared from that journal's website, I believe that the far less egregious language of SMT's Presidential Award must not be stricken from the record but, rather, must be examined for what it is: an attempt by music theory's white racial frame to take positive action with respect to racial justice, possibly framing it as "antiracism" even, while not realizing that this very action is just the opposite. And, once presented with the reasoning why this is the case—as I imagine occurred in the SMT board's "considerable discussion," as President Buchler put it in the SMT newsletter, about this award—the white frame erases the evidence from the record.[5] So, below, for the sake of posterity, I leave more or less untouched my discussion of SMT's Outstanding Publication Awards from summer 2021, so that we might all learn from the history of these awards, how music theory is framed, and how it reacts when presented with evidence of racism in the field.

The Outstanding Publication Awards

SMT's Outstanding Publication Awards have historically been reserved only for whites and whiteness, which was proven yet again in 2020, with eight new white recipients.[6] It seems SMT is incapable of seeing beyond whiteness, and it can barely see beyond cisgender men, as previous awardees show. By my count, out of 160 awardees in thirty-five years, only four were not white, which makes for nearly 98% white awardees.[7]

Ultimately, music theory's total inability to see beyond whiteness impoverishes the field. Given a few hours and a stable high-speed internet connection (a tall order here in Brooklyn, New York, I might add . . . but I digress), I could easily come up with a list of fifty articles from BIPOC scholars from the past two years that could be considered for one of our publication awards. But once the doors close and deliberations begin, many of these scholars will be crossed off the list as "not music theorists" for one reason or another, and if they are in fact music theory professors, then their scholarship will be called "not music theory." Predictably, SMT "solved" the

---

5. Buchler, "From the President."

6. They were Gregory J. Decker, Jonathan de Souza, Megan Kaes Long, Alexander Rehding, Steven Rings, Matthew R. Shaftel, Mark Spicer, and Joseph Straus.

7. Those four were Kofi Agawu (1994), Robert Hasegawa (2016), Catherine Losada (2016), and Su Yin Mak (2008)—I apologize in advance if I've misrepresented the racial identities of any of the 160 award recipients I counted.

problem of the awards' whiteness not with antiracism, that is, an acknowledgment of the awards' structural whiteness and a concerted effort to award
the existing awards to BIPOC scholars, but rather with DEI and a new
award, the "Presidential Award" for BIPOC figures in music theory. Imagine
if, on the heels of the #OscarsSoWhite movement from 2015, the Academy
of Motion Picture Arts and Sciences instituted a new Academy Award for
actors, the Oscar for "Best BIPOC Actor in a Lead Role." It would be hard
to imagine the severity of the backlash to such an award. Sadly, this is, in
effect, precisely what SMT has done with its new Presidential Award for
BIPOC figures.

On July 31, 2020, SMT president Patricia Hall emailed me about a possible new publication award intended to highlight BIPOC figures in music
theory. She began by expressing sympathy for the rage expressed at me in
volume 12 of the *Journal of Schenkerian Studies*, and then asked for my commentary on this new award. In a perfectly collegial exchange, I thanked her
for the SMT statement on volume 12, and then I responded that, in my
opinion, enacting such an award was precipitous and ill-advised. Nevertheless, SMT forged ahead with the creation of a new award:

> [The] Presidential Award honors a publication focused on composers,
> performers, critics, theorists, or other music-related agents of BIPOC
> and other geographical, regional groups historically underrepresented
> in the field of music theory in North America. The publication . . .
> exemplifies the highest qualities of original work that brings cultural
> and social perspectives to bear on music analysis, interpretation, and
> their theoretical frameworks. Publications under consideration for
> this award are also eligible for other SMT Publication Awards.[8]

This new award, far from being antiracist, is actually racist in "separate
but equal" fashion. The last line of the description of this award states, "Publications under consideration for this award are also eligible for other SMT
Publication Awards," which may lead one to believe that this is an award
like the other awards. But this represents white-framing sleight-of-hand, in
anticipation of the "separate but equal" criticism I now level at this new
award. In fact, I believe that the addition of that last sentence, that tagline,
actually proves that SMT and music theory understand the "separate but
equal" nature of this award perfectly well.

---

8. As I wrote in the prologue to this section, this language has been taken down from
SMT's website.

As I mentioned earlier, "separate but equal" was enshrined in US law with the 1896 Supreme Court ruling in *Plessy v. Ferguson*. This case began with the 1890 Separate Car Act in Louisiana, which required that blacks and whites ride in separate railway cars in the state. Homer Plessy, who was one-eighth black but easily passed for white, worked with a civil rights group to stress-test the system of racial separation in Louisiana. With the intention of getting arrested, he bought a ticket for the white's only car. Upon stating, when the conductor came for his ticket, that he was one-eighth black, he was arrested and detained. The judge in his trial was John Ferguson, and it was his ruling against Plessy that made it to the Supreme Court. *Plessy v. Ferguson* is generally considered one of the worst Supreme Court rulings in the history of the United States with respect to racial justice, as it is the ruling that enshrined racial segregationism as constitutional in the postbellum, and post-Reconstruction, United States. The written opinions in the seven-to-one decision are fascinating and relevant to my point about SMT's new Presidential Award.

In his lone scathing dissent, Associate Justice John Marshall Harlan wrote:

> It was said in argument that the statute of Louisiana does not discriminate against either race, but prescribes a rule applicable alike to white and colored citizens. But this argument does not meet the difficulty. Everyone knows that the statute in question had its origin in the purpose not so much to exclude white persons from railroad cars occupied by blacks as to exclude colored people from coaches occupied by or assigned to white persons. Railroad corporations of Louisiana did not make discrimination among whites in the matter of accommodation for travelers. The thing to accomplish was, under the guise of giving equal accommodation for whites and blacks, to compel the latter to keep to themselves while traveling in railroad passenger coaches. No one would be so wanting in candor to assert the contrary.[9]

Though it pains me to say it here, I believe that the institution of SMT's new Presidential Award is, in fact, intended to compel BIPOC to keep to themselves while traveling on the roads of American music-theoretical scholarship. In keeping with what Harlan writes in his *Plessy* dissent, the purpose of the new Presidential Award is not to exclude white persons from

9. *Plessy v. Ferguson*, 163 U.S. 537 (1896).

this new BIPOC award, nor to exclude BIPOC from the other six awards altogether, but, rather, to make it easier for SMT to continue to award the six previously existing awards—the awards "occupied by or assigned to white persons"—only to whites and whiteness. Harlan continues:

> What can more certainly arouse race hate, what more certainly create and perpetuate a feeling of distrust between these [black and white] races, than state enactments which, in fact, proceed on the ground that colored citizens are so inferior and degraded that they cannot be allowed to sit in public coaches occupied by white citizens. That, as all will admit, is the real meaning of such legislation as was enacted in Louisiana.[10]

Though it pains me to say it here, the institution of SMT's Presidential Award is, in fact, rooted in the historical idea that BIPOC are music-theoretically inferior and should not be allowed to occupy spaces that have heretofore been reserved exclusively for whites and whiteness, such as the previously existing SMT Outstanding Publication Awards. Harlan continues, "The thin disguise of 'equal' accommodations for passengers in railroad coaches will not mislead anyone, nor atone for the wrong this day done."[11] Though it pains me to say it here, the inclusion of the last sentence of the Presidential Award, stating, "Publications under consideration for this award are also eligible for other SMT Publication Awards," is meant to mislead us into thinking that the music-theoretical work by and on BIPOC will be considered to be eligible to sit in the "whites-only car" of our award infrastructure. In other words, that statement is a "thin disguise of 'equal' accommodations" for BIPOC scholars in music theory.

I encourage the reader to read the entire *Plessy v. Ferguson* ruling, which so decimated racial progress in our country, progress that had, to a small extent, seen the light of day during Reconstruction, 1865–1877. John Marshall Harlan, who became known as "The Great Dissenter" in US Supreme Court history, is considered something of a hero to many black Americans.[12] Today we might be inclined to call Harlan an antiracist and certainly not

---

10. *Plessy v. Ferguson.*

11. *Plessy v. Ferguson.*

12. See Peter S. Canellos, "Separate but Equal, the Court Said. One Voice Dissented," *New York Times*, May 18, 2021.

racist or white supremacist, yet, while it is true that Harlan's dissent seems something of a miracle today, he was still a white man with power and representative of white supremacy. He himself owned slaves earlier in life in his native Kentucky, and there is one passage in his *Plessy* dissent that is unequivocally white supremacist:

> The white race deems itself to be the dominant race in this country. And so it is, in prestige, in achievements, in education, in wealth, and in power. So, I doubt not, it will continue to be for all time, if it remains true to its great heritage, and holds fast to the principles of constitutional liberty.[13]

So it would be more accurate to call Harlan assimilationist, which is still white supremacist, based on Kendi's tripartite division of segregationism, assimilationism, and antiracism that I discussed earlier. That is, even though he was surely better than the other white-male Supreme Court justices who were clearly segregationist white supremacists, we need to be clear that white supremacy was still key to Harlan, and surely to other white men in power in the late nineteenth century as well.

Back to SMT's Presidential Award: Henry Billings Brown, writing for the majority in *Plessy*, further proves my point:

---

13. *Plessy v. Ferguson.* A final telling passage from Harlan's dissent tells of yet another historic discriminatory American horror, anti-Asian-ness: "There is a race so different from our own that we do not permit those belonging to it to become citizens of the United States. Persons belonging to it are, with few exceptions, absolutely excluded from our country. I allude to the Chinese race. But, by the statute in question, a Chinaman can ride in the same passenger coach with white citizens of the United States, while citizens of the black race in Louisiana, many of whom, perhaps, risked their lives for the preservation of the Union, who are entitled, by law, to participate in the political control of the state and nation, who are not excluded, by law or by reason of their race, from public stations of any kind, and who have all the legal rights that belong to white citizens, are yet declared to be criminals, liable to imprisonment, if they ride in a public coach occupied by citizens of the white race." From a legal standpoint, this is actually a sound argument, but from a social-justice standpoint, it's obviously disgusting. To all those who have said recently that the ugly anti-Asian activity going on in the United States since the beginnings of Covid-19 is "un-American" and "not who we are," what more proof does one need to show how wrong that idea is than to look at an otherwise just dissent from the late nineteenth century featuring bald-faced anti-Asian language? In point of fact, the United States' anti-Asian-ness is as old as the arrival of the first Asians in the country, whenever that was. White supremacy is nothing if not comprehensive in its disdain for any and all nonwhite races.

We consider the underlying fallacy of the plaintiff's argument to consist in the assumption that the enforced separation of the two races stamps the colored race with a badge of inferiority. If this be so, it is not by reason of anything found in the act, but solely because the colored race chooses to put that construction upon it. . . . The argument also assumes that social prejudices may be overcome by legislation, and that equal rights cannot be secured to the negro except by an enforced commingling of the two races. We cannot accept this proposition. If the two races are to meet upon terms of social equality, it must be the result of natural affinities, a mutual appreciation of each other's merits, and a voluntary consent of individuals.

This final point, too, is painful to acknowledge here. By instituting a new award for BIPOC figures in music theory, SMT is, in my opinion, stamping BIPOC with a badge of inferiority, whether music theory admits that or not. There is no shortage of irony when the white supremacist Brown blames the "colored race" for pointing out the structural racism of the Separate Car Act, while claiming that there is, in reality, no such racism therein. In fact, that is exactly what happened to me with volume 12 of the *Journal of Schenkerian Studies* and its aftermath. That is, many conservative voices have commented that, in fact, there is nothing antiblack or white supremacist about American music theory and its history, or about volume 12, and that I, a black man, have mistakenly "put that construction upon it."

When Brown writes that an "enforced commingling of the two races" is unacceptable, he touches on the one and only true antiracist action in striving for racial equality, namely, the idea that this equality must be forced, since a "voluntary consent of individuals" is not something that whiteness is interested in insofar as this consent would result in a loss, partial but not complete, of power and prestige for whiteness. In other words, only through forcing the issue—only through forcing music theory to recognize work by and on BIPOC figures not with a new award, but with the previously existing six awards—will we see a racially just system for recognizing outstanding scholarship in music theory.

Here we are, 126 years after *Plessy*, and white power structures are still conceiving of nonwhites and nonwhiteness in separate-but-equal terms. To prove my point we hardly need to wait for ten years of data, which will show that the six white SMT awards are still given primarily to whites and whiteness, and the single nonwhite SMT award is given primarily to nonwhites and nonwhiteness. Ultimately, what the new Presidential Award demonstrates is that SMT still cannot understand what structural racism looks like in the field, nor can it understand what a racist policy truly is, like the institution of yet another separate-but-equal method for dealing with non-whiteness in American music theory. The new Presidential Award, broadly speaking, falls under the category of "diversity initiatives" in music theory, yet, like many other contemporary diversity initiatives, this initiative is more racist than antiracist.

My analysis of SMT's Presidential Award reifies the whiteness of SMT's Outstanding Publications Awards infrastructure and shows how the institution of this new award only serves to reinforce that whiteness. Finally, I've stated unequivocally that those previous awards were reserved only for whites and whiteness—no one should dispute this simple point when considering that nearly 98% of 160 awards over thirty-five years have gone to white persons, while virtually all the topics of research were based on whiteness. In making these two points I have exposed the structural whiteness of the publication-award enterprise and modeled what true antiracist work looks like in music theory.

In my opinion, SMT should discontinue the new "Presidential Award" for BIPOC figures in music theory and openly explain why it is doing so by examining the racism in the language of the award. Further, I'd recommend that SMT actively award the previously existing six award categories to BIPOC and those who do not identify as cisgender men, and I think that benchmarks, such as a minimum percentage of BIPOC and women awardees, should be set. SMT could limit the number of awards that any one person can receive to one, maybe two, in total (several awardees have received more than one award), which would force the awards committee to look elsewhere rather than going back to the same figures for multiple awards. Finally, SMT could look back at scholarship by BIPOC beyond the two-year time limit to grant retroactive awards, since BIPOC scholars were never honestly considered for such awards in the past. SMT might even think of granting awards posthumously to BIPOC scholars. I'd begin by granting the Wallace Berry award to the 2001 fourth edition of George Russell's *Lydian Chromatic Concept of Tonal Organization*.[14] Not only would this rectify a historic wrong, but it would also allow SMT to unpack its white supremacist past, in truth-and-reconciliation fashion, apologize to those it has wronged, and explain how it will be better in the future.

---

14. George Russell, *Lydian Chromatic Concept of Tonal Organization*, 4th ed. (Concept Publishing, [1953] 2001).

In the unanimous 1954 Supreme Court ruling *Brown v. Board of Education*, which effectively overturned the 1896 *Plessy v. Ferguson* ruling, Chief Justice Earl Warren famously read from the bench, "Separate educational facilities are inherently unequal."[15] It should go without saying that separate outstanding publication awards, in any academic field, are inherently unequal as well.

How *Music Theory Online* Tried to Suppress Publication of "Music Theory and the White Racial Frame"

I was excited when I opened my email inbox on September 4, 2019. The decision had come back on my long article on white racial framing from *Music Theory Online*. In an email from then-editor Jeff Perry and signed by Perry and incoming editor David Neumeyer, along with associate editors Jon Kochavi, René Rusch, and Bryn Hughes, Perry said the following:

Dear Phil—

Thank you for submitting the article "Music Theory's White Racial Frame," for which the decision is revise and resubmit.

Both reviewers recommended publication with revisions . . .

We require revision and resubmission because much of it is written in the manner of a manifesto rather than in that of a research article.

File 5 is a partially edited version of your article that might be publishable in *MTO* with revision (though of course it would be treated as a new submission).

In brief, then, if the main point of the article is, as you say in [2.4], to debunk and confront, then it is in manifesto form and might, suitably revised, go to *CMS* [College Music Society] *Symposium* or a similar journal. . . . If it confronts the white racial frame and then explores in detail and concretely what the curriculum consequences are, then it might possibly be suitable for *JMThP* [*Journal of Music Theory Pedagogy*].

With best wishes, and thanks,

Jeff Perry and David Neumeyer, editors
Jon Kochavi, René Rusch, and Bryn Hughes, associate editors
Music Theory Online

---

15. *Brown v. Board of Education of Topeka*, 347 U.S. 483 (1954).

I note here that, though signed by five people, Perry did not CC anyone on this email. So, in short, Perry said that (1) they were overturning the decisions of the two reviewers that they themselves solicited from "accept with revisions" to "revise and resubmit" because my work was a "manifesto," (2) I may want to think about other venues for this work, like *College Music Symposium* or *Journal of Music Theory Pedagogy*, and (3) if I resubmitted to *MTO*, it would "be treated as a new submission" and, presumably, have to go through the peer-review process again.

At the time, in summer 2019, with two "accept contingent on revisions" recommendations, MTO's policy was clear, as stated in the "Submission Guidelines" on its website: "With two 'accept with revisions' decisions, the article should be considered as formally accepted and may be listed on the author's CV."[16] The wording for this policy has since changed, possibly as a result of this case. It now reads, as of July 2021: "Accept contingent on revisions. The revisions will be evaluated by the editors, who will decide if further revisions are needed."[17] This new wording has no mention of the article being "formally accepted" or listing the article "on the author's CV." The following addendum was added as well, "Please note: readers' reports and recommendations are not binding: the editors of *MTO* make the final determination on whether to offer publication, require revision, or dictate rejection," again, possibly as a result of my case.[18]

Regardless of whether these changes were the result of my case, they represent more power in the hands of the editors, not less. I believe that it was the overreach of Perry, and possibly incoming editor Neumeyer as well, that resulted in the ensuing battle over publication of "Music Theory and the White Racial Frame." What music theory needs is to make the publication process more transparent, and the powers of the editors should be reduced. When editors have too much power, it is easy for white-male structures to weed out work that challenges their authority, which is what I believe was happening in this case. Also noteworthy is Perry's characterization of my work as a "manifesto," which is similar to the many conservative outlets that have called my discussions on Schenker and his legacy an "attack." For the record, no attack, no manifesto, just scholarship, and a plea for racial (and other forms of) justice.

---

16. This wording is no longer on MTO's website and I can therefore not offer a citation, but I accessed this wording in September–October 2019.

17. See MTO, "Submission Guidelines" (https://www.mtosmt.org/docs/authors.html#Expect).

18. MTO, "Submission Guidelines."

When I forwarded this information to Joe Straus, who had self-identified as one of the two positive reviewers and with whom I was working on the SMT plenary for November 2019, he said he was angry about this, noting that there was nothing about "manifestos" in MTO's charter, and that the editors were overriding the clear recommendations of the reviewers. In addition to overturning the decisions of the two reviewers that they themselves had solicited, Neumeyer undertook an *extremely* heavy-handed edit, the likes of which I've never seen before in my career with over thirty published items, appearing in five different countries, in two languages. (Two of my published articles I wrote in Russian and published in peer-reviewed musicological journals in Russia.[19]) Virtually every sentence had edits, my punctuation and formatting were altered, and rewrites were everywhere. My epigraphs were pointless, my logic lacking, my verbs misused. In short, Neumeyer found a massive number of problems where it could reasonably be argued there were none, at least according to the several people who had already read the work to give feedback, as well as the two official reviewers that MTO had itself solicited. Frankly, Neumeyer edited the article as if I were a student and not a tenured colleague. Of course, we educators know that if you're going to fail a student's paper for any reason, you must justify the failing grade with lengthy substantive commentary. I suspect that Neumeyer's edits were undertaken in that vein, trying to build a case that my article was not really that good. Ultimately, I accepted virtually none of his edits, since I didn't think they were coming from a good place but, rather, from a white frame that does everything in its power to suppress challenges to its authority. Also, I knew that I'd have my hands full with the two extremely thorough edits and suggestions of the two reviewers who recommended publication.

I was working with the entire 2019 SMT plenary panel at the time, namely, Ellie Hisama, Yayoi Uno Everett, Betsy Marvin, and Straus, and I shared this information with them. They were disappointed, and together we plotted a plan of action. First, I had to reply to Perry to find out what the response would be when the editors were challenged about overturning the reviewers' decisions, since the website clearly indicated a different result than what I had gotten, and then I needed to determine if they'd go back

19. See Ewell, "Американская теория рядов в перспективе" (American set theory in perspective), *Музыкальная Академия* (Music academy) 2015, no. 1: 148–55, and "Почему американцы так любят Шенкера (а Римана ещё больше)" (Why Americans so love Schenker [and Riemann even more]), *Современные проблемы музыкознания* (Contemporary problems of musicology) 18, no. 1 (2018): 2–32.

to the same reviewers upon resubmission, which is standard. On September 19, 2019, I wrote to Perry asking about these two issues.[20] On September 20, Perry responded, "As to the language you mention on our website, it's always been the case that we've overruled reviewers when, in our opinion as editors, this is necessary to elicit the best possible content for MTO." And to the second point, he responded: "We will probably re-use one of the reviewers but not the other, to restore anonymity to the process," since Joe Straus had self-identified as one of the reviewers. To the first point, Perry made it sound like overturning two positive reviews was routine, which I simply do not believe. And to the second, a new reviewer, for a work such as mine, could have easily rejected the article, for reasons that should be obvious to the reader by now.

At this point I drafted a memo to Brian Alegant, the then-chair of the SMT Publications Committee, in order to press my case that the treatment I was receiving was unfair. I relayed three main points in my memo:

1. "Reader 1 (Straus) said, 'I find the article compelling and urge its publication in MTO. . . . The writing is powerful, well-reasoned, and grounded in evidence,' while Reader 2 stated, 'This article provides a necessary intervention in the field of music theory, which . . . is perennially white (and male), and significantly whiter than other academic societies in music.'"

2. "On these issues surrounding my MTO submission, I have consulted with four past SMT presidents as well as four editors of major music journals and they unanimously agreed that to overturn the two positive reviewer recommendations that the journal itself solicited breached basic editorial procedure and ethics. I therefore respectfully request that the 'revise and resubmit' decision be changed to 'accept contingent on revisions' and that my article be 'formally accepted' for publication at *Music Theory Online*."

3. "I trust that the irony is not lost on SMT's Publications Committee that these issues all now become part of the larger narrative I am telling about music theory's white frame. I would like to believe that race did not play a role in MTO's decision. But the whiteness of music theory—the very subject of 'Music Theory's

---

20. On my email I did CC all interested parties, namely, David Neumeyer, Jon Kochavi, René Rusch, and Bryn Hughes.

White Racial Frame'—and the blackness of the article's author make implicit bias a real possibility in this case. I would hope that that possibility would lend urgency to my request that MTO honor its stated policies and uphold SMT's commitment to diversity."

Soon after, Alegant reached out to me to set up a phone call, which took place on October 2, 2019. As chair of the SMT Publications Committee, he was trying to convince me to go along with the MTO decision, but I refused, since the policy clearly stated on MTO's website said that I could consider my article "formally accepted" and list it on my CV. Early in the call, Alegant asked a question often asked in situations like these which, frankly, should never be asked, namely, whether I thought this treatment was at all "racially motivated." Please, whiteness, if you're reading this and you're in a position of power, *never* ask that question of BIPOC. Resist that temptation. And BIPOC, if you're reading, please give the only correct answer to give in this position, the two-word answer I gave to Alegant on the phone, namely, "No comment." Life is hard enough as a person of color to have to explain to whiteness why things are happening the way they are. To put this another way, I certainly hope that MTO's actions were, at least in part, racially motivated because, if they weren't, that just means I wrote a crappy manifesto that didn't deserve to be published. The simple fact is that, as race scholars often note, race always plays some role; it is never not-at-all part of the picture, despite whiteness's oft-panicked race-neutral and color-blind insistence to the contrary.

Ultimately, I convinced Alegant that MTO and SMT were legally bound to follow their own policy and accept my article, and he then followed up with others in the SMT infrastructure. I'm not privy to the behind-the-scenes conversations that happened then, but in the end MTO, and SMT, capitulated, and Perry sent an email on October 6, 2019, stating, "We have received two positive reports on your submission 'Music Theory's White Racial Frame' and we are very pleased to accept it for publication in MTO pending additional revisions." I suspect the fact that I was soon to give a twenty-minute talk on this subject at the SMT plenary in November 2019, and the possibility that I could tell this story as a coda to that talk, weighed in MTO's decision to back down. (I actually drafted such a coda, which I called the "nuclear option," just in case.) I note that in the email there was no acknowledgment of the former effort to overturn the "accept with revisions" decisions or the back-and-forth with other interested parties within SMT, nor was there any formal apology to me for the stress that this situation caused. It was as if nothing had happened beforehand, and all unpleasantness was swept under the rug. In other words, the entire backstory had been colorased.

Finally, in July 2020, Jack Boss, as the new chair of the SMT Publications Committee, said on Facebook that he had advocated for publication of my article, which I pointed out in chapter 4. This was, in part, because he was being accused on Facebook, and elsewhere I presume, of taking part in the antiblackness of volume 12 as one of the ten core authors. I saw this on Facebook and asked Boss where exactly he had advocated for my article and he said that he, as the new publications chair, had been asked by the MTO editors to approve publication. So, it seems, efforts to suppress publication of my article extended well into 2020.

MTO's suppression efforts represent the behind-the-scenes antiblackness that normally goes unnoticed, that normally gets swept under the rug, normally gets colorased. It is precisely these moments that we must all interrogate in order to see how structural whiteness works in the field, and how suppressing challenges to its authority remains a key component of its basic function. And again, if there's anything worse than the erasure of blackness in American history, it's the erasure of antiblackness.

Recommendations regarding How *Music Theory Online* Tried to Suppress Publication of "Music Theory and the White Racial Frame"

SMT should consider launching a commission into the equity of its publishing decisions in the history of music theory publications. This commission could comprise outside reviewers made up of majority BIPOC scholars, at least two of whom are black, for instance. Such an investigation could determine:

1. How often, and under what conditions, do reviewer decisions get overturned by editors at SMT publications, and for what reasoning?
2. How many articles by or about BIPOC (or non-cisgender men) have been mistreated and/or rejected? What was the nature of the mistreatment and/or rejection, and how were those cases handled in terms of the language of rejection and reasons given for rejection?

3. How often do decisions on publication at SMT publications go to SMT's Publications Committee? What were the issues surrounding the appeal to the publications committee, and how often does more than one publications-committee chair get asked to approve a given article?
4. How has a history of racial and gender exclusionism affected the overall music theory publication infrastructure over the decades, and what actions can be taken to expand music theory publication beyond the current narrow confines of the field?
5. How can the peer-review process be made fairer, more transparent, and more just, and what actions have other academic societies taken to effect positive changes?

Ultimately, SMT should move to make the editorial process for its main journals more transparent and examine how this is done at other societies, and whether an open peer-review model might be appropriate.[21] As an example of racial imbalance in music theory publishing, by my count, in spring 2021, *Music Theory Spectrum* has twenty-four people on its board, twenty-three white persons and only one BIPOC, Daphne Tan. Further, out of seventy-one people listed on SMT's site on all journal boards for its five official publications—*Spectrum*, MTO, SMT-V, SMT-Pod, and the newsletter—not a single African American person is listed. Then, as I researched the archives I realized that since the inception of *Music Theory Spectrum* in 1979, the Society for Music Theory has never once had a single native-born African American black person serving in any capacity whatsoever for any of its journals or publications among the hundreds of people who have so served in forty-two years of music theory publishing.[22] The first mythology music theory's white-male frame will cite in response to such a statement is that they would have loved to include black theorists but there were none, unfortunately. But this was, and always has been, blatantly false. Here are four very early black music theorists who got a PhD in music

---

21. I thank Florida State University music theory PhD graduate Sara Everson for first suggesting open peer-review to me.

22. As of March 2021, when I write this. I put this question out to audiences for three talks I gave in January and March 2021, and then I put it out on Twitter and Facebook, in February 2021, asking for anyone to "correct me if I'm wrong" about these statistics. No one ever did, so I feel comfortable reporting this statistic as fact. If I'm wrong about this, I'm happy to hear about it. I say "native-born" here because Kofi Agawu, who is a naturalized US citizen from Ghana, once served on the editorial board for *Music Theory Spectrum*.

theory, so early in fact that theirs were some of the very first doctorates in the country. Any one of these figures would have been a great choice to help SMT understand music theory from a new, nonwhite angle:

- Horace Boyer, "An Analysis of Black Church Music with Examples Drawn from Services in Rochester, New York," PhD dissertation, Eastman School of Music, 1973
- Calvin Grimes, "American Musical Periodicals, 1819–1852: Music Theory and Musical Thought in the U.S.," PhD dissertation, University of Iowa, 1974
- Lucius Wyatt, "The Mid-Twentieth-Century Orchestral Variation, 1953–1963: An Analysis and Comparison of Selected Works," PhD dissertation, Eastman School of Music, 1974
- Jewel Thompson, "Samuel Coleridge-Taylor: The Development of His Compositional Style," PhD dissertation, Eastman School of Music, 1982

In fact, there have been many African American music theory PhDs in our country for as long as there has been the music theory PhD, which only began in the late 1960s. When confronted with this reality, white-male frameworks have dismissed such black theorists as not so significant as their white counterparts, in a second white-male mythology. Moreover, our publication infrastructure has not limited itself to actual music theorists, but has occasionally appointed musicologists to our boards. In responding to my April 2020 blog post that highlighted the white makeup of our journal boards, musicologist Mark Katz wrote in an email to me:

> Your latest post . . . particularly struck me. I've been on the *Music Theory Spectrum* board and have twice requested that I be replaced. I've never been asked to read an article and I feel like I'm just taking up space. Not only am I a white man, I'm not even a theorist! . . . Not that you need yet more examples, but I thought I'd share this with you. It's a shame that I've been on the *Spectrum* board when any number of more qualified theorists of color could be on it instead.[23]

If adding musicologists, I could submit a list of well over a hundred African American music theorists and musicologists who could have served

---

23. Mark Katz, email exchange with author, April 19, 2020.

in SMT's publication infrastructure over the past forty-two years. Clearly, in passing over black theorists to appoint white musicologists, American music theory is showing that it is more interested in upholding the structural whiteness of the field than it is in racial justice. This total lack of representation of African Americans at SMT publications is, simply put, antiblack. And, as John Marshall Harlan wrote in his *Plessy v. Ferguson* dissent, "No one would be so wanting in candor to assert the contrary."[24]

In *On Music Theory* I've primarily criticized two music theory journals, the *Journal of Schenkerian Studies* and *Music Theory Online*, though I hasten to add that *all* American music theory journals—*Journal of Music Theory, Music Theory Spectrum, Perspectives of New Music, Theory and Practice*, among others—as well as many such European journals are firmly planted in music theory's historic racial exclusionism and white supremacy. One of the key methods for overseeing this racial exclusionism in music theory publishing has been the so-called blind peer-review process, which I often refer to as the "gold standard" for policing and enforcing whiteness (and maleness, let us not forget) in academic music in the United States. And as I just outlined, it was precisely this process that figured prominently in *Music Theory Online*'s attempt to suppress publication of "Music Theory and the White Racial Frame."

Setting aside the ableist language for the moment—it could be better called "anonymous" peer review, for example—this process, which is rarely anonymous on the part of both author and reviewer, the "doubly blind" review, allows music's white-male frame to weed out work that challenges its authority, and to do so under cover of darkness, without accountability. More broadly, this policing relates to America's historic antiblackness, which is the enforcement method of white supremacy in the United States. I draw a parallel here to philosopher Kate Manne's distinction between sexism and misogyny:

> Misogyny should be understood primarily as the "law enforcement" branch of a patriarchal order, which has the overall function of *policing* and *enforcing* its governing norms and expectations. . . . Sexism

---

24. My own experience is instructive here. I've never been asked to serve on a single editorial board for any American music theory or musicology publication, yet I serve on three such boards in Europe, one in Ireland (*Global Hip Hop Studies Journal*) and two in Russia (*Современные проблемы музыкознания* and *Научный вестник Московской консерватории*). Though admittedly anecdotal, my situation shows just how loath American music theory is to recognize BIPOC and their publication achievements, even when they are almost all firmly part of its white racial frame, as my publications generally are. I'm pleased that colleagues in Ireland and Russia can see the value in my participation in their academic music publication enterprises.

should be understood primarily as the "justificatory" branch of a patriarchal order, which consists in ideology that has the overall function of *rationalizing* and *justifying* patriarchal social relations.[25]

My parallel: sexism is like racism, patriarchy is like white supremacy, while misogyny is like antiblackness, white supremacy's "law enforcement" branch that polices and enforces music theory's governing norms and expectations. And, to finish the analogy, racism is the theoretical branch of white supremacy that justifies white supremacy's racial order. In short, all American music-theoretical publishing stems from our shared historic white supremacy and the antiblackness that drove and reified its racial exclusionism.

Other Examples of Music Theory's Antiblackness

In what follows I will outline some other general instances of antiblackness in music theory. One could easily write such a section about music theory's anti-Asianness, misogyny, anti-LGBTQ+, ableism, or many other forms of discrimination that are part of music theory's history, but for now I focus on antiblackness.

How Whiteness Benefits from Blackness in Popular Music Studies

Volume 12 was not the only controversy in music scholarship in the summer of 2020. On June 12 ethnomusicologist Danielle Brown dropped an "open letter" that had a massive impact on the field.[26] Brown chronicles her career in ethnomusicology, which took her to the PhD program at New York University and then to a tenure-track job at Syracuse University, from which she resigned in 2014 because of her dissatisfaction with academia and ethnomusicology. Brown speaks of her experience at her first Society for Ethnomusicology conference, and how so many white persons were talking, with confidence and authority, about the music of various BIPOC communities in the world. Yet somehow, she writes, these white scholars just didn't really *get* it.

In the music-theoretical subfield of popular music studies, white persons,

---

25. Kate Manne, *Down Girl: The Logic of Misogyny* (Oxford University Press, 2017), 78–79.

26. Danielle Brown, "An Open Letter on Racism in Music Studies," Mypeopletellstories. com, June 12, 2020 (https://www.mypeopletellstories.com/blog/open-letter).

who make up nearly 100% of pop music scholars, especially among senior scholars, often just don't get it, as in ethnomusicology. This is especially true in musical genres that are deeply rooted in African Americanism and that have made it to the music theory mainstream, like jazz and rap/hip-hop, yet, I hasten to add, it can extend to all musical genres that could reasonably be linked to African American musical art forms like blues, disco, funk, Motown, R&B, ragtime, among many others including rock writ large, and even musical art forms that one does not commonly associate with African Americanism, like bluegrass or country. In short, whiteness benefits from and profits off of blackness in popular music studies in music theory, and profits free of charge, which is the story of our country. Addressing how one can actually "get it," Brown writes, "Getting it means understanding that an organization, whose predominantly white members by and large research people of color, *is and can be nothing other than a colonialist and imperialist enterprise.*"[27]

In music theory it's not so much that white pop music scholars are engaging in a colonialist or imperialist enterprise, as in ethnomusicology—no one is doing fieldwork in the Amazon here—but the epistemic core of that enterprise is the same: appropriation, assimilation, and profiteering, all with the intent of legitimizing the art form in question to the white framework so that the black music can continue to be mined for resources by whiteness. This happens not only in the music theory subfield of pop music studies, but with composers and musical artists as well. In "Jazz and the White Critic," Amiri Baraka speaks of the appropriation that happened when whiteness subsumed black musical genres, and how, in so doing, whiteness was able to make a formerly secretive black music "American," and thereby presentable to a mainstream audience by stripping the music of its blackness:

> The first white critics were men who sought, whether consciously or not, to understand this secret [of black music], just as the first serious white jazz musicians (Original Dixieland Jazz Band, Bix, etc.) sought not only to understand the phenomenon of Negro music but to appropriate it as a means of expression which they themselves might utilize. The success of this "appropriation" signaled the existence of an American music, where before there was a Negro music.[28]

27. Brown, "Open Letter."
28. Amiri Baraka, "Jazz and the White Critic," in Amiri Baraka, *Black Music*, reissue ed. (Akashic Books, 2010), 17.

The most egregious example of whiteness profiting off of blackness in the history of our country is of course chattel slavery, but in twentieth-century music composition it would be, in my opinion, John Powell's orchestral piece *Rhapsodie nègre*, from 1918.[29] The rhapsody features black musical genres such as ragtime, spirituals, and early jazz, and enjoyed great popularity in its time. Powell was an utterly repugnant white supremacist who in 1922 founded the "Anglo-Saxon Clubs of America," which, in turn, convinced the Virginia General Assembly to pass the Racial Integrity Law of 1924—Powell was one of the authors—which ultimately led to the famous "one-drop rule" in US history in which anyone with one drop of "negro blood" would be considered "colored." So Powell downright hated blackness and was a hardcore white supremacist, but somehow he found his way to musically benefit from blackness nevertheless. About Powell, J. Lester Feder writes:

> As revealed by analysis of his two most important symphonic works, the *Rhapsodie Nègre* (1918) and the Symphony in A (1947), Powell believed it was as critical to advance a biologically conceived notion of black/white racial difference through composition as through political rhetoric. His musical and political activities were both dedicated to the fabrication of racial difference as an absolute property of the human body that justifies and demands white supremacy.[30]

The most egregious example of whiteness profiting off of blackness in pop music, in my opinion, is blues guitarist Eric Clapton, who began his career with two early legendary British bands, the Yardbirds and Cream. In a drunken rant at a 1976 concert, Clapton infamously said:

> Stop Britain from becoming a black colony. Get the foreigners out. Get the wogs out. Get the coons out. Keep Britain white. I used to be

---

29. For more on this piece and this figure, see Stephanie Delane Doktor, "How a White Supremacist Became Famous for His Black Music: John Powell and *Rhapsodie nègre* (1918)," *American Music* 38, no. 4 (Winter 2020): 395–427; J. Lester Feder, "Unequal Temperament: The Somatic Acoustics of Racial Difference in the Symphonic Music of John Powell," *Black Music Research Journal* 28, no. 1 (Spring 2008): 17–56; and Errollyn Wallen, "A Racist Music," BBC Radio 3, *Sunday Feature*, November 24, 2019, in which I am one of the featured interviewees.

30. Feder, "Unequal Temperament," 18.

into dope, now I'm into racism. . . . The black wogs and coons and Arabs and fucking Jamaicans . . . don't belong here, we don't want them here. This is England, this is a white country, we don't want any black wogs and coons living here.[31]

This from a blues guitarist who owes his entire career to black musicians, whose most famous tune, arguably, is his 1974 cover of the Jamaican (!) Bob Marley's "I Shot the Sheriff." Of course there were immediate apologies and backpedaling, cries of "I have black friends," but the damage was already done. In "The Truth about Elvis and the History of Racism in Rock," entertainment journalist Stereo Williams tells this story, as well as other stories of racism in rock involving Presley, the Kinks, the Beatles, John Lennon (and his 1970 single, "Woman Is the Nigger of the World"), and Elvis Costello (who once said, "James Brown is a jive-arsed nigger" and "Ray Charles is a blind, ignorant nigger").[32] Williams concludes:

> These [racist rock music] incidents are evidence of so much of the troubling heritage born of rock music as a genre rife with white privilege. It can't be separated from the genre's history—not if you're having an honest conversation about that history. The quotes and lyrics range from well-intended-but-callous to careless to explicitly racist, the various musings of mostly wealthy white men whose success was directly related to their discovery and engagement in black art and experience, but who never invested in the reality behind that art and experience.[33]

Obviously, the same could be said of the white men who engage in the music-theory subfield of pop music studies, white men "whose success was directly related to their discovery and engagement in black art and experience, but who never invested in the reality behind that art and experience." This checkered history does not, however, mean that whiteness should necessarily stop analyzing or engaging with African American music altogether, yet there must be fundamental change in how it does so, in my opinion. In Jack Boss's Facebook message that I cited in chapter 4, he said that, by

---

31. Cited in Stereo Williams, "The Truth about Elvis and the History of Racism in Rock," *Daily Beast*, June 18, 2016 (https://www.thedailybeast.com/the-truth-about-elvis-and-the-history-of-racism-in-rock?ref=scroll).

32. Williams, "Truth about Elvis."

33. Williams, "Truth about Elvis."

using Schenkerian ideas to analyze a piano piece by Art Tatum, he "meant it in the spirit of celebrating the work of Black musicians," which he "understood as an antiracist activity." I've found that white pop music scholars in music theory actually believe that, by examining black pop music with white-male analytical tools, they are "celebrating," "honoring," and "uplifting" this music, that they are somehow helping the situation, and that they are, in extreme instances, even engaging in "antiracist activity."

I must speak out against these mistaken beliefs in the strongest terms possible. By pulling a piece of music originally written and performed by black musicians into the vortex of music theory's white-male frame—with its toolbox of beat/flow analysis, charts and graphic analyses, chord progressions and cadences, corpus studies, direct (truck-driver) modulations, form studies, linear progressions, triadic transformations, phrase analysis, pitch-class set analysis, and word painting—whiteness does precisely *nothing* for blackness. Broadly speaking, this represents music-theoretical assimilationism, which is racist.[34] Whiteness not only does not honor blackness by applying white-male analytical methods to black music, it does immeasurable harm, since whiteness only profits and benefits itself, while blackness doesn't benefit at all. And most shockingly, our white racial frame sometimes believes that it is doing something good, something positive, even solving the problem of racism in extreme circumstances. Inherent in this collective endeavor lies a massive amount of white entitlement and, notably, male entitlement, since a majority of white pop music scholars in the United States are, in fact, white men, especially among senior scholars. To state the obvious, if the black musicians who created the pop music that is often featured in music theory's subfield of pop music studies had never created that pop music, there would be nothing to analyze, and pop music studies in music theory, such as it is, wouldn't exist. But again, this is the history of our country—whiteness benefiting from, and profiting off of, blackness, and whiteness then framing this somehow as a noble endeavor.

I can offer two helpful suggestions. First, I suggest that white pop music scholars in music theory who are working with pop music that has some roots in African American musical art forms—and, to be clear, this is most pop music in the United States to one extent or another—make their next academic work a deep dive into race in pop music studies. Discuss the his-

---

34. For a brilliant take on assimilationism in indigenous music studies, see Dylan Robinson, *Hungry Listening: Resonant Theory for Indigenous Sound Studies* (University of Minnesota Press, 2020).

tory of pop musicians who have imitated blackness, from Elton John to the Beatles to Tom Petty to the Foo Fighters, and how blackness has always been slighted.[35] Discuss the music industry and how, because of structural racism, black musicians were shunted to the side in dealing with their own music, while often making money for whites and whiteness. Discuss all those aspects of pop music studies that racism touched, and how that racism benefited whiteness while harming blackness, along with all other nonwhite races as well. And, perhaps most important, discuss whiteness itself, what it means to you, how it has shaped your own career, and how we can rectify musical racial wrongs of the past. Such race scholarship is dearly lacking among white persons in pop music theory studies generally, and the possibilities for white music theorists to do fundamentally needed and cutting-edge research along these lines is, in my opinion, limitless.

Some of the most impactful race scholarship I've ever read is by white persons: Kathleen Belew on America's white power and paramilitary movements; Ari Berman on voting rights; Martin Bernal on the Afrocentric roots of ancient Greece and western civilization; Jane Dailey on the sexual panic behind white supremacy; Jessie Daniels and Elizabeth Gillespie McRae on the role of white women in white supremacy; Joe Feagin on white racial framing; Linda Gordon on the second coming of the KKK in the 1920s; *New York Times* journalist Nicholas Kristof and his seven-part series "When Whites Just Don't Get It"; Jonathan Metzl on how whites are willing to die to promote whiteness; Lewis Raven Wallace on the myth of journalistic objectivity in discussing race; Thomas Shapiro on how wealth perpetuates inequality for blacks; Sarah Thomas and her 2019 master's thesis for Johns Hopkins University on the history of racial exclusion at the Peabody Institute; and James Whitman on how US race law influenced the Nazis.[36] These

---

35. Wesley Morris discusses how whiteness imitates blackness in his contribution to Nikole Hannah-Jones's 1619 Project, "Why Is Everyone Always Stealing Black Music?," *New York Times*, August 14, 2019.

36. Kathleen Belew, *Bring the War Home: The White Power Movement and Paramilitary America* (Harvard University Press, 2018); Ari Berman, *Give Us the Ballot: The Modern Struggle for Voting Rights in America* (Macmillan, 2015); Martin Bernal, *Black Athena: The Afroasiatic Roots of Classical Civilization*, 3 vols. (Rutgers University Press, 1987); Jane Dailey, *White Fright: The Sexual Panic at the Heart of America's Racist History* (Basic Books, 2020); Jessie Daniels, *Nice White Ladies: The Truth about White Supremacy, Our Role in It, and How We Can Help Dismantle It* (Seal Press, 2021); Joe Feagin, *The White Racial Frame: Centuries of Racial Framing and Counter-framing*, 2nd ed. (Routledge, [2009 2013]; Elizabeth Gil-

and countless other white authors have done outstanding work in race scholarship that can rightly be called antiracist. There are no rules for who gets to do race scholarship—if someone says that you can't because you're white, tell them to go fly a kite. What America needs right now is more white persons engaging in race scholarship, not less, and music theory, which has more white scholars than most other academic fields, is ripe for new paths to be forged. True, mainstream music theory journals will not publish this material at first since it will contravene the white framing of the field, a framing that major music theory journals are still committed to upholding for the most part, so you'll likely have to find another publication venue. But good research will always find a home, and one can only control one's own excellence. It's not worth worrying about where your work might fit—doing the work first is most important. Finally, it's worth repeating here that this is not about blame or guilt but, rather, responsibility and accountability.

Second, I suggest deeply engaging with BIPOC figures for your next project. No, this does not mean doing a neo-Riemannian analysis of a tune by Aretha Franklin (there's no R-E-S-P-E-C-T in that). This means getting into the weeds of *the scholarship* by BIPOC musicians on the music in question, realizing that it does not appear in music theory publications since those publications have been effectually unavailable to BIPOC for most of the history of music theory publications, especially when engaging with African American music while not using white-male analytical tools.[37] Music theory takes many forms, and bringing in these different

---

lespie McRae, *Mothers of Massive Resistance: White Women and the Politics of White Supremacy* (Oxford University Press, 2018); Linda Gordon, *The Second Coming of the KKK: The Ku Klux Klan of the 1920s and the American Political Tradition* (Liveright Publishing, 2017); Nicolas Kristof, "When Whites Just Don't Get It," Parts 1–7, *New York Times* (August 30, September 6, October 11, November 15, November 29, 2014, April 2, October 1, 2016); Jonathan Metzl, *Dying of Whiteness: How the Politics of Racial Resentment Is Killing America's Heartland* (Basic Books, 2019); Lewis Raven Wallace, *The View from Somewhere: Undoing the Myth of Journalistic Objectivity* (University of Chicago Press, 2019); Thomas Shapiro, *The Hidden Cost of Being African American: How Wealth Perpetuates Inequality* (Oxford University Press, 2004); Sarah Thomas, "A Message of Inclusion, a History of Exclusion," Racial Injustice at the Peabody Institute, Hugh Hawkins Research Fellowship for the Study of Hopkins History, MA thesis, John Hopkins University; and James Q. Whitman, *Hitler's American Model: The United States and the Making of Nazi Race Law* (Princeton University Press, 2017).

37. I remind the reader that, in chapter 1, I list many BIPOC authors who have published on theoretical topics that would fit the bill here.

forms will only enrich what we do. Also, engaging with the history of the music in question will also make the music theory stronger. Ask a black author to coauthor a work. Form a panel at a theory conference and commit to being the only white panelist. Attend a non-music-theory conference to present your work and encourage the BIPOC present to come back and present with you at the next theory conference you attend. And then form a joint conference with a different society that may have known almost nothing of music theory beforehand. Look for music theory where you didn't before, read music scholarship outside of our main journals, attend a new concert outside of your wheelhouse, and talk with the musicians afterward. Better still, ask if you can sit in on their next rehearsal and maybe play with them. The next time you hire a music theorist, consider hiring a BIPOC figure who is outside of the narrow view of American theory, and then commit to rewriting the rules, the curricula, of what we do in the academic study of our field. Only by expanding our academic purview can we begin to expand our music theory purview. Further, the noteworthy scholarship on black music is not always written by blacks, of course. *Can't Stop Won't Stop*, by Jeff Chang, who is ethnic Chinese and Native Hawaiian, is one of the best histories of hip-hop ever written, in my opinion, while *Making Beats*, by Joe Schloss, who is white, one of the best ethnographies.[38] Schloss noted in the Q&A of a Zoom talk I attended last year that "rap has its own music theory," which is exactly right, and he touches on this theory in his work, one in which he foregrounds black voices. And, as I mentioned in my Intro, Loren Kajikawa, who is Asian American, with a Japanese father and Jewish mother, has written several outstanding works on black music, some musicological and some theoretical.[39] Expanding music theory beyond our "falsely imagined and narrowly conceived" (as the Society for Classical Studies said of their own field) version should be top of mind for us all. And, as Danielle Brown notes, "If you cannot do the most basic of things, like acknowledge the existence of the people whose lives and cultures your job is based on, you have no right to make your living off of them."[40]

---

38. See Jeff Chang, *Can't Stop, Won't Stop: A History of the Hip-Hop Generation* (St. Martin's Press, 2005), and Joseph Schloss, *Making Beats: The Art of Sample-Based Hip-Hop* (Wesleyan University Press, 2004).

39. See, for instance, Loren Kajikawa, *Sounding Race in Rap Songs* (University of California Press, 2015).

40. Brown, "Open Letter."

Why Jazz Is Not Part of the Standard Music Theory Curriculum

On its face, jazz represents the perfect genre for music theory. It has all the traits—melody, harmony, linear progressions, rich scales and modes, intricate rhythms, complicated chord progressions, and formal complexity—commonly associated with our field. Its vocal forms are plentiful, the repertoire extensive, and the lyrics poetic. Jazz spans the tonal and atonal idioms, and has a time-honored and well-developed theoretical tradition stretching back to the early twentieth century. Many of those theories could be used in tandem with typical music theory curricula. Jazz's worldwide impact is not in dispute, and many consider jazz to be, historically, America's most important music. Yet for all intents and purposes, jazz remains at the fringe in American music theory, most prominently in our undergraduate music theory core curriculum. Sure, there are jazz programs at most US music institutions now, but they are still quite outside the generic undergraduate music major, extraneous, an add-on to what is considered the essential knowledge of academic music, the "supreme geniuses" of a so-called western canon.[41]

The best way to show why jazz is not part of basic music curricula is through an analogy, this time to US health care. In her piece for Nikole Hannah-Jones's 1619 Project, *New York Times* staff writer Jeneen Interlandi unpacks the history of US health care from a racial perspective, going back to the Civil War. She speaks of how, in the late 1940s, President Harry Truman made a hard push for a national universal single-payer health care system in the United States, which initially had widespread support. The reason it ultimately failed was that the American Medical Association lobbied hard against it, claiming that government should stay out of health care. Interlandi says:

And what you have to understand about the A.M.A. is that it's an almost exclusively white [and male] organization at that time. Virtually all of its local chapters exclude black doctors completely, and just a few years earlier, the organization had refused to protest the separate but equal clause that legalized hospital segregation. Plus, this is a time when health care costs are rising and private insurance is

---

41. For an inspiring and trenchant musicological account of why jazz is not part of music theory and, more generally, classical music studies after 1945, see George Lewis, "Improvised Music after 1950: Afrological and Eurological Perspectives," *Black Music Research Journal* 16, no. 1 (1996): 91–122.

222 · ON MUSIC THEORY

really taking off. And what the A.M.A. understands is that a national health insurance program is probably going to hurt their profits. And so they've actually been fighting against this idea for years. And now, with Truman's national health insurance program, they take that fight to a whole new level. They've hired a P.R. firm. It's actually the first political consulting firm in the country. And together, they devised this plan to completely torpedo universal health care. . . . In the end, they send some 100 million pieces of literature all across the country. And what's on that literature and what's in those ads is a campaign slogan. It says, "Keep politics out of medicine." They call Truman's plan socialized medicine. They labeled Truman as a communist—and you have to remember, this is during a time when communism was a real scare—and they terrify people with this idea that if Truman gets his way, government officials are then going to be able to intervene in private medical decisions. And when they do, they're going to destroy the sacred doctor-patient relationship. And that campaign works. Popular support for the bill suddenly plummets. It fails to get through Congress, and the health care system the nation is left with at the end of this fight is still too expensive for most Americans to afford and as segregated as it has ever been.[42]

The reader has probably noticed how closely these arguments resemble those from the past ten years or so since passage of the Affordable Care Act in 2010. It's important to note that racial segregation, in hospitals or elsewhere, was not just about the racial purity of whites. Clearly, there was an economic component as well, as when Interlandi notes that profits for AMA doctors would suffer if a single-payer system, and the racial integration that would come with it, were achieved.

One significant black doctor, Montague Cobb, who taught at Howard University, took the reins of the leading black medical association, the National Medical Association, in 1963 and began advocating once again for a single-payer system, a system that would become Medicare, the US single-payer system for Americans sixty-five years of age and older. Cobb had advocated for such a system back in the late 1940s as well, so he was already well aware of all the nuances of the American system. Unsurprisingly, the AMA lobbied against Medicare in exactly the same fashion as it had lobbied

---

42. Nikole Hannah-Jones and Jeneen Interlandi, "How the Bad Blood Started," 1619 podcast series, September 13, 2019.

against universal health care in the late 1940s. But Cobb and others were able to stymie those efforts, and in 1965 President Lyndon Johnson signed Medicare into law. Of course, the 1964 Civil Rights Act and all the other social-justice activities of the 1960s helped to reframe the health care debate, including Medicare, in new ways. But importantly, hospitals did not *desegregate* after the Civil Rights Act, since they had no financial incentive to do so. Medicare changed that. Interlandi says:

> The vast majority of hospitals do nothing [after the 1964 Civil Rights Act]. They don't just suddenly desegregate, and it's unclear when—or even if—they're going to face any consequences at all for that. And this is where Medicare comes in, because Medicare is like a new pile of federal money that's dangled in front of hospitals across the country. But in order to get that money, hospitals have to comply with federal law, like the Civil Rights Act. They would have to actually desegregate. So as Congress begins to debate the bill, Montague Cobb knows that this is the moment to both create a national health insurance program and desegregate the nation's hospitals. And when he's called upon to testify, he says that after two decades of arguing and equivocating, it is past time for the nation's leaders to take, quote, "definitive action to expand access to health care."[43]

At this point those who still wished to keep hospitals segregated, like the AMA doctors, knew they had lost. The speed with which hospitals desegregated after Medicare passed was astonishing: "And so Medicare passes, and what happens is within four months of implementation, nearly 3,000 hospitals desegregate."[44]

And now for my analogy to jazz. From its beginnings, jazz has been deeply associated with African Americanism and, as such, has been segregated out of music studies. (In fact, this is the reason why all nonwhite musics have been segregated out of American music studies.) The reason why jazz was never integrated, the reason why American music studies and, especially, American music theory never truly "desegregated" to become more than just white, is simple: we in the academic study of music never had millions of federal dollars dangled in front of us saying, if you desegregate your music curriculum you can have this money, but if you don't, you can't.

---

43. Hannah-Jones and Interlandi, "How the Bad Blood Started."
44. Hannah-Jones and Interlandi, "How the Bad Blood Started."

It is a virtual impossibility that the racial views of the white-male *musicological* doctors who created our American music institutions were significantly different from the racial views of the white-male *medical* doctors who created our healthcare institutions. In music, we've never had a moment of racial reckoning, a moment whereby we were forced to face our segregationist past, such as US hospitals faced in the 1960s. Sure, everyone knows that racial disparities in health care are still rampant in the United States, but we also know that there are no longer any "black floors" (which were usually basements) and "white floors" in our hospitals. Sadly, American music theory still resides entirely, for all intents and purposes, on the "white floors" of our musical institutions, while jazz and other nonwhite musics are relegated to nonwhite floors: our American music curricula are still segregated.

So, what are we missing? In "One Line, Many Views: Perspectives on Music Theory, Composition, and Improvisation through the Work of Muhal Richard Abrams," Marc Hannaford outlines many significant twentieth-century African American theorists through whose ideas we could study music theory in our music institutions.[45] Muhal Richard Abrams, a composer, teacher, and theorist, synthesized multiple sources into a highly personal sound, and was influenced by Paul Hindemith, Bud Powell, Joseph Schillinger, Arnold Schoenberg, and Art Tatum. Mary Lou Williams—whose *Black Christ of the Andes* is considered one of the finest jazz masses in history—helped shape the modern harmonic and rhythmic materials of bebop and worked tirelessly toward a more equitable music industry. Anthony Braxton's multivolume sets *The Tri-Axium Writings* and *Composition Notes* represent two of the most detailed theorizations of his music, aesthetic framework, and philosophy of creativity. Yusef Lateef's *Repository of Scales and Melodic Patterns* and *Method on How to Perform Autophysiopsychic Music* outline a theoretical framework for creative composition and improvisation that encompass post-tonal harmonic, embodiment, and metaphysical considerations. Roland Wiggins, who influenced Quincy Jones, Lateef, Thelonious Monk, and Billy Taylor, was an official teacher of Joseph Schillinger's methods, but generated his own theoretical framework out of what he called the kinesthetic, syntactic, and semantic elements of music. Olly Wilson composed numerous articles on the relationship among western art music, contemporary music, race, timbre, and technology, among others.

---

45. Marc Hannaford, "One Line, Many Views: Perspectives on Music Theory, Composition, and Improvisation through the Work of Muhal Richard Abrams" (PhD dissertation, Columbia University, 2019).

Wadada Leo Smith published three important but largely ignored explications on experimentalism, black creativity, composition, and rhythm in the mid-1970s, and also created a personal system of graphic notation and groundbreaking theorizations and compositional implementations of interactive ensemble improvisation. Geri Allen's multilayered and formally complex compositions from the 1980s combine technological, harmonic, and rhythmic innovation in a way that foreshadows other contemporary trends. She was also known for her careful mentoring of younger musicians and sensitivity to the gendered dynamics of the jazz scene.

George Russell's *Lydian Chromatic Concept of Tonal Organization* is one of the most significant theories of tonal harmony to ever be published in the United States, and is ripe for exploration in its own right within, and not outside of, American music theory.[46] At once a practical manual, theoretical treatise on tonality, exercise book, historical narrative, discography, and improvisation workbook, *Lydian Chromatic Concept* represents a fascinating account of mid-twentieth-century practices in jazz and in tonality. Russell's "Historical Perspective" outlines the history of the modes, and touches on such figures as Hucbald, Heinrich Glarean, Gioseffo Zarlino, Palestrina, and Claudio Monteverdi.[47] Russell discusses Pythagorean tuning and other tunings systems to contextualize the equal temperament of his Concept.

Significantly, Russell intended the Concept to be applicable to all tonal music. In the "Final Comment" to his work, he writes:

> It is hoped that you have found in this course the beginnings of a chromatic technique—a way of exploring the chromatic possibilities that exist within our own traditional chord-based jazz frame. The Concept is of a jazz origin, but by no means is it applicable only to jazz music. The phase of the *Lydian Chromatic Concept of Tonal Organization* that has been presented in this course is applicable to all [tonal] music.[48]

In the fourth and final edition of *Lydian Chromatic Concept*, from 2001, Russell added analyses of works by classical composers such as Johann Sebastian Bach, Claude Debussy, and Maurice Ravel in order to show the applicability

---

46. George Russell, *Lydian Chromatic Concept of Tonal Organization* (Concept Publishing Company, 1953).

47. Russell, *Lydian Chromatic Concept*, xiii–xvi.

48. Russell, *Lydian Chromatic Concept*, 49.

of his theory of tonality to classical music.[49] It's refreshing to see a theorist analyze "Arline" by jazz pianist Ran Blake on one page and "Ondine" by Claude Debussy a few pages later.[50] But for a mixed-race music theorist like Russell—his father was white, his mother black—there was never a chance that mainstream music theory would have taken his tonal theory seriously in the mid-twentieth century when he first published his work. It is high time that we in music theory, and not only in jazz, did.

I think that the current integration of our music theory curricula—from a class in music theory fundamentals to doctoral comprehensive exams—with other nonwhite music theories is one of the most necessary and exhilarating moments in American music theory's history. Knowing now of the exclusionary nature of the racialized structures of music theory, and how unjust those structures are, we must all come together to dismantle them and forge new paths for the future. I'm always struck by how we, in the United States, can think of European music as intimately ours, but our own American music as foreign. A violinist in East Tennessee can learn all the intricacies of Tchaikovsky's Violin Concerto, written over 150 years ago some five thousand miles away, but never dare play that same violin in an Appalachian fiddling style, which happens right now in their own backyard. Our promotion of music theory's European "supreme geniuses" at the expense of so many American genres, and not just jazz and bluegrass of course, has greatly impoverished our American music institutions. We can enrich them all by understanding not only that many American and other global musics deserve our attention, but that the European "masters" were actually just composers like all others, composers who wrote interesting music also deserving of attention but not inherently better, richer, or more complex than other musics of our planet. This point is, ultimately, much larger than just music theory. The missions of our music schools, departments, and conservatories were conceived decades ago, if not more than a century ago, and the racialized hierarchical legacy of privileging European music over our own is still very much alive and well in the United States—this is something we must all confront as we forge new paths in the twenty-first century.[51]

---

49. George Russell, *Lydian Chromatic Concept of Tonal Organization*, 4th ed. (Concept Publishing, 2001), 152 (Bach), 155 (Ravel), 199 (Debussy).

50. Russell, *Lydian Chromatic Concept*, 4th ed., 194–99.

51. Two works that discuss the need for musical institutional restructuring are Loren Kajikawa, "The Possessive Investment in Classical Music: Confronting Legacies of White Supremacy in U.S. Schools and Departments of Music," in *Seeing Race Again: Countering Colorblindness across the Disciplines*, ed. Kimberlé Williams Crenshaw, Luke Charles Harris,

Antiblack Hate Directed at Me for My Antiracist Work in Music Theory

I've labeled the hate folder on my computer desktop *Ненависть*, which is Russian for "hate," a repository for all the abhorrent messages I've gotten since my SMT plenary talk in November 2019. I do this so I don't accidentally show "Hate Folder" to the many shared-screen audiences we've all gotten accustomed to during the Zoom era of the pandemic. Black ESPN sports journalist Howie Bryant calls the hate folder on his computer his "Back to Africa File," since this was one of the racist tropes he often encountered when he worked as a sports columnist for the *Boston Herald*.[52] That black race scholars need to have hate folders on their computer desktops is telling: whiteness will always reserve the right to put blackness in its place, reserve the right to enact Elijah Anderson's "nigger moment," if whiteness doesn't like blackness's account of an event.

In the following three sections I'll give examples of some of the antiblack hate that I've received since summer 2020, and I'll categorize it in three categories: mild, moderate, and severe. In offering these examples I'll not be exhaustive—I've received far more hate mail than I wish to print here—but, rather, illustrative. It's important for the reader to understand just how apoplectic whiteness can be when challenged by nonwhiteness.[53] For the record, all these commentators, whom I will not name, are white men, as far as I can discern.

MILD ANTIBLACKNESS

1. From a comment to my blog post "Beethoven Was an Above-Average Composer: Let's Leave It at That," July 31, 2020:

Daniel Martinez HoSang, and George Lipsitz (University of California Press, 2019), 155–74; and Patricia Shehan Campbell, Juan Chattah, Lee Higgins, Victoria Lindsay Levine, David Myers, David Rudge, Timothy Rice, and Ed Sarath, "Transforming Music Study from Its Foundations: A Manifesto for Progressive Change in the Undergraduate Preparation of Music Majors. Report of the Task Force on the Undergraduate Music Major," *College Music Society*, 2014 (https://www.music.org/pdf/pubs/tfumm/TFUMM.pdf).

52. Bryant, *Full Dissidence*, 175.

53. For a much more exhaustive account of antiblack hate directed at blackness for its race scholarship, I encourage the reader to read George Yancy's *Backlash: What Happens When We Talk Honestly about Racism in America* (Rowman & Littlefield, 2018), which catalogs the massive amount of hate mail that Yancy received after his famous *New York Times* piece, "Dear White America," from December 2015. Yancy does a magisterial job in explaining how whiteness can react and overreact when conversations turn to race and whiteness and when challenged about white privilege and entitlement.

What's really under attack in this article isn't whiteness. It's the idea of exceptionalism itself. I find it telling that as skeptical as the author is about Beethoven's greatness, he doesn't point to any neglected composers from the same time period. If there are composers who were marginalized due to race and sex, let's by all means discover them. This article really just seems a rant against a composer because of his race and sex. How does merely inverting the hierarchy indicate progress?

2. From another comment on my Beethoven blog post, September 14, 2020:

Sorry to sink your association chain regarding "master." The original terms were coined in German. They are Meister and therefore Meisterwerk. The term Meister stems from the system of guilds which only permitted Meister to train apprentices. As still today in Germany these Meister have to provide a specimen of their craft (Meisterstück) and pass an extensive knowledge test. Until the early 20th century art and artisanship were closely related to craftsmanship.

In the first comment, while I'm not "attacking" exceptionalism, I am most certainly challenging it, since that is one of the main rubrics offered by white-male frameworks to justify their existence, so this commentator is not entirely incorrect, but he is clearly uninterested in examining why and how exceptionalism was used as a justification to promote whiteness and maleness. The simple fact that literally 100% of the most "exceptional" composers in the western canon were white men proves that this is not coincidental. Also, his comment on "inverting the hierarchy" is one conservative voices often make about race scholars, especially black race scholars. There's just one problem: no self-respecting race scholar would ever suggest that "inverting the hierarchy," in which women of color are on top and white men on the bottom, is the solution—this is a fabrication of right-wing media. Race scholars do suggest listening to, for example, women of color, since they have rarely been listened to before, but we generally have no vertical hierarchy at all, only a very large horizontal axis of human beauty, which most certainly includes white men.

In the second comment, this person, and several others by the way, took issue with my simple suggestion that "master" and its derivatives (e.g., "masterwork") had, in part, a racist connotation, since enslaved African Americans were forced to call their owners "master" in the history of slavery in the United States. In other words, "master," from the master/slave distinction, carries a racist connotation, among other connotations. What's remarkable in all these commentaries, usually from white men and generally from Europe, is that they simply can't entertain the idea that *one* of the meanings of English "master" had racist connotations, thus sweeping the perspective of blackness under the rug, erasing blackness (and antiblackness) from existence, in another instance of what I call "colorasure." That is, the black American interpretation of that word, in *one* of its meanings, doesn't exist. I have a pretty good reading comprehension of German, and my Russian is fluent on all counts, and Russian *Мастер* is used more or less exactly as *Meister* is in German, and I understand the word and its etymology perfectly well. Unfortunately, certain white men cannot even begin to consider that the word has one other meaning in English in the United States, one that is undoubtedly racist.

MODERATE ANTIBLACKNESS

1. From my YouTube channel, September 2020 (I've removed the following message):

   Ewell is a charlatan. His rants about musical theory are worthless at best and dangerous for our culture at worst.

2. From an unsolicited email, December 24, 2020:

   I was told you resent white male greatness, here is an article that went viral, and will make you even more resentful: [URL link omitted].

3. From an unsolicited email, September 8, 2020:

   We are in such a great moment in our culture. Tearing down the work of those evil WASP and Jewish musical geniuses, who were only looking to make blacks in America miserable, is brave work sir! Jumping on the hood martyr band wagon, at this moment! Wow! So woke. Screw Vivaldi.

   I look forward to studying the great musical geniuses of sub Saharan Africa. And enjoying their works. I would also like to enjoy all art from the region . . . painting, theatre, literature, and philosophy. I'm having trouble finding anything, but I'll press onward. Stay Woke!

4. From an unsolicited email, August 14, 2021:

> Philip,
> Years ago, we spoke briefly during [time and place withheld]. . . . I found you to be a very pleasant person.
> Well, now is your time. If you listen to a classical piece of music without knowing anything about the composer, can you determine the color of the composer's skin? If you can, you have a special skill that probably ranks up there with party tricks like sticking a spoon to one's nose.
> You were born black. I was born white. According to you, I guess that means that I won and you lost. Obsess about that all you want. It is your lifetime, spend it the way you choose.
> I hear you hate Beethoven. I wait for the premiere performance of Philip Ewell's Ninth Symphony. I am sure it will put Beethoven's to shame. But it won't if Philip Ewell never writes it because he is wallowing in the pool of victimhood.
> It seems to me that decomposition is your goal, not spending every moment inspiring your students to learn all they can from past composers, no matter their color, so they may create incredible art that stands on the shoulders of those composers long dead.
> Maybe you are right and everything about this nation's past is racist. Maybe you will never achieve the lasting fame that Beethoven enjoys. Please tell that to the likes of Michael Jordan, Oprah Winfrey, Tiger Woods and Barack Obama. Maybe they missed the memo.

SEVERE ANTIBLACKNESS (CONTENT WARNING: THIS SECTION INCLUDES VILE LANGUAGE THAT THE READER MAY FIND OFFENSIVE):

1. From an unsolicited email, February 13, 2022:

> Why don't you focus on REAL black problems?
> Number one cause of young black deaths? Other black guys.
> What area has highest crime rate in any city? Black areas.
> Why are so many blacks in prison? They commit crimes.

Who is responsible for the crime and murder rate in the country? Yo' home boys.

Face of crime in America? Young black men.

67% of black kids live with only a mom as their "babies Daddy" isn't raising or supporting them.

How many other kids did he spawn?

What race does worse in school? Black kids.

I mean damn, they are now trying to dumb down or do away with test as certain "racial groups" are too dumb to take them.

I get a real kick out of black kids in Malcolm X shirts:

He didn't support smoking.

He didn't support drinking.

He didn't support taking drugs.

He didn't believe in premarital sex.

So tell me, what do black kids get from him?

How about looking in a mirror, see what the real problems are and address them?

There is a TOTAL MORAL BREAKDOWN IN THE BLACK COMMUNITY.

But it is just too easy to blame "whitey" instead of accepting responsibility.

Ya feel me?

And as far as music theory being "racist"?

Get a life.

Dumbass.

2. From my YouTube channel, in which I played a piece, "In Memoriam," with my son Kazimir, March 2021 (I've removed the following message):[54]

You sure he [my son] isn't adopted? Imagine being adopted by a racist like Ewell and then having to be raised by someone who thinks you should be ashamed of your own skin color. What a nightmare. Where's the wife? (Assuming of course). An investigation should be conducted here.

---

54. See "In Memoriam," which honors the many black lives lost to police violence in the United States, on YouTube here: https://youtu.be/GL2rql0EMKw. In this video the reader will notice that my son gives the appearance of being white.

3. From an unsolicited Facebook direct message, March 8, 2021:

> You are the dumbest piece of fuck I have ever seen. You wrote an
> article claiming that music theory was racist. I grew up studying
> music theory and I am passionate about it. You seem to want to
> break down my understanding of music and replace it with some-
> thing different. Fuck you for trying to do that. Kill yourself.

4. From an unsolicited email, August 28, 2020:

> WHY YOU FUCKIN PLAY WHITEY INSTRUMENT NIGGA?

5. From an unsolicited Facebook direct message, February 13, 2021:

> Fucking disgusting nigger.
> Fucking mutant.
> You fucking monkey piece of shit.
> Hate white people but you went after the white man's daughter
> because you know that black women are trash.
> You deserve to be beaten to death nigger.

I've worked with Hunter College's administration, security personnel, and legal advisers and they have been outstanding in support of my work and in protection of my safety. Because of this last message, I ended up talking with the FBI, and we continue to monitor the situation. (The field officer assigned to my case was a black woman, so thanks to the FBI for that I suppose.) Note this person's use of "mutant," a word directed at me because of my mixed-race heritage. Indeed, there is an entire lexicon for mixed-race antiblack hate in our country, and the most vile messages—with "mongrel" and "half-breed" the other two most common slurs—usually go down this path. Aside from the constant influx of such hate—I have received hand-written letters, voice messages, and countless unsolicited communication to email and on social media—I am often the target of hackers, on my social media accounts and otherwise online. If you'd told me some years ago that, simply by talking about race in music theory, I'd receive this kind of anger, I'd have said you were delusional, yet here we are. I include these antiblack messages to show that racial justice is a real struggle no matter what the arena, and the stakes are high. Those people who want to continue the racial status quo, usually but not always white persons and, among them, usually but not always men, are aggressively and violently lashing out at those who seek racial and other forms of justice, and we must not back down in the face of such horrors. Rather, we who stand for racial justice—we who are white, black, and of all other races—must stand united in the face of such aggressive and violent actors, and defeat them.

Final Thoughts on "On Music Theory's Antiblackness"

> To ascribe racism to an individual pathology is to move the conversation away from where it needs to dwell: the collective pathology of a field [classics] that lacks the courage to acknowledge its historical and ongoing inability to value scholars from underrepresented groups.[55]

As I've shown in this chapter, music theory's antiblackness runs far deeper than volume 12 of the *Journal of Schenkerian Studies*. And it runs the gamut, from the subtlest behind-the-scenes antiblackness to the most overt and ugly forms. In this era of Black Lives Matter, we've seen everyone in music theory emerge as allies and trumpet our cause as black Americans, yet this allyship is often superficial. But if black lives truly do matter, music theory, and its main governing body in the United States, the Society for Music Theory, will take black perspectives seriously and react to our calls to action.

In "When Culture Really Began to Reckon with White Privilege," Salamishah Tillet writes:

> While these new [antiracist] measures range from the cosmetic to the substantive, they begin to chip away at a truth that Black artists have always known: that the only way to achieve equity is to expose how white privilege exists from top to bottom in many of these cultural institutions, making it nearly impossible for artists of color to tell their stories on their own terms.[56]

In this chapter, I told stories on my own terms, without the sanitizing that always occurs when whiteness takes hold of the narrative. I told stories without whiteness interrupting and insisting that no, that's not what happened

55. Dan-el Padilla Peralta, "Some Thoughts on AIA-SCS 2019," Medium.com, January 7, 2019 (https://medium.com/@danelpadillaperalta/some-thoughts-on-aia-scs-2019-d6a480a1812a).

56. Salamishah Tillet, "When Culture Really Began to Reckon with White Privilege," *New York Times*, December 9, 2020.

there; no, Phil's interpretation is all wrong; no, race played no role in that decision. Further, I have shown how white privilege exists from top to bottom in music theory, and how that white privilege often manifests itself in antiblackness. As Tillet notes about cultural institutions, the institution of music theory has made it nearly impossible for theorists of color to tell their stories on their own terms. In her piece, Tillet was commenting on a now-famous open letter from summer 2020, which I call "the summer of open letters," from BIPOC theatermakers about white supremacy and racial injustice in the theater industry.[57] Tillet adds:

> Landing in inboxes and on Instagram soon after Black Lives Matter activists took to the streets all over the country to protest the police killing of George Floyd, this open letter—like so many others in literature, arts and journalism—set out to expose how white gatekeepers and predominantly white-led cultural institutions systematically oppress artists and audiences of color that they claim to support.

This has been one of the main goals of this chapter, to expose how white gatekeepers and predominantly white-led music theory systematically oppress artists of color *that they claim to support*. None of this is altogether easy, yet I hope that one day music theory will have many more African American and BIPOC tenured professors making these points and not just the small handful of us who are making such points now, more such voices that can stand up to our structural and institutional whiteness, so that we can all—blacks, whites, and folks of all other races—enjoy a culturally inclusive and racially diverse music theory in the future.

57. See the open letter from BIPOC theatermakers here: https://www.weseeyouwat.com

SIX

On Classical Music's Antisemitism

When we add it all up, the right conclusion is this: American white supremacy, and to some extent Anglophone white supremacy more broadly, provided, to our collective shame, some of the working materials for the Nazism of the 1930s.[1]

I was excited as I nestled into my seat at the Mariinsky Theater for Opera and Ballet, formerly the Kirov Theater for Opera and Ballet, in Saint Petersburg, Russia, on October 17, 2017, for a performance of Sergei Prokofiev's *Обручение в монастыре* (Betrothal at a monastery), which first premiered at the very same theater on November 3, 1946. I had the good fortune of spending the 2017–2018 academic year in Moscow with my wife and our son, and to see this Prokofiev opera I had traveled from Moscow to Saint Petersburg on the high-speed bullet train. (Yes, they have a network of those in Russia, which pains me to say as a train-loving American who has suffered many Amtrak-induced indignities . . . but I digress.) I was especially excited to hear two Russian operatic legends, both People's Artists of the Russian Federation, Larissa Diadkova, singing the role of the Duenna, and Sergei Aleksashkin, singing the role of Isaac Mendoza.

I knew little of the opera, set in eighteenth-century Seville, Spain, at that point, but noticed in the program that Mendoza was a "Portuguese Jew." Prokofiev's libretto was based on another libretto, by the Englishman Richard Brinsley Sheridan, for a three-act comic opera called *The Duenna*, which premiered at Covent Garden in 1775. In a bit of research on the opera, I read in Richard Taruskin's *Oxford Music Online* entry, "In particular, the character

---

1. James Q. Whitman, *Hitler's American Model: The United States and the Making of Nazi Race Law* (Princeton University Press, 2017), 145.

236 · ON MUSIC THEORY

of Mendoza is considerably softened in Prokofiev's treatment, and Sheridan's blatant anti-Semitism is as far as possible erased."[2] So I didn't think much of it beforehand, but as I watched Mendoza, a certain uneasiness set in. I could see Jewish stereotypes, caricatures, and plain old antisemitism as I watched.[3]

A famous recording of the opera from 1998, which you can find now on YouTube, is in the same staging that I saw in 2017.[4] And though most voices and the conductor were different, I was able to see and hear Diadkova and Aleksashkin as the Duenna and Mendoza in 2017 as they appear in the 1998 YouTube recording. On the recording, in Act 2, Scene 3, Louisa, played by Anna Netrebko, and Clara, played by Marianna Tarassova, discuss their amorous woes, while Mendoza, played by Aleksashkin, enters with Don Carlos, played by Yuri Shkliar. At 58'30" of the recording, notice how Mendoza is depicted, as the "Jewish Fish Merchant," as he's described in the libretto. As I saw this same depiction in 2017, peering through my opera glasses, I thought to myself: "Hang on, is that a prosthetic nose on Mendoza?" Mendoza cleans his beard and then reaches into his large nose to pull out a nose hair, in quite uncouth fashion. This remarkable depiction of Mendoza the Jew, and of Jewishness, made me squirm. I felt that this was not so different from the horrors of American blackface minstrelsy, in which blacks are similarly maligned and dehumanized. About blackface minstrelsy, *New York Times* columnist Brent Staples writes:

> The white men who donned tattered clothing and blackened themselves with burned cork introduced working-class patrons who had never so much as met an African-American to the dimwitted stereotype whose bulging eyes, rubbery lips and mangled speech would become ubiquitous in newspapers, radio, television, movies and advertising.[5]

I asked myself how this depiction of Mendoza in this production of *Betrothal* was any different. All the antisemitic stereotypes are there, and the

---

2. Richard Taruskin, "Betrothal in a Monastery," *Oxford Music Online*, 2002.

3. I, like historian Deborah Lipstadt, spell the term "antisemitism," which I take to mean, broadly speaking, hatred of Jews, with a lowercase "a" and without the hyphen. In short, there is no such thing as a "Semitic" people to be against, and the term was popularized by German journalist Wilhelm Marr in the late nineteenth century to mean, specifically, hatred of Jews, as German *Antisemitismus*. For more on this see Lipstadt, *Antisemitism, Here and Now* (Knopf Doubleday, 2019), 26–29.

4. Here is the YouTube link: https://youtu.be/BmLm-UymL24

5. Brent Staples, "How Blackface Feeds White Supremacy," *New York Times*, March 31, 2019.

intention is the same: entertainment with the purpose of dehumanizing a given group of people, portraying Jews in this case as a stereotype worthy of mockery to audiences who likely had never even "so much as met" a Jew. And when someone questions these black or Jewish caricatures, the answer always seems to be the same: Why can't you take a joke? This is all meant in jest! I suppose this works fine if you're not the one being dehumanized, though I'd certainly hope that anyone could see the injustice.

When the Kirov Opera brought this production to New York's Metropolitan Opera in 1998, James Oestreich wrote in a *New York Times* review:

> The lively Kirov production . . . scores heavily on the anticlerical front but should perhaps not be absolved so quickly in its portrayal of Mendoza, a Portuguese Jew. Sergei Aleksashkin, who sings the role, is made up with bloated facial features in too ready compliance with the tone of the libretto's dismissals of the character ("that old orangutan" and "you hairy ape," in the Met titles).[6]

To be clear, it wasn't "bloated facial features" but, rather, a prosthetic nose! That is, the Kirov's makeup artists made up Sergei Aleksashkin with a prosthetic nose and other ghastly looking makeup that, in their opinion, somehow reflected Jews and Jewishness. But in fact, in the history of classical music, in Russia and here in the United States, we are too often inclined to "absolve" all kinds of anti-Jewishness in our music academy. (And to be clear, Oestreich was not suggesting that we absolve the antisemitism of the production.) And what does this absolution, this shunting to the side of classical music's antisemitism, ultimately do? It normalizes and even legitimizes antisemitism and anti-Jewish beliefs.

Example 6.1 shows the music that accompanies Mendoza as he first notices the much younger Louisa. Between Rehearsal 204 and 205 all twelve notes of the chromatic scale sound, and the general feeling of the music is ominous and dissonant. Several tonal centers are suggested, but the excerpt is not clearly in any one diatonic key. At the beginning, the perfect harmonic fifth of A♭ to E♭ in the lower voices points to an A♭ centricity, but the toggling between C♯ and D in the middle voice clashes with that centricity. E♭ minor/major is suggested in m. 6 of the excerpt if we look at the chords in the bass clef, but the melody in the treble clef, played

---

6. James Oestreich, "Opera Review; A Bit of Bias Covered in Froth," *New York Times*, April 28, 1998. "Met titles" are the way the Metropolitan Opera does supertitles, not above the stage but on the back of every seat in the hall, to be controlled by each viewer, in order to not disturb what's happening on stage.

Example 6.1. Prokofiev, *Betrothal at a Monastery* (1946), Act 2, Scene 3, Rehearsal 204, when Mendoza notices Louisa

by the oboes in the score, suggest D or G as tonal center. At the end of the excerpt, if D is heard as ^5, G minor might be a possible key center, but the real intent here is to evoke a sinister and cloudy texture, with no clear tonality or centricity. The vocal line, equally sinister and lecherous with ascending and descending minor ninths, is quite unusual for vocal writing. Mendoza here speaks of Louisa's *мордашка* (her "mug," i.e., her face) and how she's flirting with him through her eyelashes and downturned eyes.

Example 6.2. Prokofiev, *Betrothal at a Monastery* (1946), Act 2, Scene 3, eight measures before Rehearsal 206, when Louisa enters

The music is otherworldly and, to be clear, this underhanded music is associated with Mendoza the Jew and, one presumes, Jewishness.

Example 6.2 shows the contrasting music once Louisa enters right after Mendoza, between Rehearsal numbers 205 and 206. Marked "dolcissimo," Louisa's music is indisputably in the key of D major, and features only the seven notes of the key signature once she enters on the upbeat to m. 2 of the excerpt. Though there are no strong cadences, a clear motion from the leading-tone vii° triad in first inversion to the tonic in mm. 3–4 (which I have labeled in the example), repeated in mm. 7–8, points to the clear D-major key. In her cantabile diatonic melody Louisa sings that only Mendoza is capable of showing her kindness. Her beauty and innocence are reflected in the score, a diatonic D-major section that stands in stark contrast to Mendoza's chaotic twelve-note music. At Rehearsal 206, shown in Example 6.2, we see the return of Mendoza and his menacing music, and in his text he agrees that only he can show her kindness.

When we hear the sinister, jarring, chromatic, atonal music associated with Mendoza and contrast it with the sweet-sounding, innocent, diatonic, tonal music associated with Louisa, it's not difficult to see how antisemitism is baked into Prokofiev's score. If this scene somehow represents, as Richard Taruskin wrote, a softened treatment of Mendoza in which "Sheridan's blatant anti-Semitism is erased as far as possible," I'd hate to see the original comic opera! In fact, the depiction of Mendoza traffics in so many classic antisemitic and anti-Jewish stereotypes it's hard to catalog them all: Mendoza is a powerful, rich fish merchant, and smelly fish is a recurrent theme; he is sly, cunning, and even lecherous, but duped in the end; he is called a "hairy ape" in one translation of the text; he is blamed for the problems that arise in the otherwise beautiful setting in Seville, Spain; and he is often the laughingstock of the community.

Though it's not hard to see how Prokofiev's musical depiction of Jews and Jewishness can be considered antisemitic, I don't know much else about his antisemitism. But he was hardly alone. I've always thought it strange that we in music theory so rarely speak of the antisemitism of key figures in the history of classical music, since I've known for a long time that so many of these figures were unremittingly antisemitic. It often seems that the only nineteenth-century composer whom we consistently cite as being antisemitic is Richard Wagner, and he had to write a long essay, "Das Judenthum in der Musik" (Jewishness in music)—which he published under a pseudonym, let us not forget, in 1850—in order for us to consider Wagner antisemitic today.[7] In other words, had Wagner not written this antisemitic screed in 1850, we would likely not consider him to be antisemitic, though his hatred of Jews and Jewishness would have probably been the same.

Over the past few years some commentators on *On Music Theory* have mentioned that they felt the current chapter on confronting antisemitism was somehow "out of place," extraneous to my larger project. I'd like to state for the record here my emphatic disagreement with this sentiment. Since I first conceived of this book project early in 2018, confronting antisemitism has been a part of that project. Examining classical music's historic antisemitism, and the way we have all been taught to brush off and disregard the many anti-Jewish beliefs of classical music's canonic figures, can reveal how

---

7. Richard Wagner, *Das Judenthum in der Musik* (Leipzig: Verlagsbuchhandlung von J. J. Weber, 1869). Original published under the pseudonym Karl Freigedank, "Das Judenthum in der Musik," *Neue Zeitschrift für Musik* 17, no. 19 (1850): 101–7 and 17, no. 20 (1850): 109–12.

music theory's white supremacist roots took hold and infected what we do with a hate and anger that then became normative to our field specifically and classical music generally. Through this examination we can also better understand how antiblackness, for instance, works in the field and how we can eliminate it. As I like to say when comparing academic music's historic antisemitism with its historic antiblackness, there are far more points of *convergence* than there are points of *divergence* between the two. Confronting antisemitism in classical music is every bit as important as confronting antiblackness in classical music (or other forms of hate for that matter), and no one will convince me otherwise. Or, as I wrote in a blog post from April 2020, "Antisemitism in music theory remains underexplored, and music theory should confront antisemitism with the same seriousness and fortitude that it should confront racism and sexism."[8]

Differences between Antisemitism and Racism

It's important not to confuse antisemitism with racism and to have a clear understanding of just what antisemitism is if one is to combat it. In *How to Fight Antisemitism*, journalist Bari Weiss begins by saying what antisemitism, and by extension Jewishness, is not:

> Judaism is not merely a religion, and it is not merely an ethnicity. Judaism is a people. More specifically, it is a people with a language, a culture, a literature, and a particular set of ideas, beliefs, texts, and legal practices. . . . Consider the common misunderstanding these days that anti-Semitism is a form of racism. One reason that anti-Semitism is understood as racism against Jews is because racism is at the center of America's conversation with itself.[9]

Understanding that antisemitism is not the same as racism, and something much larger than prejudice against Jews and Jewishness, is a key first step. Weiss continues:

---

8. See Ewell, "Race, Gender, and Their Intersection in Music Theory," in "Confronting Racism and Sexism in American Music Theory," April 10, 2020 (musictheoryswhiteracialframe.com).

9. Bari Weiss, *How to Fight Anti-Semitism* (Crown, 2019), 28–29.

I think of [antisemitism] as an ever-morphing conspiracy theory in which Jews play the starring role in spreading evil in the world. . . . Anti-Semitism successfully turns Jews into the symbol of whatever a given civilization defines as its most sinister and threatening qualities.[10]

I agree with Weiss that antisemitism is, first and foremost, a conspiracy theory, and one must realize what is at the core of this conspiracy theory: blaming Jews for the ills of a society, something that happens often at times of upheaval and social strife. Think here of the *Protocols of the Elders of Zion*, first published anonymously in Russia in 1903 as *Протоколы сионских мудрецов*, which contained fabricated stories of Jewish global domination and which, in many various translations, has done enormous harm worldwide. I often say that antisemitism is the conspiratorial thread that holds together white nationalism across the globe. Through falsehoods, mythologies, and flat-out lies about Jews and Judaism, many countries, peoples, and nations the world over have wrongly blamed Jews for atrocities and cooked up crazy stories of sinister global plots. Note here the QAnon conspiracy theorist and current Georgia congresswoman Marjorie Taylor Greene's fantastical belief that the 2020 California wildfires were started by a "Secret Jewish Space Laser."[11]

Perhaps most harmful is the false belief that antisemitism only affects Jews, and that those who are not Jewish, like me, are untouched by antisemitism. I personally think the most important part of confronting antisemitism is the simple idea that it affects us all, whether we realize it or not, and affects us in a most pernicious way. Weiss writes:

Remember: It is easy to think of the Jews as the sole victims of anti-Semitic hate. But another, far bigger victim is often overlooked: the culture that facilitates anti-Semitism. To tolerate anti-Semitism is to tolerate lies. A culture in which anti-Semitism thrives is a culture in which truths have been replaced with lies.[12]

---

10. Weiss, *How to Fight Anti-Semitism*, 31.

11. See Jonathan Chait, "GOP Congresswoman Blamed Wildfires on Secret Jewish Space Laser," *New York Magazine*, January 28, 2021.

12. Weiss, *How to Fight Anti-Semitism*, 48. Weiss's book generally contains much useful information for what it sets out to do, but at times it is uneven, at others, downright misleading. This is most evident during Weiss's discussion of "intersectionality," which she claims functions "as a caste system, the reverse of the caste system that has dominated Western history" (121–22). Again, this is the common false narrative of "inverting the hierarchy" that conservative writers try to attach to critical race theory. But, to be clear, neither Kimberlé

Cornell University philosopher Kate Manne has done great work in helping us understand the inner workings of sexism and misogyny, as well as male privilege and entitlement. On November 30, 2020, she posted a tweet that I believe can apply to antisemitism. Manne wrote:

> Let's remember that transphobia, like misogyny, isn't hatred in the hearts of individual bigots (though they certainly exist). It's primarily about the creation of an environment in which trans people face hostility and hatred.[13]

What if I simply substituted antisemitism and Jewish in this tweet?

> Let's remember that *antisemitism*, like misogyny, isn't hatred in the hearts of individual bigots (though they certainly exist). It's primarily about the creation of an environment in which *Jewish* people face hostility and hatred.

I think this is a useful way of thinking about antisemitism (and transphobia, and homophobia, and ableism, etc.). Are there people with hatred toward Jews in their hearts? Unfortunately, yes. But antisemitism is much larger than those individuals. Antisemitism creates a menacing environment for Jews and Jewishness, one in which Jews face hostility and hatred. And, for many centuries, hostile environments have consistently been created for Jews through fabricated conspiracy theories of global domination, banking mythologies, among many other conspiracies.

This hostility was manifest recently in our country in the horrific mass shooting at the Tree of Life Synagogue in Pittsburgh in October 2018, in which white nationalist Robert Bowers shot eleven people dead. As justification for his violence Bowers cited the fact that Tree of Life's Hebrew Immigrant Aid Society (HIAS) was helping bring Muslim refugees into the United States. Bowers wrote on social media: "Open you [*sic*] Eyes! It's the filthy EVIL jews Bringing the Filthy EVIL Muslims into the Country!! . . . HIAS likes to bring invaders in that kill our people. I can't sit by and

---

Crenshaw, whom Weiss discusses (121), nor any other self-respecting race scholar seeks to put black women at the top of a hierarchy, with white men at the bottom. We race scholars simply seek equality among all races, genders, cultures, and ethnicities, among other identities. This fallacious "inversion" argument resonates deeply with conservative Americans, but it is a mythology, and a mythology that Weiss has, unfortunately, also bought into. Consequently, her overall argument is weakened.

13. See the tweet here: https://twitter.com/kate_manne/status/1333587859350167554

watch my people get slaughtered. Screw your optics, I'm going in."[14] With this vile statement Bowers undoubtedly drew inspiration from Adolf Hitler's *Mein Kampf*:

> The Jew uses every possible means to undermine the racial founda-
> tions of a subjugated people. In his systematic efforts to ruin girls and
> women he strives to break down the last barriers of discrimination
> between him and other peoples. The Jews were responsible for bring-
> ing negroes into the Rhineland, with the ultimate idea of bastardizing
> the white race which they hate and thus lowering its cultural and
> political level so that the Jew might dominate. For as long as a people
> remain racially pure and are conscious of the treasure of their blood,
> they can never be overcome by the Jew. Never in this world can the
> Jew become master of any people except a bastardized people.[15]

These sick statements point to the fact that there is but one culprit in a horrific act like the mass shooting at Tree of Life, namely, the historic white supremacist patriarchy that has been handed down to us in our country, a supremacy that, in its most extreme state, morphs into the white national-ism that is sadly so prominent now. These statements also underscore the natural allyship between Jews and black/brown people in our shared struggle for social justice in the United States and beyond.

Examples of Antisemitism in Classical Music

The spiritual father of classical music's late nineteenth- and twentieth-century antisemitism was Richard Wagner, whose "Das Judenthum in der Musik" served as something of a *Mein Kampf* to those in classical music who sought an outlet for anti-Jewishness. I won't quote from Wagner's essay here, since it's already well-trodden material and only further highlights Wagner, which is problematic since overemphasizing this one antisemitic figure has over time led to the false impression that he was somehow exceptional in his hatred of Jews, which is simply not true when considering nineteenth- and twentieth-century European and American composers. Here are some non-Wagner examples of classical music's antisemitism:

---

14. Cited in Weiss, *How to Fight Anti-Semitism*, 5.
15. Hitler, *Mein Kampf*, trans. James Murphy (Hurst and Blackett, [1925] 1939), 254–55.

1. Fédéric Chopin once said: "I didn't expect such Jewish behavior
   from [Joseph Étienne Camille] Pleyel . . . If we have to deal with
   Jews, let it at least be with orthodox ones. . . . Jews will be Jews
   and Huns will be Huns—that's the truth of it, but what can one
   do? I'm forced to deal with them."[16]

2. Pyotr Tchaikovsky: "In a letter written in 1878, Pyotr (Peter)
   Ilyich Tchaikovsky wrote that when his train stopped at a Russian railroad station, he noticed 'a mass of dirty Yids [a slur for
   a Jew in Russian], with that poisoning of the atmosphere which
   accompanies them everywhere.'"[17]

3. Also about Tchaikovsky: "Writing [his patroness Nadezhda] von
   Meck in April, 1878, about a cottage where he's staying, he writes
   of his unhappiness about a nearby Jewish village and his relief
   that 'the Yids are not visible.' At one point, he refers to Benjamin
   Disraeli as 'that detestable Jew.'"[18]

4. Anton Webern: "Webern initially supported the Nazi party and
   the stability and order that National Socialism offered, believing
   their aggressive tactics and anti-Semitism would mellow when
   in power. However, Nazi aggression didn't seem to suppress his
   developing enthusiasm for militaristic optimism, and he wrote
   eagerly of Hitler's *Mein Kampf*, 'The book has brought me much
   enlightenment.'"[19]

5. Igor Stravinsky: "Robert Craft has described the composer's

---

16. Warren Boroson, "Chopin's Antisemitism," December 25, 2009 (https://jewishstanda
rd.timesofisrael.com/chopins-antisemitism).

17. Tom Tugend, "Tchaikovsky's 'Jewish Problem' Doesn't Make Performer Settle a Score,"
Times of Israel, July 30, 2017 (https://www.timesofisrael.com/tchaikovskys-jewish-problem
-doesnt-make-performer-settle-a-score/).

18. Allan M. Jalon, "How to Listen to Tchaikovsky While Looking Past His Anti-
Semitism," Forward.com, May 7, 2019 (https://forward.com/culture/music/423847/how-to
-listen-to-tchaikovsky-while-looking-past-his-anti-semitism). In a side note about Russian
composers and antisemitism, many significant nineteenth-century musical figures in Russia
were antisemitic, including Mikhail Glinka, Modest Mussorgsky, Mily Balakirev, Alexander
Serov, among others. In fact Richard Taruskin has noted that Rimsky-Korsakov seems to have
been an exception in that he wasn't antisemitic, and not only approved of but insisted on the
marriage of his daughter Nadezhda to his Jewish student Maximillian Steinberg, though it's
worth noting that Steinberg had to convert to Eastern Orthodox Christianity before their
Christian wedding.

19. "How Did Anton Webern Die?," *BBC Music Magazine*, September 14, 2020 (https://
www.classical-music.com/composers/how-did-anton-webern-die).

antisemitism as 'lifelong and undying,' and Richard Taruskin has argued that Stravinsky's antisemitism may have stemmed from his rivalry with Jewish composer Maximilian Steinberg, whose early career outshone the young Stravinsky's when they were studying together with Rimsky-Korsakov in St Petersburg."[20]

6. About American composer Carl Ruggles, Jake Cohen writes: "To cite merely two instances, in a 1933 letter to Henry Cowell, Ruggles referred to 'that filthy bunch of Juilliard Jews,' and Lou Harrison distanced himself personally from Ruggles following a 1949 lunch in which Ruggles publicly shouted racist and anti-Semitic slurs in New York City."[21]

7. Percy Grainger: "No, my horror at the helping hand held out to the Jews has nothing to do with dislike of Jews or due to any feeling on my part that Jews behave badly. My horror arises out of a wish to see nature realise her dreams—horror at needless destruction of nature's dreams. . . . I bow to her aims & dreams, as far as I understand them. And I can see that nature has given birth to peace, kindliness, impersonality, tenderness, wistfulness, etc., in one race: the Nordic."[22]

8. Richard Strauss was the president of Hitler's Reichsmusikkammer (Reich Music Chamber), a position he had taken up in November 1933 at the request of Joseph Goebbels, Adolf Hitler's right-hand man.[23]

9. As I mentioned in chapter 3, Heinrich Schenker, for instance, once wrote in his diary, "The Jews top the list as Germany's enemies," and I also mentioned Schenker's letter in praise of Adolf Hitler from May 1933, four months after Hitler ascended to the German chancellery.[24]

10. Alexander Serov: "They [Jews] keep all musical activity in both St. Petersburg and Moscow under continual siege. Soon, with

20. Abaigh McKee, "Igor Stravinsky," *Music and the Holocaust*, no date (http://holocaustmusic.ort.org/politics-and-propaganda/igor-stravinsky) (accessed July 4, 2022).

21. Jacob A. Cohen, "Constructions of New England Identity and Place in American Music, 1885–1935" (PhD Dissertation, CUNY Graduate Center, 2017), 232.

22. Matthew Guerrieri, "Percy Grainger," *Red Bull Music Academy*, July 17, 2017 (https://daily.redbullmusicacademy.com/2017/07/percy-grainger-feature). From this quote it seems that nature has not, however, bestowed upon Grainger the ability to write good English.

23. Clemency Burton-Hill, "Richard Strauss: A Reluctant Nazi," *BBC Culture*, June 9, 2014 (https://www.bbc.com/culture/article/20140610-richard-strauss-a-reluctant-nazi).

24. *Schenker Documents Online*, OJ 14/45, [22], transcr. Marko Deisinger, trans. Scott Witmer, and OJ 5/7a, [46], formerly vC46, transcr. and trans. William Drabkin.

the founding of the conservatoire they desired for themselves as the future breeding ground for talentless musical civil servants, they begin to throw their weight around in the province they have acquired in a thoroughly despotic manner, trying to crush any musical talent in Russia that does not spring from within their own Yankel [another slur for a Jew in Russian, from Russian 'Yakov' (i.e., 'Jacob')] ranks. Out of a hatred of all that is Russian, they are doing all they can to nip in the bud any true and natural development of Russian musical talent."[25]

Having just mentioned the Russian opera composer Alexander Serov, who was part Jewish himself and a personal friend of Richard Wagner, I should pause here and make mention of the powerful work that my fellow Russianist Richard Taruskin has undertaken over the years in exposing anti-semitism in our field.[26] Whether in Johann Sebastian Bach's *St. John's Passion*, a cantata by Igor Stravinsky, or John Adams's opera *The Death of Klinghoffer*, Taruskin has been at the forefront of showing us how these and other works, usually universally lauded for their artistry, can bear traces of antisemitism that are often not so noticeable at first glance, especially if the antisemitism is buried in a foreign text, as is the case with *St. John's Passion.*[27] Notably, the response to Taruskin's efforts to combat antisemitism have often been met with the same race-neutral exceptionalism arguments that my own race scholarship has been met with, that we shouldn't be bringing up such arguments that detract from the greatness of the piece in question, that the composers were simply "products of their time," that they "had Jewish friends," or that things have changed for the better now so we don't have to think about the prejudices of yesteryear's great composers. I for one am grateful to Taruskin for his important work in exposing antisemitism and other forms of hate in academic music, since only by acknowledging such hate can we ever hope to eliminate it. Finally, I would be remiss if I didn't also mention the compelling work that Michael Marissen has done to expose antisemitism in the works of Johann Sebastian Bach and George Friedrich Handel.[28]

---

25. Stuart Campbell, ed. *Russians on Russian Music, 1830–1880* (Cambridge University Press, 1994), 81–82.

26. Taruskin died on July 1, 2022, aged 77. Rest in peace Richard.

27. See, for instance, Richard Taruskin, "Music's Dangers and the Case for Control," *New York Times*, December 9, 2001, and "Stravinsky's Darkness and Light," *New York Times*, August 9, 1992.

28. See, for instance, Michael Marissen, *Tainted Glory in Handel's "Messiah"* (Yale University Press, 2014), and *Bach & God* (Oxford University Press, 2016).

Overcontextualizing Antisemitism

Unsurprisingly, authors, writers, and scholars have breezily dismissed anti-semitism in American classical music studies in strikingly similar fashion to the ways in which they have dismissed antiblackness and other forms of racism and hate. This has been done in order to sustain the mythologies of white-male greatness. In the same sources with examples of various compos-ers' antisemitic statements above, the authors also give mitigating instances for the composers. So, for example, Tom Tugend says about Tchaikovsky:

> Hershey Felder—a playwright, actor and composer . . . added that Tchaikovsky's putdown of "Yids" was countered by his actions. He provided a scholarship from his own pocket for the young Jewish vio-linist Samuli Litvinov; he maintained a deep friendship with composer-conductors Anton and Nikolai Rubenstein; and he defended Felix Mendelssohn against Richard Wagner's anti-Semitic slurs.[29]

In his piece about Percy Grainger, Matthew Guerrieri speaks of how gen-erous and considerate the composer was, and tells the story of how, in the summer of 1919, there was a race riot in Chicago—I mentioned earlier in a footnote at the beginning of chapter 4 that these race massacres, which numbered in the dozens in 1919, were referred to as "red summer"—and that Grainger helped one of his black students by sending her food since black residents were under lockdown.[30] Thus this is a mitigating counternarrative to the antisemitic remarks that Grainger had uttered before.

About Richard Strauss, in his piece entitled "Richard Strauss: A Reluc-tant Nazi," Clemency Burton-Hill writes:

> There are no easy answers when it comes to the question of art, biog-raphy and morality; and the line between resistance, passivity and collaboration in Nazi Germany is arguably the murkiest of all. On the occasion of his 150th birthday, as we marvel anew at music in which beauty and truth and humanity seem to defy any other judgment, perhaps we may finally allow ourselves to tip our hats to Richard Strauss.[31]

---

29. Tugend, "Tchaikovsky's 'Jewish Problem.'"
30. Guerrieri, "Percy Grainger."
31. Burton-Hill, "Richard Strauss: A Reluctant Nazi." I note that this title itself is a soft-pedaling of Strauss's antisemitism.

Again, we see the desire to overcontextualize the antisemitism of one of the "great" composers of classical music so that we might continue to lionize him.

Perhaps the most classic defense against any type to discrimination is the claim to have friends of the group being discriminated against. So, in her piece on Stravinsky, Abaigh McKee writes, "However, Stravinsky did maintain friendships with Jewish musicians including violinist Samuel Dushkin and composer Arthur Lourié."[32]

In the entry for "Richard Wagner" on Wikipedia, the two most basic tropes for defending antisemitic behavior—that the given figure was just "a product of the times" and that they "had Jewish friends" are on full display:

> Wagner's hostile writings on Jews, including *Jewishness in Music*, corresponded to some existing trends of thought in Germany during the 19th century; despite his very public views on these themes, throughout his life Wagner had Jewish friends, colleagues and supporters.[33]

I quote from the unscholarly Wikipedia here not because it's definitive—it is not, and should never be cited as authoritative in academic writing for obvious reasons. Rather, I cite it because it does represent, in its freewheeling anyone-can-edit openness, a certain consensus, a very troubling consensus, that believes having certain friends can absolve someone from prejudice, which is absurd, of course. Indeed, the idea of the "Jewish friend" seems to be the most common response to charges of antisemitism, one that has worked as a defense for bad behavior against marginalized groups the world over. Having a friend of a certain race, gender, ethnicity, or other identity doesn't mean that you can't discriminate against such identities. My favorite example of this ridiculousness is when cisgender-male politicians stand at a lectern claiming they can't possibly be sexist because they have a mom, wife, and two daughters, before voting to pass some horribly misogynistic legislation. As I said earlier, these discriminations are not primarily about hate but, rather, about the creation of hostile environments in which hatred can flourish.

As a final example of overcontextualizing antisemitism, I'll quote from a 2006 book on Franz Liszt, and the final long chapter in that book by the conductor and longtime president of Bard College, Leon Botstein, who writes that Liszt's

---

32. McKee, "Igor Stravinsky."
33. Wikipedia, s.v. "Richard Wagner."

views on the Jewish question can be contrasted with Wagner's. Liszt's anti-Semitism was of a more ordinary nineteenth-century social character, akin to Schumann's and Max Bruch's. Liszt's anti-Semitism is perhaps best expressed in his relief that Sophie Menter chose not to marry a Jew. This reflected less racialist thinking than concern for potential conflict in terms of mutual understanding and social status. Jewish identity seemed a historical barrier to the task of transcending the barriers of birth through art, an unnecessary and unwelcome social stigma for the non-Jew. . . . Liszt's anti-Semitism is reflective of an eighteenth-century variant that despised the Jew as socially disfigured but redeemable.[34]

Botstein is a thoughtful writer who has also written about the atrocious aspects of Heinrich Schenker and Schenkerism, for instance, and I don't wish to suggest that he is outright excusing Liszt's antisemitism.[35] Rather, I wish to highlight how easily authors have sought to overcontextualize what are, in fact, fairly straightforward hateful and, indeed, antisemitic aspects of our "great composers." Is the antisemitism of a "social character," as Botstein writes, really that much better than the "racialist" antisemitism of a figure like Wagner? Possibly, but they're both pretty bad. This closely mirrors the distinction between cultural and biological racism that I wrote about in chapters 3 and 4. I wonder how Botstein might moderate his language now given the time that we're currently living through? Liszt's antisemitism here is like the racism that one might hear if a white person brings home a new black partner to meet the parents and the parents later say, for instance: "I'm not racist of course, but I'm just thinking about how difficult it will be for you in our society, dear, if you choose to stay with Latisha!" I'd still call that racism, the same way I'd call Franz Liszt's beliefs antisemitic.

Before I turn to a few recommendations, let me reiterate here that antisemitism is, primarily, not racism but a conspiracy theory that has targeted Jews and Jewishness for centuries in order to scapegoat one group of people for the bad behavior of others. To live in a world of conspiracy theories is to live in a world of lies, and a world of lies is one in which the powerful

34. Leon Botstein, "A Mirror to the Nineteenth Century: Reflections on Franz Liszt," in *Franz Liszt and His World*, ed. Christopher H. Gibbs et al. (Princeton University Press, 2006), 555.

35. See Leon Botstein, "Schenker the Regressive: Observations on the Historical Schenker," *Musical Quarterly* 86, no. 2 (2002): 239–47.

gain more power while the marginalized become more marginalized. Consequently, democracy, the voice of the people, suffers. So it's not difficult to see that antisemitism and the environments that nurture it are corrupting and destructive for everyone, Jew and non-Jew alike. Or, as historian Deborah Lipstadt puts it:

> When expressions of contempt for one group become normative, it is virtually inevitable that similar hatred will be directed at other groups. Like a fire set by an arsonist, passionate hatred and conspiratorial worldviews reach well beyond their intended target. They are not rationally contained. But even if the antisemites were to confine their venom to Jews, the existence of Jew-hatred within a society is an indication that something about the entire society is amiss. No healthy society harbors extensive antisemitism—or any other form of hatred.[36]

When thinking of the horrific antiblack and, especially recently but always present, anti-Asian violence in our American society, is it any wonder that we see upticks in antisemitic violence as well. When Lipstadt writes, "No healthy society harbors extensive antisemitism—or any other form of hatred," we get the sense that the United States of America, currently, is a most unhealthy society, since so many forms of hatred flourish here among us now. Again, there is but a single culprit in this American conflagration of hate: the patriarchal white supremacy that has formed our country since its founding in 1776, a supremacy rooted in mythologies of white-male greatness and exceptionalism.

Antisemitism and Divisiveness in Music Theory

When Timothy Jackson wrote in his response to my SMT plenary talk in November 2019, "Ewell's scapegoating of Schenker, Schenkerians, and Schenkerian analysis, occurs in the much larger context of Black-on-Jew attacks in the United States. . . . Ewell's denunciation of Schenker and Schenkerians may be seen as part and parcel of the much broader current of Black anti-Semitism," he is clearly trying to drive a wedge between blacks

---

36. Lipstadt, *Antisemitism, Here and Now*, 9.

and Jews, thus dividing two logical historical allies in the struggle for social justice in the United States, a common tactic in the white-male frame. Though the antiblack sentiment of Jackson's comment is obvious, a less obvious sentiment is the antisemitic one. With this statement, Jackson seeks, in my opinion, to divide not only blacks and Jews, but Jews themselves into two groups, namely, those who will defend Schenker and Schenkerians, and those who will defend Philip Ewell. This subtler message, with the intent of dividing Jews is, simply put, antisemitic, and such attempts at division should be called out when they rear their ugly head. Bari Weiss puts it succinctly toward the end of *How to Fight Antisemitism* when she says, "Don't trust people who seek to divide Jews. Even if they are Jews."[37]

Perhaps the best example in music theory's history of a Jew who sought to divide Jews into good and bad was, of course, Heinrich Schenker, who once wrote in his diary:

> Galician Jews: they are criticized for having such difficulty in linking up with other nations, of assimilating themselves to them. And one attributes to them, with some anxiety, manners and gestures that they continue to retain after they have come into contact with better circles of people. But I think that the racial question plays the smallest role in their isolation; for me, the one and only cause for this is their boundless poverty. . . . They are like soldiers on the battlefield: filled with concerns for their life and in a constant state of warfare. But one should instruct the fighting soldier on the battlefield to adopt and exercise the good manners of a man who is wealthy and enjoys the full security of the moment. They simply cannot recover their breath, and for that reason cannot be thinking at all of good manners. Indeed, they would not at all even be conscious that such things were necessary for them in battle! . . . How it is otherwise easier, however, for Jews to adopt good manners is something one can see among those who have become wealthy: that which still remains as a Jewish residue can surely only be reckoned as a racial factor.[38]

37. Weiss, *How to Fight Anti-Semitism*, 174.

38. *Schenker Documents Online*, Diary entry, September 29, 1915, transcr. Marko Deisinger, trans. William Drabkin. Galicia, where Schenker was from originally, is a historic region that now lies right at the border between Poland and Ukraine.

Schenker's beliefs in "better circles of people," Jews' lack of "good manners," and an undesirable "Jewish residue" are remarkably antisemitic sentiments, and Schenker's antisemitism remains remarkably underexplored. But there can be no question that Schenker believed in the idea of good and bad Jews. As I mentioned at the end of chapter 3, to leave not only Schenker's antisemitism but his racism, nationalism, and sexism untouched is to implicate millions of Jews in the same horrific beliefs when, in fact, this is largely untrue. But pointing this out would contravene the white-male narrative and do damage to Schenkerism, which is why the mythologies surrounding the man were so important or, to put it in terms of philosopher Charles Mills's epistemological ignorance, this is why the teaching of "knowledge-avoidance" has been so key to promoting the musical theories of Heinrich Schenker.

Recommendations for Confronting Classical Music's Antisemitism

What follows are some ideas about confronting antisemitism in classical music. In many ways, they could be thought of as applying to other forms of discrimination that occur in classical music. First, when you hear of the antisemitism of a composer or other music figure from the past, don't gloss over that antisemitism and treat it as unimportant, and, for heaven's sake, don't say that it's fine because the person in question "had Jewish friends." I often point out when discussing, for example, Tchaikovsky, that I know of someone for whom Tchaikovsky's antisemitism was anything but irrelevant, for whom his antisemitism was actually quite important. And that person's name is Pyotr Tchaikovsky. Indeed, the antisemitic utterings of the persons themselves should be enough to convince anyone that their antisemitism deserves further scrutiny, and definitely should not be swept under the rug as has so often been the case.

Second, when people try to divide natural allies, like blacks and Jews, or Jews among themselves, realize that and call it out. Nothing makes white-male frameworks happier than to see racialized, gendered, minoritized, and otherwise marginalized groups fight among themselves, and often white cisgender men encourage this fighting, like the conservative activist Edward Blum, who has worked tirelessly to turn African Americans and AAPI against each other in, for example, the recent federal lawsuit against Harvard University and their admissions policies. In a piece for the American Civil Liberties Union, staff attorney Sarah Hinger writes, "Blum's cynical attempt to use members of the Asian-American community seeks to pit people of color against one another. This is the direct antithesis of race-conscious admissions programs, which endeavor to create richly diverse college campuses."[39]

Third, immerse yourselves in literature on how we can confront anti-semitism and think of joining groups that are committed to combating anti-Jewishness in all its forms. This will allow you to better distinguish between falsehood and truth when it comes to Jews and Jewishness. There are so many falsehoods out there that we must all arm ourselves with the best sources, and then we must push back when we hear the conspiracy theories that so often accompany and underlie antisemitism.

Fourth, if undertaking a commission or study of institutional racism, sexism, or other forms of discrimination, make sure to include an exhaustive section on institutional antisemitism in the study. Antisemitism is one of the oldest forms of discrimination on our planet, and one that has shaped academic music in the United States to a much larger degree than is generally acknowledged. Think, for instance, of music theory's heavy emphasis on Christian hymns or Bach chorales and cantatas—with titles like "Liebster Jesu, mein Verlangen" (Dearest Jesus, my desire) or "Jesu, meine Freude" (Jesus, my joy)—or how eagerly we perform Requiem masses by composers like Giuseppe Verdi or Wolfgang Amadeus Mozart. Indeed, Christian theology runs deeply through much of what we do in the academic study of music, and this hidden Christianity requirement can easily fall under the rubric of antisemitism as well. Commissioning a study of these issues could go a long way to uncovering not just past antisemitic activities, but other past injustices as well.[40]

Finally, find your allies and build coalitions! This is fairly self-evident, but sometimes underestimated. I've seen many significant changes happen in American music studies as the result of banding together for a shared purpose. We should all seek to confront and dismantle institutional anti-semitism, and through coalitions we will have a better chance at success.

---

39. Sarah Hinger, "Meet Edward Blum, the Man Who Wants to Kill Affirmative Action in Higher Education," ACLU.org blog, October 18, 2018 (https://www.aclu.org/blog/racial-ju stice/affirmative-action/meet-edward-blum-man-who-wants-kill-affirmative-action-higher).

40. The influence of Christian theology on music theory specifically, and the academic study of music generally, is an extremely important topic that deserves its own monograph, yet it's beyond the scope of my work here. It need be said, however, that, in the history of patriarchal white supremacy in the United States and across the globe, proselytizing Christianity was of the utmost importance to those in power, and was intricately involved in white-male power structures.

Final Thoughts on "On Classical Music's Antisemitism"

Howard Hanson, an ethnic Swede born in Nebraska, became the head of music theory and composition at the University of the Pacific conservatory of music at the age of nineteen, in 1916, and then he became its dean in 1919. Hanson would go on to become the head of the Eastman School of Music, in Rochester, New York, for forty years until his retirement in 1964. Importantly, Hanson was active in national music-education organizations, like the National Association of Schools of Music, so his influence was massive in the twentieth century. Following the death of American composer David Diamond in 2005, classical music critic Michael Steinberg had this to say about the year that Diamond spent as a student at Eastman: "Hanson disliked Jews and he disliked homosexuals and he disliked modernists, and David Diamond qualified in all of those categories. And it must have been a pretty unhappy year, and I think it's significant that Diamond left the place after a year."[41] Current Eastman professor of musicology Roger Freitas said, about Hanson, "That nexus of liberal, Jewish, gay was, by extension, the opposite of what Hanson stood for," adding that it was "mainly an atmosphere here at Eastman that was anti-gay. There was not a lot of evidence that Hanson himself was involved. But he did not interfere with people being drummed out of the school."[42]

Hanson seemed to have played his antisemitic and homophobic cards somewhat close to his vest, which is often the case, but Hanson's antisemitism is today not in doubt. Hanson was a well-known American nativist, as evidenced by his letter to the editor of the *New York Times* from 1941, entitled "Problem of Adjustment: Clashing Interests between Native Musicians and Refugees Come to America from Overseas."[43] He begins by saying that he has just returned from the annual meeting of the National Association of Schools of Music, and that there was a large problem often discussed, namely, the "foreign guests," as he put it, who had become so present in music studies in America. Of course, this being 1941, with World War II quickly ramping up across the globe, the ethnicity of these foreign guests should be clear—they were largely Jewish. To be fair to Hanson, he does mention that "the assimilation of these personalities into the artistic bloodstream of our country should serve as an enrichment of our cultural life."

---

41. Jeff Spevak, "From the Archive: The House That Hanson Built," *Democrat and Chronicle*, April 6, 2014 (https://www.democratandchronicle.com/story/lifestyle/art/2014/04/06/house-hanson-built/7343473).

42. Spevak, "From the Archive."

43. Howard Hanson, letter to the editor, *New York Times*, January 19, 1941.

Yet he also strikes a nativist tone when he says, about opportunities for these foreign guests, "At the same time we must realize that such opportunities must not be at the expense of the development of the native composer and artist." I wonder what the tone of Hanson's letter would have been if the majority of these foreign guests were not Jewish? In other words, to what extent were Hanson's comments driven not by a genuine concern for "native" Americans, but by antisemitism? I also wonder who exactly in terms of racial and gender identification qualified as "native" in Hanson's estimation (obviously, not Native Americans, that is, indigenous people). Defenders will quickly point out Hanson's support for black American composer William Grant Still, for example, but this will always be the case. Do those same defenders honestly think that Hanson would have put Still's works on par with the "supreme geniuses" of the white western canon? John Marshall Harlan could easily see the folly in the majority ruling in *Plessy v. Ferguson* in 1896, but he still held, as I showed in chapter 5, clear white supremacist beliefs, and I wouldn't be at all surprised if Harlan's discrimination extended to Jews as well. Most historical accounts of Howard Hanson and his time at Eastman remain quite hagiographic, in keeping with the tendency of white-male frameworks to whitewash uncomfortable truths from the past.[44]

Toward the end of her brilliant monograph *The Music Libel against the Jews*, musicologist Ruth HaCohen writes:

> Moving beyond the Jewish scene, it should be once again emphasized that the seemingly unruly sonic-performative practices that have characterized it are far from being a unique Jewish Spécialité. "Clapping, screaming and shouting that may seem jarring to the untrained ear" characterize other groups, maybe similarly engaged in cohesive solidarities and spontaneous communicative norms, sounding as noise to outsiders. The last quotation is, in fact, Barack Obama's autobiographical account of his cherished affiliation with the Trinity Church in Chicago. This, however, brings us back to Jewish predilections: it points to a long-term affinity between African-American and Jewish-American sonic cultures that brought about glorified moments of

---

44. One notable exception is Appendix E from the Eastman School of Music's Eastman Action Commission for Racial Justice from October 2020. See https://www.esm.rochester.edu/diversity/report. That appendix also cites a work that gives a compelling account of Hanson's time at Eastman, namely, Emily Abrams Ansari, *The Sound of a Superpower: Musical Americanism and the Cold War* (Oxford University Press, 2018). See especially chapter 1, "The American Exceptionalists: Howard Hanson and William Schuman."

musical collaborations and coalescences throughout the twentieth century.[45]

I would add to HaCohen's astute observation on the affinities between "African-American and Jewish-American sonic cultures" and suggest that they extend far beyond just music. Those affinities extend to our shared experiences, painful experiences of seizures of property, forced relocations, forced labor, and unspeakable violence and horror. Which is why I consider the allyship between American blacks and American Jews to be so very important to social justice in the United States. I couldn't have been happier to see those bonds work in tandem to win two US Senate run-offs in January 2021 in the state of Georgia, which saw the election of its first black senator, Raphael Warnock, and its first Jewish senator, Jon Ossoff, in the state's history.[46]

Finally, while there have certainly been Jewish successes in the history of academic music in our country, especially since the mid-twentieth century, this does not mean that it's somehow less important to confront classical music's antisemitism. If anything, this makes it more important, since one can easily be lulled into the false belief that antisemitism in academic and classical music doesn't exist, which is simply not true. Just ask yourself, aside from Richard Wagner, which of the musical figures mentioned in this chapter—Johann Sebastian Bach, Mily Balakirev, Max Bruch, Frédéric Chopin, Mikhail Glinka, Percy Grainger, George Friedrich Handel, Howard Hanson, Franz Liszt, Modest Mussorgsky, Sergei Prokofiev, Carl Ruggles, Heinrich Schenker, Robert Schumann, Alexander Serov, Richard Sheridan, Richard Strauss, Igor Stravinsky, Pyotr Tchaikovsky, or Anton Webern—did you know to be antisemitic to one extent or another? Too often excuses are made for the antisemitism in music theory and musicology, and we must all find the fortitude to understand and confront antisemitism in our work. In so doing, we can create a welcoming and safe environment not only for Jews, but for everyone.

45. Ruth HaCohen, *The Music Libel against the Jews* (Yale University Press, 2011), 371.
46. Warnock often refers to Ossoff as "my brother from another mother."

OUTRO

On a Path Forward and Music Theory's Future

> What if the thing we need some citizens to give up is a sense of superiority, a sense that they are—or ought to be—first among equals? And what if they refuse? What do we do about our democracy when one group of citizens, or at least its chosen representatives, rejects the egalitarian ideal at the heart of democratic practice?[1]

On March 18–19, 2021, I was invited for a virtual two-day residency at the Eastman School of Music, one of our country's finest. I met with a theory pedagogy class and a DEI committee, and I gave a talk with a Q&A afterward. It was invigorating, I was pleased to see old friends and new in my Zoom gallery, and I was honored to take part. As I prepped for the meetings, I logged onto Eastman's music theory web page to remind myself who was on the faculty, and, of the twenty-one names listed, I noticed that all twenty-one persons were white.[2] I need to make two points accordingly. First, Eastman is not *at all* exceptional in this regard. Just visit the websites of any of music theory's storied programs—the CUNY Graduate Center, Florida State University, Harvard University, Indiana University, McGill University, Northwestern University, University of British Columbia, University of Chicago, University of Michigan, University of Texas, or Yale University, among others—and do a quick demographic check for race and you'll find at least 90% white faculty, if not 100% as at Eastman. These numbers might change depending on how the program is defined, and whether theory is

1. Jamelle Bouie, "It Started with 'Birtherism,'" *New York Times*, November 24, 2020.
2. See the list of Eastman's music theory faculty here: https://www.esm.rochester.edu/theory/faculty

taken together with composition, but the point remains: the music theory faculty at our main institutions are remarkably white, especially faculty with true power, that is, with tenure.

Second, and this is the more important point, the solution to this radical racial imbalance is not finding one BIPOC music theorist so that the racial makeup of the theory faculty, say at Eastman, becomes 5% BIPOC and 95% white. That might seem like the solution, but even though it can help in some regards, I believe it does more harm than good. In hiring a BIPOC theorist, music theory's white-male frame is looking for someone who fits the mold of the frame. For most of my career, I have been such a theorist. My PhD is from Yale University, one of the strongest music theory programs in the country; my main advisers were Carl Schachter, Allen Forte, and Yuri Kholopov, three of the most significant music theorists from the last half century; and my research areas, Russian music theory, Russian opera, pitch class set analysis, and modal and tonal theory, all comport with the framing of our field. Over the past years I have spoken with two senior theorists who told me, to my face, that they would love to have more BIPOC theorists (to interview for a job, give an award to, serve on a non-DEI committee, apply for admission to a theory program, whose scholarship they could publish, etc.) but they just didn't see any qualified BIPOC theorists out there. Ironically, they were saying this to me, which means one of two things: either they don't consider me to be BIPOC, or they don't consider me and my scholarship to be qualified (I suspect it was a bit of both).

The solution is not in finding the one BIPOC theorist who conforms to the white-male frame of the field but, rather, the solution lies in *changing the framing of the field itself.* Eastman's music theory faculty shouldn't be 5% BIPOC—*it should be 50% BIPOC*, as the theory programs at all other major institutions should be. Once again, for a final time, I invoke the language of the Society for Classical Studies:

> As scholars and teachers, we condemn the use of the texts, ideals, and images of the Greek and Roman world to promote racism or a view of the Classical world as the unique inheritance of a *falsely-imagined and narrowly-conceived* western civilization.[3]

---

3. Helen Cullyer, "Public Statement from the SCS Board of Directors," Society for Classical Studies, November 28, 2016 (https://classicalstudies.org/scs-news/public-statement-scs-board-directors) (italics mine).

Currently, our conceptions of American music theory fit squarely into these falsely imagined and narrowly conceived notions of a superior western canon of music. Some will quickly point out all the new directions music theory has taken over the last, say, decade, interdisciplinary directions that have pushed the field to forge new paths. I certainly can't deny that these new directions exist, but this is misleading. The epistemic core of the American music major, which always consists of at least two but usually four to six semesters of undergraduate music theory, as well as the core of the field itself, still centers the west and all the mythologies of greatness contained in a falsely imagined and narrowly conceived western civilization.

The 1855 Project

Nikole Hannah-Jones's 1619 Project continues to draw ire and acclaim, yet critics and advocates alike rarely mention their own race. Instead, clad only in black text on a white page, identities are hidden, biases ignored. Hannah-Jones, who is black, assembled a multiracial collective to help reframe American history from an African American perspective, one that gives the arrival of the first enslaved Africans, in August 1619, as the true beginnings of the United States. Five prominent white historians pushed back in a critical letter to the *New York Times*.[4] Historians Thavolia Glymph and Nell Irvin Painter, who are black, were asked to sign that letter, but notably refused.[5] Perhaps the time has come to weigh the voices of those involved depending on how one benefits from any given racialized structure. To be blunt: for all their talk of colorblindness, critics of the 1619 Project are overwhelmingly white. Should we not therefore grade, for example, journalist Bret Stephens's critique of 1619 on a curve since he, a white person, most benefits from keeping in place the dubious historical American narrative—one of a constant march of racial progress—as it currently exists?[6]

Certain reactions to my race scholarship in music theory quite resemble some of the conservative reactions to 1619. All the ten core volume 12 authors were white men, for instance, yet other negative reactions to my work from

4. Victoria Bynum, James M. McPherson, James Oakes, Sean Wilentz, and Gordon S. Wood, "Letter to the Editor: We Respond to the Historians Who Critiqued the 1619 Project," *New York Times*, December 20, 2019.

5. Adam Serwer, "The Fight over the 1619 Project Is Not about the Facts," *The Atlantic*, December 23, 2019.

6. Bret Stephens, "The 1619 Chronicles," *New York Times*, October 9, 2020.

BIPOC scholars have been remarkably muted, almost nonexistent in fact. So, with volume 12, did I get 1619-ed? I quite welcome honest debate over any position I take in a scholarly venue, so long as that debate remains collegial and respectful. Yet we would all do well to interrogate exactly whose voices get most amplified in these debates. There has been—and should be—sustained critique from BIPOC of structural racism and the methods for dismantling it within any scholarly discipline that is historically white like music theory. But the only dissenting voices in the music academy that I've heard so far to my race scholarship are, in fact, white (and male) voices, and those voices display an utterly predictable level of colorblindness and entitlement.

One of the most compelling aspects of the 1619 Project was to rethink the founding of our country, moving its beginning from 1776 to 1619, highlighting the impact that slavery has had on our history. In the entry for "Theory" in *Oxford Music Online*, David Carson Berry and Sherman Van Solkema place the beginning of music theory in the United States at 1960.[7] This is when figures like Milton Babbitt and Allen Forte were beginning to make their "scientific" explorations and discoveries in the field. But as with the 1619 Project, I'd like to offer a different starting point for music theory, both in the United States and Europe: 1855, the year the French aristocrat and race pseudoscientist Arthur de Gobineau finished his four-volume *Essai sur l'inégalité des races humaines* (Essay on the inequality of human races).[8] This work, which developed the theories of the Aryan master race that were used by the Nazis in the twentieth century, also gave musicians working materials with which to build racialized structures in the study of music.

As I have already pointed out, three significant musical figures drew inspiration from Gobineau's *Essai*, among other writings by Gobineau: François-Joseph Fétis, Richard Wagner, and Heinrich Schenker. As outlined in Thomas Christensen's *Stories of Tonality in the Age of François-Joseph Fétis*, Fétis was greatly influenced by Gobineau late in life and, with respect to the *Essai*, Christensen writes that "Fétis owned a copy of Gobineau's notorious tract and evidently made much use of it."[9] Wagner met Gobineau briefly in Rome in 1876, and they became friends until Gobineau died in 1882. Further, Wagner and his wife Cosima carried on a lengthy correspondence

---

7. David Carson Berry and Sherman Van Solkema, "Theory," *Oxford Music Online*, 2013.

8. Arthur de Gobineau, *Essai sur l'inégalité des races humaines* (Essay on the inequality of human races), 4 vols. (Paris, 1853–55).

9. Thomas Christensen, *Stories of Tonality in the Age of François-Joseph Fétis* (University of Chicago Press, 2019), 204. Also, generally, see chapter 5 in *Stories of Tonality*. I also pointed this out in my Intro.

with Gobineau in the early 1880s.[10] Schenker mentioned Gobineau in "The Mission of the German Genius," as well as in his diaries five times in 1918.[11] These three men, two music theorists and one composer, were extremely influential in the history of music and music theory in both Europe and the United States, and their beliefs in the racial hierarchies of white supremacy are not in doubt. Specifically, Schenker provides an explicit link between the European white supremacy espoused by Gobineau and American music theory. Connecting their beliefs, through the countless musicians whom Fétis, Wagner, and Schenker influenced, to racial injustice in the field is actually not that difficult once one gets going, and one could undoubtedly write a great dissertation or monograph on this topic. But my point here is much more modest: I'm suggesting that American music theory did not really begin in the 1960s but, rather, with the nineteenth-century intensification of a fallacious race science that sought to prove white superiority and black inferiority, an intensification that reached an apex of sorts with the fourth and final volume of Gobineau's *Essai* in 1855. Who now will write music theory's 1855 Project, which would foreground music theory's racialized structures that account for the hostile environments that BIPOC face in the field? That's a work I for one would be eager to read.

Recommendations

I have one general overarching recommendation: namely, through organizing and collective action, keep the pressure on existing power structures in music theory, and in academic music, to effect substantive antiracist and antisexist changes, and not just superficial "diversity" changes that often only reinforce the whiteness and maleness of what we do. Change is happening faster than I thought possible when I started this work several years ago. I now hear defenders of the status quo crying "academic freedom" when they're told that they have to include more diverse music and music theorists in the classroom, for instance. I consider this a great victory, since historically those who support the white-male status quo have never had to justify their classroom content at all, simply claiming it was the greatest,

10. See Eric Eugène, ed., *Richard et Cosima Wagner / Arthur Gobineau: Correspondance, 1880–1882* (Nizet, 2000).

11. Heinrich Schenker, *Der Tonwille: Pamphlets in Witness of the Immutable Laws of Music, Offered to a New Generation of Youth*, trans. Ian Bent, William Drabkin, Joseph Dubiel, Timothy Jackson, Joseph Lubben, and Robert Snarrenberg (Oxford University Press, [1921–23] 2004), vol. 1, 13.

most exceptional music and music theory of all time, in race-neutral and gender-neutral fashion. Their retreat to "academic freedom" means that the old mythologies of white-male greatness are no longer working, and this is when we must all keep the pressure on, for the simple reason that no one has the academic freedom to be racist in the classroom (see the Civil Rights Act of 1964 here), just like no one has the academic freedom to be sexist in the classroom (see the Title IX civil rights legislation of 1972 here).

Also, insist on *forcing* the inclusion of BIPOC into the structure of academic music. Only by forcing white-male structures to acknowledge the work of BIPOC can we begin to see the change we seek. One instructive case comes from my mother's country. In 2003 antisexist forces in Norway had had enough. Sexists were spinning their hackneyed idea of "how hard it is to find qualified women" for company boards of directors, so the antisexist government acted, passing a law requiring that all publicly held companies have minimum 40% women on their boards. The law took effect in 2006 and gave companies until 2008 to make the change or risk liquidation. Guess what happened? They found the women.[12] Imagine that. Other countries followed, like Finland, France, Germany, Iceland, and Spain, for instance. Sexist countries have criticized Norway's actions and tried to spin it negatively, since Norway's success would imply similar action should be taken elsewhere.

Such forced inclusion is needed in music theory to change power structures. The Society for Music Theory could set benchmarks like Norway did. Here's how a statement might read:

> By 2030 we at SMT vow to make the society minimum 50% people who do not identify as cisgender men, and minimum 40% BIPOC. We will do this by aggressively recruiting such persons to run for office and serve on boards and committees, and not just diversity committees where they have historically served. We will set benchmarks with respect to the number of such persons who are involved in our governing structures, and we will grant our Outstanding Publication Awards with the same benchmarks in mind.

Only through forcing the issue will music theory diversify with respect to race and gender—it will not happen organically. Because of self-interest, those in power will not cede power by themselves.

---

12. Morten Huse, Silvija Seres, and Cathrine Seierstad, "Lessons from Norway in Getting Women onto Corporate Boards," *The Conversation*, March 6, 2015 (https://theconversation .com/lessons-from-norway-in-getting-women-onto-corporate-boards-38338).

A note to students of all levels. You have power, more than you know. If you've read *On Music Theory* and agree with its content, I encourage you to find your allies, build coalitions, and organize in order to press faculty and administrators to address the issues I've written about, since those faculty and administrators are accountable to you. I often lament neoliberalism, in which we treat our institutions of higher learning as corporations, everything judged by the bottom line, but this is actually one thing that is good about our American neoliberal academy. Students banding together to request and even demand action can actually lead to positive change. By contrast, in Russia, a country I know quite well, it would be unthinkable that students banding together to request fundamental, say curricular, changes, would result in anything but possibly those students being punished by the administration.

Another general recommendation, one that I've highlighted in various ways throughout *On Music Theory*, concerns the necessity of finding allies to band together to act collectively. Allyships and coalitions are extremely important in trying to bring change to fields like music theory that are resistant to change. By banding together with like-minded individuals, I've seen positive change happen. As an example, one master's degree jazz student wrote to me in 2020 from a university in California and explained how my writings had had a positive impact in making change through collective action. The student had been accepted to the university in fall 2020 as a graduate jazz performance major and was being asked to take a "music theory and history placement test," which consisted almost entirely of classical "western" music. The student refused to take the test and, instead, wrote a letter of protest to the administration, noting that, for the only question not based on classical white-male music—who wrote "Take the 'A' Train"?—the faculty misidentified the composer as Duke Ellington (it's actually Billy Strayhorn). This student banded together with all other graduate jazz students, that is, found allies, built a coalition, and demanded change. The student shared with me the redacted correspondence that the group had with administrators—a fascinating read—and, ultimately, the group was successful. The administrators agreed to three major changes: they (1) disbanded the use of placement/diagnostic tests for *all* entering graduate students (after all, such students have already been accepted for an MA degree—if they were somehow deficient they should not have been accepted in the first place), (2) disbanded the use of remedial courses for grad students, and (3) created two graduate-level jazz seminars (formerly they did not have any, and students needed to take courses in classical music to fulfill requirements). Needless to say, this email made my day, realizing that something I had written helped students in their quest for graduate degrees in music. Through collective action, change is possible, and students have more power than they might realize.

My African American father would often say that those who stand to gain the most from racial justice are white persons, in "The truth shall set you free" fashion. White persons, especially white men, bear an enormous unnecessary burden in sustaining the many myths of whiteness and maleness in music theory. Since my SMT plenary talk in November 2019 I have been struck by how many people, thousands from all over the world, have reached out on various platforms to thank me for my talk and my work. At first I was struck by comments from women and BIPOC, but after reflection I have been perhaps more struck by comments from white men, who were generally thankful that I had begun this discussion. The divide is, to a large extent, generational. Young scholars, irrespective of racial or gender identity, generally support my race scholarship. Indeed, I have never been more convinced that these young scholars are eager to undertake this type of work and turn the page on music theory's irrepressible promotion of whiteness and maleness.

However, senior scholars are more likely to be skeptical of the positions I have taken, since they have power in the field, and if some of the changes I suggest are made, they will lose some (but certainly not all) of that power. In other words, by opposing my positions they are acting in their own self-interest, which freezes them into inaction. Also, senior scholars often overcontextualize racial and gender matters and offer bothsides explanations with respect to serious antiracist or antisexist measures. Sure, overcontextualizing Schenker is an extreme case, since he was so manifestly horrible, but any and all racial, gender, or other injustice is often overcontextualized by senior scholars in the field, and calling out that overcontextualization is paramount to achieving social justice in the academic study of music. Also, if someone avoids direct racial language, call that out too, since avoiding such language is a key component of framing the issues. In music theory's white-male frame, and America's white-male frame for that matter, direct racial and gender language is frowned upon—colorblindness and gender neutrality reign supreme—and underlying matters about racism and sexism go misunderstood as a result. Upton Sinclair saw this long ago when he famously wrote, "It is difficult to get a man to understand something when his salary depends on his not understanding it."[13]

---

13. See https://www.goodreads.com/quotes/21810-it-is-difficult-to-get-a-man-to-understand-something

Table Outro.1. The Distinction between DEI and Antiracism/Antisexism
(read points left to right)

Diversity, Equity, and Inclusivity	Antiracism/Antisexism
• Staging Shirley Graham Du Bois's opera *Tom Tom: An Epic of Music and the Negro* (1932)	• Writing an academic work explaining why *Tom Tom* has been ignored because of structural racism/sexism
• Forming a committee to discuss various aspects of race/gender in an academic music program	• Voting in committee to discontinue a racist/sexist exclusionist structure, like a graduate German-language requirement for musicians
• Allowing a student to pass a musicianship proficiency by substituting, say, the oud for the piano, as an exception to a piano-proficiency requirement	• Discontinuing the piano-proficiency requirement altogether, having realized that it itself is a method of policing and enforcing a commitment to whiteness and maleness
• Adding a Jewish or Kwanzaa song to your winter holiday concert	• Examining the legacy of Christianity associated with such concerts, and the potentially exclusionary aspects of a hidden Christianity requirement therein
• Admitting a woman, transgender man/woman, or gender-nonconforming person into your doctoral orchestral conducting program	• Committing, in writing, to have minimum 50% such persons within a given timeframe, say five years, in your doctoral orchestral conducting program at all levels, from incoming students to senior faculty

Finally, before my general list of recommendations, it's of the utmost importance to consistently keep in mind the distinction between DEI and antiracism/antisexism, since all too often DEI is mistaken for antiracism/antisexism—the two are even conflated at times—and only by understanding this paramount difference can we move beyond the simpler additive activities of DEI to bolder antiracist/antisexist actions.[14] I've used Table O.1 in a recent talk in order to outline this difference. On the left I list a DEI version of an action, and on the right the bolder antiracist/antisexist similar action. So read the bullet points left to right.

Too often DEI activities act as a smokescreen in order to allow music theory's (and academic music's) white-male structures to maintain and reinforce their power. By taking DEI actions, white men often (though not always) seek to decelerate or otherwise impede antiracist/antisexist progress.

---

14. For more on problems with DEI in higher education, see Sara Ahmed, *On Being Included: Racism and Diversity in Institutional Life* (Duke University Press, 2012).

And when such DEI activities are taken, they must be understood clearly and called out as the stalling tactics they are often intended to be.

Here are some other general recommendations:

1. Push for your institution or academic society to conduct a racial- and gender-justice commission, something like the recent commission undertaken by the Eastman School of Music, the "Eastman Action Commission for Racial Justice," from October 2020.[15] Though such commissions can't solve all racial problems, they can establish a baseline of historical injustices and give direction on what actions can be taken in the future to right these injustices. True, such commissions often fall under the rubric of DEI and not antiracism, but through them we can often begin discussions about antiracism, and such commissions often lead to further actions and studies that can continue the momentum of racial and gender justice in our American musical institutions.

2. If there are classes in which 100% of the figures studied are white men, like a typical History of Music Theory graduate seminar in doctoral programs, insist that those classes are optional, not required, and cite the possible infringement of the 1964 Civil Rights Act and the 1972 Title IX legislation as a reason to do so. If the curricula for those classes are then required to change, set minimum benchmarks for BIPOC figures, as well as those who do not identify as cisgender men, including not only cisgender women but transgender men and women and gender nonconforming persons as well.

3. Push to change music proficiency requirements, especially piano proficiency requirements. Piano is yet another way music theory polices and enforces a commitment to whiteness and maleness in the field. Is it any surprise that all "master" composers of a so-called western canon were pianists? Of course, any and all instruments deserve a seat at the table, and those who want to check students' musicianship can listen to them perform on their instrument, including voice. And with respect to teaching theory and the ability to play piano, I'm of the firm opinion that one can teach music theory quite effectively and *never touch* a piano keyboard in class. One can also play piano in class, but it

---

15. See https://www.esm.rochester.edu/diversity/report

is not a requirement for effective music theory teaching in the twenty-first century.

4. If revamping doctoral admissions policies, consider requiring that one of the writing samples primarily feature figures who are not both white and male.

5. Consider doing away with graduate "placement" or "diagnostic" exams, since they are only ways in which to police and enforce a commitment to whiteness and maleness.

6. Consider doing away with Graduate Record Examinations (GRE) requirements, if your program still has them, since the history of standardized tests is deeply rooted in racial exclusionism and segregationism.[16]

7. Consider eliminating all graduate foreign-language requirements, since they can be so clearly linked to the many mythologies of greatness that undergird the "western canon" in music, and are also so clearly linked to racial and gender exclusionism. Let's not forget that, in music theory, there are historically only five "official" such languages—ancient Greek, Latin, Italian, French, and German, here listed in chronological order in the western narrative. This tracks exactly the western mythologies that I outlined in chapter 2. And if the word "German," for instance, is simply removed from in front of "foreign-language requirement," point that out as white-racial-framing sleight-of-hand, since the existing German-French-Italian structure will obviously still be favored. As I wrote earlier, I often say that requiring graduate *music* students to pass foreign-language proficiency exams would be like requiring graduate students in German to pass a clarinet-performance proficiency exam. Sure, playing the clarinet is great, but obviously not necessary to study German languages and literature, the same way studying German (or French or Italian) is not necessary to study music theory.

8. If your graduate music theory program has required classes in Schenkerian analysis, consider making such classes optional and

---

16. For a clear example of, in this instance, keeping black men away from white women through standardized testing, see once again Thomas Russell, "'Keep Negroes Out of Most Classes Where There Are a Large Number of Girls': The Unseen Power of the Ku Klux Klan and Standardized Testing at the University of Texas, 1899–1999," *SSRN Electronic Journal*, April 5, 2010.

not required. Schenkerian theory and analysis, a racialized and gendered structure of music theory's white-male frame, benefits white men while disadvantaging all others. Because we have consistently whitewashed Schenker's racism and sexism, this results in colorblind racism and gender-neutral sexism, which seeks to erase any explicit discussions about racism and sexism, all of which can create hostile environments for those who do not identify as white men. By making such classes optional you are making a clear statement that you are not *requiring* students to participate in such a highly racialized and gendered structure, as no student should be required to do. Finally, note that classes in Schenkerian analysis are now being rebranded as "linear," "prolongational," or, most common, "tonal" analysis. This amounts to white-male framing sleight of hand, an obfuscation tactic, and should be called out as such. Shockingly, those who effect such changes sometimes actually believe that they are being antiracist, when in fact it's just the opposite. Such obfuscation tactics have one primary goal: to keep in place the existing racist and sexist structure so that whiteness and maleness can continue to enjoy the privileges to which they feel entitled. Changing the title of your class in Schenkerian analysis does the same work as removing "German" from in front of "language requirement" for graduate students in music, namely, obfuscation in service of whiteness and maleness.

9. Consider opening up different music-major tracks, so that the major does not only cater to, or center solely around, those who've played classical instruments for years. Such tracks might include, for instance, sound recording and engineering, pop music studies, music copyright law (possibly in conjunction with a law school), music business (possibly in conjunction with a business school or MBA program), global music traditions, video and gaming music, or turntablism and beat making.

10. For capstone projects, whether for a bachelor's, master's, or doctoral degree, consider allowing other forms of scholarship aside from written papers. Such forms might include a podcast series, a thematic CD or album, a YouTube video or documentary, or other forms of media production. This is not to say that writing compellingly should not be a goal of our educational institutions. Rather, it is acknowledging that such writing can

be expressed in many ways in the twenty-first century, ways that highlight trends in technology and social media, ways in which so many of our students are already conversant.[17]

11. Begin to rebrand doctoral music theory programs to reflect the reality that graduating students are unlikely to get full-time tenure-track jobs in the field. This clear-eyed accounting of music theory (and musicology and ethnomusicology) will allow for new conversations with administrators about what careers such doctorates might lead to in our new environment. There is still a place for music doctorates even if they are not part of academia, and we should embrace that reality in order to give the best advisement to our graduate-student colleagues.

12. Consider rebranding "ethnomusicology" as, simply, "musicology," which it is of course, since the distinction arose as yet another form of racial exclusionism in the late nineteenth and early twentieth centuries.[18]

13. If you are a member of the leadership of a music theory society, regional or national, in North America or in Europe, for instance, consider crafting a statement like that of the Society for Classical Studies that I've cited in my work, and note specifically that, not only does your society support efforts to include many different styles and genres of our planet's music theories, it believes that music theory applies to studies far beyond a "falsely imagined" and "narrowly conceived" western music theory.

14. Break the bizarre cycle of boycotting academic conference sites based on state politics. I recently had an interesting back-and-forth with a friend about potential Society for Music Theory boycotts of conference sites, based on the recent Supreme Court *Dobbs v. Jackson Women's Health Organization* decision.

---

17. As an example, see A. D. Carson's thirty-four-song rap album, which served as his PhD dissertation, "Owning My Masters: The Rhetorics of Rhymes & Revolutions" (PhD dissertation, Clemson University, 2017). For more on this, see Michel Martin, "After Rapping His Dissertation, A. D. Carson Is UVa's New Hip-Hop Professor," *All Things Considered*, National Public Radio, July 15, 2017.

18. For a compelling account of ethnomusicology's questionable past as *Vergleichende Musikwissenschaft* (comparative musicology), see Pamela Potter, "The Concept of Race in German Musical Discourse," in *Western Music and Race*, ed. Julie Brown (Cambridge University Press, 2007), 49–62.

I consider a potential SMT boycott as at least three things. (1) Antiblack, since many of the top boycott destinations are in the south, which has the largest black population in the country. If blacks had not been so completely shut off from the ballot box there, who knows where those places would be politically at the moment? An SMT boycott of southern states rewards white power structures, which don't want (white) progressives there anyway, while punishing black/brown people who need the business, and who have virtually no voice. (2) Myopic, since I could hop on my bike in Brooklyn and get to a neo-Nazi rally on Staten Island in less than 60 minutes. But no, let's meet in New York, NY, which is "more in line with SMT's core values." (3) Most important, holier-than-thou, since if SMT boycotts a place because "it's not in line with our core values," I'd retort, "what, white supremacy and patriarchy?" Channeling my anti-racist killjoy, I will challenge any such boycott up until that time when music theory can look at the mirror and honestly tell the lengthy story of its own history of hate, anger, and exclusion.[19]

15. If someone says that enacting any of my recommendations represents a "lowering of standards," push back against that language. Usually, a lowering of standards is code for becoming less white and less male. In fact, to the racial assimilationist, a lowering of standards quite literally means becoming less white, since whiteness represents the highest and most sophisticated standard in music to the assimilationist. That is, enacting true antiracist change equates to a lowering of standards to the racial assimilationist and, if someone speaks in this coded language,

19. For my money, I'd suggest that the next SMT meeting should be in Birmingham, Alabama. It's a beautiful town, over 65% black, with a rich (musical) history of resistance and perseverance, and we could make a statement about so much more than the latest American tragedy (in this case the overturning of *Roe v. Wade*) by meeting there. SMT boldly going to Birmingham, and explaining in depth why it is doing so, would make SMT a society to be proud of. Frankly, it could be a model for others, and it could break the crazy mold of progressives throwing a fit about meeting in "bad" places, without acknowledging or even realizing that our very own place is quite problematic to begin with. Or, how about meeting in a city near a sizable indigenous territory and population—Billings, MT, Flagstaff, AZ, and Tulsa, OK, come immediately to mind—and actively engage with those people and their rich music (theoretical) traditions, if they'd be so kind to invite us as guests of course, if only for a moment.

they should be called out for it. Finally, I could make exactly
the same argument that enacting antisexist change equates to a
lowering of standards to the gender assimilationist, who believes
that the cisgender man is the highest and most sophisticated
standard among genders.

16. If you are a BIPOC individual, and a person in power asks you
if the treatment you are receiving is "racially motivated," refuse
to answer that question and say, "No comment." It should not
be your duty to explain to power structures the racial dynamics of music education. The same goes for comments such as
"motived by sexism, homophobia, transphobia, Islamophobia,
etc." And if you're in a position of power and someone comes to
you for help, never ask if the situation in question was "racially
motivated"—presume that's the case and work from there.

17. If you are a member of a minoritized and marginalized group
and you are being discriminated against, to the point of losing your position through a denial of tenure or reappointment,
being denied your graduate degree in your program, or undergoing any other matter of injustice because of that discrimination,
consider the following steps:

    (a) Stop the electronic paper trail. This means no email, social
    media, text messages, and the like regarding your case. Limit
    your discussions of the discrimination to verbal encounters
    with your partner or close friends, but stop writing openly
    about it. Even folks you thought you knew can surprise
    you in their lack of support—or even support for your
    abuser—so conservatively narrow your circle of friends more
    than you think is necessary.

    (b) Document. Write clear timelines for yourself and your allies
    documenting all of the antiblack, antiwoman, Islamophobic,
    transphobic, homophobic, antisemitic, ableist, etc., actions
    taken against you, and be prepared to present the timelines
    when necessary. You're playing a long game here, collect-
    ing evidence, and you never know what new material may
    emerge.

    (c) Wait. As much as you might want to act, bide your time by
    waiting until the situation plays out. One thing that frus-
    trates white-male power when it acts maliciously is when the

target of the discrimination doesn't play by the white-male playbook. Wait weeks or months if necessary—you never know what things might change in the meantime.

(d) If possible and appropriate, seek legal advice. Lawyers are wonderfully dispassionate when it comes to these situations, and they can see them much more clearly as a result. This said, be as dispassionate as you can possibly be yourself, as hard as that may be to do.

(e) Don't go to the DEI office or the Title IX office prematurely. Existing power structures consider a person's appeal to DEI or Title IX officials, to an extent, a victory—since they can then claim "he said, she said" or "I'm not a racist/sexist" nonsense—so don't give them that victory prematurely. This goes along with my general advice to wait out the process and to stay quiet. Of course there may come a time to go to those offices, and it's good that they're there. Just don't go prematurely.

(f) Remain unflappable. This might be the hardest one of all, since being discriminated against for simply being who you are is so very unjust. Again, existing power structures often consider a breakdown on the part of the person being discriminated against a victory, so don't give them this victory.

(g) Move on. Once you emerge victorious, move on to greener pastures. Dwelling on the painful past is probably not worth it, unless you can turn your experience into a learning moment to those around you somehow, through academic or other work.[20]

(h) Help others. One thing I've felt after my battles with antiblack actors, and certainly after I gained tenure, is a responsibility to help others who face racial, gender, and other injustices brave the storm, and I hope that you can do the same on the other side of whatever nonsense you went through. My mentorship (I don't much care for this term, since I learn so much from my mentees) of those who have been wronged by existing power structures has been, in fact, one of the most rewarding aspects of my career over these

---

20. Turning such painful experiences into learning moments is the topic of Sara Ahmed's latest book *Complaint!* (Duke University Press, 2021).

past several years. Also important, many of my mentees are in fact white men since they can be collateral damage in the white-male structures of music theory. In other words, white men are not a monolith, and countless white men are, obviously, some of the best allies out there. And, as I've said many times, no blame, no guilt, but responsibility and accountability, for everyone.

18. If you are undertaking an academic research project in music, consider making an examination of race and racial issues part of the project. There will always be a racial angle to any musical topic if you wish to make it part of the project.

19. If you're planning a concert, consider putting musical genres and styles that are not normally programmed together on the same concert. For instance, you could plan a concert entitled "The 1870s" and include various pieces of music from the planet that were written in the 1870s, like a given Mariachi piece from Mexico, a traditional gamelan composition from Indonesia, a piano piece by a composer from Austria, and a traditional choral piece from Ghana. Such a concert would connect various musics of the world and present them on equal terms, as they should have always been presented. (Of course, you yourself will not play in all such pieces—this type of concert I offer more from a programming perspective.)

20. If you are part of music theory publishing, consider instituting an open peer-review process. So-called blind (an ableist term for "anonymous") peer review is often a way that white-male structures can weed out work that challenges their authority, under cover of darkness, without accountability. An open peer-review process provides for a higher level of accountability, which is something we should all welcome. And, if someone says that this represents a "lowering of standards," examine whether that comment is from someone who laments the field becoming less white and less male.

21. If you are BIPOC or another minoritized person, consider refusing to serve on diversity committees that exist only to buttress the whiteness and maleness of an organization. Of course, some diversity committees do good work, which should be supported by all involved. But too often such committees are formed only to justify existing power structures. I often say that

diversity committees are the oxygen that whiteness and maleness need in order to justify their existence and maintain power
in the twenty-first century. If declining service is not an option,
consider insisting on BIPOC representation of other "power"
committees, those that are not diversity committees, those that
actually set the policies that govern a given structure.[21]

22. Consider instituting what I call a "flipped mentoring program."
Over these past several years I have learned tremendously from
folks who are junior to me, including even high school students who have reached out to me to discuss my race scholarship. Unfortunately, when mentoring programs are instituted
in music theory, such as those at the Society for Music Theory,
for example, they are very much top-down enterprises, that is,
junior scholars are meant to learn from senior scholars, and
what they are meant to learn, for the most part, is the white-
male methods for succeeding in the field. In other words, we
mentor whiteness and maleness whether we realize that or not.
But what happens when the junior scholars are those who know
more about something—social justice in this case—that inter-
sects with music theory? In my flipped program I would assign
two or three junior scholars with one willing senior scholar who,
together, work on a project that reframes music theory from a
social-justice perspective. Perhaps such meetings, probably over
Zoom, could take place with a certain amount of anonymity,
because of the power imbalance, and then results could be discussed at the next major conference. Too often we senior scholars don't avail ourselves of the great wealth of knowledge that
our junior scholars can offer. I mean no disrespect to the several
eminent senior music theorists I've studied with since the 1990s,
but, honestly, I have learned no less about music theory in the
past few years in my interactions with those who are junior to
me—in fact, it has been one of the most exhilarating aspects of
my career.

---

21. Alan Henry calls the distinction between power committees and diversity committees
"glamor work" vs. "housework." See Henry, "How to Succeed When You're Marginalized or
Discriminated against at Work," *New York Times*, October 1, 2019.

23. Don't let music theory's white-male frame draw you into bad-faith arguments. If you play on the field of white-male framing, you've lost the game before it began—this game, to coopt the language of the right, is rigged. For instance, you'll never convince anyone, anywhere, that Joseph Bologne (1745–1799), who was black, was as good or a better composer than Franz Joseph Haydn (1732–1809), who was white—it can't be done within the white racial frame, which is to say within academic music theory. Not that Bologne was a better composer than Haydn—he wasn't. Or he was. Which is to say it's purely a matter of opinion. For my money, I'm a fan of neither Haydn's nor Bologne's music—the difference here is that I'm willing to acknowledge that my dislike of their music is purely my opinion and nothing more, while music theory has convinced us all that Haydn is a better composer than Bologne because of measurable "scientific" data, that this is not subjective but "objective," and that it has nothing to do with race, just exceptionalism (to the racial assimilationist) or that it is indeed most certainly linked to race (to the biologically racist segregationist). Which is all utter hogwash of course.

   I have two pieces of advice here. Either smile, wish your would-be debater a good day, and walk away, or leave the white-male playing field altogether and invite your interlocuter to come and play on your field of social justice. Then, respectfully and collegially, ask them about the various racialized (and/or gendered) aspects of classical music, and whether they've ever considered any of them before. Don't let them bring the conversation back to white-male talking points but, rather, insist on playing the game according to your rules, rules that highlight past injustices in the field and the ramifications of ignoring those injustices throughout music theory's entire history. This makes for a much fairer and more invigorating game.

24. Finally, don't be scared! If you've read *On Music Theory* until this point, you know that the reactions of conservative voices in music to genuine antiracist and antisexist work in the field, voices that are usually but not always white and, among them, usually but not always male, can range from mildly disapproving to completely untethered, but this must not dissuade you from

pressing on to make real substantive change in music. Such conservative voices have, above all, one goal in mind: shutting down adult conversations on race and gender (and other social-justice matters) in order to keep in place music's whiteness and maleness, which benefits themselves while disadvantaging all others. Stay strong in the face of such ridiculousness and injustice, and find solace knowing that you are on the right side of history.

Final Thoughts on *On Music Theory*

This is no time to engage in the luxury of cooling off or to take the tranquilizing drug of gradualism. Now is the time to make real the promises of democracy. Now is the time to rise from the dark and desolate valley of segregation to the sunlit path of racial justice. Now is the time to lift our nation from the quicksands of racial injustice to the solid rock of brotherhood. Now is the time to make justice a reality for all of God's children.[22]

Having expressed my thoughts about the contemporary state of American music theory, and the academic study of music more generally, over an Intro and six chapters, I can now say that I might have reasonably subtitled *On Music Theory* "How the Many Mythologies of the Western White-Male Musical Canon Have Created Hostile Environments for Those Who Do Not Identify as White Cisgender Men." But I've not buried the lede by saying so at the end of my book, since there are still so many who believe in those very same mythologies, and, had I said so at the outset, I'd have lost readers early on. Old habits die hard. And even if the reader has stayed with me until this point, it'll still be difficult to unlearn beliefs about the superiority of the Beethovens, the genius of the Riemanns, or the ineffability of Italian opera or German lied. This is not to say, and it has never been to say, that Beethoven, Riemann, Puccini, or Schubert didn't write significant work that is compelling and beautiful. I have always supported those who wish to study and discuss such work, as I have myself for my entire career. Yet those who want to maintain the status quo—those who still believe the mythologies—will doggedly try to make this a zero-sum game, try to obfus-

---

22. Martin Luther King, "I Have a Dream" speech, in "'I Have a Dream' Speech, In Its Entirety," *National Public Radio*, January 18, 2010 (https://www.npr.org/2010/01/18/12270 1268/i-have-a-dream-speech-in-its-entirety).

cate my basic positions. But no amount of obfuscation will change the basic outlines of my argument. White supremacy and patriarchy are mythologies that were used by white men to create the entire concept of the west, western civilization, and the western canon in music, with the most intense efforts coming in the nineteenth and early twentieth centuries. These mythologies, in turn, were used to reinforce and enshrine white-male dominance in the academic study of music, which resulted in the power to form our American music institutions beginning, again, in the nineteenth century. And conservative reactions to me, as a black person, making these simple points are deeply rooted in the antiblackness—the flip side of white supremacy—that is baked into our American DNA.

Panic. The best word to describe how large swaths of America's white population have viewed racial integration with nonwhites and, especially, with blacks in the history of the United States is panic. I write this Outro one hundred years after the Tulsa, Oklahoma, race massacre that killed roughly three hundred black Americans, and injured and displaced thousands more. But this is, ultimately, the reaction of whiteness when blackness gains some power, prestige, or wealth: panic. The reaction from conservative music theorists to my race scholarship as it applies to the academic study of music in the United States can also be summed up by panic. Panic that I'm ruining the foundations of the field (with no acknowledgment that those very foundations are falsely imagined and narrowly conceived); panic that I'm dividing us along racial lines (when in fact music theory itself, since its inception, has done exactly that with composers, musicians, and musical genres); panic that the most cherished part of a beloved music academy is in jeopardy because of ridiculous wokeness, the intrusion of critical race theory into discussions of music, and cancel culture run amok. But this conservative music-theory panic serves only to prove the basic outlines of my argument again and again. No cancel culture or wokeness here. (I'm not cool enough to be woke.) No "inversion of the hierarchy," with white men now at the bottom—no self-respecting race scholar would ever advocate for that. No race or gender is superior, and none inferior. I quite welcome any and all white men into my discussions on race and gender, and I'm happy and honored that countless white men have taken me up on those discussions.

Respect. The most important thing that is lacking in American music theory is respect. First and foremost, respect for all the rich musical traditions of our planet that could rightly count as music theory. And, of course, respect for the people who made those music theories. Our field's unflagging promotion of both whiteness and maleness is disrespectful to so many musicians and musical cultures of our planet, and we desperately need to begin respecting all peoples and cultures regardless of race and gender. I always marvel at critics who tell me that there are white men, from other European cultures for instance, whose music and music theories have been neglected, critics who try to use this as proof that there is nothing racist about our current system. Of course there are, since there are many places on earth where the people who have become known as white can reside. But this is an extremely facile argument, the most facile argument I've encountered in fact, and a diversion that completely ignores the entire five-hundred-year history of white supremacy and the patriarchy—as old as human history itself—that necessarily accompanied that white supremacy. By showing humility about our own beliefs and respecting all other musical cultures, not just with words but with actions, we will all benefit from this respect, and the human dignity that that respect will engender.

Love. We cannot love what we don't respect, and only through love, of our fellow musicians and colleagues across the globe, and the musical traditions of all cultures, can we turn away the panic, the anger, the hate, and look to a better future. I myself have been guilty of musical disrespect in my life, disrespectful of musical cultures that I somehow thought didn't measure up, and I have shown indifference, not love, to other musical peoples as a result. But that's on me and me alone. Note that mine is not a plea to enjoy and respect bad music. Any musical culture can produce that. It is, rather, a plea to understand that the best music of any culture is as worthy and rich as any other, that there is no universal hierarchy for "best music of the planet."

I've found that, especially among younger scholars and musicians, people are learning the racial history of the United States anew and beginning to understand how race has affected the academic study of music in our country. Consequently, these young people have emancipated themselves from the nineteenth- and twentieth-century mythologies that I was taught about music. And, with courage and charisma, they have vowed not to return to the way things were. But this awakening, while in one sense linear—the vast majority of the country, myself included, only learned of the Tulsa race massacre in the last several years, for instance—is also cyclical, and we must be mindful that we could all slip back into complacency, to the way things were, which we must not let happen.

In an open letter to Angela Davis in 1971 while she was in prison, commenting on the racial progress of the time, James Baldwin wrote, "What has happened, it seems to me, and to put it far too simply, is that a whole new generation of people have assessed and absorbed their history, and, in that tremendous action, have freed themselves of it and will never be victims again."[23] Let us all—black persons, white persons, and those of all other races—honestly and openly assess and absorb music theory's history anew as well, free ourselves of its many mythologies while retaining its intrinsic beauty, and resolve to never be victims again.

---

23. James Baldwin, "An Open Letter to My Sister, Miss Angela Davis," *New York Review of Books*, January 7, 1971.

Bibliography

"An Act for Suppressing Outlying Slaves." April 1691. *Encyclopedia Virginia.* https://en cyclopediavirginia.org/entries/an-act-for-suppressing-outlying-slaves-1691/

Agawu, Kofi. "Tonality as a Colonizing Force in Africa." In *Audible Empire: Music, Global Politics, Critique,* ed. Ronald Radano and Tejumola Olaniyan, 334–55. Duke University Press, 2016.

Ahmed, Sara. *Complaint!* Duke University Press, 2021.

Ahmed, Sara. *Living a Feminist Life.* Duke University Press, 2017.

Ahmed, Sara. *On Being Included: Racism and Diversity in Institutional Life.* Duke University Press, 2012.

Aldwell, Edward, Allen Cadwallader, and Carl Schachter. *Harmony and Voice Leading.* 4th ed. Schirmer, 2011.

Alexander, Michelle. *The New Jim Crow: Mass Incarceration in the Age of Colorblindness.* New Press, 2012.

Allen, Theodore W. *The Invention of the White Race.* 2nd ed. 2 vols. Verso, 2012.

Alpern, Wayne. "Music Theory as a Mode of Law: The Case of Heinrich Schenker, Esq." *Cardozo Law Review* 20 (1999): 1459–1511.

Alpern, Wayne. "The Triad of the True, the Good, and the Beautiful: Schenker's Moralization of Music and His Legal Studies with Robert Zimmermann and Georg Jellinek." In *Essays from the Fourth International Schenker Symposium,* ed. L. Poundie Burstein, Lynne Rogers, and Karen M. Bottge, vol. 2, 7–48. Georg Olms Verlag, 2013.

Anderson, Carol. *White Rage: The Unspoken Truth of Our Racial Divide.* Bloomsbury, 2016.

Anderson, Elijah. *Black in White Space: The Enduring Impact of Color in Everyday Life.* University of Chicago Press, 2022.

Anderson, Elijah. "The White Space." *Sociology of Race and Ethnicity* 1, no. 1 (2015): 10–21.

André, Naomi. *Black Opera: History, Power, Engagement.* University of Illinois Press, 2018.

Anku, Willie. "Principles of Rhythm Integration in African Drumming." *Black Music Research Journal* 17, no. 2 (Autumn 1997): 211–38.

Ansari, Emily Abrams. *The Sound of a Superpower: Musical Americanism and the Cold War*. Oxford University Press, 2018.

Appiah, Kwame Anthony. *The Lies That Bind: Rethinking Identity*. Liveright Publishing, 2018.

Appiah, Kwame Anthony. *Lines of Descent: W. E. B. Du Bois and the Emergence of Identity*. Harvard University Press, 2014.

Appiah, Kwame Anthony. "Mistaken Identities: Creed, Country, Color, Culture." *The Reith Lectures*. 2016. BBC Radio 4. https://www.bbc.co.uk/programmes/b080twcz

Appiah, Kwame Anthony. "There Is No Such Thing as Western Civilisation." *The Guardian*, November 9, 2016.

Baker, Kendall. "NBA Leads Big Sports Leagues in African American Representation in Non-player Roles." *Axios.com*, June 9, 2020. https://www.axios.com/african-american-representation-sports-leagues-nba-e0537610-d3da-45e8-ac56-c4d6c2ae25e7.html

Baldwin, James. "As Much Truth as One Can Bear." *New York Times*, January 14, 1962.

Baldwin, James. *The Fire Next Time*. Michael Joseph, 1963.

Baldwin, James. "An Open Letter to My Sister, Miss Angela Davis." *New York Review of Books*, January 7, 1971.

Baraka, Amiri. "Jazz and the White Critic." In Amiri Baraka, *Black Music*, Reissue ed., 15–26. Akashic Books, 2010.

Barthes, Roland. *Mythologies*. Les Lettres nouvelles, 1957.

Beach, David. "Schenker—Racism—Context." *Journal of Schenkerian Studies* 12 (2020): 127–28.

Becker, Judith. "Is Western Art Music Superior?" *Musical Quarterly* 72, no. 3 (1986): 341–59.

Belew, Kathleen. *Bring the War Home: The White Power Movement and Paramilitary America*. Harvard University Press, 2018.

Benjamin, William. "Schenker's Theory and the Future of Music." Review of Schenker's *Der Freie Satz. Journal of Music Theory* 25, no. 1 (1981): 155–73.

Bent, Ian, William Drabkin, et al. *Schenker Documents Online*. http://www.schenkerdocumentsonline.org/index.html

Benward, Bruce, and Marilyn Saker. *Music in Theory and Practice*. 9th ed. 2 vols. McGraw Hill, 2015.

Berman, Ari. *Give Us the Ballot: The Modern Struggle for Voting Rights in America*. Macmillan, 2015.

Berger, Maurice. "Using Photography to Tell Stories about Race." *New York Times*, December 6, 2017.

Bernal, Martin. *Black Athena: The Afroasiatic Roots of Classical Civilization*. 3 vols. Rutgers University Press, 1987.

Berry, David. "Hans Weisse and the Dawn of American Schenkerism." *Journal of Musicology* 20, no. 1 (2003): 104–56.

Berry, David, and Sherman Van Solkema. "Tonality." *Oxford Music Online*, 2013.

Bleiberg, Edward, and Yekaterina Barbash. Wall text for "Ancient Egypt: An African Culture." *Ancient Egyptian Art*, Egyptian Galleries, Third Floor, Morris A. and Meyer Schapiro Wing, Brooklyn Museum, Brooklyn, New York (as of June 8, 2022).

Blumenbach, Johann Friedrich. "De generis humani varietate nativa" (On the natural variety of mankind). PhD dissertation, University of Göttingen, 1775.

Bogage, Jacob. "Leo Frank Was Lynched for a Murder He Didn't Commit. Now Neo-Nazis Are Trying to Rewrite History." *Washington Post*, May 22, 2017.

Bond, Sarah Emily. "History from Below: Hold My Mead: A Bibliography for Historians Hitting Back at White Supremacy." 2017. https://sarahemilybond.com/2017/09/10/hold-my-mead-a-bibliography-for-historians-hitting-back-at-white-supremacy/

Bonilla-Silva, Eduardo. *Racism without Racists: Color-Blind Racism and the Persistence of Racial Inequality in America.* 5th ed. Rowman & Littlefield, [2003] 2018.

Bonilla-Silva, Eduardo. "Rethinking Racism: Toward a Structural Interpretation." *American Sociological Review* 62, no. 3 (1997): 465–80.

Boroson, Warren. "Chopin's Antisemitism." December 25, 2009. https://jewishstandard.timesofisrael.com/chopins-antisemitism/

Boss, Jack. "Response to P. Ewell." *Journal of Schenkerian Studies* 12 (2020): 133–34.

Botstein, Leon. "A Mirror to the Nineteenth Century: Reflections on Franz Liszt." In *Franz Liszt and His World*, ed. Christopher H. Gibbs et al., 516–67. Princeton University Press, 2006.

Botstein, Leon. "Schenker the Regressive: Observations on the Historical Schenker." *Musical Quarterly* 86, no. 2 (2002): 239–47.

Bouie, Jamelle. "It Started with 'Birtherism.'" *New York Times*, November 24, 2020.

Bow, Leslie. "Difference without Grievance: Asian Americans as the 'Almost' Minority." In *Written/Unwritten: Diversity and the Hidden Truths of Tenure*, ed. Patricia Matthew, 67–79. University of North Carolina Press, 2016.

Bower, Calvin M. "The Transmission of Ancient Music Theory into the Middle Ages." In *The Cambridge History of Western Music Theory*, ed. Thomas Christensen, 136–67. Cambridge University Press, [2002] 2008.

Boyer, Horace. "An Analysis of Black Church Music with Examples Drawn from Services in Rochester, New York." PhD dissertation, Eastman School of Music, 1973.

Brett, Philip, Elizabeth Wood, and Gary C. Thomas, eds. *Queering the Pitch: The New Gay and Lesbian Musicology.* Routledge, 1994.

Brown v. Board of Education of Topeka, 347 U.S. 483 (1954).

Brown, Danielle. "An Open Letter on Racism in Music Studies." Mypeopletellstories.com, June 12, 2020. https://www.mypeopletellstories.com/blog/open-letter

Brown, Jenine. "Annual Report on Membership Demographics." Society for Music

Theory, October 2019. https://societymusictheory.org/sites/default/files/demograph
ics/smt-demographics-report-2019.pdf

Brown, Julie, ed. *Western Music and Race*. Cambridge University Press, 2007.

Bryant, Howard. *Full Dissidence: Notes from an Uneven Playing Field*. Beacon Press, 2020.

Buchler, Michael. "From the President." *SMT Newsletter* 45, no. 1 (February 2022): 1–2.

Burkhart, Charles. "Response to Philip Ewell." *Journal of Schenkerian Studies* 12 (2020): 135.

Burstein, L. Poundie, and Joseph N. Straus. *Concise Introduction to Tonal Harmony*. Norton, 2016.

Burton-Hill, Clemency. "Richard Strauss: A Reluctant Nazi." *BBC Culture*, June 9, 2014. https://www.bbc.com/culture/article/20140610-richard-strauss-a-reluctant -nazi

Bynum, Victoria, James M. McPherson, James Oakes, Sean Wilentz, and Gordon S. Wood. "Letter to the Editor: We Respond to the Historians Who Critiqued the 1619 Project." *New York Times*, December 20, 2019.

Cadwallader, Allen. "A Response to Philip Ewell." *Journal of Schenkerian Studies* 12 (2020): 137–40.

Cadwallader, Allen, and David Gagne. *Analysis of Tonal Music: A Schenkerian Approach*. 3rd ed. Oxford University Press, 2010.

Campbell, Patricia Shehan, Juan Chattah, Lee Higgins, Victoria Lindsay Levine, David Myers, David Rudge, Timothy Rice, and Ed Sarath. "Transforming Music Study from Its Foundations: A Manifesto for Progressive Change in the Undergraduate Preparation of Music Majors. Report of the Task Force on the Undergraduate Music Major." College Music Society. November 2014. https://www.music.org/pdf /pubs/tfumm/TFUMM.pdf

Campbell, Stuart, ed. *Russians on Russian Music, 1830–1880*. Cambridge University Press, 1994.

Canellos, Peter S. "Separate but Equal, the Court Said. One Voice Dissented." *New York Times*, May 18, 2021.

Carson, A. D. "Owning My Masters: The Rhetorics of Rhymes & Revolutions." PhD dissertation, Clemson University, 2017.

Chait, Jonathan. "GOP Congresswoman Blamed Wildfires on Secret Jewish Space Laser." *New York Magazine*, January 28, 2021.

Chang, Jeff. *Can't Stop, Won't Stop: A History of the Hip-Hop Generation*. St. Martin's Press, 2005.

Cheng, William. "Gaslight of the Gods: Why I Still Play Michael Jackson and R. Kelly for My Students." *Chronicle of Higher Education*, September 15, 2019.

Chiari, Mike. "Kyrie Irving Explains Flat Earth Stance, Says There Is No Real Picture of Planet." Bleacherreport.com. November 1, 2017. https://bleacherreport.com/ar ticles/2741935-kyrie-irving-explains-flat-earth-stance-says-there-is-no-real-picture -of-earth

Christensen, Thomas, ed. *The Cambridge History of Western Music Theory*. Cambridge University Press, [2002] 2008.

Christensen, Thomas. "Music Theory and Its Histories." In *Music Theory and the Exploration of the Past*, ed. Christopher Hatch and David W. Bernstein, 9–40. University of Chicago Press, 1993.

Christensen, Thomas. *Stories of Tonality in the Age of François-Joseph Fétis*. University of Chicago Press, 2019.

Clark, Suzannah. "The Politics of the Urlinie in Schenker's 'Der Tonwille' and 'Der freie Satz.'" Review article, *Explaining Tonality: Schenkerian Analysis and Beyond* by Matthew Brown. *Journal of the Royal Musical Association* 132, no. 1 (2007): 141–64.

Clendinning, Jane, and Elizabeth Marvin. *Musician's Guide to Theory and Analysis*. 3rd ed. Norton, 2016.

Coates, Ta-Nehisi. *Between the World and Me*. Spiegel & Grau, 2015.

Coates, Ta-Nehisi. "The Case for Reparations." *The Atlantic*, June 2014.

Coates, Ta-Nehisi. "The First White President." *The Atlantic*, October 2017.

Coates, Ta-Nehisi. *We Were Eight Years in Power: An American Tragedy*. One World, 2017.

Cohen, Jacob A. "Constructions of New England Identity and Place in American Music, 1885–1935." PhD dissertation, the CUNY Graduate Center, 2017.

Cook, Nicholas. "Response to Philip Ewell." *Journal of Schenkerian Studies* 12 (2020): 153–56.

Cook, Nicholas. *The Schenker Project: Culture, Race, and Music Theory in Fin-de-Siècle Vienna*. Oxford University Press, 2007.

Cook, Nicholas. "Schenker's Theory of Music as Ethics." *Journal of Musicology* 7, no. 4 (1989): 415–39.

Crawford, Richard. *The American Musical Landscape*. University of California Press, 1993.

Crenshaw, Kimberlé. "Demarginalizing the Intersection of Race and Sex: A Black Feminist Critique of Antidiscrimination Doctrine, Feminist Theory and Antiracist Politics." *University of Chicago Legal Forum* 140 (1989): 139–67.

Crenshaw, Kimberlé. "The Panic over Critical Race Theory Is an Attempt to Whitewash U.S. History." *Washington Post*, July 2, 2021.

Crenshaw, Kimberlé. "The Urgency of Intersectionality." TED Talk, October 2016. https://youtu.be/akOe5-UsQ2o

Crenshaw, Kimberlé, et al., eds. *Seeing Race Again: Countering Colorblindness across the Disciplines*. University of California Press, 2019.

Cullyer, Helen. "Public Statement from the SCS Board of Directors." Society for Classical Studies. November 28, 2016. https://classicalstudies.org/scs-news/public-state ment-scs-board-directors

Curry, Marshall. "When 20,000 American Nazis Descended upon New York City." Video from *The Atlantic*, October 10, 2017. https://www.theatlantic.com/video/ind ex/542499/marshall-curry-nazi-rally-madison-square-garden-1939

Dailey, Jane. *White Fright: The Sexual Panic at the Heart of America's Racist History.* Basic Books, 2020.

Daniels, Jessie. *Nice White Ladies: The Truth about White Supremacy, Our Role in It, and How We Can Help Dismantle It.* Seal Press, 2021.

Derrida, Jacques. *Margins of Philosophy.* Harvester Wheatsheaf, 1982.

Devaney, Johanna. "Eugenics and Musical Talent: Exploring Carl Seashore's Work on Talent Testing and Performance." *American Music Review* 48, no. 2 (Spring 2019): 1–6.

Doktor, Stephanie Delane. "How a White Supremacist Became Famous for His Black Music: John Powell and *Rhapsodie nègre* (1918)." *American Music* 38, no. 4 (2020): 395–427.

Drabkin, William. "Heinrich Schenker." In *The Cambridge History of Western Music Theory*, ed. Thomas Christensen, 812–43. Cambridge University Press, 2002.

Du, Jincheng, Francisco Guzman, John Ishiyama, Matthew Lemberger-Truelove, and Jennifer Wallach. *Ad Hoc Panel Review: Report of Review of Conception and Production of Vol. 12 of the* Journal of Schenkerian Studies. November 25, 2020.

Du Bois, W. E. B. *Black Reconstruction: An Essay toward a History of the Part Which Black Folk Played in the Attempt to Reconstruct Democracy in America, 1860–1880.* Harcourt, Brace and Company, 1935.

Du Bois, W. E. B. "The Souls of White Folk." In *The Oxford W. E. B. Du Bois Reader*, ed. Eric Sundquist, 497–509. Oxford University Press, 1996.

"Editorial: An Examination of the *Times*' Failures on Race, Our Apology and a Path Forward." *Los Angeles Times*, September 27, 2020.

Eidsheim, Nina Sun. *The Race of Sound: Listening, Timbre, and Vocality in African American Music.* Duke University Press, 2019.

Eligon, John. "A Debate over Identity and Race Asks, Are African-Americans 'Black' or 'black'?" *New York Times*, June 26, 2020.

Eugène, Eric, ed. *Richard et Cosima Wagner / Arthur Gobineau: Correspondance 1880–1882.* Nizet, 2000.

Ewell, Philip. "Американская теория рядов в перспективе" (American set theory in perspective). *Музыкальная Академия* (Music academy) 2015, no. 1 (2015): 148–55.

Ewell, Philip. "Confronting Racism and Sexism in American Music Theory." 2020. Musictheoryswhiteracialframe.com

Ewell, Philip. "Erasing Colorasure in American Music Theory, and Confronting Demons from Our Past." RILM's *Bibliolore* blog series, March 25, 2021.

Ewell, Philip, ed. "Forum: Ethnic Diversity in Music Theory: Voices from the Field." *Gamut: Online Journal of the Music Theory Society of the Mid-Atlantic* 2, no. 1 (2009).

Ewell, Philip. "Music Theory and the White Racial Frame." *Music Theory Online* 26, no. 2 (2020).

Ewell, Philip. "Music Theory's White Racial Frame." *Music Theory Spectrum* 43 (2021): 1–6.

Ewell, Philip. "On Rimsky-Korsakov's False (Hexatonic) Progressions outside the Limits of a Tonality." *Music Theory Spectrum* 42 (2020): 1–21.

Ewell, Philip. "On the Russian Concept of Lād, 1830–1945." *Music Theory Online* 25, no. 4 (2019).

Ewell, Philip. "Russia's New Grove: Priceless Resource or Propagandistic Rubbish?" In *Music's Intellectual History, RILM Perspectives* (2008): 659–70.

Ewell, Philip. "Scriabin's Dominant: The Evolution of a Harmonic Style." *Journal of Schenkerian Studies* 1 (2006): 118–48.

Ewell, Philip. "Symposium on Kendrick Lamar's *To Pimp a Butterfly*." *Music Theory Online* 25, no. 1 (May 2019).

Ewell, Philip. "Почему американцы так любят Шенкера (а Римана ещё больше)" (Why Americans so love Schenker [and Riemann even more]). *Современные проблемы музыкознания* (Contemporary problems of musicology) 18, no. 1 (2018): 2–32.

Ewell, Philip, and Megan Lyons. 2022. "Don't You Cry for Me: A Critical-Race Analysis of Undergraduate Music Theory Textbooks." Forthcoming in *Teaching and Learning Difficult Topics in the Music Classroom*.

Eybl, Martin. "Heinrich Schenker's Identities as a German and a Jew." *Musicologica Austriaca: Journal for Austrian Music Studies*, September 21, 2018. http://www.musau.org/parts/neue-article-page/view/54

Eybl, Martin. *Ideologie und Methode Zum ideengeschichtlichen Kontext von Schenkers Musiktheorie*. Hans Schneider, 1995.

Fannin, Mike. "The Truth in Black and White: An Apology from the *Kansas City Star*." *Kansas City Star*, December 20, 2020.

Feagin, Joe. *The White Racial Frame: Centuries of Racial Framing and Counter-framing*. 2nd ed. Routledge, [2009] 2013.

Feagin, Joe, and Kimberley Ducey. *Elite White Men Ruling: Who, What, When, Where, and How*. Routledge, 2017.

Feder, J. Lester. "Unequal Temperament: The Somatic Acoustics of Racial Difference in the Symphonic Music of John Powell." *Black Music Research Journal* 28, no. 1 (Spring 2008): 17–56.

Flaherty, Colleen. "Countering Allegations of Racism—in Court." *Inside Higher Education*, January 28, 2021. https://www.insidehighered.com/news/2021/01/28/professor-counters-allegations-racism-court

Foti, Silvia. "No More Lies. My Grandfather Was a Nazi: In Lithuania, He Was Celebrated as a Hero. But We Can't Move On until We Admit What He Really Did." *New York Times*, January 27, 2021.

Fricker, Miranda. *Epistemic Injustice: Power and the Ethics of Knowing*. Oxford University Press, 2007.

Giergiev, Valerii. Sergei Prokofiev's *Betrothal at a Monastery*. Kirov [Mariinsky] Theater of Opera and Ballet. Phillips Recording, 1998.

Gillespie McRae, Elizabeth. *Mothers of Massive Resistance: White Women and the Politics of White Supremacy.* Oxford University Press, 2018.

Giovetti, Olivia. "Origin Myths: The Middle Eastern Heritage of Opera." *Van Magazine,* April 4, 2019. https://van-magazine.com/mag/origin-myths/

Giovetti, Olivia, and Jeffrey Arlo Brown. "Music, in Theory." *Van Magazine,* January 28, 2021. https://van-magazine.com/mag/schenker-lawsuit

Gobineau, Arthur de. *Essai sur l'inégalité des races humaines* (Essay on the inequality of human races). 4 vols. Paris, 1853–55.

Goetz, Rebecca Anne. *The Baptism of Early Virginia: How Christianity Created Race.* Johns Hopkins University Press, 2012.

Gordon, Linda. *The Second Coming of the KKK: The Ku Klux Klan of the 1920s and the American Political Tradition.* Liveright Publishing, 2017.

Grimes, Calvin. "American Musical Periodicals, 1819–1852: Music Theory and Musical Thought in the U.S." PhD dissertation, University of Iowa, 1974.

Gross, Jenny. "6 Dr. Seuss Books Will No Longer Be Published over Offensive Images." *New York Times,* March 4, 2021.

Grout, Donald J. *A History of Western Music.* Norton, 1960.

Grout, Donald J., and Claude Palisca. *A History of Western Music.* 4th ed. Norton, 1988.

Grout, Donald J., Claude Palisca, and J. Peter Burkholder. *A History of Western Music.* 7th ed. Norton, 2006.

Grout, Donald J., Claude Palisca, and J. Peter Burkholder. *A History of Western Music.* 10th ed. Norton, 2019.

Guerrieri, Matthew. "Percy Grainger." Red Bull Music Academy, July 17, 2017. https://daily.redbullmusicacademy.com/2017/07/percy-grainger-feature

HaCohen, Ruth. *The Music Libel against the Jews.* Yale University Press, 2011.

Hale, Mike. "Telling the Story of the Tulsa Massacre." *New York Times,* May 30, 2021.

Hall, Anne. "From the Committee on Diversity." *SMT Newsletter* 19, no. 1 (February 1996): 7.

Hall, Stuart. "New Ethnicities." In *Stuart Hall: Critical Dialogues in Cultural Studies,* ed. David Morley and Kuan-Hsing Chen, 442–51. Routledge, [1996] 2005.

Han, Karen. "John Oliver Teaches Fellow White People What They Need to Know about Black Hair." *Brow Beat,* Slate.com, May 10, 2021. https://slate.com/culture/2021/05/john-oliver-black-hair-last-week-tonight-video.html

Hanna, Alex, Nikki L. Stevens, Os Keyes, and Maliha Ahmed. "Actually, We Should *Not* All Use They/Them Pronouns: A Response to a Recent *Scientific American* Essay." *Scientific American, Voices* blog, May 3, 2019.

Hannaford, Marc. "One Line, Many Views: Perspectives on Music Theory, Composition, and Improvisation through the Work of Muhal Richard Abrams." PhD dissertation, Columbia University, 2019.

Hanson, Howard. Letter to the Editor. *New York Times,* January 19, 1941.

Harris, Samantha. "At the University of North Texas, the Mob Comes Calling for a Music Theorist." Nationalreview.com, July 31, 2020. https://www.nationalreview .com/2020/07/at-the-university-of-north-texas-the-mob-comes-calling-for-a-mus ic-theorist/

Hayes, Chris. "The Whiteness of Wealth with Dorothy A. Brown." *Why Is This Happening* podcast, April 20, 2021.

Healy, Kieran. "Fuck Nuance." *Sociological Theory* 35, no. 2 (2017): 118–27.

Hegel, Georg Wilhelm Friedrich. *The Philosophy of History*. Trans. J. Sibree. Batoche Books, 2001.

Heng, Geraldine. *The Invention of Race in the European Middle Ages*. Cambridge University Press, 2018.

Henry, Alan. "How to Succeed When You're Marginalized or Discriminated Against at Work." *New York Times*, October 1, 2019.

Hesse, Barnor. "Racialized Modernity: An Analytics of White Mythologies." *Ethnic and Racial Studies* 30, no. 4 (2007): 643–63.

Hinger, Sarah. "Meet Edward Blum, the Man Who Wants to Kill Affirmative Action in Higher Education." ACLU.org blog, October 18, 2018. https://www.aclu.org/bl og/racial-justice/affirmative-action/meet-edward-blum-man-who-wants-kill-affirm ative-action-higher

Hisama, Ellie. "Getting to Count." *Music Theory Spectrum* 43, no. 2 (2021): 1–15.

Hitler, Adolf. *Mein Kampf.* Trans. James Murphy. Hurst and Blackett, [1925] 1939.

"How Did Anton Webern Die?" *BBC Music Magazine.* September 14, 2020. https:// www.classical-music.com/composers/how-did-anton-webern-die/

Hu, Zhuqing. "From Ut Re Mi to Fourteen-Tone Temperament: The Global Acoustemologies of an Early Modern Chinese Tuning Reform." PhD dissertation, University of Chicago, 2019.

Huse, Morten, Silvija Seres, and Cathrine Seierstad. "Lessons from Norway in Getting Women onto Corporate Boards." *The Conversation*, March 6, 2015. https://theconve rsation.com/lessons-from-norway-in-getting-women-onto-corporate-boards-38338

Hyer, Bryan. "Tonality." In *The Cambridge History of Western Music Theory*, ed. Thomas Christensen, 726–52. Cambridge University Press, 2002.

"Ibram X. Kendi Likes to Read at Bedtime." *New York Times*, "By the Book" series, February 25, 2021.

Interlandi, Jeneen. "Why Doesn't the United States Have Universal Healthcare? The Answer Has Everything to Do with Race." *New York Times*, August 14, 2019.

Interlandi, Jeneen, and Nikole Hannah-Jones. "How the Bad Blood Started." 1619 podcast series, September 13, 2019.

Ishizuka, Katie, and Ramón Stephens. "The Cat Is Out of the Bag: Orientalism, Anti-blackness, and White Supremacy in Dr. Seuss's Children's Books." *Research on Diversity in Youth Literature* 1, no. 2 (2019): Article 4.

Itten, Johannes. *Kunst der Farbe*. Otto Maier Verlag, 1961.

Itten, Johannes. *The Elements of Color*. Ed. Faber Birren. Trans. Ernst van Hagen. Van Nostrand Reinhold, 1970.

Jackson, Timothy. "Escaping from a Black Hole: Facing Depression in Academia." *Music Theory Online* 15, nos. 3–4 (2009).

Jackson, Timothy. "A Preliminary Response to Ewell." *Journal of Schenkerian Studies* 12 (2020): 157–67.

Jalon, Allan M. "How to Listen to Tchaikovsky While Looking Past His Anti-Semitism." May 7, 2019. Forward.com. https://forward.com/culture/music/423847 /how-to-listen-to-tchaikovsky-while-looking-past-his-anti-semitism/

Jamnia, Naseem. "The Dangers of the Gender Binary." Medium.com, January 9, 2016. https://medium.com/the-coffeelicious/the-myth-of-the-gender-binary-72ed2428 c955

Kajikawa, Loren. "Leaders of the New School? Music Departments, Hip-Hop, and the Challenge of Significant Difference." *Twentieth-Century Music* 18, no. 1 (2020): 45–64.

Kajikawa, Loren. "The Possessive Investment in Classical Music: Confronting Legacies of White Supremacy in U.S. Schools and Departments of Music." In *Seeing Race Again Countering Colorblindness across the Disciplines*, ed. Kimberlé Williams Crenshaw, Luke Charles Harris, Daniel Martinez HoSang, and George Lipsitz, 155–74. University of California Press, 2019.

Kajikawa, Loren. *Sounding Race in Rap Songs*. University of California Press, 2015.

Kalib, Sylvan. "Thirteen Essays from the Three Yearbooks 'Das Meisterwerk in der Musik' by Heinrich Schenker: An Annotated Translation." 2 vols. PhD diss., Northwestern University, 1973.

Keldysh, Yuri. *Музыкальная энциклопедия* (Music encyclopedia). 6 vols. Sovetskaia Entsiklopediia, 1991.

Kendi, Ibram X. "Denial Is the Heartbeat of America." *The Atlantic*, January 11, 2021.

Kendi, Ibram X. "The Heartbeat of Racism Is Denial." *New York Times*, January 13, 2018.

Kendi, Ibram X. *How to Be an Antiracist*. One World, 2019.

Kendi, Ibram X. "Our New Postracial Myth." *The Atlantic*, June 22, 2021.

Kendi, Ibram X. *Stamped from the Beginning: The Definitive History of Racist Ideas in America*. Nation Books, 2016.

Kennedy, Rebecca Futo. "On the History of 'Western Civilization,' Part 1." *Classics at the Intersections* blog, 2019. https://rfkclassics.blogspot.com/2019/04/on-history-of -western-civilization-part.html

Kennedy, Rebecca Futo. "Race/Ethnicity Bibliography." *Classics at the Intersections* blog, 2017. https://rfkclassics.blogspot.com/p/bibliography-for-race-and-ethnicity -in.html

Kennedy, Rebecca Futo. "We Condone It by Our Silence: Confronting Classics' Complicity in White Supremacy." *Eidolon*, May 11, 2017. https://eidolon.pub/we-condo ne-it-by-our-silence-bea76fb59b21

King, Martin Luther. "I Have a Dream" speech. In "'I Have a Dream' Speech, in Its Entirety." 1963. *National Public Radio*, January 18, 2010. https://www.npr.org/2010 /01/18/122701268/i-have-a-dream-speech-in-its-entirety

King, Martin Luther. "Letter From a Birmingham Jail." 1963. https://www.africa.upe nn.edu/Articles_Gen/Letter_Birmingham.html

Kostka, Stefan, Dorothy Payne, and Byron Almén. *Tonal Harmony*. 8th ed. McGraw Hill, 2018.

Koza, Julia Eklund. *"Destined to Fail": Carl Seashore's World of Eugenics, Psychology, Education, and Music*. University of Michigan Press, 2021.

Kristof, Nicolas. "When Whites Just Don't Get It." Parts 1–7. *New York Times*, August 30, September 6, October 11, November 15, November 29, 2014; April 2, October 1, 2016.

Laitz, Steven G. *The Complete Musician: An Integrated Approach to Theory, Analysis, and Listening*. 4th ed. Oxford University Press, 2014.

Lang, Paul Henry. *Music in Western Civilization*. Norton, 1941.

Lefkowitz, Mary. *Not Out of Africa: How "Afrocentrism" Became an Excuse to Teach Myth as History*. Basic Books, 1997.

Lefkowitz, Mary, and Guy MacLean Rogers, eds. *Black Athena Revisited*. University of North Carolina Press, 1996.

Lerdahl, Fred. "Cognitive Constraints on Compositional Systems." In *Generative Processes in Music: The Psychology of Performance, Improvisation, and Composition*, ed. John A. Sloboda, 231–59. Oxford University Press, 2000. Reprint from Oxford Scholarship Online, 2012.

Levitz, Tamara. "The Musicological Elite." *Current Musicology* 102 (2018): 9–80.

Lewis, Anthony. "'Bakke' May Change a Lot While Changing No Law." *New York Times*, July 2, 1978.

Lewis, George. "Improvised Music after 1950: Afrological and Eurological Perspectives." *Black Music Research Journal* 16, no. 1 (1996): 91–122.

Lipstadt, Deborah E. *Antisemitism, Here and Now*. Schocken Books, 2019.

Lumsden, Rachel, and Jeffrey Swinkin, eds. *The Norton Guide to Teaching Music Theory*. Norton, 2018.

Mann, Michael. "Schenker's Contribution to Music Theory." *Music Review* 10 (1949): 3–26.

Manne, Kate. "Brett Kavanaugh and America's 'Himpathy' Reckoning." *New York Times*, September 26, 2018.

Manne, Kate. *Down Girl: The Logic of Misogyny*. Oxford University Press, 2017.

Manne, Kate. *Entitled: How Male Privilege Hurts Women*. Crown Publishers, 2020.

Mannes, David. *Music Is My Faith*. Norton, 1938.

Marissen, Michael. *Bach & God*. Oxford University Press, 2016.

Marissen, Michael. *Tainted Glory in Handel's "Messiah."* Yale University Press, 2014.

Martin, Michel. "After Rapping His Dissertation, A. D. Carson Is UVa's New Hip-Hop Professor." *All Things Considered*, National Public Radio, July 15, 2017.

Matthew, Patricia A., ed. *Written/Unwritten: Diversity and the Hidden Truths of Tenure*. University of North Carolina Press, 2016.

McClary, Susan. *Feminine Endings: Music, Gender, and Sexuality*. University of Minnesota Press, 1991.

McCoskey, Denise Eileen. "Black Athena, White Power: Are We Paying the Price for Classics' Response to Bernal?" *Eidolon*, November 15, 2018. https://eidolon.pub/bla ck-athena-white-power-6bd1899a46f2

McCreless, Patrick. "Music Theory and Historical Awareness." *Music Theory Online* 6, no. 3 (2000).

McGhee, Heather. *The Sum of Us: What Racism Costs Everyone and How We Can Prosper Together*. One World, 2021.

McKee, Abaigh. "Igor Stravinsky." *Music and the Holocaust*. http://holocaustmusic.ort .org/politics-and-propaganda/igor-stravinsky/ (accessed July 5, 2022).

McWhorter, John. "Is Music Theory Really #SoWhite?" *It Bears Mentioning* Substack newsletter, February 16, 2021. https://johnmcwhorter.substack.com/p/is-music-the ory-really-sowhite

McWhorter, John. "Stay Woke. The Right Can Be Illiberal, Too." *New York Times*, January 25, 2022.

McWhorter, John. *Woke Racism: How a New Religion Has Betrayed Black America*. Portfolio/Penguin, 2021.

Meeùs, Nicolas, et al. "Open Letter on Schenker's Racism and Its Reception in the United States." September 28, 2020. https://heinrichschenker.wordpress.com/open -letter-on-schenkers-racism-and-its-reception-in-the-united-states/

Metzl, Jonathan M. *Dying of Whiteness: How the Politics of Racial Resentment Is Killing America's Heartland*. Basic Books, 2019.

Miller, Karl Hagstrom. *Segregating Sound: Inventing Folk and Pop Music in the Age of Jim Crow*. Duke University Press, 2010.

Mills, Charles W. "Epistemological Ignorance." In *Fifty Concepts for a Critical Phenomenology*, ed. Gail Weiss, Ann V. Murphy, and Gayle Salamon, 107–13. Northwestern University Press, 2019.

Mills, Charles W. *The Racial Contract*. Cornell University Press, 1997.

Molk, Dave, and Michelle Ohnona. "Promoting Equity: Developing an Antiracist Music Theory Classroom." *New Music Box*, January 29, 2020. https://nmbx.new musicusa.org/promoting-equity-developing-an-antiracist-music-theory-classroom

Moore, Robin D., ed. *College Music Curricula for a New Century*. Oxford University Press, 2017.

Morris, Wesley. "Why Is Everyone Always Stealing Black Music?" *New York Times*, August 14, 2019.

Morrison, Matthew. "Race, Blacksound, and the (Re)making of Musicological Discourse." *Journal of the American Musicological Society* 72, no. 3 (2019): 781–823.

Mputubwele, Ngofeen, and Britta Greene. "Ukraine, War Refugees, and the Problem of White Empathy." *New Yorker Radio Hour*, May 6, 2022.

Neely, Adam. "Music Theory and White Supremacy." Adam Neely's YouTube channel, September 7, 2020. https://youtu.be/Kr3quGh7pJA

Nir, Sarah Maslin. "How 2 Lives Collided in Central Park, Rattling the Nation." *New York Times*, June 14, 2020.

Nir, Sarah Maslin. "White Woman Is Fired after Calling Police on Black Man in Central Park." *New York Times*, May 26, 2020.

Oestreich, James. "Opera Review; A Bit of Bias Covered in Froth." *New York Times*, April 28, 1998.

Oliver, John. *Last Week Tonight*. Season 8, Episode 5, March 14, 2021.

Oluo, Ijeoma. *So You Want to Talk about Race*. Seal Press, 2018.

Padilla Peralta, Dan-el. "Some Thoughts on AIA-SCS 2019." Medium.com, January 7, 2019. https://medium.com/@danelpadillaperalta/some-thoughts-on-aia-scs-2019-d6a480a1812a

Painter, Nell Irvin. *The History of White People*. Norton, 2011.

Palfy, Cora, and Eric Gilson. "The Hidden Curriculum in the Music Theory Classroom." *Journal of Music Theory Pedagogy* 32 (2018): 79–110.

Plessy v. Ferguson, 163 U.S. 537 (1896).

Pomeroy, Boyd. "Schenker, Schenkerian Theory, Ideology, and Today's Music Theory Curricula." *Journal of Schenkerian Studies* 12 (2020): 179–82.

Poser, Rachel. "He Wants to Save Classics from Whiteness. Can the Field Survive?" *New York Times*, February 2, 2021.

Potter, Pamela. "The Concept of Race in German Musical Discourse." In *Western Music and Race*, ed. Julie Brown, 49–62. Cambridge University Press, 2007.

Powell, Michael. "Obscure Musicology Journal Sparks Battles over Race and Free Speech." *New York Times*, February 14, 2021.

Powell, Michael. "'White Supremacy' Once Meant David Duke and the Klan. Now It Refers to Much More." *New York Times*, October 17, 2020.

Radano, Ronald. *Lying Up a Nation: Race and Black Music*. University of Chicago Press, 2003.

Radano, Ronald, and Philip V. Bohlman, eds. *Music and the Racial Imagination*. University of Chicago Press, 2000.

Radano, Ronald, and Tejumola Olaniyan, eds. *Audible Empire: Music, Global Politics, Critique*. Duke University Press, 2016.

Ramsey, Guthrie P., Jr. *Race Music: Black Cultures from Bebop to Hip-Hop*. University of California Press, 2004.

Riemann, Hugo. *Vereinfachte Harmonielehre, oder Die Lehre von den tonalen Funktionen der Akkorde*. Augener, 1893.

Robinson, Dylan. *Hungry Listening: Resonant Theory for Indigenous Sound Studies*. University of Minnesota Press, 2020.

Robinson, Dylan. "To All Who Should Be Concerned." *Intersections* 39, no. 1 (2019): 137–44.

Roig-Francolí, Miguel. *Harmony in Context*. 2nd ed. McGraw Hill, 2010.

Ross, Alex. "Antonio Salieri's Revenge." *New Yorker*, May 27, 2019.

Ross, Alex. "How American Racism Influenced Hitler." *New Yorker*, April 23, 2018.

Ross, Alex. "The Rediscovery of Florence Price." *New Yorker*, January 29, 2018.

Rothstein, William. "The Americanization of Heinrich Schenker." *In Theory Only* 9, no. 1: (1986): 5–17.

Russell, George. *Lydian Chromatic Concept of Tonal Organization*. Concept Publishing, 1953.

Russell, George. *Lydian Chromatic Concept of Tonal Organization*. 4th ed. Concept Publishing, 2001.

Russell, Thomas. "'Keep Negroes Out of Most Classes Where There Are a Large Number of Girls': The Unseen Power of the Ku Klux Klan and Standardized Testing at the University of Texas, 1899–1999." *SSRN Electronic Journal*, April 5, 2010.

Saguy, Abigail C., and Juliet Williams. "Why We Should All Use They/Them Pronouns." *Scientific American, Voices* blog, April 11, 2019. https://blogs.scientificameric an.com/voices/why-we-should-all-use-they-them-pronouns

Salzer, Felix, and Carl Schachter. *Counterpoint in Composition*. Columbia University Press, [1969] 1989.

Sanneh, Kalefa. "The Limits of 'Diversity.'" *New Yorker*, October 9, 2017.

Schachter, Carl. "Elephants, Crocodiles, and Beethoven: Schenker's Politics and the Pedagogy of Schenkerian Analysis." *Theory and Practice* 26 (2001): 1–20.

Schachter, Carl. *Unfoldings: Essays in Schenkerian Theory and Analysis*. Ed. Joseph N. Straus. Oxford University Press, 1999.

Schellhous, Rosalie. "Fétis's 'Tonality' as a Metaphysical Principle: Hypothesis for a New Science." *Music Theory Spectrum* 13, no. 2 (1991): 219–40.

Schenbeck, Lawrence. *Racial Uplift and American Music, 1878–1943*. University Press of Mississippi, 2012.

Schenker, Heinrich. *Counterpoint: A Translation of Kontrapunkt by Heinrich Schenker*. Ed. John Rothgeb. Schirmer Books, [1910 and 1922] 2001.

Schenker, Heinrich. *Der freie Satz*. Trans. and ed. Ernst Oster. Longman Publishers, [1935] 1979.

Schenker, Heinrich. *Der Tonwille: Flugblätter zum Zeugnis unwandelbarer Gesetze der Tonkunst einer neuen Jugend dargebracht von Heinrich Schenker*. Georg Olms Verlag, 1990.

Schenker, Heinrich. *Der Tonwille: Pamphlets in Witness of the Immutable Laws of Music, Offered to a New Generation of Youth*. Trans. Ian Bent, William Drabkin, Joseph Dubiel, Timothy Jackson, Joseph Lubben, and Robert Snarrenberg. Oxford University Press, [1921–23] 2004.

Schenker, Heinrich. Diary entry. 1923. *Schenker Documents Online*, OJ 14/45, [22]. Transcr. Marko Deisinger. Trans. Scott Witmer.

Schenker, Heinrich. *Harmony*. Trans. Elisabeth Mann Borgese. Ed. Oswald Jonas. University of Chicago Press, [1906] 1954.

Schenker, Heinrich. Letter to Felix-Eberhard von Cube. 1933. *Schenker Documents Online*, OJ 5/7a, [46], formerly vC46. Transcr. and Trans. William Drabkin.

Schenker, Heinrich. *The Masterwork in Music*. Vol. 3. Trans. Ian Bent, Alfred Clayton, and Derrick Puffett. Ed. William Drabkin. Dover Publications, [1930] 2014.

Schenker, Heinrich. *Piano Sonata in C minor, Op. III.* Vol. 3 of *Beethoven's Last Piano Sonatas: An Edition with Elucidation.* Trans. and ed. John Rothgeb. Oxford University Press, 2015.

Schenker, Heinrich. *Selected Correspondence.* Ed. Ian Bent, David Bretherton, and William Drabkin. Boydell Press, 2014.

Schloss, Joseph Glenn. *Making Beats: The Art of Sample-Based Hip-Hop.* Wesleyan University Press, 2004.

Serwer, Adam. "The Fight over the 1619 Project Is Not about the Facts." *The Atlantic,* December 23, 2019.

Shapiro, Thomas. *The Hidden Cost of Being African American: How Wealth Perpetuates Inequality.* Oxford University Press, 2004.

Shrage, Laurie. "Confronting Philosophy's Anti-Semitism." *New York Times,* March 18, 2019.

Slottow, Stephen. "An Initial Response to Philip Ewell." *Journal of Schenkerian Studies* 12 (2020): 189–94.

Spevak, Jeff. "From the Archive: The House That Hanson Built." *Democrat and Chronicle,* April 6, 2014. https://www.democratandchronicle.com/story/lifestyle/art/2014/04/06/house-hanson-built/7343473/

Staples, Brent. "How Blackface Feeds White Supremacy." *New York Times,* March 31, 2019.

Staples, Brent. "How the White Press Wrote Off Black America." *New York Times,* July 10, 2021.

Stephens, Bret. "The 1619 Chronicles." *New York Times,* October 9, 2020.

Straus, Joseph. "From the President." *SMT Newsletter* 19, no. 1 (February 1996): 2–3. https://societymusictheory.org/sites/default/files/newsletters/19-1.pdf

Sullivan, Shannon, and Nancy Tuana, eds. *Race and Epistemologies of Ignorance.* State University of New York Press, 2007.

Sumarsam. "Inner Melody in Javanese Gamelan Music." *Asian Music* 7, no. 1 (1975): 3–13.

Taruskin, Richard. "Betrothal in a Monastery." *Oxford Music Online,* 2002.

Taruskin, Richard. "Catching Up with Rimsky-Korsakov." *Music Theory Spectrum* 33, no. 2 (Fall 2011): 169–85.

Taruskin, Richard. "Music's Dangers and the Case for Control." *New York Times,* December 9, 2001.

Taruskin, Richard. *The Oxford History of Western Music.* 5 vols. Oxford University Press, 2005.

Taruskin, Richard. "Stravinsky's Darkness and Light." *New York Times,* August 9, 1992.

Tenzer, Michael, ed. *Analytical Studies in World Music.* Oxford University Press, 2006.

Thomas, Sarah. "A Message of Inclusion, a History of Exclusion: Racial Injustice at the Peabody Institute." Hugh Hawkins Research Fellowship for the Study of Hopkins History. MA thesis, John Hopkins University, 2019.

Thompson, Jewel. "Samuel Coleridge-Taylor: The Development of His Compositional Style." PhD dissertation, Eastman School of Music, 1982.

Thurman, Kira. *Singing Like Germans: Black Musicians in the Land of Bach, Beethoven, and Brahms*. Cornell University Press, 2021.

Tillet, Salamishah. "When Culture Really Began to Reckon with White Privilege." *New York Times*, December 9, 2020.

Tomlinson, Brett. "Faculty Members Propose an Anti-racism Agenda." *Princeton Alumni Weekly*, July 13, 2020. https://paw.princeton.edu/article/faculty-members-propose-anti-racism-agenda

Tommasini, Anthony. "Trump Is Wrong if He Thinks Symphonies Are Superior." *New York Times*, July 30, 2017.

Tucker, Sherrie. "Big Ears: Listening for Gender in Jazz Studies." *Current Musicology* 71–73 (2001–2): 375–408.

Tugend, Tom. "Tchaikovsky's 'Jewish Problem' Doesn't Make Performer Settle a Score." *Times of Israel*, July 30, 2017. https://www.timesofisrael.com/tchaikovskys-jewish-problem-doesnt-make-performer-settle-a-score/

Wagner, Christoph. *Johannes Itten*. Great Masters in Art. Hirmer Publishers, 2019.

Wagner, Richard. *Das Judenthum in der Musik*. Verlagsbuchhandlung von J. J. Weber, 1869. Original published under the pseudonym Karl Freigedank, "Das Judenthum in der Musik." *Neue Zeitschrift für Musik* 17.19 (1850): 101–7 and 17.20: 109–12.

Walden, Daniel. "The Politics of Tuning and Temperament: Transnational Exchange and the Production of Music Theory in 19th-Century Europe, Asia, and North America." PhD dissertation, Harvard University, 2019.

Wallace, Lewis Raven. *The View from Somewhere: Undoing the Myth of Journalistic Objectivity*. University of Chicago Press, 2019.

Wallen, Errollyn. "A Racist Music." BBC Radio 3, *Sunday Feature*, November 24, 2019.

Weiss, Bari. *How to Fight Anti-Semitism*. Crown, 2019.

White, Chris. "Beethoven Has a First Name: It's Time to 'Fullname' All Composers in Classical Music." Slate.com, October 24, 2020. https://slate.com/culture/2020/10/fullname-famous-composers-racism-sexism.html

Whitman, James Q. *Hitler's American Model: The United States and the Making of Nazi Race Law*. Princeton University Press, 2017.

Wiener, Barry. "Philip Ewell's White Racial Frame." *Journal of Schenkerian Studies* 12 (2020): 195–206.

Williams, Mary Frances. "How I Was Kicked Out of the Society for Classical Studies Annual Meeting." Quillette.com, February 26, 2019. https://quillette.com/2019/02/26/how-i-was-kicked-out-of-the-society-for-classical-studies-annual-meeting/

Williams, Stereo. "The Truth about Elvis and the History of Racism in Rock." *Daily Beast*, June 18, 2016. https://www.thedailybeast.com/the-truth-about-elvis-and-the-history-of-racism-in-rock?ref=scroll

Wyatt, Lucius. "The Mid-Twentieth-Century Orchestral Variation, 1953–1963: An Analysis and Comparison of Selected Works." PhD dissertation, Eastman School of Music, 1974.

Yancy, George. *Backlash: What Happens When We Talk Honestly about Racism in America*. Rowman & Littlefield, 2018.

Yancy, George. "Dear White America." *New York Times*, December 24, 2015.

Young, Damon. "Yeah, Let's Not Talk about Race: Unless You Pay Me." *New York Times*, July 10, 2020.

Zamudio-Suarez, Fernanda. "Race on Campus: What Does 'Latinx' Mean?" *Chronicle of Higher Education*, March 16, 2021.

Index

antisemitism (*continued*)
racism and, 241–44; music theory and, 20, 248–56; in nineteenth-century Europe, 17; overcontextualizing, 248–51; in philosophy, 113; recommendations for confronting, 253–54; Schenker's, 120, 246, 257; use of term, 236n3; Wagner's, 20, 28, 116, 240, 244, 249–50, 257. *See also* Jews and Jewishness
antisexism, 85, 87, 263–64, 266–67, 273, 277
Appiah, Kwame Anthony, 55–57, 71
appropriation, 214
Arabs, 54, 64
Aristoxenus, 22, 81
art and design, 69, 93–95
Ashe, Arthur, 53
Asian American and Pacific Islanders (AAPI), 27, 42, 131–32, 201n13, 251, 253–54
assimilationism: antiblackness and, 130–32, 146; black music and, 214; cultural racism and, 155; exceptionalism and, 277; lowering of standards and, 272–73; in music theory, 132–38, 149–50, 171, 217; white supremacy and, 52–53, 201. See also *Journal of Schenkerian Studies,* vol. 12 (JSS affair)
Atlantic, 190
Austria, 76

Babbitt, Milton, 262
Bach, Johann Sebastian, 38, 77, 225, 247, 254, 257
Bakke, Allan, 2
Bakulina, Ellen, 129
Balakirev, Mily, 245n18, 257
Baldwin, James, 20, 44, 280–81
Baraka, Amiri, 214
Barthes, Roland, 11n24
Bartók, Béla, 78
Battle, Kathleen, 53
Beach, David, 147, 188; "Schenker—Racism—Context," 139–43
Beatles, 216, 218

Beaudoin, Richard, 129–30
Becker, Judith, 72–73
Beethoven, Ludwig van, 38, 76, 79, 85, 87, 89, 145, 190, 227–28, 230, 278; Schenker on, 101, 153–54
Belew, Kathleen, 218
Benjamin, William, 101
Berger, Maurice, 69n50
Berman, Ari, 218
Bernal, Martin, 57–61, 74, 97, 218
Berry, David Carson, 21–22, 262
bias and emotionality, 61–62, 124
biological racism, 93, 98–99, 106, 114, 154–55, 250, 262–63, 277. *See also* racial purity
BIPOC (black, indigenous, and people of color), use of term, 3n7
black, use of term, 2n2
Black Athena (Bernal), 57–61
black composers and artists, 2–3, 35, 38–43, 160–61, 219–20, 256
blackface minstrelsy, 236–37
Black Lives Matter movement, 143, 190, 233–34
black musical genres, 97–98, 213–17
Black Music Research Journal, 32
blackness, 1–2; advancement and success, 53, 126; agency and, 176; color theory and, 94; erasure of, 3, 27, 68, 99, 124, 209, 229; popular music studies and, 213–20; whiteness profiteering from, 214–18. *See also* antiblackness
Black Opera (André), 34
Blake, Ran, 226
Blanchard, Terrance, 3n5, 135n21
Blow, Charles, 183n124
bluegrass, 214, 226
blues, 214, 215–16
Blum, Edward, 253–54
Blumenbach, Johann Friedrich, 59n29
Boethius, 81
Bohlman, Philip, 27, 32, 154
Bologne, Joseph, 38n47, 41, 277
Bond, Sarah Emily, 62, 64
Bonilla-Silva, Eduardo, 8, 41, 62–63, 174

Boss, Jack, 130, 189, 209, 216–17; "Response to P. Ewell," 143–47
bothsidesing: defined, 6; JSS affair and, 174–83; Schenker and, 121, 266; Trump and, 6n11
Botstein, Leon, 249–50
Bouie, Jamelle, 183n124, 259n1
Bow, Leslie, 131–32
Bower, Calvin, 75
Bowers, Robert, 243–44
Boyer, Horace, 35, 211
Brahms, Johannes, 78, 91
Braxton, Anthony, 224
Brent, Paul, 136–37
Brett, Philip, 7n13
Brown, Danielle, 213–14, 220
Brown, Dorothy, 123n1
Brown, Henry Billings, 201–2
Brown, Julie, 28, 32
Brown v. Board of Education, 137, 204
Bruch, Max, 257
Bryant, Howie, 227
Buchler, Michael, 196–97
Buckley, William F., 180
bullying, 152
Burkhart, Charles, "Response to Philip Ewell," 147–48
Burkholder, J. Peter, 67–72
Burton-Hill, Clemency, 248

Cadwallader, Allen, 171, 173; "A Response to Philip Ewell," 148–53
California State University, Northridge, 170
Cambridge History of Western Music Theory, 73–74
Canarsee people, 69
cancel culture, 118, 180, 185–86, 190, 192, 279
canon, European/western. *See* western canon
Carson, A.D., 35
Caucasian, use of term, 59n29
censorship, 172–73, 180–81
Chang, Jeff, 220
Charlottesville, Virginia, "Unite the Right" rally in, 64
Chauvin, Derek, 19, 175
Cheng, William, 113
Chopin, Frédéric, 99, 163, 245, 257
Choron, Alexandre-Étienne, 115
Christensen, Thomas, 28–32, 73–75, 92, 262
Christianity, 67, 71, 254
Cincinnati Conservatory of Music, 89n2
cisnormativity, 6–7, 10, 81, 112, 268
citations, 14
citizenship, 50–51
City University of New York, 8; Mid-Career Faculty Fellowship Program, 10–11
Civil Rights Act (1964), 95, 223, 264, 268
Civil Rights movement, 66
Clapton, Eric, 215–16
Clark, Suzannah, 129–30
classical, use of term, 77
classics, 60–65, 69. *See also* Society for Classical Studies
coalitions, 254, 265–66. *See also* allyship
Coates, Ta-Nehisi, 10n22, 85–86, 128, 181, 183n124
Cobb, Montague, 222–23
coded language, 11, 89n2, 139–40, 272–73
Cohen, Jake, 246
Cold War, 66
Cole, Andrew, 196n2
College Music Symposium, 204–5
colonialism, 58, 69, 84, 132; in Africa, 34, 110; musical, 72–73; white supremacy and, 58, 86, 170
color (in art and design), 93–95
colorasure (erasing blackness), 209, 229
colorblindness, 13, 63, 150, 208, 261, 266
colorblind racism, 45, 92, 144, 174, 270
commissions for racial and gender justice, 268
complexity (in music), 72–73
composers: BIPOC, 2–3, 35, 38–43, 160–61, 256; in music theory textbooks, 37–44, 189; names of, 77n68; white racial frame and, 24–25; women, 38–43. *See also* western canon; *specific composers*
concerts, 275

inclusion, 223, 264. *See also* diversity, equity, and inclusion (DEI)
incrementalism, 137
Indiana University, 89n2, 259
Indigenous peoples, 69
inequality, 96; hierarchies and, 148–49. *See also* hierarchies
"Inner Melody in Javanese Gamelan Music" (Sumarsam), 32
Inside Higher Education, 167
Interlandi, Jeneen, 221–23
interracial relationships, sexual, 4, 48–50, 98, 184
Irving, Kyrie, 182
Italian language, 80–82, 269
Italy, 76
Itten, Johannes, 93–95

Jackson, Timothy, 127–30, 139, 145, 171, 189; "A Preliminary Response to Ewell," 156–63, 251–52; lawsuit filed by, 129n14; in Powell's *New York Times* article, 174–75, 178–80; "whimpathy" toward, 184–86
Jackson, Travis, 35
jazz, 214, 215; music theory curricula and, 221–26, 265
Jews and Jewishness, 10, 103n44; Jewish-black relations, 157–58, 178–80, 244, 251–53, 257; racism and, 118–19; Schenker's views on, 252–53; stereotypes and hatred of, 236–40. *See also* antisemitism
Jim Crow racism, 137
John, Elton, 218
Johnson, Lyndon, 223
Jonas, Oswald, 100, 107
Jones, Quincy, 224
Joplin, Scott, 3, 41
Journal of Music Theory, 212
Journal of Music Theory Pedagogy, 204–5
Journal of Schenkerian Studies, vol. 1, 190
Journal of Schenkerian Studies, vol. 12 (JSS affair), 11–12, 123–93; analysis of core response essays, 138–66; antiblackness and, 12, 125–29, 141–

42, 147–53, 156–76, 178–83, 186–88, 191; antiracism and, 34, 190–93; assimilationism and, 156–62, 165, 175, 178–82, 186, 191; background, 125–30; editorial management, 127–28; European reactions to, 169–74; global reactions, 166–67; histories, stories, and testimony, 123–25; media responses, 167; *New York Times* article on, 162, 174–83, 190n132; racism in, 130–32; Society for Music Theory and, 188–90; "whimpathetic" reactions to, 183–88

Kajikawa, Loren, 34, 192n134, 220
Kansas City Star, 177
Kant, Immanuel, 82–83, 113
Katz, Adele, 23
Katz, Mark, 211
Kavanaugh, Brett, 184
Kendi, Ibram X., 25n12, 42, 44–45, 50, 79, 82n74, 120, 132–34, 158–59, 161, 181, 183n124, 188, 190, 201
Kennedy, Rebecca Futo, 54–55, 64, 66
Kernodle, Tammy, 35
Kholopov, Yuri, 260
Kielian-Gilbert, Marianne, 128
King, Martin Luther, 151, 278n22
Kinks, 216
Kinney, L. Viola, 38n49
Kirov Opera, 235–37
Kochavi, Jon, 204, 207n20
Koslovsky, John, 192
Kristof, Nicholas, 218
Ku Klux Klan, 136–37

Lang, Paul Henry, 76
Laplanders. *See* Sámi
Lateef, Yusef, 224
Latin, 80, 269
Latinx people, 27
Lavengood, Megan, 151–52
Lavik, Viola, 4, 53
"Leaders of the New School?" (Kajikawa), 34
Lefkowitz, Mary, 60–61

Music in Western Civilization (Lang), 76
musicology, 22, 26–28, 35, 73, 211–12, 271
music theorists: BIPOC, 14, 31–32, 35, 211–12, 224–26, 234; white, 16, 19, 24–25, 31
music theory: beginning of, 262–63; definitions of, 21–23; demographic data, 35–37, 189, 259–60; as European/western, 21–23, 73–74 (*see also* western canon); historical/theoretical divide, 92–93; love and, 280; panic over race scholarship, 279; race and gender in, 1–14, 278–81 (*see also* white-male frame); recommendations for changes in, 263–78; respect and, 279–80; as study of "notes on the page," 7, 21, 26, 45; western, 73–74. *See also* curricula; *Journal of Schenkerian Studies,* vol.12 (JSS affair); publications; white-male frame in music theory
Music Theory Online, 11, 156, 204–13
Music Theory Society of New York State (MTSNYS), 168–69
Music Theory Spectrum, 128, 210–12
Mussorgsky, Modest, 245n18, 257
Myanmar, 132
mythologies. *See* white mythologies

National Association of Schools of Music, 255
National Medical Association, 222
National Public Radio, 167, 176
National Review, 167, 180
naturalization law, 50–51
Nazi Germany, 28, 119–20, 157n66, 244–45, 248, 262; American white supremacy and, 10, 235; Schenker and, 102–3, 107, 120
Neff, Severine, 128
neoliberalism, 265
Netrebko, Anna, 236
Neumeyer, David, 204–6, 207n20
New England Conservatory, 83, 135
New Musicology, 6–7n13
New Yorker, 167
New York Philharmonic, 2, 83, 135

New York Times, 52, 167; 1619 Project and, 261; Hanson's letter to, 255–56; "Obscure Musicology Journal Sparks Battles over Race and Free Speech" (Powell), 162, 174–83, 190n132; review of Prokofiev opera, 237
New York University, 213
Noreika, Jonas, 119
Norman, Jessye, 53
North Africans, 48n4
Northwestern University, 90n2, 259
Norway, 76
notational systems, 21–22
Nuremberg Laws, 10

Oberlin College Conservatory of Music, 189
objectification, 99
objectivity, 61–62, 124, 176–77, 218, 277
Oestreich, James, 237
Oluo, Ijeoma, 51
"one-drop rule," 215
"Open Letter on Schenker's Racism and Its Reception in the United States" (Sept. 28, 2020), 169–74
opera, 34
Orientalism, 30–31
#OscarsSoWhite, 198
Ossoff, Jon, 257
Oster, Ernst, 100, 107, 163
othering, 196
overcontextualization, 139–42, 248–51, 266
Oxford History of Western Music (Taruskin), 76
Oxford Music Online, 21–23, 262

Padilla Peralta, Dan-el, 62–64, 196n2
Painter, Nell Irvin, 48, 54, 261
Palestrina, 225
Palisca, Claude, 66–72
Parkhurst, Bryan, 192
paternalism, 174
patriarchy, 6, 25, 27, 87, 212–13. *See also* gender; maleness; misogyny; sexism
Peabody Institute, 83, 135–38

Rameau, Jean-Philippe, 81
Ramsey, Guthrie, 28, 35
rap, 214, 220, 271n17
Ravel, Maurice, 225
R&B, 214
Reagan, Ronald, 160
"Red Summer," 124n3, 248
Reed, Teresa, 35
Regents of the University of California v. Bakke, 2
responsibility, 15, 16, 219
revisionism, 119–21, 182, 188
Riemann, Hugo, 22, 81, 114, 278
Rimsky-Korsakov, Nikolai, 77–79, 245n18
Rittenhouse, Kyle, 184
Robinson, Dylan, 3n4
Robinson, Vicki Sue, 38n49
rock music, 214
Rogers, Lynne, 128
Romani, 64
Romans, ancient, 55–56, 64–67, 81
Ross, Alex, 41, 110
Rothgeb, John, 100–101, 163
Rothstein, William, 102–3, 107, 163
Rousseau, Jean-Jacques, 82–83
Ruggles, Carl, 246, 257
Rusch, René, 204, 207n20
Russell, Bertrand, 53
Russell, George, 203, 225–26
Russian language, 80
Ruwet, Nicolas, 72

Sámi, 64, 76
Sands, Rosita, 35
Sanneh, Kalefa, 2
Scarlatti, Domenico, 78, 99, 116, 163
Schachter, Carl, 45, 105–6, 111, 116, 141, 163–65, 260
Schenker, Heinrich, 89–121; antisemitism and, 120, 246, 257; epistemology of knowledge-avoidance and, 85, 253; German nationalist beliefs, 90, 96, 102–3, 172; Gobineau's racial theories and, 30, 86–87, 262–63; influence and legacy of, 22, 89–90,

114–21, 163, 178, 191–92; Jewishness, 118–20, 155–56, 178–79, 190, 252–53; musical theories (*see* Schenkerian analysis); Nazi Germany and, 102–3, 107, 120; perceived "attack" on, 125, 128, 138, 148, 162, 166, 171, 205; racist beliefs, 30, 45–46, 86–87, 89, 91, 93, 96–99, 101–21, 140, 144–45, 148, 153–55, 163, 165, 171–72; reframing of, 105–8; sexist beliefs, 111–12; supernatural revelations and, 115–16. See also *Journal of Schenkerian Studies*, vol.12 (JSS affair); western canon
—WORKS: *Der freie Satz*, 100, 102, 155; *Der Tonwille*, 98, 106n54; *Harmonielehre*, 111; *Kontrapunkt*, 100, 111; "Von der Sendung des deutschen Genies" (Mission of the German Genius), 30, 87, 98, 140, 263
Schenker Documents Online, 96
#SchenkerGate, 167
Schenkerian analysis: black composers and, 145–46; black pop music and, 217; courses in, 89n2, 113, 164–65, 269–70; fundamental line *(Urlinie)*, 110, 116, 149; fundamental structure, 110–11; hierarchies and, 101–5, 108–11, 116–17; as institutionalized racialized structure, 90, 165, 270; overview of, 90–91; teaching of, 112–14, 192. *See also* Schenker, Heinrich; tonal analysis
Schillinger, Joseph, 224
Schloss, Joe, 220
Schmalfeldt, Janet, 23
Schoenberg, Arnold, 78, 114, 224
Schubert, Franz, 278
Schumann, Robert, 257
Scott, Tim, 181
Seashore, Carl, 30
Segall, Christopher, 129–30
segregationism, 132–38; biological racism and, 155; economics and, 222–24; "separate but equal," 198–204. *See also* desegregation; racism
Sells, Marcia, 2
Senegal, 98–99